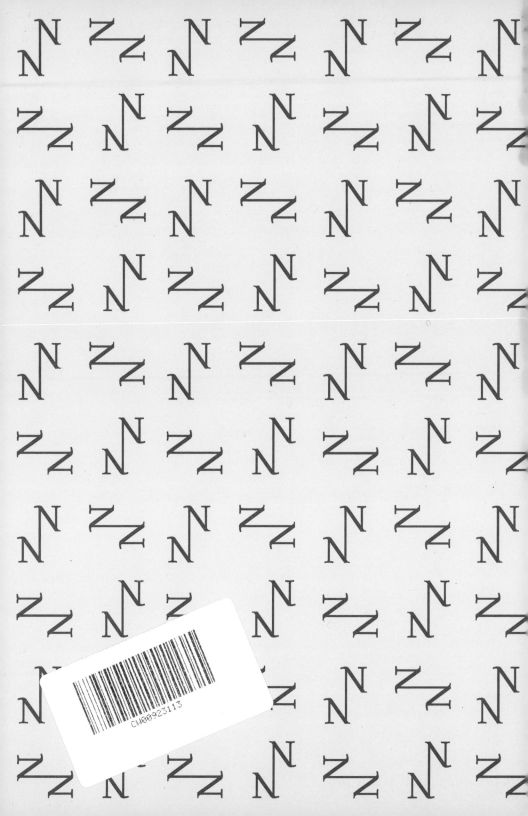

THE NEW NATURALIST LIBRARY

A SURVEY OF BRITISH NATURAL HISTORY

NATURE IN TOWNS AND CITIES

THE NEW NATURALIST LIBRARY

NATURE IN TOWNS AND CITIES

DAVID GOODE

WILLIAM COLLINS

This edition published in 2014 by William Collins,
An imprint of HarperCollins Publishers

HarperCollins Publishers
77–85 Fulham Palace Road
London W6 8JB
WilliamCollinsBooks.com

First published 2014

A CIP catalogue record for this book is available
from the British Library.

Set in FF Nexus, designed and produced by
Tom Cabot/ketchup

All photos by the author unless otherwise credited.

Maps are based on OS OpenData and contain Ordnance Survey data
© Crown copyright and database right 2014.

Extract from 'The Swifts' by Ted Hughes (1982, from *Selected Poems 1957–1981*)
reprinted by permission of Faber & Faber, copyright © the Estate of Ted Hughes

Printed in Hong Kong by Printing Express

Hardback
ISBN 978-0-00-724239-9

Paperback
ISBN 978-0-00-724240-5

Contents

Editors' Preface

I N 1945, WHEN LARGE PARTS OF London and Britain's other major cities still lay in ruins after World War II, the New Naturalist series, which was itself then new, chose *London's Natural History* as one of its first titles. There could have been no more poignant example of the destructive effect of humans on their environment than the urban bomb sites of that period, but *London's Natural History* revealed that nature is resilient and even opportunist. The rosebay willowherb that colonised bomb sites in profusion occasioned an increase in the elephant hawk-moth whose caterpillars feed on its leaves.

Sixty-nine years later, the Editors are delighted that we are at last able to revisit urban natural history, this time painted on a larger canvas that covers *Nature in Towns and Cities* throughout the United Kingdom. David Goode, whose lifelong passion for natural history began at 14, is a pre-eminently qualified author on this subject. In 1982 he became Senior Ecologist at the Greater London Council, later Director of the London Ecology Unit and ultimately Head of Environment at the Greater London Authority. In the 1990s, he helped develop programmes for urban nature conservation in China and Chile. David is a keen photographer and has illustrated this book mainly with his own photographs. He writes very engagingly about the kinds of habitats that most of us encounter daily, but where the unexpected can still frequently be found.

Although Dr Goode was privileged to have a bird's- and indeed a birder's-eye view of the natural history of the capital from a lofty position in the city's government, he is just as familiar with the more intimate scale of nature in the City of Bath where he now lives. Anyone reading David's description of the nature of that city will be infected by his delight in the detail of everyday encounters with house sparrows hiding in garden hedges or the lichens to be found on walls and pavements. For those with more aerial tastes, there are peregrine falcons nesting in a church tower and indeed the whole story reads like an urban idyl. Bath is a special city, there is no doubt, but this book will also take you to many more places up-and-down the land that are just as rich in wildlife and full of surprise. How many people realise that our rarest native trees can be seen from the Clifton Suspension Bridge in the City of Bristol? Or that kittiwakes nest in the centre of Newcastle?

Urban natural history is not just about native species, but also about incomers and change. Parakeets have become familiar birds in many suburbs and parks. Some native animals like the fox and the pied wagtail have moved, just as people once did, from the country into the town. We live in a crowded island, but there is nature all around us, even in the midst of our towns and cities. Urban living would be hugely impoverished if we could not share our human habitat with plants and wildlife. This book will help us all see it, appreciate it and protect it.

Author's Foreword and Acknowledgements

I
T IS ALMOST SEVENTY YEARS since publication of Richard Fitter's seminal book on *London's Natural History* in 1945. It was one of the earliest volumes (No. 3) in the New Naturalist series and one of the first attempts anywhere to investigate urban natural history in all its facets. His aim was to demonstrate the effects of human activities on nature, and the ways that nature responds, within a great city. He did it well. His book has remained authoritative and inspirational for generations of Londoners, scholars and naturalists ever since.

This is the first New Naturalist book to address the broad field of urban natural history since Fitter's book. But it is very different. It tells two stories. The first deals with urban natural history from an ecological perspective, looking at a range of habitats and species that flourish in towns and cities and investigating the ecological processes involved. It is not intended to be a comprehensive account of urban natural history. Rather it traces the origins of the main types of habitat and their associated species and attempts to explain why particular conditions prevail. These are the ordinary habitats that we see every day, from railwaysides and cemeteries to parks and domestic gardens, as well as fragments of the wider world that have become caught up in the urban sprawl. Some species have been chosen to illustrate changes that occur through colonisation. Others were chosen because they are declining. These choices also reflect my personal interests and I make no apology for the strong emphasis on birds as they are the group that I know best.

The second story deals with the growth and development of urban nature conservation and the application of ecological knowledge to the design of new urban landscapes. Much has happened in the past thirty years and I have been fortunate to be closely involved throughout. I remember standing on Westminster Bridge in 1982 looking at London with new eyes having just been offered the job of Senior Ecologist with the Greater London Council. Little did I know that I was to be plunged into a maelstrom of activity as wildlife conservation spread into the cities and urban ecology suddenly became fashionable among academics. I witnessed many novel ideas becoming adopted as mainstream, including creation of the first ecological parks and early attempts to turn town parks into wildflower meadows. More radical when first proposed was the idea that we should value urban wastelands and use them as a model for habitat creation. Recently we have seen construction of major new nature reserves such as the London Wetland Centre and a proliferation of green roofs and other new habitats within the built environment as people look for sustainable solutions. New initiatives have been part of life.

I am writing this as I pass through Didcot on the train and catch a glimpse of a red kite quartering suburban gardens for food. What better symbol could there be? A bird brought back from the brink that is now recovering its place in towns and cities, to the great delight of residents. Its just one of the many stories.

A great deal has happened since 1982 and I hope that I have done justice to the enthusiasms and dedication of those involved. Which brings me to a third strand that runs all through the book. The story would not be complete without reference to the people who have made it all happen. The ecologists involved in unravelling the life histories of urban foxes, investigating bird populations of London's squares or delving into the intricacies of ancient trees, provide the nuts and bolts of urban ecology. Then there are those involved in campaigns to protect important wildlife sites, the social scientists investigating the value of nature to people living in towns and cities, and landscape designers applying ecological knowledge and developing novel solutions for management of urban landscapes. They all have a story to tell. In a sense this book is a social history; a biography of a movement. Some of those involved have been particularly significant as visionaries. Max Nicholson, George Barker, Tony Bradshaw, Oliver Gilbert and Chris Baines stand out as leaders in a field that is full of dynamic individuals who have brought about changes in our relationship with urban nature. I have been fortunate to work with many of them.

It has been an extraordinarily rewarding period to be working as an urban ecologist and I am thankful for that. If this book helps to promote greater understanding and appreciation of the subject then it will have done its job.

ACKNOWLEDGEMENTS

This book would not have been possible without the help and encouragement of many people. Some provided guidance on places that they know well, others contributed on specialist topics, yet others helped with locating published material, to all of whom I am extremely grateful. I value the time spent with enthusiasts in various parts of Britain exploring the local natural history and I can only apologise in those cases where material has not been used owing to lack of space. The following is a list of people who have assisted and if there are others who I have inadvertently missed I beg your indulgence: John Archer, Simon Atkinson, Hilary Ash, Helen Baker, George Barker, Leo Batten, David Bevan, Catherine Bickmore, John Box, Lynda Brooks, Richard Bullock, Sara Carvalho, Rai Darke, Ed Drewitt, Mathew Frith, Niall Fuller, Meg Game, Jean Hansell, David Ingram, Lynda Lake, Mandy Leivers, Mike LeRoy, Grant Luscombe, Edward Mayer, Edward Milner, Dick Newell, Philip Oswald, Laura Palmer, Mike Poulton, William Purvis, Rob Randall, Peter Rock, Richard Scott, Peter Shirley, Chloe Smith, Matthew Thomas, and Ian Trueman. Thanks are also due to Wildlife Trusts, regional biological record centres and city ecologists in many places, especially Birmingham and the Black Country, Bristol, Edinburgh, London, Manchester and Sheffield. Thank you, too, for help from staff at Buglife, particularly Jamie Robins, Sarah Henshall and Steven Falk.

I am particularly grateful to people who have contributed photographs, especially Paul Wilkins; also Buglife, the Hawk and Owl Trust (Hamish Smith), the Parks Trust, Milton Keynes (Liz Woznicki), RSPB (Michael Szebor), Wildlife Trusts (Anna Guthrie) and the Wildfowl and Wetlands Trust (Catherine Beazley). Photo credits are included in the captions. Thanks are also due to Mike Wells and his staff at Biodiversity by Design in Bath who provided much debate and allowed me the freedom of their library. Special thanks too to those who commented on sections of the book in draft, especially Malcolm Rush whose comments were invaluable.

The book has been strongly influenced by the work of the London Ecology Unit. I am mindful of the tremendous wealth of material on urban ecology and nature conservation generated by members of the Unit over many years and would like to pay tribute to their endeavours. Thanks are due to all those whose work has found its way into the book.

I would like to thank Jonathan Silvertown of the New Naturalist Editorial Board and Julia Koppitz at HarperCollins for their patience and encouragement and also Tom Cabot for his skilful design. To Robert Gillmor, my thanks for a lovely illustration for the jacket.

Finally I thank Johanna and Tom for their prolonged support and Helen for sharing the journey.

In memory of Diana

CHAPTER 1

The Nature of Towns and Cities

TOWNS AND CITIES OF THE British Isles provide a huge range of conditions where nature can thrive. Every place is different and the opportunities for nature to co-exist with human activities vary enormously. The effects of historic development, together with local variations in geology, geomorphology and climate all play their part in influencing the diversity of nature that can occur. We tend to know individual towns and cities by their characteristic buildings or architecture. The dreaming spires and colleges of Oxford, Georgian Edinburgh and Bath, mill towns of Lancashire and West Yorkshire, seaside spas of Scarborough and Torquay, ports of London, Lowestoft and Liverpool, the granite city of Aberdeen, hillside terraces of the South Wales valleys, and business parks of Basildon and Basingstoke. The variations are endless.

But equally towns and cities can be recognised by their natural features. So Norwich might be known as the city in the fen, sitting as it does at the head of the Broads that still permeate the city. Conversely Edinburgh is a city of hills and crags with Arthur's Seat, Castle Rock and other smaller islands of volcanic rock rising above the urban sprawl. Salisbury and Oxford have their water meadows, Sheffield, Durham and Glasgow their ancient wooded valleys. Some, like Bristol, Newcastle, Harrogate and London still have extensive commons. Edinburgh and Belfast are unusual in having everything from seacoast to mountaintop within their boundaries. Other coastal towns, such as Yarmouth, Lancaster and Truro, have an intimate mixture of urban and maritime, where saltmarsh comes right up to the high street and you can watch redshanks and turnstones from the bus stop.

All our towns and cities are different, not only in their cultural features but also in the natural world that they accommodate. So where do we start in attempting to describe the nature of towns and cities?

NATURE IN A SMALL CITY

Perhaps the simplest thing to do is to take you on a walk around my home city of Bath. It is a relatively small city of about 90,000 people near Bristol and lies in a saucer, with the River Avon winding through the middle and wooded hills around the edge. Stand on almost any street in the city centre and you will see woodland rising above the rooftops not far away. Indeed when Bath was being considered for World Heritage status, principally on account of its Roman and Georgian heritage, the great proximity of the city to its wooded surroundings was recognised as an important asset.

But nature is not restricted to the edges. There is much to discover in the heart of the Georgian town. Those who live in the centre cannot fail to be aware of the gulls nesting on the rooftops, for there are lots of them. Their population has grown enormously over the past twenty years and there are now over a thousand pairs of gulls treating the city as their own. Their strident calls provide an early morning wake up call as the birds perform their daily rituals. Early morning for them is four or five a.m. in the summer! Later in the day they drown the voices of tourist guides and steal food from your plate at outdoor restaurants. So dominant are they that at times one tends to forget other species. But the buildings and

FIG 1. The City of Bath from Bathwick Meadows.

FIG 2. Small courtyards in the Georgian town support a variety of garden birds, including this robin which came into my house for mealworms.

squares of the Georgian town support a variety of birds, including swift, crow, jackdaw, magpie, woodpigeon and, of course, the ubiquitous town pigeon. The city is small enough to have tawny owls nesting close to the centre, their hoots reverberating around the grand buildings of the Circus. The collared dove, normally a bird of leafy suburbs, can also be seen here. Even quite small courtyards have their resident pairs of robins, wrens, dunnocks and blackbirds. Some still have small colonies of house sparrows, though the population is tiny compared with what it was 20 years ago. Those that remain are confined to courtyards where there are plenty of shrubs or where walls are covered in bushy growths of ivy, Virginia creeper or Russian vine. Blackcaps are regular visitors to these courtyards in winter, and brown long-eared bats live in buildings nearby. Buzzards and ravens can often be seen passing over the rooftops and occasionally red kites appear!

The Georgian town has numerous deep basements and small courtyards at the front of the buildings, many of which have become colonised by a great variety of plants, including garden escapes or aliens, which give a particular botanical character to the city. Red valerian, ivy leaved toadflax, wall lettuce, yellow corydalis, herb Robert and Mexican fleabane (or wall daisy) are particularly abundant. Two species of bellflowers have colonised the steps and walls. The Adria and trailing

FIG 3. Plants on basement walls, red valerian, yellow corydalis and wall daisy.

bellflower were both introduced as garden plants from the former Yugoslavia and the latter is fast becoming dominant. All these plants bring a remarkable amount of colour to the streetscapes, and provide an abundance of nectar for bees and other insects. These basement walls also support many ferns including wall rue, hart's tongue, male fern and several introduced species of ribbon fern, most commonly *Pteris cretica*, which have recently become naturalised. Maidenhair spleenwort grows in some of the shadier spots. In deeper underground recesses of the Roman Baths, lit for the benefit of tourists, there was until recently a thriving colony of the much rarer maidenhair fern.

In the middle of the city the buildings can be baking hot in summer, but wherever there are leaking drainpipes, or holes in the masonry, buddleia and red valerian find a niche. Several species of lichen commonly occur on low walls beside the pavement, especially *Caloplaca flavescens*, and others cover paving stones in places where few people walk. Tiny plants of common whitlowgrass manage to thrive between cobble-stones of the Royal Crescent, turning the road white with their flowers in spring. Buildings afford relatively few opportunities for invertebrates, but jumping spiders occur on the walls, and other spiders lurk in holes in the stonework. The funnel spider *Segestria florentina*, an introduction from southern Europe, is particularly fond of corners under pediments and balustrades where the characteristic spokes of its web can be seen. In some deeper basements and culverts under the city lives the cave spider *Meta menardi* one of our largest British spiders. Each female spider sits on its large egg sac hanging from the roof in complete darkness.

By the river the steeple of St John's church boasts recent arrivals, a pair of peregrine falcons now resident through the year. Down below are cormorants, also relatively recent newcomers since the early 1990s, which have become a regular sight fishing the river in the city centre where local anglers catch chubb, bream, eel, perch, roach and pike. Where the ancient culvert from the Roman baths empties into the river huge carp gather line-astern in the never ending torrent of hot water. Swans nest by the Riverside Café and there are odd pairs of Canada and greylag geese, some of which interbreed. All day long in spring and summer there is a continuous procession of herring and lesser black-back gulls coming down to the weir by Pulteney Bridge to drink and bathe. Each

FIGS 4 & 5. Common whitlowgrass (above left) grows between the cobbles in the Royal Crescent. Peregrine falcons can be seen every day in the centre of the city (above right). This immature bird was ringed at the nest on St John's Church. (Mark Coller)

FIG 6. Bath has 1,100 pairs of gulls nesting in the city. They are quick to seize the opportunity when refuse bags are put out for collection. Feral pigeons follow suit.

bird spends an average of only four minutes on its ablutions and then it is off, yet birds are present throughout the day. This part of the river is favoured for feeding by house martins, and kingfishers are seen regularly by the railway bridge. Here too are grey wagtails, and occasionally a common sandpiper might appear on migration. Otters are on the increase, with frequent sightings even in the centre of the city where one recently spent a day catching ducklings. A potter with his studio on one of the bridges sees them regularly, as do early-morning drivers at the bus depot further downstream. The riverside walk from the town centre out to the countryside at Newbridge takes you through a cross-section of the city's habitats and you can always return by bus.

Along the riverside there was until recently an old gasworks that had lain derelict for many years. A new housing development has now taken its place, but before that it was used as a car park where a host of plants, many of them aliens, managed to colonise rubble and concrete in the spaces between the cars, and with them came insects and other small invertebrates of urban wasteland. Soldier beetles and hoverflies were particularly abundant on flower heads. Thickets of buddleia grew around the edges, often covered with old man's beard. Where the concrete was more intact cracks became colonised by plants such as Oxford

FIG 7. A great variety of plants grew in the remnants of the old gasworks, including Canadian goldenrod, evening primrose, hemp agrimony and buddleia.

ragwort, Canadian goldenrod, hemp agrimony, wild carrot and ribwort plantain. Brambles spread across the concrete trying to find a foothold. This was a hot, dry environment in the summer, with no soil and little in the way of plant nutrients, yet it supported a remarkable range of species. Many of these plants are adapted to surviving in conditions of ecological stress and are particularly characteristic of such a harsh urban environment. The result was a remarkably diverse mixture of species, creating some very colourful assemblages. They are attractive too to many invertebrate species, including bees, solitary wasps and a huge variety of flies. Even tiny patches of derelict land can play host to a rich array of plants. An abandoned plot under the railway arches that was once a stone-mason's yard now has a fine show of greater celandine and old man's beard.

Old graveyards in the heart of the city harbour a very different set of species. St Mary's burial ground by Cleveland Bridge is a good example. Rich humus, with lots of nutrients, supports cow parsley, green alkanet, red campion, nettle and white dead nettle. Tombstones and monuments are covered in lichens, mosses and ferns. One of the large chest tombs is being undermined by an extensive badger sett. Badgers are well established in Bath and this is just one of nearly 100 setts in the city.

FIG 8. The Kennet and Avon Canal provides a popular walk along the towpath as well as having valuable wetland habitats.

A short distance south of here the Kennet and Avon canal winds its way through the south side of the city before descending by a series of locks to join the River Avon. The leaky lock gates are colonised by a tangle of water-loving plants including gypsywort, skullcap, pendulous sedge and wild angelica, with a profusion of liverworts covering the woodwork at the lower levels. Hart's tongue fern, wall daisy and pellitory-of-the-wall grow on the lock walls, whilst the towpath edge has white dead nettle, shepherd's purse, knotweed, nipplewort, herb Robert, soapwort and hedgerow cranesbill. Winter heliotrope and tansy cover the canal banks in places and in autumn the tangled hedges are festooned with old man's beard, snowberry and arboreal ivy. This is a popular route for dog walkers and nettles are prolific as a result of nitrogen enrichment. Gardens and allotments come down to the water's edge along much of the canal's route through the town, providing a broad green corridor. Coot, moorhen and mallard frequent this stretch of the canal. Herons, kingfishers and dabchicks regularly fish where it broadens out for boats to turn. One heron, oblivious to passers by, has learnt to wait patiently by the lock gates where it catches small fish carried through the leaky gates. Another equally tame bird visits the small ornamental fishpond in the sensory garden of a local park.

Another green corridor is the disused railway line, now converted into a parkland walk, which runs along the backs of houses in the otherwise densely built-up suburb of Oldfield Park. This enclave of Victorian terraces bounded by privet hedges is one part of Bath where house sparrows still survive in good numbers. A cycle track and footpath run along the old railway track, but trees have grown along both sides, so that as you walk this route you are totally cut off from the urban environment, only a stone's throw away. Speckled wood butterflies have become well established, and in places there are slow worms in the walls. Keep walking through the old railway tunnel, nearly a mile long but well lit and with piped music, until you emerge at Tucking Mill Nature Reserve, a real wetland with dragonflies and dabchicks. From here you can walk back over the hill into town.

On the northern flanks of the city is Royal Victoria Park, which has the distinction of being one of the earliest public parks in Britain. Established in 1830 it was protected from development by public subscription and includes a botanical garden with a fine collection of specimen trees dating from the mid-1800s. The garden contains several champion trees, including the tallest hornbeam in Britain and a weeping lime 150 feet high. In places there are survivors from older habitats; one grassy bank regularly supports a variety

FIG 9. The mixture of old trees, rich herbaceous borders and attractive glades means that the Botanical Garden has a good diversity of birds and insects.

of orchids, including pyramidal and bee orchids. Another bank supports
newcomers. It is riddled with the holes of a huge colony of ivy mining bees,
a species that has only recently become established in Britain. Every year in
September hundreds of these bees forage nearby on late flowering ivy. Grey
squirrels abound in the botanic garden, where jays are remarkably tame. Tree
creepers roost in the soft bark of giant redwoods and badgers live under the
rockery. Kingfishers and herons visit the fishpond. The mixture of mature
trees, glades and dense shrubberies supports a good variety of birds including
goldcrest, blackcap, nuthatch, chaffinch and greenfinch. Sparrowhawks regularly
hunt in the gardens. Green woodpeckers search for ants on the greens of the
adjacent mini golf course, which is also just the place for mistle thrushes and
jackdaws, and for the occasional migrating wheatear in the spring. Severe winter
weather brings large flocks of redwing and fieldfare, together with occasional
parties of meadow pipits.

   Domestic gardens and allotments provide many different habitats and
can attract a remarkable number of species. A town garden only 800 m south
of the city centre is a good example. The owners are keen members of Bath
Natural History Society and have diligently recorded the species they have seen

FIG 10. A tiny domestic garden in Bath where 44 species of birds have been recorded.
(Alan Barrett)

in the garden since 1991. Their sightings of birds, butterflies, dragonflies and other insects demonstrate the wealth of species that can occur, including some unexpected visitors. The 44 species of birds include sparrowhawk, bullfinch, marsh tit and redpoll, as well as four species of warbler. Their tally exceeds some of the best of our town parks. Butterflies total 20 species, of which the white letter hairstreak is the most unusual. Both scarlet and garden tiger moths occur, together with hummingbird, convolvulus and elephant hawk-moths. Other insects include speckled and oak bush crickets, and seven species of bumble bee. A small pond built in 1998 has since attracted seven common species of damselfly and dragonfly, and also supports frogs, toads and both common and palmate newts. These records provide some indication of what is possible in a town garden managed to encourage wildlife (Barrett, 2009).

Wedges of open land extend in from all directions towards the centre of the city. These include extensive meadows and woodlands as well as golf courses, cemeteries and some notable gardens. The Widcombe valley just south of the railway station has a distinctly rural atmosphere with pony paddocks and hay meadows. A stream that flows down through these leafy suburbs has a rich assemblage of water-loving plants. Purple loosestrife, marsh marigold, figwort and horsetails grow alongside a mixture of umbelliferous species including hemlock water-dropwort, lesser water parsnip and fool's watercress. The local garden centre boasts a fine green roof covered in stonecrop. Amazingly a pair of buzzards has nested for the past few years in a secluded domestic garden near here. One morning the owners were delighted to find all the young birds perching on chairs on their veranda shortly after they had fledged! Nearby is the Abbey Cemetery, one of the earliest Victorian cemeteries in the country, now overgrown with a mixture of meadow and wasteland plants supporting over 20 species of butterflies and a strident population of grasshoppers and crickets. Lesser spotted woodpeckers are known to occur and ravens, a recent arrival in the city, nest in a tall wellingtonia tree. Roe and muntjack deer are regularly seen grazing the rides in the evening. They have become frequent visitors to many suburban gardens on the south side of the city.

Further up the valley, but still well within the confines of the city, is the landscape garden of Prior Park, now managed by the National Trust. Originally laid out in the late 1700s by Ralph Allen, owner of the stone mines that gave Bath its distinctive buildings, it has a fine landscape of woodland, glades and meadows, with ornamental lakes and a beautiful Palladian bridge. The woods are famous for their wild garlic, whilst the meadows are full of primroses and cowslips, with a variety of orchids later in the year. Meadows are grazed under a countryside stewardship scheme and it was recently found that the numerous

FIG 11. Prior Park landscape garden is a mixture of grand design and wild nature. It brings a more rural atmosphere into the city .

anthills of yellow meadow ant are at least 160 years old. Yet again there are badgers, and a small colony of herons nest near the Palladian Bridge and in the adjacent grounds of Widcombe Manor. Stock doves and tawny owls nest in some of the older trees. In recent years cormorants have become regular visitors, attracted by an easy source of food. They could well breed here before long. Another recent incomer is the American crayfish which is causing havoc by burrowing into the banks of the ornamental lakes so that they have had to be reinforced. Lesser horseshoe bats occur in the icehouse and grass snakes lay their eggs in the compost heap.

A little further up these southern slopes we come to the suburb of Combe Down where stone was mined to build the city. Parts of the old workings have been retained, at considerable cost, to provide a breeding site for greater horseshoe bats. With about 70 individuals it is one of the larger colonies in Britain. The mines also have a roosting colony of over 100 lesser horseshoe bats, together with a variety of other species. This part of the city is also important for its woodlands, many of which are relics of ancient woodland with wild service tree, spindle, spurge laurel, wood sanicle, yellow archangel, and stinking iris. A few rarer species also occur, notably coralroot, toothwort, Solomon's seal and Bath asparagus. Several of these woods are only 2 km from the city centre and their stillness and antiquity provide an extraordinary contrast with the urban scene immediately below.

Almost all of the open land on slopes around the city is specially protected to retain the mixture of woodland and meadows which is so appealing. Relics of old farmland penetrate down into the suburbs where they are caught up within the urban sprawl. The meadows at Bathwick start just above the canal only 15 minutes walk from the Abbey. These provide open amenity grassland much used by dog walkers. But the fields have rough edges rich in crickets and grasshoppers; dark bush cricket and long-winged coneheads have been recorded. Overgrown hedgerows are thick with blackthorn, and an abundance of hips and haws. These meadows are grazed at times by cattle, bringing a rural atmosphere to the city. More surprising is the patch of grassland below Lansdown Crescent in the Georgian town still grazed by a flock of sheep! Other meadows have cattle or ponies, and Bath City Farm now occupies one small group of fields in Twerton, completely surrounded by post-war housing estates. Here there are goats, pigs, ducks, Soay sheep and several rare breeds of chicken. A local farmer brings Aberdeen Angus cows to graze in the summer. It is said that barn owls still hunt here and there are great-crested newts in the pond. The city farm is a great favourite with school children. But things do not always go according to plan. One year just before Christmas, whilst a mothers and toddlers group was there, a fox appeared and made off with one of the chickens!

Not far above is Twerton Roundhill, a limestone knoll on the southern rim of the city surrounded by suburbia, which has a particularly rich flora with fairy flax, pepper saxifrage, greater knapweed, common centaury, cowslip and bee orchid. The richness of its flora has led to it being designated as a Local Nature Reserve by the city council. Further along the southern edge of the city is the park-and-ride bus terminus, where limestone grassland by the car park supports a good population of small blue butterflies. On the opposite rim of the city the Kingswood School rugby field at Lansdown is notable for the presence of green winged orchids which have persisted from the time when this was permanent pasture. In winter golden plovers, common gulls and lapwings gather on sports pitches and on the nearby racecourse, along with flocks of fieldfares, redwings, starlings, meadow pipits and skylarks. A footpath takes you back down into suburbia through Primrose Hill Community Woodland which was recently planted on arable fields, bringing a new lease of life to this part of the green belt.

FIG 12. Winter flocks of waxwings forage for berries in city car parks. (Duncan Usher)

During periods of particularly severe weather large numbers of winter thrushes invade suburban gardens in search of food, stripping berries from ornamental shrubs. At such times flocks of finches appear in gardens well into the centre of the city where urban goldfinches and chaffinches may be joined by bullfinches and even bramblings. Large parties of siskins descend on alder catkins in riverside trees behind the railway station. In some years waxwings have suddenly appeared in suburban streets and city-centre car parks, feasting on berries of cotoneaster and holly. The last major invasion in Bath was in 2005 when flocks of up to 100 birds were seen in the city. But there is one gathering of birds that you can be sure of seeing every winter. This is the pied wagtail roost in the new shopping centre. Flocks of wagtails fly in at dusk from all directions. They congregate in rows on top of the buildings before diving into the only tree in the centre, where they spend the night in the warmth of the city. Mallard ducks that live in the city centre go one step further. During very cold spells they have taken to visiting the Roman Baths where they up-end with great excitement in the hot spa water.

URBAN NATURAL HISTORY

So what can we learn from Bath about the natural history of towns and cities? Perhaps the most striking thing is the great diversity of wildlife to be found in a small city. The range of habitats is enormous but there is a clear distinction between those which owe their origins to the landscape on which the city has grown and those which are strictly part of the urban scene. That distinction applies in towns and cities wherever they occur. The pre-existing landscape and local climatic conditions continue to provide a template for each individual place.

Bath is fortunate in retaining many vestiges of its earlier landscape in the form of ancient woodlands, meadows and even the River Avon itself. These habitats are long established and some have retained the characteristic species that make them so special. Others have been modified more acutely by their urban surroundings and have gradually become less diverse. Not all cities have such a wealth of long established habitats, but most have some vestiges of the landscape that was there before the city developed.

Habitats stemming directly from urban activities include a great mixture from parks and gardens to the hard surfaces of the built environment. There are many different substrates ranging from the fertile soils of gardens and allotments, to urban wasteland with its almost complete lack of soil. At the extreme end of the spectrum is the built environment where walls and roofs support only those species capable of surviving the harsh conditions. Each of these different habitats, whether it be garden pond, canal, disused railway line or inner city graveyard, has its own particular suite of species. These are the places where nature thrives. Because the city is so heterogeneous, with a great mixture of different ecological conditions, it is not surprising that a considerable variety of wildlife is able to exist.

From this brief excursion around Bath it is clear that one of the key factors in urban ecology is change. Wherever there are opportunities there will be species to exploit them and the urban environment is full of opportunities. Recent changes in Bath include the enormous growth in the population of roof-nesting gulls, successful breeding of peregrine falcons, colonisation of Georgian courtyards by a host of alien plants, the quiet occupation of nooks and crannies in buildings by funnel spiders from the Mediterranean, and the equally quiet presence in suburban gardens of muntjack deer from China. These are just a few of the great variety of species that have successfully colonised the city. One of the particular features of truly urban areas is the high proportion of alien species that have been introduced by human activities.

Another all-important factor is the extent to which places are protected. Bath is fortunate in that most of the woods and meadows forming the backdrop to the city are protected as part of the World Heritage Site. Some of the best habitats are managed by the National Trust to provide public access and also promote nature conservation. But, as can be seen from our brief excursion, many other areas are rich in wildlife and much depends on sympathetic management for it to survive. The tiny private garden in Widcombe where 44 species of birds have been recorded provides an indication of what is possible (Fig. 10).

Perhaps the most significant thing about the city is that all of this happens cheek by jowl with people. Species that are relatively timid and easily disturbed in wild places can be remarkably tolerant of people in the city environment. In fact the city offers some of the best opportunities for seeing wildlife at close quarters. Whether it is a kingfisher sitting on a bridge by the supermarket, herons fishing in the park lake, peregrine falcons sitting for hours on end right next to a busy street, or a badger's sett in the botanic garden, all of these are part of daily life in Bath. Every town and city has particular species that have become so accustomed to people that they are now a normal part of the urban scene.

THE WIDER PICTURE

Looking at towns and cities elsewhere it becomes clear that Bath provides a microcosm of what can be found in many other places. In fact the broad pattern of urban development in Britain shows a great deal of consistency and, in ecological terms, most towns and cities have many features in common. The majority have a densely built-up town centre, surrounded by areas of suburban residential or commercial development. Within this is a patchwork of green spaces and water bodies which have originated in a great variety of ways. Those that owe their origins to the landscape on which the town developed may have a long ecological history. Those resulting directly from urban activities are often of

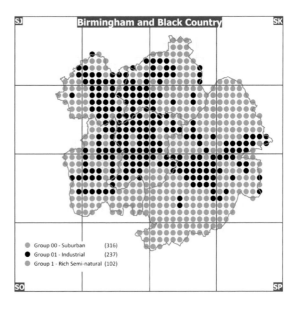

FIG 13. Map of Birmingham and the Black Country showing the distribution of the three main landscape types identified by twinspan analysis of plant records. From Trueman *et al.*, 2013. (EcoRecord/ Contains Ordnance Survey data © Crown copyright and database right 2013)

very recent origin. In general the amount of green space increases outwards from the centre towards the edge of the urban area where it often forms a significant proportion of the townscape.

The picture becomes more confused where towns and villages have merged to form extensive conurbations, as in London, Birmingham, Manchester, Merseyside and West Yorkshire. Here the patchwork of habitats depends on the historical development of local areas; especially industrial development. Nowhere is this better demonstrated than in Birmingham and the Black Country where plant records in the recent *Flora* (Trueman *et al.*, 2013) were used to classify and interpret the urban landscape (Fig. 13). The analysis shows a patchwork made up of three main elements; suburban, industrial and rich semi-natural. Whilst much of the conurbation is predominantly suburban, other parts are mainly industrial. But small scale industrial landscapes are also scattered throughout the urban matrix, with canals, abandoned mineral workings and remains of derelict industries sitting cheek by jowl with residential and commercial districts. Their distribution is closely linked with the canal network. The third category includes surviving pockets of encapsulated countryside, with some larger areas around the edge of the metropolis.

Vestiges of long established habitats, and unofficial wild land, through to formal gardens, town squares, tree-lined streets and even the built environment, together form the ecological matrix of a city. Open land along river corridors and transport routes creates linear green networks that may provide important linkages, whilst other elements form a less regular patchwork of green spaces. In many towns and cities the total amount of greenspace is very considerable. For example, two thirds of Greater London is green space or water and only one third is covered by buildings and hard surfaces, such as roads and car parks. Private gardens cover nearly a fifth of the land area and extensive tracts of woodland, heath and downland occur in the outer boroughs (Fig. 14).

Open spaces that have their origins in the pre-existing landscape may include river valleys and woodlands, patches of heath, or downland, rocky hills, marshland and even fragments of farmland caught up within the urban sprawl. Some of these can be remarkably natural in character despite their urban context. But as urban development intensifies many of these vestiges of the countryside gradually become modified. Rivers and streams are canalised or culverted and most are polluted to some degree. Most heaths and commons that survive have lost their heather and gorse as a result of urbanisation, becoming rather drab expanses of grassland, barely distinguishable from civic parks. Similarly where ancient woodlands survive many have lost their natural ground flora through trampling and compaction. The critical indicators of ancient woodland are either much reduced or have gone completely. Evidence of their antiquity now only

FIG 14. London's land cover (from GLA 2002, www. london.gov.uk).

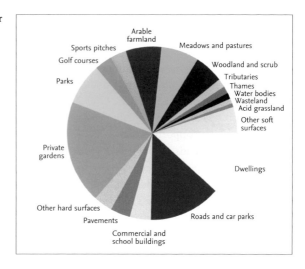

survives in wood banks, ancient pollarded trees and boundary stones. Marsh and bog habitats caught up within urban areas frequently suffer from drying out and pollution, so that the vegetation is much modified. Despite such changes there are numerous examples of long established habitats encapsulated within towns and cities that still have strong affinities with the wild. They support a great variety of wildlife that would not otherwise exist within an urban area. Frequently these habitats contrast very strongly with their urban surroundings and many are now managed as town nature reserves. Long established landscape gardens and the larger historic parks that are now surrounded by suburbia, like Richmond Park in London and Sutton Park in Birmingham, provide an even greater contrast. Because of their antiquity and the protection afforded over the centuries these places may still support relict assemblages of plants and insects that are now extremely localised. The so called 'royal beetles' associated with ancient oaks of Windsor Great Park and other hunting forests are a good example.

Then there are open spaces created as a direct result of urban development each of which has very specific uses. The full spectrum includes town parks and botanic gardens, sports fields, golf courses and other recreation areas, graveyards and cemeteries, city squares and tree-lined boulevards, private gardens and allotments, city farms and sewage farms, reservoirs and waterworks. The extent to which these places are colonised by nature depends largely on the rigour of their management. All have a variety of wildlife associated with them and where this is positively encouraged they can be remarkably rich in species. Golf courses illustrate this very well. Many of them provide a mixture of habitats that have close affinities with the original countryside from which they were developed. Where they are derived from coastal sand-dunes systems, or calcareous grassland, they can support a rich flora with many notable species. These may include national rarities, such as the lizard orchid that grows on the Royal St George's Golf Course at Sandwich in Kent. But all golf courses, even in the most urban of surroundings, offer the possibility of maintaining a great variety of habitats from close-mown turf, through rough grassland, to wetlands and woodland. The opportunities for wildlife to thrive on golf courses are well known, but all depends on the policy of individual clubs (Stubbs, 1996). Whilst some accept green woodpeckers foraging on the fairways others have a more clinical approach that excludes nature as far as possible. Given the amount of land devoted to golf courses in towns and cities they have the potential to contribute significantly to urban wildlife.

Most urban areas contain some wild places that have developed unintentionally, providing a suite of habitats that are truly urban in character. Like the disused gasworks in Bath, these habitats are typically found in places that have been abandoned for a good few years. They include the flower rich communities of urban wasteland and areas of industrial dereliction. Some of the richest are waste dumps of Victorian industries, now colonised by spectacular swathes of orchids and other unlikely plants. But urban areas have many other pockets of unused land such as quarries and gravel pits that gradually became colonised over the years and ended up as mature scrub or secondary woodland. The patchwork of woodland, scrub and grassland alongside railways and canals is typical. Some of these urban habitats have a rich assemblage of plants, and associated invertebrates, and are a particularly fascinating feature of urban ecology. Such areas have been referred to as 'Urban Commons' (Gilbert, 1983), or 'Unofficial Countryside' (Mabey, 1973).

It is not a great step from the flora of derelict land to the natural colonisation of pavements, walls and roofs within the built environment. A study of plants growing on the pavements and buildings of Mayfair and Soho (Hadden, 1978) identified 157 species that had managed to establish themselves in all sorts of odd corners within London's West End. Others have studied the plant life of streetscapes in Aberystwyth and Cambridge (Chater et al., 2000). Some of the commonest native species are groundsel, chickweed and dandelion, along with annual meadow grass, greater plantain, procumbent pearlwort, smooth sow-thistle, wall lettuce and hairy bitter-cress. Alien species include rosebay willowherb, Oxford ragwort, Canadian fleabane, ivy-leaved toadflax and buddleia. In the streets of Cambridge, Philip Oswald recorded 241 species of which nearly 100 were aliens, many of garden origin.

The flora of walls has attracted the attention of botanists throughout Europe and elsewhere and it is well known that old walls can support a diverse range of species. Recent surveys of Colchester's Roman walls revealed over sixty species of higher plants and 125 species of lichens (Wheater, 2011). The ecology of walls is admirably summarised by Darlington (1981) but it is a subject that would repay more detailed study. What is clear is that long-established floras and the associated invertebrates depend on sensitive maintenance. Buildings provide micro-habitats suitable for rather specific invertebrates, especially spiders, capable of tolerating extremes of temperature and lack of water. If left for a few years without maintenance, roofs and walls will be colonised by a variety of plants. Stone surfaces and roof tiles are gradually covered by lichens and mosses and ultimately by distinct assemblages of higher plants and associated invertebrates. The species that thrive depend on local climatic conditions and to a large extent on local building materials. Those growing in Bath's basements are dependent on lime-rich stone in a west-country climate. Elsewhere different combinations will occur, bringing local character to each and every place.

But plants are not alone in making the most of opportunities. As we have seen in Bath even densely built-up town centres support their own range of birds, including feral pigeons, jackdaws, crows, swifts, herring gulls, pied and grey wagtails, kestrels and nowadays even peregrine falcons. All are attracted by different sources of food and many make use of buildings and other artificial structures for nesting or roosting.

In considering urban natural history one becomes acutely aware of the key physical factors that influence ecological processes. These include the urban heat island effect, the particular characteristics of urban drainage and the unusual nature of urban soils. At a broad level these three factors determine how urban ecosystems work and why they are different from more natural landscapes. They also provide keys to sustainable management of urban habitats in the face of climate change. I shall digress for a moment to explain.

It is well known that the ambient temperature of towns and cities can be up to 7°C higher than in surrounding rural areas due to the heat island effect. The larger the city the more intense is this effect. It is caused essentially by the high proportion of buildings and roads, which have very different thermal properties from natural areas. Concrete, brick and stone afford less evaporative cooling than is the case with trees, vegetation and water. Solar heat stored in the urban fabric is released gradually resulting in higher night-time temperatures. This process is exacerbated by heat released from heating and cooling systems and from transport. But, by increasing tree cover by 25 per cent, afternoon air temperatures can be reduced by 6–10°C. and vegetation in streets

FIG 15. Urban soils can be entirely anthropogenic in origin: the Thames foreshore at Wapping contains concrete, bricks, charred wood, bones and oyster shells.

may reduce temperatures by 2°C. Comparisons of temperatures in city parks and surrounding urban areas have shown differences of 2.5 to 4°C. The fact that green spaces in cities have an important function in ameliorating local climatic conditions is now widely appreciated. Similarly the effect of street trees, particularly their value for shading buildings, is widely understood. Ecological landscaping, including green roofs and walls together with green areas within the urban fabric, is now being used to reduce deleterious effects of climate change on UK towns and cities (Goode, 2006).

Drainage patterns are similarly modified in the urban environment. Under natural conditions rivers are dynamic systems continually moving and interacting within their floodplain. Where towns and cities have been built within the flood plain, rivers have generally been heavily modified to provide maximum space for housing and industry and to provide the subsequent flood protection required. In most urban areas in Britain the solution has been to straighten the river channel and contain it by canalisation or culverting. But river management within urban areas also presents other challenges apart from loss of flood plains. The high proportion of sealed surfaces in heavily built-up areas causes more rapid and increased volume of run-off, and higher peak flows than in less urbanised surroundings. Peak flows frequently overload drainage systems causing flash flooding and may cause foul sewers to overflow. Urban run-off also carries a range of pollutants from the surfaces of buildings and streets into watercourses reducing river water quality. In recent years it has been recognised that environmental improvements along urban river corridors can have both

FIG 16. Giant hogweed, an invasive alien, especially along river valleys.

environmental and social benefits and more sustainable approaches to the management of urban watercourses are now being widely promoted. This is addressed more fully in Chapter 15.

The third factor is soil. Urban soils have several notable characteristics. They are extremely varied in composition, from the rich loams of gardens and fertile ground of cemeteries, to the bare surfaces of brick rubble and concrete of urban wastelands. This great heterogeneity results in a huge variety of ecological conditions. However, soil compaction and the intensity of urban drainage means that the majority of urban soils are at the dry end of the spectrum and wetland habitats tend to be limited. As already mentioned, industrial areas can have soils that are entirely artificial, resulting from waste deposits of various kinds that may be limiting to plant growth. The significance of different soil types is explored further in Chapter 5.

A particular feature of urban habitats is the abundance of alien species, well known examples of which are Japanese knotweed, buddleia, Himalayan balsam, giant hogweed and Oxford ragwort. But these are just the tip of an enormous iceberg. In fact urban areas have for long been the receptors for colonisation by such species and the list is very long. Many are particularly characteristic of urban wastelands, where intimate mixtures of native and alien species bring an unusual, exotic quality to the plant communities. The very nature of urban development, with cycles of growth and dereliction, leads to new and varied substrates becoming available for colonisation and this is one of the reasons why urban areas are so receptive to aliens. Another key factor is trade. Importation through the docks led to whole assemblages of new species becoming established and naturalised. Every port in the country has a list of incomers that colonised areas around the docks, assiduously recorded by local botanists. Many species were associated with the centres of particular industries. Aliens derived from wool shoddy were a specific group, which resulted in a large number of species becoming naturalised in Britain, not only around the docks but far inland around the centre of the wool industry, and in the rhubarb fields of Bedfordshire where the waste 'shoddy' was used as a fertiliser. Trade goes on today in different ways through garden centres and horticultural suppliers, which are responsible for the introduction not only of plants but also of a great variety of insects and other invertebrates associated especially with imported shrubs. Domestic gardens themselves provide another major source of alien plants, especially in suburbia. The heat island effect of large towns and cities encourages species from warmer climates to become established. With the influence of climate change large urban centres provide a springboard for northward moving species to become naturalised in Britain.

Some species have moved into towns and cities as a result of social and cultural changes. With the post-war decline in game management, birds of the crow family spread into areas where they benefited from protection rather than persecution, and so we now have magpies, jays and crows as common birds of town parks. In recent years ravens have followed this trend and are now breeding in Liverpool, Shrewsbury, Cardiff and Bath and have even been seen in Cambridge. Foxes are perhaps the best known of these new colonisers, and are now well established as part of urban life. Not so well publicised, but in some places equally prevalent, are the badgers that have survived in urban surroundings. Other beneficiaries have been birds of prey, several of which have colonised urban areas over the past thirty years, the most notable being the peregrine falcon, which is now firmly established as an urban species. Garden birds too have generally benefited from greater public interest. Their populations have grown significantly following the huge increase in use of garden feeders over the past twenty years. Those that have increased include chaffinch, goldfinch, nuthatch and long-tailed tit. Others, notably the house sparrow, starling, greenfinch and song thrush, have declined.

The story of urban wildlife is ever changing. Colonisation of London's bombsites during World War II by black redstarts, and the more successful colonisation of post-war gravel pits by little ringed plovers, were two of the most exciting ornithological events of that period (see Chapters 8 and 9). But similar things are happening today. Peregrines, parakeets, mandarin ducks, Chinese mitten crabs and American crayfish are all part of this ever-changing scene. Not all these changes are seen as beneficial by urban dwellers. People who live near a parakeet roost complain bitterly about the incessant noise, as do those with herring gulls nesting on their roofs. Gardeners are well aware of the damage done to their roses by deer, and others who encourage garden birds with feeders may find that they are also providing ready meals for sparrow hawks. Herons are hated by proud

FIG 17. Greenwich Peninsula Ecology Park is a good example of a newly created habitat that was part of a major urban development.

owners of well stocked fish-ponds, and cormorants have wreaked havoc on some commercial fisheries. Urban foxes are tolerated if not encouraged by many people who enjoy seeing them in their garden, but it only takes a few tragic incidents of babies being attacked for there to be calls for their extermination. Some issues posed by wild species that have recently become pests are addressed in future chapters, but these do not include traditional pests of human habitation, such as mice, rats, fleas, bed-bugs and cockroaches. They merit another book.

In this overview of urban natural history one must also include places that are being created specifically to bring nature back into the urban environment. Habitat creation is a major part of urban nature conservation, with the construction of ecological parks, butterfly gardens, green roofs, and even extensive new wetland ecosystems. Designed specifically to promote opportunities for city dwellers to connect with nature these are new and expanding features of urban design. This new approach has developed spontaneously in many countries during the past thirty years and such features are likely to grow in significance in the future.

PART ONE

Urban Habitats

FIG 18. Ancient hazel coppice woodland with ramsons (wild garlic) at Smallcombe Wood in Bath.

CHAPTER 2

Encapsulated Countryside: Ancient Woodlands

T HE GREAT NORTH ROAD CLIMBS up through leafy suburbs of north London, passing East Finchley underground station where there is a small park called Cherry Tree Wood. Like many other local parks it has a children's playground, tennis courts and football pitch surrounded by cherry trees. But there is something different about this park that sets it apart, for much of it is woodland. The tarmac path weaves its way between large trees of

FIG 19. Cherry Tree Wood, an ancient woodland in north London, now a town park.

oak and hornbeam with clumps of midland hawthorn, holly and hazel beneath. Most of the hornbeams have multiple trunks, a clear sign that they were coppiced in the past, but they have been left to grow for over 100 years. Many lean at odd angles, creating a strange vista of criss-crossed trunks and branches. In contrast the oaks stand straight and tall. There is a dense canopy throughout the wood, resulting in few woodland flowers, but some plants manage to survive around the edges, including bluebell, wood anemone, wild garlic, wood sedge, lesser celandine, cow parsley and lords and ladies. The presence of some of these plants, together with an obvious history of coppicing, suggests that the park might be a remnant of ancient woodland. That is exactly what it is.

Cherry Tree Wood is only a tiny fragment, yet it demonstrates perfectly the changes that have affected so many ancient woodlands that survive in urban areas. The wood is shown on Rocque's map of 1754 at its present size, but it was once part of the Bishop of London's great Hornsey Park which dates from the thirteenth century. At that time it was probably managed as part of an extensive piece of wood pasture. Later, as the park became fragmented and converted to farmland, small patches of woodland were enclosed against grazing and managed as coppice, supplying woodland products for the local wood and timber trade. Coppicing provided a regular supply of timber and wood over the years, while avoiding the need to fell a wood and plant new trees. Hazel and hornbeam were cut just above the ground, leaving the base of the trunk and roots undisturbed to form a coppice stool from which new stems would sprout. Most woodlands of this kind were divided into separate compartments, known as falls, which were cut in rotation, each block being allowed to grow for ten to fifteen years. With sufficient compartments in a wood a continuous supply of coppice products was assured. Hazel produced long straight poles used for posts, fencing and hop poles, as well as baskets, hurdles, hoops and stakes. Hornbeam, being very hard, was used to make wagon wheels and agricultural machinery. Brushwood was collected into faggots for firewood or for making charcoal. In most areas of coppice woodland some of the oaks were allowed to grow into mature trees known as standards. Such a wood had a two-layered structure, known as coppice with standards, with a scattering of high oaks above the coppice compartments at different stages of development. Oak trees provided substantial pieces of timber, in the form of beams and planks, for use in buildings, shipbuilding and river defences.

Cherry Tree Wood was one of these small coppice woodlands. In the early 1800s it was known as 'Dirthouse Wood', a reference to the nearby White Lion public house which was frequented by carters bringing out night soil from London and taking hay back for the city's horses. At that time the wood was still a significant part of the local rural economy. But as the demand for woodland

FIG 20. Queens Wood, a Local Nature Reserve run by the Borough of Haringey.

products waned during the latter half of the century many of these small coppice woodlands were no longer managed, and the trees were left to grow. So it is that the old hornbeam coppice has turned into mature trees, with thick trunks taking the place of the last crop of coppice poles.

Other much larger pieces of ancient woodland survive nearby, including Highgate Wood, Queen's Wood and Coldfall Wood. There are smaller fragments too. Turner's Wood, a private nature reserve, lies hidden behind houses of Wildwood Road, and two smaller patches called Big Wood and Little Wood still survive in Hampstead Garden Suburb. Silvertown (1978) traced the history of these north London woodlands from Tudor times to 1974. He demonstrated that proximity to London was all-important in their continued economic exploitation, and more recently in their preservation. The woods are part of an oak–hornbeam province extending from London northwards and eastwards from Hertfordshire into Essex. In north London many of the woods were called 'Falls', implying that individual woods were managed as single compartments in the coppice cycle. Coppicing seems to have been rotated between several woods to provide a constant supply of fuel and woodland products. In 1580 State Papers recorded that the Bishop of London received £1,466. 0s. 4d. in two years from the sale of wood and timber. It is clear that considerable quantities of wood were sent to London from the Bishop's land.

Silvertown found that the amount of woodland remained fairly constant until the late nineteenth and early twentieth century, a period that saw the biggest changes in the size and economic importance of these woods. The rapid expansion of London's new suburbs posed a threat to any open land. Some woodlands that had been part of Hornsey Park since the thirteenth century were felled, the largest of these being Bishop's Wood which was cleared in the 1920s to make way for housing and a golf course. Many other smaller woods disappeared and others were fragmented. But London's expansion brought with it a wave of protest against such clearances, which resulted in formation of the Commons Preservation Society in 1865. In Epping Forest the City of London Corporation brought a successful lawsuit against those responsible for enclosing the forest. Since the Epping Forest Act of 1878 the forest has been used for the free enjoyment of the people of London. During the next ten years pressure mounted on Highgate and Queen's Woods, which were unique as the most accessible surviving woods close to the city, and which had already become a favourite place for recreation. A campaign to save them for public enjoyment was remarkably successful. The Ecclesiastical Commissioners bequeathed Highgate Wood to the Corporation of London in 1885, to be managed as public open space. A *Times* leader pointed out that one factor in that decision was fear that property values would fall if the district lost its woods which were regarded as an amenity. In 1898 Queen's Wood was sold to Hornsey Rural District Council (later Haringey Council) and was designated as a Local Nature Reserve in 1990.

The railway came to East Finchley in 1867 and by 1900 Dirthouse Wood was surrounded by new suburbs. It only survived because the local council bought it in 1914 for use as a public park. A year later it was renamed Cherry Tree Wood and the council set about providing public facilities. The centre of the wood had been cleared of trees some fifty years earlier when construction of the railway caused localised flooding. This was now turned into a playing field and ornamental cherry trees were planted. A pavilion was built, together with tennis courts, a children's playground, tarmac paths, seats, signboards, a café and toilets. It soon had all the trappings of a public park. Over the years the woodland has been heavily trampled by many feet, and this, together with the dense tree canopy, has ousted most of the woodland flowers. All that survive now are the bare bones of the wood. But it is possible that these trees have a continuous link with the natural woodlands which existed here for several millennia. For those with eyes to see, it remains a fascinating remnant of the wildwood.

Over a third of the woodland cover of London is thought to be ancient, that is woods which have been in existence continuously since 1600. A survey by the Nature Conservancy Council (NCC, 1984) identified nearly 200 ancient woods

FIG 21. Hornbeam coppice that has grown into large trees creates extraordinary shapes in Cherry Tree Wood.

larger than two hectares, which totalled about 2600 hectares. They are well distributed through the outer suburbs, particularly in Bromley, Hillingdon, Barnet and Waltham Forest, and a few occur in the inner boroughs. The total is made up of many small woods, but some very significant woodlands have survived. The group known as Ruislip Woods is one of the most impressive. It is almost surrounded by the outer suburbs of Ruislip, and Northwood in northwest London. Four extensive woods, Park Wood, Copse Wood, Mad Bess Wood, and Bayhurst Wood together form a woodland complex that is remarkably diverse in both species and woodland structure. Covering over 300 hectares this is by far the largest block of ancient woodland in Greater London. These woods consist predominantly of old and neglected hornbeam coppice, with standards of both pedunculate and sessile oaks and, unusually, hornbeam and beech. Several other trees associated with ancient woodland are widespread, including field maple, wild service tree, wild cherry and aspen, and the shrub layer has much Midland hawthorn. Park Wood has probably the largest stand of aspen in London, a tree that spreads readily by suckering and is not liked by deer. Old hornbeam coppice with its dense canopy has much bare ground, or the ground flora is dominated by bramble, but where there are clearings the flora includes species such as wood melick, common cow-wheat, moschatel, hairy woodrush and southern woodrush. Woodland birds include breeding sparrowhawk, tawny owl, and even woodcock together with the occasional wood warbler and hawfinch.

These woods formed part of a 'park for wild beasts of the forest' recorded in the Domesday Book and traces of a wood bank that enclosed the park are visible in Park Wood. Mad Bess Wood has many banks and ditches resulting from a long history of coppicing. Records show that these woods have long been of great importance to the local rural economy and there is evidence of continuous use over many centuries. They supplied timber for the Tower of London and the Palace of Westminster in the fourteenth century. Thirty men worked in Park

Wood in the 1700s and it is said that by 1880 women and children were able to make more money selling firewood for Londoners than men could make working on local farms (Goode, 1986). Since then trade in woodland products declined and the woods became neglected. Fortunately these woods were on the very fringe of London when post-war Green Belt legislation halted further expansion of the suburbs, and so they have survived.

By the time that the Nature Conservancy was established in 1949 their importance for nature conservation was already recognised and one year later the woods were designated as a Site of Special Scientific Interest. It took a good deal longer for the NCC to realise that these woods should be a National Nature Reserve (NNR). They were not even listed in the Nature Conservation Review (Ratcliffe, 1977), which aimed to identify all areas that merited NNR status. I suspect this was simply because the woods were in London, the prevailing view at that time being that urban sites were not of sufficient quality. However wisdom eventually prevailed and Ruislip Woods were designated as a National Nature Reserve (NNR) in 1997. Bayhurst Wood, has long been managed as a Country Park with recreational facilities including a nature trail, information centre, woodland craft museum and even facilities for barbecues, which takes some of the public pressure away from the other woodlands.

But surely Epping Forest is bigger than Ruislip Woods I hear you say. Yes that is true, but though large parts extend southwards into the built-up areas of east London, the majority of the forest lies outside the capital in Essex. Covering nearly 2500 hectares, Epping Forest is by far the largest semi-natural wooded landscape in eastern England. It was made a Royal Forest in 1132 and over the centuries was managed largely as wood pasture with dense stands of ancient pollards of oak, beech and hornbeam, under which commoners grazed their livestock. Wood pasture was simply a means of growing new wood out of reach of grazing animals. Trees were lopped at a height of seven to ten feet above the ground and new growth sprang from the top of old pollard boles. In Epping compartments were cut every 10 to 13 years. It is probable that pollarding rights pre-date the Norman Conquest and that many individual pollard boles are hundreds of years old. At one time there were at least 500,000 pollards in the forest, but even today with 50,000 remaining there are more pollards here than in any other woodland in Britain (Dagley, 2007). Many of these ancient trees have hollow interiors or cavities and they contain much rotten wood which supports a distinct assemblage of insects, particularly beetles and flies, which are only found in trees more than 300 hundred years old. The fauna is similar to that of ancient trees in Richmond Park and Windsor Great Park (see Chapter 7).

It was the long established commoners rights of pollarding and grazing which led to the protection of Epping Forest when it was threatened by destruction from London's expansion in the 1860s. Tom Willingale, one of the commoners, became famous for lopping trees in a protest against the Lord of the Manor who illegally prevented commoners from exercising their rights. Illegal enclosures were already taking place when the City Corporation, backed by the Commons Preservation Society, brought the successful lawsuit that led to the Epping Forest Act of 1878. The forest was protected from development, but it still needed to be managed if it was to retain its ecological diversity. After the City Corporation acquired the Forest it allowed pollarding to lapse and the trees have grown to such a size that re-instating traditional pollarding now presents many difficulties. If the Corporation had continued pollarding on a regular basis the woodlands would be in a much healthier state today. But as Rackham (2006) points out the early conservators understood little about woodland history or ecology and were not interested in pollarding. Fortunately not all is lost. Since 1982 the Corporation has embarked on a serious attempt to re-instate pollarding. Over 1500 of the ancient hornbeams have been re-pollarded with considerable success and there are now areas where the coppice cycle has been reinstated. Oak and beech still pose problems (Dagley, 2007).

Despite its considerable size and long history of traditional management, Epping Forest was another of London's woodlands that was under-valued in the Nature Conservation Review. It only made it into the second tier of sites with the words 'in view of the pollution and public pressure the site is not considered to merit grade one status'. There is no doubt that Epping Forest is one of the most important woods in the country. It has the largest area of wood pasture in the UK, totalling at least 1400 hectares. Its importance has now been recognised through designation as a Special Area of Conservation (SAC), particularly for its beech woods and because it supports a significant population of stag beetles. The recent work of Helen Read and Jeremy Dagley on re-instating pollarding has received international acclaim from those concerned with the management of ancient trees.

FIG 22. Large populations of stag beetle occur in Epping Forest and Richmond Park, but they are also frequently seen in private gardens in south London. (Penny Frith)

Let us move now from the largest of London's woods to one of the smallest. In the western suburbs near Wembley is a small patch of ancient woodland sandwiched between the Grand Union Canal, Central Line tube, an industrial estate and suburban housing. This is Perivale Wood, an example of oak–ash woodland with many field maples, crab apples and wild service trees, and an understorey of hazel coppice. The wood only survives because of the actions of the Selborne Society, a body founded in 1885 to celebrate and emulate the work of Gilbert White of Selborne. The society was particularly active in west London where members of its Brent Valley Branch were keen to investigate the natural history of Perivale Wood, a fine piece of ancient countryside on their very doorstep. They managed to establish one of the earliest official sanctuaries for wildlife in the country in 1902 (Bender & Edwards, 1981). Harry Quarterman was appointed as keeper in 1905 with the daunting job of 'maintaining the hedges, coppicing the wood, and keeping out poachers, egg collectors, bird catchers, flower hawkers and sundry other trespassers'. He also constructed a range of nest boxes for woodland birds. In 1922 the wood was bought by the Selborne Society and became the Gilbert White Memorial Reserve. It was still managed commercially as coppice woodland until the late 1930s and small-scale coppicing has continued throughout the past fifty years in order to open up glades for woodland flowers.

FIG 23. For most urban dwellers the primrose is one of the first signs of spring.

FIG 24. Wood anemones can be surprisingly abundant in some ancient woods in urban areas, especially those managed as Local Nature Reserves.

Bird life of the wood was much studied during the early years of the reserve. In 1924 it was reported that surveys over the previous 19 years showed a total of 49 breeding species, many of which are still breeding today. But a number that were once regular breeders no longer occur. Several have declined in numbers nationally and no longer breed in London. In the early 1900s dozens of tree sparrows nested in boxes on the reserve. Now they are very scarce and localised as a breeding species in London. Other species which no longer occur are nightjar, nightingale, red-backed shrike, cuckoo, turtledove, yellowhammer and wryneck. Hole nesting birds such as woodpeckers and nuthatch have increased, together with the introduced ring-necked parakeet. Because of its long history as a nature reserve the wood was designated as an SSSI in 1954 and was officially recognised as one of London's first Local Nature Reserves by the Borough of Ealing in 1974. It is famous locally for its spring flowers and is open to the public on one day each year, when bluebells are at their best.

In the mid-1980s the Greater London Council carried out a review of London's woodlands to select those that deserve protection as Sites of Metropolitan Importance for Nature Conservation (see Chapter 14). The work was done by Meg Game who had worked previously with George Peterken in identifying plant species which could act as ancient woodland indicators. Twenty-three woods were selected, totalling nearly 1,400 hectares, the largest being Ruislip, and Perivale one of the smallest. These woods demonstrated a huge range of variation including oak–hornbeam woods of north London; hornbeam pollards and wood pasture of Epping and Hainault Forests; sessile oak and sweet chestnut of Lesnes Abbey and Oxleas Woods in Greenwich; oak and hazel on the Crystal Palace ridge that was once covered by the Great North Wood; beech hangers on the southern chalklands; and alder woods along spring-lines, and in river valleys such as the Colne and Ingrebourne (GLC, 1986).

Many of these woods have a remarkably rich flora with numerous ancient woodland indicators. A splendid example is Kings Wood in Croydon which is composed of oak, birch and ash with an understorey of hazel and holly. The rich ground flora includes dog's mercury, wood sorrel, sanicle, wood anemone, early purple orchid and yellow archangel. All three British woodpeckers breed here, and there may still be wood warblers, now a rare bird for London. Nearby is Selsdon Wood, another ancient oak–hazel coppice, which has been managed as a nature reserve since 1936. Both these woods have some of the finest displays of bluebell in London, despite being surrounded by Croydon's outer suburbs. Similarly woods at Lesnes Abbey in Greenwich are famous for their swathes of wild daffodils and wood anemones. Old Park Wood in Hillingdon has a particularly rich flora, including wood spurge, yellow pimpernel, sanicle and rarities such as coralroot and thin-spiked wood sedge. On the chalk hills in the south some of the woods are equally rich in species, but here they host a very different assemblage of plants including broad-leaved helleborine, twayblade, spurge laurel, toothwort and stinking hellebore. Though technically within Greater London they lie on the very edge of the metropolis and hardly count as urban woods.

FIG 25. Highgate Wood in north London: a very popular venue which suffers from soil compaction that affects the older trees. Coppicing ceased 150 years ago and hornbeams now stand tall.

What do we learn from this perambulation through London's ancient woods? There seem to be several factors influencing the ecology. First is the recent history, especially the cessation of traditional woodland management, which resulted in long established coppice woods and pollards being left neglected for most of the twentieth century. Many woods now have a dense canopy, resulting in heavy shade and loss of woodland flowers. Second is the recreational pressure from suburban Londoners and their dogs. The effects of trampling pressure and disturbance have reduced the woodland flora and fauna, but the magnitude of such changes varies greatly between

FIG 26. New coppicing at Coldfall Wood in Haringey.

different woods. Third is the extent to which individual woods were protected in the face of London's expansion during the late nineteenth and first half of the twentieth centuries. Then there are the ecological consequences of recent plantings, where native trees were cleared to make way for exotic species, either for commercial forestry, game coverts or simply in an attempt to beautify the woods of private estates. A further factor is the spread of exotic plants, and finally there is the possible effect of climate change, which is thought by some to be responsible for dieback of oaks in Highgate Wood.

Virtually all the ancient woods in London suffer from being over mature. Epping Forest is an extreme example, but the oak–hornbeam woods of north London have also suffered from lack of management and here again there have been efforts to reinstate traditional management, in this case coppicing, which ceased at Queen's Wood in the mid-nineteenth century, and at Coldfall Wood in the 1930s. David Bevan, who was for many years responsible for nature conservation issues in the Borough of Haringey, has described the effects of recent coppicing in both these woods (Bevan, 2011). The botanical diversity of the two woods dramatically increased. In the case of Coldfall Wood the number of species recorded almost doubled within five years of coppicing, increasing from 128 to 249 species. Although many of the early colonists were transient ruderal plants, other shade-tolerant species may well become permanently established.

FIG 27. Low chestnut paling fences in Lesnes Abbey Woods in east London help to protect woodland flowers including wild daffodils and wood anemones.

One of the most remarkable effects of opening these areas to the light was the reappearance from the seed bank of several woodland species that had not been seen for many years. These include foxglove, heath groundsel, two species of St John's wort, three woodland sedges, yellow pimpernel and the diminutive three-nerved sandwort. Primroses also increased dramatically. One year after coppicing the largest clump in Queen's Wood had 27 flowers. A year later it had almost 400 flowers. At Coldfall Wood almost all of the coppiced hornbeam regenerated successfully, but at Queen's Wood regrowth of hornbeam was much slower, probably because of the much longer period since these trees were last coppiced.

The impact of public pressure varies a great deal. Most of London's ancient woodlands are freely accessible and some that I have already mentioned, like Cherry Tree Wood, Highgate Wood and much of Epping Forest, have suffered as a result of too much trampling. But many of the ancient woods have retained a variety of woodland plants, despite being surrounded by suburbia and used daily by hundreds of people for informal recreation. Some woods have been able to withstand these pressures better than others through the design and layout of paths. The fine displays of wild daffodils, wood anemones and other spring flowers at Lesnes Abbey woods owe their survival to low rustic fences which keep walkers to the paths. The woods have been managed in this way since the 1930s. Similarly at Kings Wood in Croydon there are well-established rides and smaller paths which most people stick to, even if their dogs do not! With the exception of the hornbeam forests in north London it seems that impacts of recreation are most pronounced in woods situated nearest to the centre of the capital, where the pressures are greatest. Highgate Wood has been seriously affected by compaction of the soil due to its many visitors. Compaction prevents water movement through the soil and where it occurs around the roots of large trees they can become seriously deprived of water. Many of the large oaks, for which the wood is so famous, are now suffering severe stress as a result.

Historical factors also vary enormously. In view of the successful campaigns of the late 1800s that led to the saving of Epping Forest and Highgate woods it seems extraordinary that the much larger Bishops Wood was destroyed in what would now be regarded as an act of vandalism, particularly as much of it was converted to a golf course. To an extent the woods that survived were those that posed most problems for house builders. Hilly land and wet valley bottoms were avoided. Thereafter it depended on the strength of feeling and influence of local people. Those living in the leafy suburbs of Hampstead, Highgate and Dulwich had considerable influence and were able to mount successful campaigns. Lesnes Abbey Woods were saved after a public appeal was launched in 1927. Local authorities gave their support and the London County Council, which provided the bulk of the funding, became responsible for managing the woods in 1931. Many small woods elsewhere were lost without trace. However, the post-war Green Belt legislation had a profound effect. Many woods around the edge of London, which would otherwise have been up for grabs, were suddenly protected from urban development. Since the 1980s a large number of these have been managed as nature reserves, either by local boroughs or by the London Wildlife Trust.

The story of ancient woodlands caught up in the nineteenth-century expansion of towns and cities is repeated in many places, but nowhere has it been investigated with greater enthusiasm and rigour than in Sheffield. It may come as a surprise that Sheffield, despite its history as a major centre of heavy industry, still has at least thirty-five ancient woodlands within its boundary. Mel Jones, and others, have traced the history of these woods by searching through documentary archives going back hundreds of years. They also built up a picture of recent changes through detailed studies of the ecology and archaeology of individual woods. The popular account of Sheffield's Woodland Heritage (Jones, 2009) appeals equally to woodland specialists and the wider public.

FIG 28. Ancient woods form a backdrop to the city in Bath.

Their research shows that at the time of Domesday all the woodlands in the Sheffield area were wood pasture and many were still managed in this way in 1300, but by the late middle-ages coppice with standards emerged as the general practice. In Sheffield coppice woods were known as spring woods, and were normally divided into compartments which were cut at different times. Standards were referred to according to their age. Young trees, aged about twenty years, were called wavers; those that had grown through at least two coppice cycles (aged forty to fifty years) were known as black barks; and trees older than sixty years were called lordings. Jones quotes a review of 1799 which states that for every acre of newly cut coppice it was customary in the West Riding to reserve 180 wavers, ten black barks and another ten lordings. The older trees were kept until there was a demand for the timber. In addition to the coppice woods there were many so called 'holly hags' which provided winter fodder for sheep and deer.

As in London traditional coppice woodlands were a vital component of the rural economy from late medieval times until the nineteenth century. Coppice products in Sheffield had a multitude of uses. Wood was used for most domestic implements and in many industrial processes. Barrels, wheels, carts and baskets were all made from wood. Clog making was a major activity and the larger coppice poles provided pit props. Oak bark was used extensively in leather tanning, and the production of charcoal was a significant local industry, providing fuel for iron and lead smelting. Another lesser-known product was 'white coal', small pieces of wood baked in kilns in the woods, and used together with charcoal in lead smelting. Remains of over 150 white coal kilns have been found in Ecclesall Woods in Sheffield (Jones, 2009).

As the industrial revolution progressed coppicing went into a steady decline, particularly in the late nineteenth century, and virtually disappeared in Sheffield by the beginning of World War I. This was largely a response to national trends, but local factors also played their part. Increasing use of coal as a domestic fuel in place of wood was a major factor. New factories provided mass-produced domestic implements made of metal that rapidly replaced wooden products. Local self-employed craftsmen making wood products soon went out of business. Use of bark for tanning declined with cheaper imports and chemical substitutes. Charcoal was replaced by coke as smelting grew to an industrial scale. The presence of valuable coal and ironstone reserves beneath many local woods led to their destruction. With the rapid growth of Sheffield many woods with a long history of coppicing disappeared under housing and industrial development. One example mentioned by Jones (2009) is Burngreave Wood 'now only a few stunted trees over a patch of bluebells in Burngreave Cemetery'. Others have gone completely leaving only their name such as Hall Carr Wood. Jones comments that other local factors affecting the ecology of these woods were the increasing amount of trespass from the growing urban population, and the pall of pollution that hung over the city.

As the value of coppice wood plummeted in the 1890s landowners in Sheffield responded by turning the woods to commercial timber production. Jones describes it as 'a change from woodmanship to forestry'. This was achieved either by letting the best stem of a coppice stool grow into a standard tree, or by planting up coppices with new trees, many of which were not native to the area. These included beech, sweet chestnut, lime, sycamore and larch. Nurse crops of conifers were used extensively. The result was to change the character of these woods dramatically. Around the turn of the century many of the former coppice woods came into the ownership of the city council, either as gifts or by purchase. The Duke of Norfolk bequeathed two of his woods to the City, Roe Wood in 1897 and Wincobank Wood in 1904. Others, including Bowden Housteads and Ecclesall Woods, had already been converted to forestry before being sold to the city council. By the end of the twentieth century most of these city woods were managed as amenity woodlands, but almost all of them have been neglected for many years since the time of their purchase. Jones calls it a 'care and maintenance basis' but there seems to have been little care. They have grown dark, over-mature, and the shrub layer is greatly diminished or has disappeared completely. Vandalism and neglect have taken their toll in the more accessible woods and there are still development pressures in others.

One of the most interesting changes that has occurred is the colonisation of these woods by non-native plants. Ecclesall Wood in the western suburbs of Sheffield is a good example. Housing reached the edge of the wood in the early 1920s and it was protected as a public open space in 1928. In the 1990s Oliver Gilbert found a total of 89 introduced plants growing in the wood, representing

FIG 29. Deep valleys protect urban woodlands as at Jesmond Dene in Newcastle.

39 per cent of the flora. But these plants were not evenly distributed throughout the wood. They were concentrated around the margins where they formed a distinct urban ecotone. The most prevalent were montbretia, garden solomen's seal, Welsh poppy, Spanish bluebell, Himalayan balsam, Irish ivy and horticultural varieties of daffodil. Some others, notably lesser periwinkle, variegated yellow archangel and pick-a-back-plant had established dense patches up to 10 m across. Gilbert found that the greatest number of introduced plants occurred in parts of the wood adjacent to back garden fences and minor roads, precisely the places where people dispose of weeds and other unwanted vegetation (Gilbert & Bevan, 1997).

Bevan recorded forty introduced species in new areas of coppice at Coldfall Wood in London in the 1990s. Early colonisers were ruderal species, most of which had gone after three years. Other more shade-tolerant species may well become established as part of the woodland flora. These include garden blackberries, Himalayan cotoneaster, holm oak, Swedish whitebeam and tutsan. Most of these were spread by birds from nearby gardens. In the more recent coppices at Queen's Wood and Coldfall Wood about 20 per cent of the colonising plants found by Bevan were non-native, which he says 'reflects the urban nature of the woods'. Himalayan honeysuckle is widespread, together with Himalayan giant blackberry, cut-leaved blackberry, firethorn and various species of cotoneaster, all of which have originated from local gardens. The establishment of some of these species in urban woodlands could well become a future problem. Bevan concludes that Himalayan honeysuckle, Indian balsam and yellow-flowered strawberry may need to be controlled, but at present the rapid spread of goat willow, a native species, is more cause for concern (Bevan, 2011). Because of the greater extent of edge effects small fragments of ancient woodland within urban areas will be most seriously affected by such changes.

FIG 30. Leigh Woods National Nature Reserve is a fine tract of ancient woodland on Bristol's doorstep in the Avon Gorge.

Gilbert (1989) suggests that a number of large cities such as Manchester, Birmingham, Leicester, Leeds, Liverpool and Hull contain fewer vestiges of ancient woodland because the woods had already been destroyed by intensive farming before the spread of the cities. But in cities with steep-sided valleys, woods have a greater chance of survival and there are some spectacular examples such as Jesmond Dene in Newcastle, the National Nature Reserves of Castle Eden Dene near Peterlee in Durham and Leigh Woods on the edge of Bristol. Other examples are found along the river valleys of Glasgow and Cardiff, and in the Cloughs of Skelmersdale New Town in Lancashire. Cotterill Clough in the valley of the River Bollin in south Manchester was protected as a bird sanctuary in 1934 as a memorial to the Cheshire naturalist T. A. Coward. Almost overwhelmed by expansion of Manchester Airport this tiny woodland has survived despite the odds, protected as an SSSI and managed by the Cheshire Wildlife Trust.

FIG 31. Shenley Wood is one of several ancient woodlands managed by the Parks Trust in Milton Keynes.

The nature conservation value of ancient woodlands has become more widely appreciated since the 1980s, prompted nationally by the work of Peterken and Rackham, and there has been a concerted approach to develop an overall strategy for woodland conservation in urban areas. The programmes developed in Sheffield and London are replicated on a lesser scale in many other places.

CHAPTER 3

Encapsulated Countryside: Meadows, Marshes, Heaths and Hills

WOODLANDS WERE NOT THE ONLY ancient habitats to survive urbanisation. Fragments of other long established habitats can still be seen in many towns and cities. They include heathland, hay meadows and water meadows, freshwater marshes and coastal grazing marshes. Most of these were vital components of the rural economy in the landscape where a city grew. But they were gradually overtaken by urbanisation. Their survival depended largely on local geography and, as with woodlands, many of these habitats would have been destroyed were it not for the protection afforded by commoners rights and more recently by green belt and other local planning constraints.

Again London has many examples. Before 1800 much of the landscape surrounding the city contained extensive tracts of semi-natural habitats. To the west large areas of the Tertiary sands and gravels of the Thames basin were covered in heathland. Eastwards grazing marshes occupied the Thames valley from the Pool of London to the salt marshes of Essex and Kent. Most of the tributaries of the Thames that still survived on the surface were fringed by freshwater marshes. In the clay lands of Middlesex were swathes of hay meadows and to the south were chalk downlands. As the city expanded dramatically during the nineteenth century most of these habitats were engulfed by burgeoning new suburbs. The story of their demise is told in detail elsewhere (Goode, 1986). Despite all the pressures of urban development remarkable examples have survived, although it must be said some only just made it.

MARSHLAND

Grazing marshes were particularly affected by urban development and hardly any now survives within the confines of London. Vast areas of grazing marsh were created from the thirteenth century onwards by reclaiming coastal saltmarshes, including those of the Thames estuary which supported huge flocks of sheep even in the late medieval and Tudor period. This wet pasture-land was drained by brackish-water dikes, which over the centuries developed a characteristic flora and fauna, including a range of invertebrates dependent on different levels of salinity. Redshank, lapwing, yellow wagtail and snipe were abundant as breeding species. In the late 1700s such marshes still existed close to the city at Rotherhithe and Limehouse and also covered the whole of the Isle of Dogs and Greenwich Peninsula. Further east, marshes on the north bank of the river were, in places, over a mile wide and extended without a break to merge with the coastal saltmarshes of Essex. However, great changes occurred in the first half of the nineteenth century with the construction of London's docks, all of which were built on grazing marshes. At this time bitterns and bearded tits still nested on Plumstead Marshes and marsh harriers by the Surrey Canal in Bermondsey. Over the next hundred years residential and industrial developments spread relentlessly eastwards. The huge swathe of grazing marsh along the north side of the Thames was gradually developed. Dagenham Marsh provided the site for the Ford Motor Company factory and further east at Rainham the marshes became an army firing range. On the south bank too marshes were lost to industrial development stopping just short of Crayford Marshes where the boundary of London's Green Belt was drawn. Strangely, although Rainham marshes were still open land, they were excluded from the Green Belt because of their military use.

So, apart from a few relict patches of dykes and old sea walls caught up among the Thames-side industrial landscape, only two significant pieces of grazing marsh have survived in London. They both lie on the very edge of the metropolis, at Rainham and Crayford, and both are now protected as SSSIs. Crayford Marshes cover nearly 100 hectares. Despite adjacent housing and industrial developments they are remarkably intact and still support a number of notable species. The system of ditches and dykes separating the fields still forms a single hydrological unit, with a distinct salinity gradient across the marshes from freshwater to brackish. The aquatic invertebrate fauna of these ditches is exceptional, with many nationally rare and scarce species, especially the water beetles. There is also a thriving population of water voles, one of very few in London. Among the plants too there are nationally rare species, such as marsh sow-thistle and divided sedge, together with brookweed, brackish water-crowfoot, marsh and sea arrow-grasses, golden dock, and marsh dock all of which have a very restricted distribution in London. Despite their limited extent Crayford Marshes supports nearly half the total number of wetland plants recorded from the whole of the north Kent marshes. Breeding birds still include redshank, lapwing, yellow wagtail, shelduck and skylark, and in winter the marshes attract short-eared owls and hen harriers.

Across the river to the north is the much larger expanse of wetland popularly known as Rainham Marshes, which exceeds 400 hectares. Parts are still intact as grazing marsh, which support many of the same species found at Crayford Marshes, but here there has been a greater variety of past land uses, including lagoons used for holding silt dredged from the river, the remains of military ranges and long established domestic refuse tips. Despite these impacts the area has retained a wealth of wetland species. Most of the area is now being managed as a wetland nature reserve by the RSPB (see Chapter 6).

MEADOWS

Hay meadows fared rather better than many of London's habitats. In this case rather more of them have survived. Perhaps the need for hay to feed the vast numbers of horses during Victorian times had some influence in retaining productive meadows close to the capital. Their survival also depended on the

FIG 32. Richmond Hill and Petersham Meadow by the Thames in Richmond.

FIG 33. Brook Farm Open Space a popular local nature area in Barnet. From Totteridge and Whetstone tube station you can follow the Dollis Brook through the meadows and return via High Barnet (above left). Flower-rich meadows and old hedgerow trees (above right) at Brook Farm Open Space.

pace of development in different parts of London, which depended in turn on proximity to the newly developing rail network. Some parts of north London away from the tube lines remained undeveloped well into the twentieth century and it is here that we find the most extensive areas of hay meadow and old pasture still surviving today. Totteridge Fields, tucked away between Barnet and Edgware, remains one of the finest of these areas of ancient countryside. Here the unimproved hay meadows have a very rich flora, including numerous locally uncommon plants. Devil's-bit scabious, sneezewort, ragged robin, harebell, saw-wort, pepper-saxifrage and greater burnet-saxifrage are mixed with a great variety of grasses and at least seven species of sedge. Ecologists will be familiar with the vegetation of these fields as types MG 5 and 6 of the National Vegetation Classification. Networks of old hedgerows contain numerous species of shrubs and trees. Among the predominant hawthorn, blackthorn and suckering elm are hornbeam, ash, field maple, crab apple, dog rose, guelder-rose and even wild service trees. The number of woody species suggests that these hedges have existed for several hundred years. This whole landscape is ancient and has only survived because it lies within London's Green Belt. Elsewhere such landscapes have mostly been converted to intensively managed agriculture and it comes as something of a surprise to find these enclaves of old England still intact within the suburbs of London.

Totteridge is not the only example. In 1988 the London Ecology Unit carried out a review of London's meadows and pastures to select those that deserved protection as Sites of Metropolitan Importance for Nature Conservation (see

Chapter 14). The list included fifteen examples of ancient grasslands. Horsenden Hill in Ealing is one of the finest examples with fields full of meadow flowers separated by hedges of medieval age. Others include Arrendine Open Space in Barnet, Fryent Country Park in Brent and Bentley Priory Open Space in Harrow. One small patch of wet fields along the Yeading Brook in west London is surrounded by suburban housing yet still retains rare plants such as the adder's tongue fern and the national rarity, narrow leafed water-dropwort. Because of the danger of flooding these fields were never built over, and they are now managed by the London Wildlife Trust as a nature reserve (Hare, 1988).

Ancient water meadows have survived in other cities and provide extraordinary examples of *rus in urbe*. Constable's painting of the water meadows at Salisbury is one of the most famous of such views. Since Roman times these meadows have been managed to provide a hay crop and grazing for sheep. They are still grazed today and the wildlife is quite exceptional for an area only a few minutes walk from the town centre. Water levels are controlled by a series of sluices and dykes linked to the River Avon and the smaller River Nadder. The flora includes marsh marigold, lady's smock, fleabane, early marsh orchid, meadow cranesbill, common spike rush, amphibious bistort and the introduced monkey flower which has become established along so many of our rivers. Water rails, reed buntings and sedge warblers nest along the dykes, whilst the meadows

FIG 34. Harnham water meadows in Salisbury.

provide feeding grounds for swallows, house martins and swifts. Herons and little egrets fish the dykes. Orange tip butterflies are abundant early in the year when lady's smock is in flower. In July the waterways are full of banded agrion damselflies. Otters are seen with increasing frequency and Daubenton's bat hunts by night. The meadows are managed as a nature reserve by the Friends of Harnham Meadows and the Dean and Chapter of Salisbury Cathedral.

Some urban meadows are particularly striking. The famous displays of fritillaries at Magdalen College, Oxford have been known since 1785. Others may seem ordinary in comparison, but they make up for it by the longevity of their management regime. Port Meadow, also in Oxford, has been pastured by horses and cattle since the Domesday survey of 1085 and evidence suggests a grazing regime of greater antiquity. It was given to the Freemen of the City by King Arthur in AD 885. The meadow covers 132 hectares dominated by various grassland communities, with a relatively low diversity of associated species when compared with nearby hay meadows. A notable plant is the Red Data Book species creeping marshwort (*Apium repens*) for which this meadow is the only known site in Britain. It is registered as Common Land and also as an SSSI on account of its great antiquity and the considerable body of research relating to grazing management. The meadow supports large numbers of birds during winter floods, with over 1,000 wigeon and 1,000 snipe, together with teal, pintail, shoveler and large flocks of lapwing.

FIG 35. Betony in the meadows at Alt Yr Yn, a Local Nature Reserve run by Gwent Wildlife Trust in Newport South Wales.

Then there is the area known as Bog Meadows in Belfast which stands out as an extraordinary piece of encapsulated countryside so close to a city centre (Scott 2004). This is the remaining fragment of a once much more extensive tract of flood-plain meadowland along the River Blackstaff just 3 km from the centre of Belfast. Now hemmed in between the M1 motorway and the Falls Road it has become one of the most prized nature reserves of the Ulster Wildlife Trust. In the early 1800s, when the city was much smaller, the floodplain of the river covered over 400 hectares. It was renowned for the large flocks of waterfowl, together with corncrake, snipe, curlew and golden plover. At that time it was much favoured for wildfowling. From the late 1800s onwards development of the city resulted in gradual encroachment on the meadows through housing estates along the Falls Road and construction of Milltown Cemetery. Even in the 1950s a sizable tract of wet meadows survived and records show that it was still important for wetland birds. But new developments threatened its survival, particularly after a major drainage improvement scheme, and construction of the motorway in 1972. By the 1980s the importance of the meadows was becoming recognised and the local community campaigned vigorously to protect them. The Friends of Bog Meadows later joined with the Ulster Wildlife Trust and in 1998 were successful in obtaining sufficient funding from the European Union Programme for Peace and Reconciliation to purchase the meadows that remained. The City Council went one step further in 2001 by designating the area as a Local Nature Reserve.

The sixteen hectares of Bog Meadows that survived include wet meadow, marsh, reedbed, open water and alder woodland. Marsh and fen plants include wild angelica, celery-leafed buttercup, lesser spearwort, marsh ragwort, marsh marigold and watercress. Birds include heron, water rail, snipe, curlew, lapwing, skylark, reed bunting and sedge-warbler, as well as linnet and stonechat in the drier parts. Grasshopper warblers are also known to occur. Short-eared owls hunt over the meadows in winter when there may be up to three hundred snipe feeding in the fields.

HEATHS AND COMMONS

Heathlands and commons have a special story to tell. The number of ancient commons that still exist as public open spaces in London is extraordinary. Their survival is due to the positive action which was taken to protect them, rather than the chance factors that determined the fate of so many other habitats. In 1800 there were nearly 7000 hectares of common land in Middlesex, most of it open heathland and rough pasture grazed by cattle, sheep and horses. Like the woodlands described earlier, local residents had commoners rights, particularly for grazing, but also for gathering furze and even digging peat. During the eighteenth century many of London's commons suffered some degree of encroachment. Expensive villas were built around Hampstead Heath, Wimbledon Common and the village commons of Clapham, Wandsworth, Streatham and Tooting. As London spread during the first half of the nineteenth century these commons were subject to enormous changes. Common grazing gradually declined. Excavations for sand and gravel proliferated, most notably at Hampstead Heath and Mitcham Common. The new railways also took their toll by splitting commons into smaller fragments that were no longer viable for grazing. As they became surrounded by built-up areas some of the commons acquired a new function as places where working people of London found space for recreation. The Surrey botanist Ted Lousley (1971) describes the multitude of changes affecting Mitcham Common during the nineteenth century, including golf courses, gravel winning and refuse dumps.

Pressure for development was the greatest threat. Landowners saw the opportunity to enclose their commons and sell the land for building. Countless disputes arose and many Bills were debated in Parliament regarding the future of particular tracts of common. A typical case is Tooting Common, described in the New Naturalist volume on Common Lands (Hoskins & Stamp, 1963). In 1861 a local man bought the manor of Tooting Graveney and began proceedings for enclosure of the common. A committee of local residents opposed his plans, but he went ahead and enclosed about ten hectares. In 1868 commoners took action and broke down the fences, whereupon the lord of the manor responded with legal action for trespass. Commoners retaliated with a lawsuit seeking clarification of their rights and an injunction against the enclosure. In 1870, after a long legal battle, their common rights were upheld and the common has remained a valuable open space for the people of Tooting ever since.

FIG 36. Hampstead Heath, one of London's most popular open spaces. The fight to protect the heath led to formation of the Commons Preservation Society in 1865.

The 1860s was a crucial period and proved to be a turning point for the future of the commons. People all over London were fighting to save their local patch. The battles to save Hampstead Heath and Wimbledon Common are two of the most famous episodes in the history of London's commons. Whereas previously they had been the subject of isolated disputes, now they became central to a national campaign. In 1864 Lord Spencer, lord of the manor of Wimbledon, made public his plans to convert most of the common into an enclosed park and build houses on the rest. It was the publicity surrounding his private enabling bill that brought the plight of the London commons to wider public attention. In 1865 a House of Commons Select Committee was set up to 'inquire into the best means of preserving, for the use of the public, the commons, open spaces and forests in the vicinity of London.' Much of the dispute concerning Lord Spencer's plans was fought out before the Select Committee. After several years of negotiations a lawsuit between Lord Spencer and the commoners was settled amicably in 1870. The Wimbledon and Putney Commons Act of 1871 transferred all the rights of the lord of the manor to eight Conservators who became responsible for ensuring that the commons 'remained open, un-enclosed, and available for the purposes of exercise and recreation for the public and local people'.

The story of Hampstead Heath is told in great detail by Alan Farmer (1984), who recounts the repeated attempts from 1829 onwards by the lord of the manor Thomas Wilson to obtain Parliament's approval for his plans to enclose the Heath, all of which were thwarted by local public opposition. From his evidence to the Select committee in 1865 it is clear that he still believed the heath to be his private property. Having already destroyed much of it by extraction of sand he started building houses in 1866. The Heath Defence Group responded by taking legal action, on behalf of the commoners, led by eminent Hampstead resident Gurney Hoare. It seems likely that a long drawn out legal battle would have ensued, were it not for the death of Thomas Wilson in 1868. Agreement was then reached remarkably quickly with his successor for the heath to be bought on behalf of Londoners by the Metropolitan Board of Works. The Hampstead Heath Act of 1871 stated that 'the Board shall for ever keep the Heath open, unenclosed and unbuilt on'. The Board was also required 'to preserve, as far as may be, the natural aspect and state of the Heath, and to that end shall protect the turf, gorse, heather, timber and other trees, shrubs and brushwood thereon.' (Farmer, 1984).

During the course of these disputes, a number of those concerned became convinced of the need for a national body to co-ordinate action to protect the nation's heritage of common land. Evidence presented to the Select Committee in 1865 was compelling and this led one of its members, George Shaw-Lefevre, along with others to set up a new body, The Commons Preservation Society.

The Society was rapidly called upon to assist with the major disputes in London, including Epping Forest, Hampstead and Wimbledon, together with Tooting and many others, and it quickly extended its activities to protect commons elsewhere throughout the country. The outcome of many individual disputes depended on this new society throwing its weight behind local commoners. Success also depended on having powerful civic leadership. London certainly had that in both the Corporation of London and the relatively new Metropolitan Board of Works, but many other towns and cities did not. In the Midlands growth of industrial towns was so rapid in the late 1700s that scant regard was paid to the ancient commons and in Birmingham the last few acres were enclosed in 1799. Similarly Oldham in Lancashire, which was no more than a small township in the late 1700s, was still surrounded by commons. But in 1803 an Act was passed to enclose them. Within four years eight cotton mills and over two hundred houses replaced one of the local commons. Preston was rather different. It had a long established Corporation which acquired the local Moor in 1253 by Royal Charter and in 1867 managed to resist the pressure for development by converting it into a Victorian park (Hoskins & Stamp, 1963). Newcastle still has its Town Moor and Harrogate the Stray, but both have been converted to grazing land.

Although many of London's commons were saved as public open spaces few remain as true heathlands. Blackheath, Clapham, Peckham Rye, Streatham and Tooting all have their commons, but they have lost their heathland character to become rather ordinary expanses of amenity grassland. Urbanisation has resulted in them becoming little more than town parks. Wandsworth Common faired rather better and still has remnants of acid grassland and birch woodland. Vestiges of the original heath can still be seen in patches of gorse, broom and bracken on banks of railways crossing the common. Other commons that have been left ungrazed and unmanaged have turned into secondary woodland. Barnes Common is one of these. Apart from some areas being converted into sports pitches most of the common, which covers about fifty hectares, is still very wild in character. Much of it is still acid grassland with typical grasses such as common bent, wavy-hair grass, mat grass and fescues, and a number of heathland plants including heath bedstraw and creeping willow. Since grazing ceased in the nineteenth century substantial areas have become colonised by pedunculate oak and silver birch, with a ground layer of bramble and patches of bracken, cow parsley and ivy. Many of the oaks are now sizeable trees. The wildness of the common is much appreciated by local people and it became a Local Nature Reserve in 1992. There was fierce opposition later when Richmond Council decided to clear some of the birch to encourage open areas of acid grassland and heather. The council's ecologist had a hard time persuading people that open heath vegetation can be more important than trees.

FIG 37. Patches of acid grassland survive on Barnes Common in Richmond.

FIG 38. Since grazing ceased, much of the open heath on Barnes Common has turned to oak woodland with a ground layer of bramble.

FIG 39. The blackcap is now one of the commonest warblers on Wimbledon Common. (Paul Wilkins)

The Conservators of Wimbledon Common and Putney Heath have rather more on their hands when managing these commons. The whole area amounts to about 450 hectares, of which nearly a quarter is open heathland dominated by heather and another quarter acid grassland. Most of the remainder is secondary woodland, but there are a number of other important habitats including Sphagnum bog and small oligotrophic ponds. Most of the area is designated as an SSSI, particularly for the wet heath communities, but many rare and restricted species still survive in the other habitats, making this one of the most outstanding wildlife sites in the capital. It is beautifully described in a book produced by the Conservators (Drakeford & Sutcliffe, 2000) which provides a detailed picture of the natural history and management of a common that is now treasured by many people.

Since the Act which guaranteed their survival in 1871 the commons have been managed by a Board of Conservators who have to balance the many recreational uses of the commons with the needs of nature conservation. Grazing was stopped towards the end of the nineteenth century and ever since then the greatest threat to the heath has been succession to secondary birch and oak woodland. Mechanical cutting and selective burning are now used to maintain a variety of growth stages in the heather, and to keep this and the acid grassland free from saplings of birch. If it were left it would rapidly become colonised by birch and eventually oak in the same way as Barnes Common.

But ecological management is only one aspect of the work of the Conservators. Managing people occupies a great deal of time. The commons can attract up to 10,000 people a day on sunny weekends and bank holidays. Recreational pursuits no longer include the Victorian obsession with rifle ranges, when thousands gathered for the annual competition of the National Rifle Association! But today there are many different uses falling under the title of 'exercise and recreation'. They include walking, dog walking, running, cycling, horse riding, golf, football and picnicking, as well as quietly enjoying contact with nature. Bye-laws have been imposed to prevent the use of four-wheel drive vehicles, and metal detectors, and the practice of commercial dog-walking has been stopped. At one stage this had resulted in packs of up to forty dogs being exercised on the heath by one person! Removal of litter and other rubbish remains a major issue. Staff employed by the Conservators spend nearly a third of their time dealing with removal of waste material, including fly tipping (Drakeford & Sutcliffe, 2000).

Heath communities at Wimbledon are dominated by heather with small amounts of cross-leaved heath and bell heather in places. It is a dramatic sight in August when the whole of the plateau seems to be covered in purple heather. Other heath plants include bracken, heath bedstraw and creeping willow. Like Barnes Common the acid grassland contains a rich variety of grasses such as wavy hair grass, mat grass, Yorkshire fog, purple moor grass, meadow foxtail and Timothy. Associated with these are soft rush, heath rush, yarrow, adder's tongue fern and the nationally scarce yellow vetchling. One area of bog still has three species of Sphagnum moss forming an undulating mossy lawn. These are *Sphagnum palustre, S. recurvum* and *S. squarrosum* all of which are tolerant of some nutrient enrichment. Other plants of the bog include common reed, yellow-flag iris, reedmace, marsh pennywort, lesser skullcap and bogbean. The area is spring-fed and the range of species is characteristic of an oligotrophic flush rather than a true bog. The boggy patches and small ponds support a remarkable number of dragonflies and damselflies. Nineteen species have been recorded including the black darter and keeled skimmer. Similarly the Commons support a large number of butterfly species. Twenty-eight species were recorded between 1982 and 1999. Twenty-two of these are long-term residents, of which seventeen are very common. Woodland species are particularly significant, especially the purple hairstreak and the rare white-letter hairstreak. Other notable insects include the stag beetle, which is abundant where old tree stumps persist.

The birds were studied in great detail by David Wills and Ron Kettle, plus others, over many years (Wills & Kettle, 1997). Their records show a gradual decline in the number of breeding species since the 1970s, but the decline has been going on for much longer. Like Perivale Wood a range of species disappeared as a result of national declines early in the twentieth century, including red backed shrike and nightjar, which were both resident on the heaths in 1900. More recently about another fifteen species are known to have been lost as breeding species, again linked to national declines. Spotted flycatcher, wood lark, cuckoo, tree sparrow, redpoll and willow tit are just a few of those that have gone. Sadly since the 1980s the ground nesting birds such as skylark, meadow pipit and tree pipit have also been almost entirely lost, probably as a result of disturbance by dogs. Some species have increased in numbers including both green and great spotted woodpeckers, and the number of magpies has also grown considerably since the 1980s. Blackcaps too have become much more common. With about 100 breeding pairs they now far outnumber the willow warbler which was once the commonest warbler. A few new species have become established, including mandarin duck nesting in old trees along the Beverley Brook, ring-necked parakeet, sparrowhawk and recently the hobby. The total list of breeding birds now includes forty six species, compared with nearly seventy in 1900. A spectacular feature of the bird life is the nightly gathering of crows, especially in autumn and winter. In mid-winter up to 1,000 birds fly in from miles around at dusk to roost in woodlands on the common. Dusk is also the time to see bats. Six species are known to occur, including Daubenton's, noctule, brown long-eared, serotine and both species of pipistrelle (Drakeford & Sutcliffe, 2000).

There are few examples of heathland surviving the Victorian period in towns and cities elsewhere, but Mousehold Heath in Norwich is one that did. This is the last remaining fragment of a vast heath covering 2400 hectares which once stretched from Norwich to South Walsham. Most of it was enclosed in 1801 for agriculture, but within the city the heath was left unenclosed and was exploited for gravel and flint. In 1880 the remaining seventy four hectares were gifted to the citizens of Norwich by the Dean and Chapter of Norwich Cathedral, to be kept as an open space for use by the public. Since then the heath has been managed by the city council through a Board of Conservators and it recently became a Local Nature Reserve. But it is yet another example of a heath that has suffered in the absence of management. Like so many other urban commons grazing stopped after it was acquired by the city and much of it subsequently turned into oak woodland. Now the conservators are fighting a constant battle to encourage open areas of heather, and to maintain patches of gorse which suffer frequently from fires. Stripping of the topsoil has been used in some areas

FIG 40. Canford Heath SSSI in Dorset: nationally important heathlands are suffering as a result of urban development.

to promote re-colonisation by heather. Considerable efforts are being made to control encroachment of trees on the small amount of open heathland that remains. Lying only 2 km from the city centre Mousehold Heath is surrounded on all sides by urban development, yet it still manages to retain its wild character and is much loved by the people of Norwich. Some fear that as the city grows the heath will gradually become more urbanised. However, the recent management plan from Norwich City Council in 2010, with its strong emphasis on improving public awareness of heathland ecology, is a positive signal.

Far more serious is the recent impact of urban development on heaths around Poole and Bournemouth where rapid growth of this large conurbation has encroached on some of the most significant heathlands in the UK. New housing schemes now sit cheek by jowl with top quality nature reserves and there are already serious ecological implications, particularly through fragmentation and the effects of destructive fires. Haskins (2000) reports that only a few heaths of more than 100 hectares now survive around the edge of the urban area. Canford Heath, Upton Heath, Parley Common and Christchurch Town Common are substantial fragments, but most are small patches, of less than five hectares, which are now caught up within the urban areas. Fragmentation has resulted in the loss of a number of critical species from the remaining patches, especially the sand lizard, smooth snake and silver-studded blue butterfly, and impoverishment of invertebrate populations has also occurred. The other major impact is fire. There were nearly 200 fires between March and July 1995 on heaths within the urban area of Poole. Canford Heath suffered ninety fires during the two years 1995–6. Fire has become a persistent feature of these urban heathlands, whereas on the more rural heaths in Dorset fires are few and far between. Human activity is likely to be the cause, whether through negligence or intent. On small urban sites a substantial proportion of the total area can be affected very quickly, and on larger sites individual fires have on occasions destroyed over twenty hectares of heath. During periods of hot weather the fires burn very deep affecting all aspects of the ecosystem. Reptiles are particularly vulnerable, but destruction of stands of gorse also affects the number of Dartford warblers. Following extensive fires in the 1976 drought their population was much reduced and recent fires have had similar effects. Individual severe fires are known to promote rapid colonisation of birch, or gorse and there is evidence that repeated fires encourage a more permanent change to grass-dominated heath. The changes affecting these heaths today are simply repeating what happened to London's commons in the late 1800s.

The influence of large numbers of people is something that affects all these semi-natural habitats caught within the urban environment. Yet some have survived rather better than others. If there is one that really deserves the term encapsulated countryside it is Hampstead Heath. This is a most extraordinary piece of London's former countryside, only 5 km from Trafalgar Square, which has been preserved from urban development to become one of the capital's most treasured open spaces. The area that was first protected in 1871 was only a quarter the size of the Heath we know today. Many campaigns and battles were fought in succeeding years to acquire surrounding areas. Parliament Hill Fields, the Kenwood Estate, Heath Extension, Golders Hill Park and a number of small but significant gardens have all been added over the years. The Hampstead Heath Protection Society, formed in 1897, was crucially important in promoting public appeals to acquire the land. Protection of the Heath arouses enormous passions in local people and under its new guise as the Heath and Old Hampstead Society this body continues to provide a powerful voice for local people on all aspects of the Heath's management. Hunter Davies (1983) considered the protection of Hampstead Heath to be 'perhaps the greatest achievement that any preservation lobby has ever had'. The Heath now covers over three hundred hectares, with an intimate mixture of ancient and formal landscapes. These include ancient woodlands, hay meadows, old hedgerows, marshes and strings of ponds and lakes, together with remnants of the original heathland vegetation. The whole area is designated as a Site of Metropolitan Importance for Nature Conservation

FIG 41. Patches of heather and bell heather are being encouraged on Hampstead Heath.

and parts are an SSSI. But nature conservation is only one element in the vast array of recreational activities that occur on the heath.

The ancient woodlands of Kenwood contain an exceptional number of veteran trees, providing dead wood habitat for a range of specialist invertebrates, including the nationally rare jewel beetle (*Agrilus pannonicus*). Similar ancient trees occur along old hedge lines some of which mark long-established parish boundaries. Many of the fields are now managed again as hay meadows, leaving long grass until July or August. Several areas have been successfully reseeded to create wildflower meadows that have been welcomed by many people. The boundary between old hedges and meadows is a contentious issue. Left to themselves these hedges develop a belt of scrub and bramble that gradually extends out into the fields. Such areas provide perfect habitat for birds such as garden warbler, whitethroat and blackcap and are vigorously protected by birdwatchers. However, there are also those who are adamantly opposed to bramble, who want it strictly controlled. Meetings to resolve such differences can be acrimonious and the issue is unlikely to go away.

In a few places there are patches of acid grassland with notable species such as pignut and heath bedstraw. Within the original heath, now mostly colonised by secondary woodland, there are a few places where heathland restoration is being attempted. Efforts to establish heather plants from seedings are regularly thwarted by someone who dislikes the idea so much that all the seedlings are removed within a day or two of planting! Some relicts of the original heath still remain, including the tube-web spider (*Atypus affinis*) which was rediscovered in 1995. Milner (2006) considers that recent changes in the spider populations reflect a partial ecological recovery as open areas once heavily mown are now encouraged to revert to rough grassland. Royal fern planted recently is spreading in some of the marshy tracts. Grass snakes occur in the bird sanctuary, which also supports reed warblers and kingfishers. In February 2012 a bittern spent two

FIG 42. Long-eared bats roost under the pergola of the Hill Garden, one of the wonders of Hampstead Heath.

weeks investigating all the new areas of reedbed and delighted many people by roosting in the same tree every evening (a habit that became known to the heath regulars as *exhibitternist*). Long-eared bats roost under the pergola in the Hill Garden. There are of course introduced species. Muntjack deer occur in the bird sanctuary and Mandarin ducks breed in old trees by the lady's bathing pond and by the concert pond at Kenwood. Two kinds of crayfish have become abundant, Turkish crayfish and the American red marsh crayfish. Terrapins too occur in most of the ponds. Ring-necked parakeets are now well established nesting in the many old trees along hedges and in Kenwood.

It does seem extraordinary that Hampstead Heath has seven million visitors a year, with many organised recreational activities from football to cross country running, yet despite all this the Heath retains a wealth of wildlife and its many visitors still enjoy the natural features of the area. The great variety in the landscape means that it can absorb many people without seeming to be overcrowded. Even those who know it well may still get lost! The Heath has been skilfully managed to integrate nature conservation and other recreational pursuits since it was taken over by the Corporation of London in 1989 and it remains one of the most outstanding wildlife areas in the capital.

CLIFF FACES, ROCKY HILLS, MOORS AND MOUNTAINS

Relatively few towns and cities in the UK have rocky hills or cliffs within the urban sprawl, but where they do these places can be some of the richest botanical sites despite being part of a big city. An outstanding example is the Avon Gorge in Bristol. This spectacular feature was cut through carboniferous limestone as an overflow channel from a large lake during the Ice Age. On its eastern side the cliffs rise almost vertically in places to almost 100 m. These cliffs provide a range of habitats, including rock ledges and patches of limestone grassland, together with scrub and secondary woodland. The somewhat gentler western side is largely covered with extensive woodland, including Leigh Woods National Nature Reserve, but there are steep cliffs in places as a result of quarrying.

As the suburbs of Bristol spread westwards, the gorge brought further expansion to an abrupt halt, and today the residential districts of Clifton and Sneyd Park extend to the very edge of the gorge. Between them is Clifton Downs, an extensive area of open grassland. Because the gorge lies less than 2 km from the city centre it has inevitably been affected by all kinds of urban activities. Extensive quarrying occurred along both sides from the 1600s until the late

1800s. A major road runs along the east side and a railway and cycle path along the other. The most dramatic feature is, of course, Brunel's suspension bridge, completed in 1864, which spans the gorge at its southern end.

Despite these impacts the Avon Gorge remains one of the hot spots for botanical diversity in the UK. It has a remarkable number of rare plants, including twenty seven that are nationally rare or scarce. Some are endemic species. Bristol whitebeam and Wilmott's whitebeam occur nowhere else in the world, and Bristol rock cress and round headed leek nowhere else in Britain. Red data book species include honewort, little robin, compact brome and nit grass, along with another fifteen national rarities

FIG 43. The Avon Gorge in Bristol is one of the UK's richest botanical 'hot spots'.

FIG 44. National rarities in the Avon Gorge include spiked speedwell ...

such as green flowered helleborine, ivy broomrape, Hutchinsia, spring cinquefoil, rock stonecrop, and spiked speedwell. As well as these exceptionally rare species there are many other notable plants such as lily-of-the-valley, lesser meadow rue, bloody cranesbill, autumn squill and wasp orchid. The total list of plants exceeds 500 species.

Why is the gorge so rich in species? It is thought that the rather unusual conditions of limestone ledges and crannies favoured plants of open habitats, and that the gorge provided a refugium for plants of open conditions throughout post glacial times when the rest of Britain was becoming wooded. Many of the rare plants are at the northern limit of their range in Europe and depend on these rather special conditions for their survival. The gorge has been famous among botanists for its rare plants ever since the sixteenth century herbalist William Turner discovered honewort in 1562. But the environment has changed greatly over the years. In addition to the very dramatic effects of quarrying there have been equally significant impacts on the landscape as a result of changes in grazing pressure. The earliest documentary evidence of grazing rights is contained in an Anglo Saxon charter of AD 883, and it is known that the gorge, together with the adjacent Clifton Downs, was still heavily grazed by sheep until the mid- to late nineteenth century, and by rabbits until the 1950s. Watercolour paintings from the 1800s and photographs early last century show a much more open landscape almost devoid of trees.

Since then, in the absence of grazing, the rocky slopes of the gorge have gradually been colonised by trees. Holm oaks have become established through jays carrying acorns from nearby gardens where these trees were planted in Victorian times. Other trees, especially black pines, were deliberately planted

FIG 45. ... and Wilmott's whitebeam.

in the late nineteenth century in an attempt to beautify the gorge. Many of these are now substantial trees, which have shaded out valuable populations of rare plants. There have been other changes too. A large number of non-native species have become established, many of them as seeds from adjacent gardens, but some of them deliberately. A few pose serious problems, especially Alexanders, winter heliotrope, Japanese knotweed and garden varieties of garlic, all of which compete successfully with the less vigorous rarities (Myles, 2000). Cotoneaster is also proving to be a problem.

Although the botanical importance of the Avon Gorge has long been well known, it is only relatively recently that the rare plants have been investigated in detail to assess their populations and to develop appropriate measures for their conservation. Local botanist Libby Houston has been one of the key figures in the precarious business of checking individual populations, when rock climbing ability and taxonomic knowledge are equally important. Building on the pioneering work of Dr Lewis Frost of Bristol University, she and others now undertake a regular census of all the plant rarities, one of the most detailed for any botanical site in Britain. In addition to the rare plants of the limestone crags, the woodlands on the west side are also of considerable significance. Other important wildlife include a number of notable invertebrates, such as the silky wave moth in one of only three known localities in Britain. Lesser horseshoe bats have winter roosts in some of the caves, and both raven and peregrine falcon regularly breed on cliff ledges.

The gorge is protected as an SSSI and also as a Special Area of Conservation under the European Habitats Directive. In 2010 the Avon Gorge and Downs Wildlife Project published a management plan for the Bristol side of the Avon Gorge, which set out detailed plans for conservation of wildlife. This work was co-ordinated by Bristol City Council, in partnership with Bristol Zoo, Natural England, Merchant Venturers, Bristol University and the Downs Committee. One of its proposals was to re-introduce grazing to control woody vegetation and this was done in 2011. A section of the cliffs was fenced to provide an enclosure

3.5 hectares in extent, within which rare tree species were protected and a small refuge was also created to allow tree seedlings to regenerate. Six goats were then brought in, but not any old goats. They were specially selected from a herd of cashmere goats that graze the Great Orme. These goats prefer woody species and according to biodiversity officer, Mandy Leivers, they seem to be doing a good job.

For a city council to be directly involved in the management of an internationally important botanical site is most unusual, and this reflects the extraordinary significance of the gorge to the people of Bristol. It is by far the most notable landmark in the city, attracting hundreds of thousands of visitors every year, most of whom go to see the suspension bridge and the dramatic scenery of the gorge. A small rocky garden by the bridge has examples of some of the rare plants, so it is now possible for people to see them without having to abseil down the gorge. There are also display boards at intervals along the cliff top explaining the ecological history of the area. Increasingly people come to see the peregrine falcons which have nested on a cliff ledge since the 1990s. From the peregrine watch point it is possible to see ravens at their nest on the other side of the river. The Avon Gorge is equally famous as a centre for rock climbing. On popular weekends the cliffs and quarry faces attract numerous parties of climbers from all over the country. The local climbing club helps with botanical survey work on the steeper parts of the gorge, and with the annual ringing of peregrine chicks. They also make it clear that certain routes are out of bounds to climbers during the nesting season.

Another city notable for its dramatic scenery is Edinburgh where hills of ancient volcanic rock rise above the city, the most prominent being Arthur's Seat and Salisbury Crags in Holyrood Park and the crag on which Edinburgh Castle stands. Similar rocks form Blackford Hill and Craiglockhart Hill, creating islands of natural vegetation within the southern suburbs of the city. All these hills have steep rocky slopes and some impressive cliffs of volcanic rocks, mainly basalt, which are base-rich in places and support a range of notable plants. The sticky catchfly (*Lychnis viscaria*), a nationally rare relative of ragged robin, is one of these. It was first recorded in Britain from Holyrood Park in 1668. At one time it was known to grow on the Castle Rock and is said to have been the favourite flower of King James VI of Scotland. It has declined in numbers over the years and by 1993 was reduced to only three plants growing on Arthur's Seat. Since then it has been included in the Royal Botanic Garden's project on Scottish Rare Plants. Plants propagated from local seed were re-introduced in order to ensure a more sustainable population in Holyrood Park. More recently attempts have been made to establish plants on Blackford Hill and on Castle Rock. Sadly those on Blackford Hill were eaten by rabbits and the plant is also particularly vulnerable to fire. Another scarce plant, well established on Arthur's Seat, is the forked

FIG 46. Arthur's Seat, Edinburgh: view from Blackford Hill.

spleenwort which likes the dry, south-facing crags of columnar basalt known as Samson's Ribs. Here too there are patches of another unusual fern, the southern polypody. Holyrood Park also has one of the scarce species of whitebeam, in this case the rock whitebeam (*Sorbus rupicola*). Other specialities of these dry south-facing rocky slopes are spring sandwort, maiden pink, spring cinquefoil and purple milk-vetch. The latter may also still survive in a tiny patch on the top of Blackford Hill, despite the impact of large numbers of walkers. These basalt hills also support several rare species of mosses, including one, *Grimmia anodon*, that is only found in Britain on Arthur's Seat.

Edinburgh is one of the few cities in Britain to have a Habitat Action Plan (see Chapter 14) for Rock Faces to promote the conservation of critical species. In addition to the plants already mentioned it includes a small and rather disparate group of species, including the sieve toothed moss (*Coscinodon cribrosus*), a micro moth called *Glyphipterix minorella*, the blind white snail (*Cecilioides acicula*), together with species of ant, jumping spider and plume moth. All of these are at the northern edge of their range in the UK and several are found nowhere else in Scotland. The presence of these species far beyond their normal range in southern England is probably due to the presence of base-rich volcanic rocks, and steep south-facing slopes which together provide favourable conditions.

Botanists tell me that over five hundred plant species are recorded from Holyrood Park and that it is by far the most extensive area of unimproved grassland in the Lothians. But for me its greatest value is because it is such a wild landscape to have right in the middle of a city. No other place in the UK has anything to match it. Though only 250 m high the rugged top of Arthur's Seat, and spectacular cliffs of Salisbury Crags, seem more akin to mountain habitats and it is always a great pleasure to scale their heights to look down on Edinburgh from above. It is a place of meadow pipits and skylarks, where you can see kestrels hunting voles within a few minutes walk of Holyrood Palace.

But go across the water to Belfast and there you find a city that has grown until it is right up against the hills. The dramatic crags of Cave Hill rise high above north Belfast. The summit of Divis, the highest of these hills at 428 m, overlooks the Falls, and the quarried slopes of Blackmountain form a backdrop to south Belfast. Robert Scott describes these hills in *Wild Belfast* (2004), one of the best recent descriptions of a city's natural history. The lower slopes are largely covered in scrub, supporting a variety of small birds such as blackcap, linnet, willow warbler and stonechat. Further up are rocky slopes and steep cliffs, with patches of herb-rich grassland amongst more extensive rough grazing and dry upland heath. Some of these hills are well known for their orchids. Slievenacloy has twayblade, frog orchid, greater and lesser butterfly orchids and the rare Irish lady's-tresses. Other plants in the wet meadows here include heath speedwell and moonwort. One of the eighteenth-century botanists, John Templeton, found the rare thyme broomrape on Cave Hill. Other notable plants, mossy saxifrage and lesser wintergreen, were found by the famous Irish botanist Lloyd Praeger in the 1920s. All these can still be found today. Upland heath includes wet and dry facies with heathers and bilberry in drier parts and cross-leaved heath, purple moor grass and Sphagnum moss in wetter places. There are patches of blanket bog too, with cotton grass, bog asphodel and lousewort. Devil's-bit scabious is widespread and Slievenacloy has a local population of the rare marsh fritillary butterfly, which is dependent on the scabious as its food plant (Scott, 2004).

The birds of the Belfast hills are typical upland species, the last thing you would expect to find in a city! Skylarks and meadow pipits abound, together with wheatear, snipe and even a few red grouse and ring ouzels. Kestrels are the commonest birds of prey, but a number of other species occur including buzzard, peregrine, sparrowhawk and both long and short-eared owls. Ravens range widely over the hills and their deep croaks can be heard from many parts of the city.

RIVERS

We end with one habitat that occurs in virtually every town or city: rivers and streams. Many watercourses running through urban areas have been heavily modified either by canalisation or culverting. Yet there are many that still retain their natural features and these river valleys now provide some of the richest urban habitats. Those that flow in well-defined valleys like the River Wear in Durham have survived particularly well. The River Kelvin in Glasgow and Water of Leith in Edinburgh are also fine examples. Both have riverside paths that take you on a mysterious journey where every bend opens to a new vista and the whole ecology is a mixture of native species such as goosanders, dippers, grey wagtails, herons

FIG 47. The Water of Leith at Dean Village in Edinburgh.

and kingfishers, alongside great swathes of Himalayan balsam and giant hogweed. They have a special atmosphere, cut off from the rest of the city, yet an integral part of it. In the city centre of Cardiff the same birds, together with cormorants, are found on the River Taff where it runs past Bute Park arboretum. Like many other rivers in industrial areas it was heavily polluted, but water quality has improved significantly over the past thirty years and both salmon and sea trout can now be seen leaping the Blackweir or going through the fish pass. Otters are found on all three of the main rivers running through the city, but especially on the River Ely. In her exploration of the River Taff, Gillham (2002) follows the river through the city, providing a detailed account of its natural history, and traces the fate of many patches of riverine wetland now lost to development. Like the grazing marshes in London those in Cardiff are long gone, but here there has been another loss; the conversion of the intertidal habitats of Cardiff bay into a freshwater lagoon.

The Thames and its tidal tributaries in London are recognised as a Site of Metropolitan Importance for Nature Conservation. The river supports a great variety of wildlife, with large populations of wildfowl and waders on intertidal reaches downstream of Greenwich. It also supports over 100 species of fish, and many of the tidal creeks are important fish nurseries, including some species that are fished commercially (Wheeler, 1979). In the upper reaches of the river west of Kew Gardens there are numerous small islands, some of which have large heronries. In a few places, such as Syon Park, the river still has a natural bank

FIG 48. Turnstones on discarded cockle shells at Leigh-on-Sea, Essex.

FIG 49. An estuary in the town with curlews and oystercatchers: Teignmouth, Devon.

with tidal creeks, where two nationally rare species of snails manage to survive in a few isolated pockets of suitable habitat. These are the German hairy snail (*Perforatella rubiginosa*) and the two lipped door snail (*Balia biplicata*). The flood meadow here is scheduled as an SSSI and another example at Barnes railway bridge is a Local Nature Reserve.

Further down the Thames estuary near Southend is the centre of operations for the cockle industry where small-scale factories occupy the shoreline and piles of empty cockle-shells are deposited every day. Turnstones and gulls invade the yards to feast on fragments of cockles left in the shells; rich pickings indeed. The range of opportunities for wildlife associated with coastal towns, especially fishing ports and those next to estuaries, is very considerable. But space does not allow me to elaborate. The turnstones will have to suffice.

CHAPTER 4

Canals, Cemeteries and Railways

S OME OF THE MOST STRIKING urban habitats that we find today arose as by-products of the industrial revolution. Canals, cemeteries and railways have all left their mark on towns and cities. Each has a particular legacy of man-made landscapes and habitats that now provide places where nature can thrive. This was not intended. In some cases colonisation by nature came about directly as a result of economic failure that led to magnificent Victorian edifices being abandoned, falling into disuse, going wild. In other cases where they are still in use nature has capitalised on opportunities presented by new uses and different management regimes. In all these places change has been instrumental in allowing nature to take over. The stories differ in each case, but the underlying ecological processes are remarkably similar.

CANALS

One of the greatest legacies of the Industrial Revolution is the intricate network of canals that were built during the late 1700s and early 1800s. The first in the UK was the Newry Canal in Northern Ireland built in 1742, and the first in England came nearly twenty years later with the St Helens Canal and Bridgewater Canal, both of which were opened in 1761. The Bridgewater Canal took coal directly from the mines at Worsley in South Lancashire to the industrial heartland of Manchester. Its success resulted in a rush to build canals to provide easy access to other manufacturing centres. They brought immediate benefits through the carriage of huge quantities of raw materials for industrial processes and an efficient way of distributing the products. Many leading manufacturers promoted construction of particular canals, such as the Trent and Mersey Canal funded in part by Josiah Wedgwood.

Within a few years after completion of the Bridgewater Canal a national network was well underway. It was an extraordinary period. Canals soon connected all the major industrial conurbations and some, like the Grand Union, Leeds and Liverpool, and the Kennet and Avon, provided links between navigable rivers, notably the Thames, Severn, Trent and Mersey. In Scotland the Forth and Clyde Canal linked all the larger industrial towns of the central belt, as well as connecting the two main estuaries. Major industrial conurbations such as Birmingham and the Black Country, and Greater Manchester were riddled with canals. Birmingham still has over 220 km of canals. Some follow the contours, like the Wyrley and Essington Canal in Birmingham which curls its way around Walsall, whilst others rely on tunnels, locks and aqueducts to find routes through industrial landscapes. One of the last canals to be built was the Manchester Ship Canal. Opened in 1894 it allowed ocean-going ships to pass from the Mersey estuary to the docks at Salford Quays in central Manchester. For a time this enabled Manchester to become the country's third largest port, despite being over 60 km inland.

The period from 1770 to 1830 was the great age of canals. At their maximum extent the inland waterways amounted to about 6,400 km of canals and navigable rivers. They were a major factor in promoting the industrial revolution. But such was the pace of change they had hardly become established before being overtaken by the next major advance in transport, the railways. Because most of the canals were designed for narrow boats, only 2.3 m wide, there were limits to the amount of cargo that could be carried and compared to the railways barge traffic moved at snail's pace. The railways quickly gained an advantage, added to which railway entrepreneurs bought out canal companies to eliminate opposition to their parliamentary Bills for new railways. Competition was rife from 1840 onwards and by 1850, when the railways were well established, the amount of cargo on canals had fallen by two thirds. Few new canals were built after 1830 and many fell into disuse in the late nineteenth and early twentieth centuries. During the first half of the twentieth century freight traffic gradually dwindled and by 1950 only a few canals still carried any freight. Some factories persisted with deliveries of coal where it was economic to do so, but the last significant freight traffic ceased by the 1960s.

By 1962 the canal system had shrunk to only 3,000 km. Six years later when canals became the responsibility of the British Waterways Board (BWB) there was an annual deficit in running costs of £1 million. In 1968 the Transport Act recognised three kinds of waterways: those that were still commercially viable which were mainly navigable rivers; those with potential for recreational use, including cruising, fishing and other leisure pursuits; and the remainder which

FIG 50. Birmingham and Fazeley Canal in Birmingham City Centre with new waterside development along the towpath and colonisation of the far side by emergent aquatics and shrubs growing on the wall.

were considered to provide few clear benefits. Many canals in the third category suffered from fragmentation by new urban developments, or construction of motorways. Some were converted into roads or linear parks and in some cases local groups sprang up to fight their closure. The majority of canals fell into the second category, the 'cruiseways'. BWB recognised the considerable potential for a new commercial use based on recreation and gave much support to this new activity. The burgeoning growth of recreational boat traffic, primarily narrow boats with their associated marinas, has since revitalised the canal network, and some canals which had been unused for many years, such as the Kennet and Avon, were restored.

More recently canals in some inner cities have provided a focus for new commercial and residential waterfront developments. Gas Street Basin in Birmingham, Castlefield Basin and Salford Quays in Manchester, Victoria Quays in Sheffield, and Limehouse and Battlebridge Basins in London have all been remarkably successful in retaining the industrial archaeology of the canals alongside modern commercial uses. Wigan Pier on the Leeds and Liverpool Canal is another example where the industrial heritage has been restored.

FIG 51. Birmingham Canal Path.
The city has 220 km of canals.

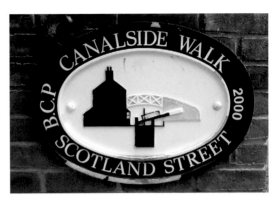

The other big change affecting urban canals is the intensive use made of them as linear parks. Away from busy roads the towpaths provide quiet routes that are used by huge numbers of people for walking, jogging, cycling and quiet recreation. They have become one of the most valuable 'natural' features of the urban scene. Very often canals provide vital links with surrounding areas of countryside. Towpaths are frequently modified to cater for these various activities.

Such are the changes that have affected canals over the past 250 years. What we are left with is a legacy of the original canals with all their associated structures, such as bridges, locks, tunnels, cuttings, aqueducts, wharves,

FIG 52. Birmingham Canal Old Line – a very popular canalside walk.

FIG 53. Great willowherb on the Lancaster Canal.

docksides and retaining walls that have survived over the years, providing remarkable continuity over a substantial period. For many towns and cities canals provide some of the oldest surviving elements of the built environment. Given the range of habitats involved, both aquatic and terrestrial, it is not surprising to find that they support a great variety of wildlife. The habitats of urban canals can be conveniently divided into those of the towpath, the canal itself and the 'far bank'. In the most heavily built-up stretches buildings may form hard edges on both sides, but more often than not there is a narrow zone of vegetation forming a verge on either side of the towpath and a wilder strip along the far bank that is generally inaccessible. Bridges, lock-gates and tunnels each provide their own set of ecological conditions.

Canals combine the properties of ponds, backwaters and lowland rivers, but with fixed water levels and very low flow rates they have no truly natural counterparts (Briggs, 2012). Their ecology is influenced to a great degree by recreational use. Within the canal itself the density of boat traffic is crucially important in determining the amount of aquatic vegetation. In areas with most boat traffic the water is murky owing to the regular stirring-up of bottom sediments which creates rather turbid conditions. This together with direct disturbance by boats precludes growth of floating vegetation. In such circumstances the species that manage to survive best are Canadian waterweed and fennel pondweed, with a sporadic fringe of reed sweet-grass, which tends to recover quickly after damage. Canadian waterweed was introduced from Canada, first appearing in 1836 and rapidly spreading by fragments being carried throughout the canal system. In places it caused great problems by choking canals and even prevented boats from getting through. At times the filamentous alga *Cladophora glomerata* may also become dominant, producing dense mats across the surface, eradicating all other water plants. Although the water quality

FIGS 54 & 55. Hemlock water dropwort along the Regents Canal in London (above left); Flowering rush and mare's-tail grow along less disturbed parts of the Wyrley and Essington Canal in Birmingham (above right).

may appear to be reduced, the range of fish species indicates that this is not so. An example is the Regents Canal in Camden where anglers catch eel, dace, roach, carp, perch and even some very large pike. The introduced Turkish crayfish is also abundant. In some of the wider stretches where there is less disturbance by boats other aquatic plants survive, including soft hornwort, curled pondweed and white water lilies, the latter often planted intentionally.

Where boat traffic is less severe a greater variety of floating-leaved pondweeds may be found along the margins of the central channel, sometimes with patches of yellow water lily. A well established zone of emergent aquatic species occurs in the shallows along both edges. This includes some of the characteristic plants of the canals such as water plantain, arrowhead, branched bur-reed, yellow flag and purple loosestrife. In those sections where there is very little boat traffic a much greater variety of floating aquatic plants occur. As well as the commoner species, such areas may also support the small, curled and perfoliate pondweeds, rigid hornwort, spiked water milfoil, common water-starwort and several species of duckweed. Narrow leaved water-plantain and flowering rush may also increase in abundance. The aquatic willow moss and introduced water fern can both become dominant at times (Murphy & Eaton, 1983). Less frequently one may find floating plants of water soldier and frog-bit in backwaters, as for example in Broads Dock in west London.

Where there is very little boat traffic both sides of the channel can develop fringes of emergent aquatic species which may vary from dense beds of reed sweet-grass to more mixed communities of bur-reeds and taller reedswamp with common reed and bulrush in places. Generally this grades back into tall-herb fen with great willowherb, yellow iris, hemp agrimony, water dock, meadowsweet

FIG 56. Water plantain and amphibious bistort occur where there is very little boat traffic.

and lower growing plants such as watercress, ragged robin and marsh marigold. A good example of one of the more species-rich urban canals is the Wyrley and Essington Canal in Walsall (Trueman et al., 2013). Here the central channel has good populations of water crowfoot, amphibious bistort, spiked water milfoil, arrowhead and water plantain, with a variety of other floating leaved plants including curled, perfoliate, fennel and shining pondweeds. One of its specialities is the floating water plantain which is abundant in places. Common and ivy-leaved duckweeds cover the water at times, as do yellow and white water lilies. Emergent plants along the margins include tall stands of common club-rush, bulrush, yellow iris and cyperus sedge. Within this zone are soft rush, branched and unbranched bur-reed and hemp agrimony. Several umbellifers are commonly found including, watercress and fool's watercress, lesser water parsnip and hemlock water-dropwort. Water mint, water forget-me-not, gypsywort and flowering rush complete the picture.

Canals with very little boat traffic can be particularly rich in a range of aquatic invertebrates and several urban canals have been designated as SSSIs, some for their dragonflies, others for their molluscs. A section of the Leeds and Liverpool canal running through Leeds has a particularly good assemblage of molluscs, including the introduced zebra mussel. Some canals in Manchester and Birmingham still hold populations of the native white-clawed crayfish. One plant that is particularly significant is the floating water-plantain, *Luronium natans*. This is a declining species in Europe which depends largely on certain canals in the Midlands and northern England for its survival in the UK. It is a plant of moderately acidic water, low in nitrogen and phosphorus, and suffers from increased eutrophication and turbidity. The plant is protected by European legislation and several canals have been designated as Special Areas for

FIG 57. White water lilies are an attractive feature on the Grand Union Canal in London.

Conservation, including the Rochdale Canal and the Cannock Extension Canal where special measures are taken to ensure its survival during canal restoration. On the Rochdale Canal a dual-channel was constructed, with a geotextile fabric running between the two, to maintain a channel relatively free from silt.

Oddities include Sowerby's freshwater jellyfish (*Craspedacusta sowerbii*), a native of tropical Central and South America which was first found in the wild in Britain in 1928, but has spread significantly since the 1990s and is now known from a number of urban canals from Exeter to Sheffield. There are also instances of particular species being dependent on local factories for their survival. In the 1970s a breeding population of the tropical fish *Tilapia* flourished in a stretch of the St Helens Canal in Lancashire where the water was heated by effluent discharged from the Pilkington glassworks. The fish became established in the canal in 1963 following liberation of the stock after a tropical fish shop closed down (Lever, 1977).

Canals in urban areas provide important habitats for water birds. Even the most built-up sections of inner city canals often support mallard duck, mute swan, coot and Canada goose and it requires only the slightest fringe of emergent vegetation for moorhen to find a niche. The relatively undisturbed nature of the 'far-bank' provides opportunities for all of these to nest, as can be seen at Gas Street Basin in the centre of Birmingham and along the Regents Canal just north of Kings Cross station in London. Coot and occasionally tufted ducks may also breed in such places. Where there are more extensive patches of fringing reedswamp with bulrush and common reed it is possible for reed and sedge warblers to breed, even in central areas of cities. Broader basins for turning boats and holding water for locks often have more extensive patches of reedbed and willow carr, providing opportunities for dabchick and reed bunting

FIG 58. Coot use any scraps of rubbish in the water to build their nest.

to nest. Kingfishers have thriving populations on some urban canals, despite the lack of natural banks for nest holes. They will use all manner of artificial holes, particularly drainage pipes in walls. In some places artificial kingfisher banks have been constructed.

Other birds catch fish in urban canals, especially herons. I have seen anglers on a canal in the middle of Amsterdam hand their catch to a waiting heron which sidled up to take the fish. These birds have become remarkably tame in British towns and cities over the past thirty years and it is no surprise now to see them along canals in the centre of London or Birmingham. Cormorants are relative newcomers to the urban scene, but they too have taken to fishing in less busy stretches of urban waterways, such as the Regents Canal near Paddington and along the Lee Navigation in the Olympic Park. The common tern is another bird that is fast becoming established in cities, fishing along canals and nesting on rafts provided specially for them in disused docks and other water bodies. But for me the one bird which I expect to see when I walk a canal is the grey wagtail. It seems totally at home feeding around lock gates and canal banks, and finds ideal nest holes in dilapidated Victorian masonry, especially under canal bridges. One other bird that seems to favour the canal environment of some inner cities is the black redstart. It has been suggested that its close association with waterways in London can be explained by the abundance of chironomid midges in such areas.

FIG 59. Backwaters and holding ponds provide habitats for dragonflies such as the common darter.

In many places urban canals still support good populations of water vole, a species that has been depleted in many parts of the country through predation by American mink. Otters may find too much disturbance for them to colonise urban canals, but their recent recovery and spread throughout lowland Britain has been facilitated by canals providing a network of waterways linking river systems.

Many water-loving plants found along canal sides also manage to gain a foothold within the vertical stonework of canal walls and lock gates. Gilbert (1989) points out that the lush growth of plants on these walls is not seen elsewhere in the urban environment. Some of the commonest are gypsywort, skullcap, purple loosestrife, water dock, marsh woundwort and hemlock water-dropwort, together with a variety of introduced species such as London bur-marigold, beggarticks, monkey flower, Himalayan balsam and garden angelica. Ferns frequently colonise the walls, especially male fern, common buckler and lady fern, with polypody and hart's tongue in more westerly districts.

Lock gates create a rather special habitat. Because of the constant flow of water through ill-fitting gates they provide ideal conditions for liverworts which colonise the wooden surfaces and create opportunities for other bryophytes to become established.

Urban canals that fall into disuse may initially become rich in aquatic species. As lock gates gradually disintegrate water levels are no longer maintained throughout the canal and each section becomes an independent pond. Some canals retain open water for many years, but eventually they succumb to the urban equivalent of hydroseral succession. Pools of standing water not only become choked with aggressive plants such as reedmace, reed sweet grass and yellow flag, but they also become filled with car tyres, shopping trolleys, bottles, broken umbrellas, bicycles, plastic bags and all the other paraphernalia of urban life. If left to itself this temporary phase would eventually give way to colonisation by a variety of woody species, predominantly willows and alder. But generally other plans are hatched long before that happens, either to restore the canal to its former glory or perhaps convert it to a linear park, or worse. What is certain is that once a canal is no longer maintained it will change its character very quickly.

For a botanist urban canal towpaths offer untold treasures. They seem to attract a rather special assemblage of species, many of which are aliens. Because they have been there for up to 250 years there have been countless opportunities

for colonisation, which are still going on today. Although many of the plants can also be found in urban wastelands their presence at your feet as you walk the towpath makes them all the more accessible. They make the towpaths one of the botanical highlights of towns and cities. Some are everyday plants of pavements and roadsides, others rare and exciting newcomers.

The narrow strip lying between the canal and the towpath, known to botanists as the canal verge, supports species that can withstand constant trampling, forming a low herb-rich grassy belt merging into the plants that have colonised the top of the wall. Commonly occurring species include oat-grass, cocksfoot, wall barley and bents, with yarrow, clovers and trefoils. Both ribwort

FIG 60. Disused canals quickly fill with aquatic vegetation: the Monmouth and Brecon Canal at Newport is mostly colonised by bulrush.

FIG 61. Common mallow on the towpath edge.

and greater plantain can become almost completely dominant in the thin layer of soil over brickwork, producing an extremely attractive spectacle when they are in flower.

But it is the verge on the other side of the towpath that is particularly special. Where canals pass through areas of derelict industry as in parts of Glasgow, Manchester, Birmingham and the East End of London this habitat may be only a few inches wide, yet it can contain a multitude of plants. In the East End it includes cultivated flax, feverfew, cornflower, fodder burnet, wild parsnip, lupin, buckwheat, thornapple, chicory, California brome, soapwort, Mexican tea and even marijuana. Some, like London rocket and lucerne, have been well established in the capital for a very long time. Many others may have originated from cargos carried on the canals. More recent invaders include Guernsey fleabane which has spread rapidly throughout the London area in recent years. Another example is the isolated patch of water finger-grass (*Paspalum distichum*), a native of tropical South America which was found on the towpath of the Regents Canal in Hackney in 1984. These London towpaths, hemmed in by buildings, also support taller plants typical of urban wasteland such as mugwort, common mallow, black horehound, bristly oxtongue and evening primrose, which are remarkably adept at surviving in the chinks and crannies of masonry (GLC, 1986).

As mentioned in Chapter 1 the strong links between the flora of urban wasteland and canals is illustrated rather well in the new flora of Birmingham and the Black Country (Trueman *et al.*, 2013). An association analysis of the 1,500 plants by their presence in individual 1 km squares shows that a quarter of the squares fall into a clearly defined category characterised by industry and canals (see Fig. 13, Chapter 1). Post industrial habitats are indicated by the presence of wormwood, toadflax and weld, and canals by hemlock water-dropwort, gypsywort and water dock. These six species together define this group of squares referred to as the industrial category. Two other major categories were identified, a suburban group covering 55 per cent of the area and a group containing semi-natural habitats covering 20 per cent.

FIG 62. The derelict wharves of Port Dundas in Glasgow support common knapweed, wild carrot, yarrow, Oxford ragwort and even eyebright.

This link between post-industrial landscapes and canals can be seen in central Glasgow where the derelict docks and quays of Port Dundas, which once formed the bustling city terminal of the Forth and Clyde Canal, are now covered in a great variety of plants rooted in the stonework. Yarrow, red clover, common knapweed, wild carrot, common ragwort, and perforate St John's wort grow alongside eyebright, red bartsia, heathrush and bird's-foot trefoil. Particularly unusual are the fine clumps of royal fern growing on a derelict quayside wall. Some canal banks are covered in the yellow umbels of Alexanders whilst large areas of the old docks are dominated by bracken. There is little distinction between the canal flora and that of post-industrial dereliction.

Walking a canal towpath through town you will find that the far side of the canal, known as the off-side, is more generally overgrown and tangled with vigorous growths of bramble, bindweed, everlasting pea, honeysuckle and even bracken in places. If left for a few years these banks become colonised by woody species, especially buddleia and elder, but other typical species can include danewort and bladder-senna. This side tends to be less accessible and often forms a refuge for water birds to nest, notably swan, moorhen, mallard, Canada goose and feral greylag goose. Water voles and kingfishers benefit from the presence of soft banks.

Bridges and walls support a variety of ferns, including wall-rue, black spleenwort, hart's tongue and male fern. Sides of lock basins have gipsywort, skullcap, hemp agrimony and pellitory of the wall. There will always be oddities, like common broomrape on a canal wall in Camden and ploughman's spikenard growing in lime-rich mortar of a bridge at Bumble Hole in Birmingham. Tunnels offer a rather special environment for bats and some have been designated as SSSIs for this reason. In some places dock basins have become nature reserves as at East India Dock in London which now forms part of the Lea Valley Regional Park. The basin is brackish and at times has mud banks in the

FIG 63. Rusty-back fern growing in lime mortar on a canal wall.

middle, providing feeding and roosting areas for black headed gulls, shelduck, cormorant, tufted duck, mallard and common terns which nest on floating rafts which rise and fall with the tide. Despite its urban situation several hundred teal often occur in winter and kingfishers and herons regularly fish in the basin. The area also supports black redstarts.

The most recent change to affect canals was the decision by the UK government in 2012 to abolish the British Waterways Board and transfer the canals to a new Charitable Trust, the Canal and River Trust which has taken responsibility for managing most of the canals in England and Wales. There seems to be an acceptance that the emphasis on navigation will be broadened to encompass a wider range of recreational activities including wildlife conservation. Only time will tell.

CEMETERIES AND BURIAL GROUNDS

Ask any urban wildlife trust for a list of its best nature areas and it will probably include one or two cemeteries. Some Victorian cemeteries have also been designated by local authorities as Local Nature Reserves. They are among the most spectacular of urban habitats. Kensal Green, Nunhead and Highgate cemeteries in London, Southampton Old Cemetery, Arnos Vale in Bristol and the Necropolis in Glasgow are perhaps the most striking examples. But every town and city has burial grounds and each contributes in its own particular way to the local ecology.

They are rather special habitats with an unusual mixture of ecological conditions. Gravestones and monuments with their many different types of stone provide a variety of microhabitats, especially for lichens, ferns and mosses, and they have been invaluable as outdoor laboratories for the study

FIG 64. Nunhead Cemetery near Peckham Rye in south London: secondary woodland of sycamore and ash now covers much of the cemetery.

of air pollution through the distribution of lichen species. Open grassland habitats are particularly important, especially those which have their origins in ancient unimproved meadows and pastures, which may include plants such as great burnet, adders tongue fern and green winged orchid which have long since disappeared elsewhere in the local area. In many cases open areas between the graves have turned into flower-rich meadows dominated by plants such as meadowsweet, hemp agrimony, common knapweed, ox-eye and Michaelmas daisies, sneezewort and evening primrose. Cemeteries with extensive areas of such grassland are rich in insect life and may support over twenty species of butterflies. Veteran trees often feature prominently, as many ornamental specimen trees were planted

FIG 65. A fine assemblage of lichens colonising a headstone in Smallcombe Cemetery, Bath (also see Fig. 238, p. 400).

when cemeteries first became established in the early 1800s. Some of these trees have now achieved considerable stature.

But the overwhelming feature of most of these old cemeteries is the dense growth of secondary woodland, mostly dominated by sycamore and ash, where trees and monuments are festooned in ivy, bindweed and old man's beard. Paths and rides are colonised by swathes of cow parsley, comfrey and green alkanet. Many of the cemeteries dating from early Victorian times, especially those unmanaged for long periods, are now completely dominated by such woodland. It smothers the serried ranks of gravestones and tombs and creates an almost impenetrable tangle of trees and ivy amongst the stonework. These are strange and eerie places, both grotesque and beautiful, and they provide one of the most unusual of any habitat in Britain.

It isn't just the mixture of natural elements that makes these places special. They benefit too from being cut off from surrounding urban areas behind high walls, forming sanctuaries where nature can thrive. They have in effect become nature reserves simply because they were left alone and nature has taken its course. Many are now greatly valued by local people as wild places which provide freedom to get close to nature. These natural sanctuaries provide an unusually tranquil environment distant from the hubbub of city life. How they have become the wild oases that they are today is one of the most intriguing stories of all urban habitats.

FIG 66. Narrow paths wind through a sea of cow parsley in the dense ash woodland at Nunhead.

The story commences with the enormous growth in population associated with the industrial revolution. During the early 1800s the population of many towns and cities in Britain, especially industrial areas, grew at a prodigious rate. In Liverpool the population grew from 75,000 in 1800 to nearly 500,000 by 1860. London's population also increased dramatically, driven by the huge growth of commercial and financial activity. Between 1800 and 1830 it rose from 856,000 to over one and a half million, and as in other major cities this posed an acute problem. There was insufficient space to bury the dead. In London the number of burials exceeded 50,000 a year and existing small churchyards could no longer cope with the numbers involved. By 1820 many of these long established burial grounds were so full of bodies that they had become a hazard to public health. The whole issue became a public scandal and a radical solution was needed.

The answer was to provide new burial grounds. Cemeteries had already become well established in many European towns and cities. But, as it happens, the first cemeteries in Britain were prompted not by public health issues, but rather by the needs of nonconformists who required their own dedicated burial grounds. The Rosary in Norwich opened in 1819, and was quickly followed by others in Liverpool, Manchester and Newcastle. One of these was the Liverpool Necropolis. Set up in 1825 by a new 'joint-stock' company it produced remarkably good returns for its shareholders and quickly attracted attention from investors. The nonconformist's need for their own burial grounds, separate from churchyards, had inadvertently provided a new model that led to a massive development of cemeteries over the next fifty years.

A London barrister, George Carden, began campaigning for burial reform after visiting the Père Lachaise cemetery in Paris in 1821. Inspired by his visit, and no doubt aware of the success of the Liverpool Necropolis, he was largely responsible for setting up a new enterprise called the General Cemetery Company, which bought fifty-four acres of land at Kensal Green near Paddington in 1831. Only a few months later Britain's first major cholera epidemic hit the capital and Parliament needed little persuasion to pass an Act enabling establishment of 'a general cemetery for interment of the dead in the neighbourhood of the metropolis'. This was the first of a series of Acts allowing many large new cemeteries to be created around London and in other major cities (Curl, 2001).

Kensal Green Cemetery was opened in 1832 and became an immediate success. It was modelled broadly on Père Lachaise which was opened in 1804, with extensive lawns and avenues lined with cedars which, together with many other ornamental trees produced an attractive though somewhat formal landscape. Prints of the time illustrate stiffly dressed couples perambulating along winding

FIG 67. The Necropolis in Glasgow: formal rows of monuments contrast with wild ivy-covered cliffs of the old quarry.

walks, edged with formal flower beds. Strategically placed evergreen or weeping specimen trees brought a pleasing sense of melancholia to the scene and the Doric Temple provided a fine classical backdrop (Latham, 1984).

It was not long before other cemetery companies followed and by 1841 seven large new cemeteries were operating around London. At that time the built-up area of London was relatively confined. These new cemeteries were all situated in open countryside forming a ring around the capital some four to five miles from Charing Cross. Since that time London has spread enormously and they are all now surrounded by densely built-up suburbs. Norwood Cemetery (1838), was closely followed by Highgate (1839), Abney Park, Brompton and Nunhead (1840) and Tower Hamlets (1841). Meanwhile cemetery companies were springing up in other cities, where enthusiastic investors were getting in on the act. Birmingham, Sheffield, Nottingham, Bristol and York were some of the first, with York Cemetery opened in 1837 and Arnos Vale in Bristol in 1839. Exeter City Council was the first to fund a cemetery publicly through the rates in 1837; Southampton followed with the Old Cemetery opened in 1846. The Abbey Cemetery in Bath, designed by J. C. Loudon and opened in 1844 was unusual in being run by the Anglican church rather than a cemetery company. One of the most extraordinary cemeteries of this period is the Necropolis in Glasgow completed in 1833. Its development was funded by the Merchants House in Glasgow, the layout being designed by John Strang who published a detailed description, *Necropolis Glasguensis*, in 1831. A second wave of cemetery construction followed the Burial Acts of 1852–53 when most small city churchyards were finally closed. Many of these later Victorian cemeteries are still in use today.

The founders of the first cemetery companies in London were quick to recognise that they were in competition with one another to attract potential clients. Their cemeteries had to be attractive places where people would want to be buried. At the first meeting of the London Cemetery Company it was announced that Highgate and Nunhead 'would not only rival all other cemeteries in their public utility but provide most interesting ornaments to the suburbs of this great metropolis, and be an honour to the country' (Waite *et al.*, 1993). They recognised that for a cemetery to succeed it needed to be more beautiful and unusual than any potential rival. So the companies employed designers and architects to create attractive new landscapes. But what were these to be? The objective was entirely new and there were few examples to follow. These places were being created before there was any tradition of public parks, and the existing formal landscapes of great country houses were hardly appropriate.

Most of the designers promoted informal landscapes of a rather special kind. Instead of formal avenues and lawns Arnos Vale, Nunhead, Abney Park and Highgate had more intimate landscapes of winding paths and shrubberies. Thousands of exotic trees and shrubs were planted, using evergreens and weeping specimen trees to create an atmosphere of peace and tranquillity. Some of the most popular trees were cypress, cedar, swamp cypress, false acacia, Indian bean tree, weeping ash and lime, ginkgo and monkey puzzle, together with a great variety of ornamental shrubs including many evergreens such as privet, box, laurel and holly. Abney Park Cemetery in Hackney, designed by George Loddiges, became famous as an arboretum based on the *gardenesque* style promoted by Loudon, which used many exotic species. Some 2,500 varieties of trees and shrubs were planted creating a magnificent display. Arnos Vale in Bristol was famous for its avenue of Irish yews along the Ceremonial Way and other specimen trees included Austrian pines, western red cedars and Himalayan cedar. This cemetery forms a natural amphitheatre on a hillside overlooking the city and the landscape is still one of the most spectacular of all the old cemeteries.

Loudon had an enormous influence on the design and development of cemeteries. It was he who set the pattern for the new London cemeteries when he advocated in 1830 that the capital should have several cemeteries equidistant from each other and from the centre of the metropolis, and that they should be laid out and 'planted with every sort of hardy trees and shrubs'. He suggested that they should become Botanic Gardens and was extraordinarily forward looking, recognising that all cemeteries once filled should be closed for burial and later opened as public walks or gardens. The new cemeteries 'ought to be made sufficiently large to serve at the same time as breathing spaces … the greater the number of present cemeteries, the greater the number of future public gardens.' His ideas were brought together in a comprehensive treatise *On the Laying Out, Planting, and Managing of Cemeteries* (Loudon, 1843), which provided the basis of cemetery design and management for the next fifty years.

The new cemeteries provided an opportunity for Victorian embellishment on a grand scale, which certainly pandered to the wealthy. Elaborate tombs, monuments and even catacombs became the order of the day, and nowhere were they developed to better effect than at the Old Highgate Cemetery where they can still be seen today. The centrepiece is a most extraordinary series of elaborately decorated vaults built into the summit of the hill. It is entered through an ornate Egyptian-style archway leading via the Egyptian Avenue to the Circle of Lebanon, a sunken lane lined with rows of vaults, surrounding a 300-year-old cedar tree. The whole structure creates an aura of antiquity, intended to encourage a sense of awe and timelessness. The cemetery was beautifully described and illustrated by Felix Barker and John Gay in 1984 when rampant nature held sway and the avenue of catacombs covered in buddleia, clematis and ferns had all the appearance of an ancient city lost in the jungle. At the time when it was built it must have been spectacular. It remains one of the wonders of London today.

Highgate certainly lived up to the aspirations of its sponsors. It became a very fashionable place to be buried. Prestigious burial space was much sought after, and many great family names appear on the tombstones, monuments and mausolea. But it was not alone. All these early Victorian cemeteries proved to be extremely successful businesses. The land at Highgate was bought for only £3,500 and early projections based on 30,000 graves suggested a potential return of £225,000. In fact there were nearly 170,000 burials in about 52,000 graves. Tower Hamlets was more densely filled. By 1889 there had been 247,000 burials, the vast majority being common graves costing twenty-five shillings each. Shareholders were delighted, and even more so after the City burial grounds were closed in 1852. For many years the cemeteries raised substantial incomes and the companies were able to employ an army of gardeners to ensure that these special landscapes remained attractive. In Highgate alone 28 gardeners were employed to look after a landscape that was rapidly turning to woodland.

After a time two things conspired to change the face of these cemeteries. The key factor was the rapidly diminishing amount of space, resulting in fewer

FIG 68. The dense growth of ivy-covered trees at Nunhead is typical of these early Victorian cemeteries.

burials and a declining income to the cemetery companies. As space became restricted specimen trees were removed to make way for more graves, which were also placed along paths and rides. Eventually there came a point when some of the cemeteries were no longer economically viable. But long before this a second factor came into play. This was the rapid encroachment of trees and shrubs. In the early years it was possible to control their growth, but as the cemeteries matured the need for maintenance increased. Mature trees produced seedlings in profusion and gardeners were faced with a continuous battle to stem the tide of woody plants. With declining incomes the cemetery companies could no longer afford to pay the gardeners and it was only a matter of time before some cemeteries reached crisis point. By 1896 large parts of Tower Hamlets Cemetery had become sadly neglected with '… a regular ocean of tombstones, many of which are lying about apparently uncared for and unclaimed; in fact most of the graves except those at the edges of the walks look utterly neglected …' (Holmes, 1896). The death knell for most of the cemeteries was World War I when gardeners were no longer available and nature ran riot. Some still managed to survive until the 1940s, after which they became derelict. Others are hanging on today with a few burials and a massive job coping with rampant vegetation.

FIG 69. At Arnos Vale in Bristol gravestones disappear under the rampant growth of ash saplings.

Virtually all these early Victorian cemeteries are now being looked after by groups of 'Friends' who have set up charitable Trusts for this purpose. The details differ for each place, but the essence is the same. After long periods of neglect local people have stepped in to ensure that the cemeteries survive. Highgate is a good example. The cemetery had become extremely neglected when the owners suddenly announced in 1981 that it was to be sold for development. Local people campaigned for it to be protected and lobbied successfully against development. The Friends bought it for £50. Similarly York Cemetery had been in decline since the 1940s and after the company went into liquidation in 1966 the whole place became a derelict wilderness. A group of concerned citizens set up the York Cemetery Trust, which bought it in 1987. In other cases cemeteries have been acquired by local authorities. Arnos Vale was the subject of a heated local campaign before being bought through compulsory purchase by Bristol City Council and leased to the Friends. Nunhead, Abney Park, Tower Hamlets in London and the Abbey Cemetery in Bath, are all managed by local councils in partnership with 'Friends' groups.

All these groups recognise that the cemeteries have considerable value for wildlife and most are committed to managing them to maintain as much diversity as possible. In those that have become almost entirely dominated by secondary woodland there have been attempts to open up glades and create meadow habitats, with a particular emphasis on encouraging butterflies. Other cemeteries still have extensive open areas of tall-herb grassland, with patches of shorter turf where intensive management still prevails. In broad terms there are four main types of habitat, dense secondary woodland, small woodland glades, more extensive areas of open grassland and paths and rides. In addition there are many micro-habitats associated with graves, tombstones and monuments.

The secondary woodland is remarkably similar in all these early Victorian cemeteries, being dominated mainly by dense thickets of sycamore and ash, often mixed with horse chestnut. Other colonisers include birch, hawthorn, snowberry, woody nightshade, bramble and elder. Evergreen shrubs of holly, spotted laurel, Portugal laurel and Japanese privet probably came from the original plantings, together with a wide range of specimen trees including hornbeam, evergreen and Turkey oaks, lime, beech, weeping ash and many other ornamental species such as ginkgo and monkey puzzle. In one cemetery an avenue of old sweet chestnut trees, all long dead and riddled with woodpecker holes, still stands amidst a forest of new green sycamore poles. In most of these woodlands ivy is dominant, smothering tombstones and monuments and festooning the trees to the exclusion of almost everything else. Yet even here plants such as dog's mercury, celandine, lords and ladies, pendulous sedge and herb robert may persist; and the parasitic ivy broomrape has been found in Highgate and Arnos Vale cemeteries. Where tree cover is less dense the ground layer may include bluebell, cow parsley, hogweed, hedge mustard, rosebay willowherb, white deadnettle, red campion, foxglove and greater celandine, together with impenetrable patches of bramble and bindweed. Clearings made in an attempt to diversify the habitat have often become colonised

FIG 70. Green alkanet, an introduced species originating mainly from gardens, is one of the most successful colonisers of old burial grounds.

by Japanese knotweed, notably at Abney Park, Tower Hamlets and Arnos Vale, but also in many other places. This plant is now a major problem for cemetery managers because of the difficulties of eradication once it is firmly established among the graves and tombs.

Older glades within the woodland, kept open by rabbit grazing, may have well-developed grassland swards with red and white clover, meadow cranesbill, common knapweed, bird's-foot-trefoil, melilot and possibly even chamomile; producing an attractive and colourful contrast to the ivy dominated woodland. Winter heliotrope has colonised some of these glades. Other small clearings, created more recently, may have open woodland-edge or grassland habitats with a variety of plant species including primrose, wood sage, red and white campion, tufted vetch, lady's bedstraw, creeping jenny, greater stitchwort and meadow vetchling. Shaded woodland paths and rides have a particular range of species including cow parsley, green alkanet, comfrey and hogweed (Game & Whitfield, 1996; Archer *et al.*, 1989).

A few of these old cemeteries have remained relatively open and are now dominated by grassland communities rather than woodland. Kensal Green and Morden Cemetery in London, Abbey Cemetery in Bath and the Glasgow Necropolis are good examples. The first of these was studied in great detail by Latham (1984) and later by Tim Freed (1997 & 2001) whose description of the natural history remains the most detailed for any of the Victorian cemeteries.

Kensal Green Cemetery was developed on low-lying neutral grassland, a distinctive type of damp grassland with its own characteristic suite of plants. Because there was no pressure for agricultural improvement the grassland of the cemetery was spared the use of chemicals and so retained many ancient grassland species. Plants recorded by Latham in the 1980s, which are particularly notable, included great burnet, common valerian, sneezewort, pepper-saxifrage, wild basil and grey sedge. Other plants, characteristic of unimproved damp pasture, include meadowsweet, cuckooflower, meadow cranesbill, burnet saxifrage, zigzag clover and pignut. Many commoner grassland plants were also found, such as oxeye daisy, common knapweed, hoary ragwort and goat's beard. Extensive patches of wood anemone, bluebell, bugle, common dog violet and primrose indicate links with old woodland or hedgerows. Throughout the cemetery there are numerous anthills of yellow meadow ant indicative of long-established grassland. Meadow pathways are open and sunny with bird's-foot trefoil, clovers, creeping

FIG 71. Kensal Green Cemetery near Paddington retains meadow habitats more than most, but even here there are parts that are swamped by secondary woodland.

buttercup and red bartsia. The variety of species is quite extraordinary given that the cemetery lies only a short walk from Paddington station.

Several other cemeteries are known to retain the flora of old meadowland, including some unusual species. One is Morden Cemetery in south London where several hundred plants of green winged orchid were discovered in 1979 when the mowing regime was relaxed. Other plants included pyramidal orchid, trailing St John's wort, common broomrape and cowslips. Similarly Broadway Cemetery in Peterborough supports the largest population of meadow saxifrage in Cambridgeshire and has been protected as a County Wildlife Site since 1990. The Rosary in Norwich is another example with heather and wood speedwell surviving from the time when it was heathland. In Glasgow the Necropolis has records of heath pearlwort, soapwort and stag's horn clubmoss growing in the close mown lawns. Adder's tongue fern, another survivor of old meadowland, has been found in the City of London Cemetery.

In a detailed study of butterflies at Kensal Green from 1989–97, Freed (1997) recorded 23 species, of which 19 were breeding. Commonest of the grassland

FIG 72. Broadway Cemetery in Peterborough: famous for its splendid show of meadow saxifrage. (David Withrington)

species was the meadow brown, but others included small copper, common blue and gatekeeper, as well as three species of skipper (the small, large and Essex). The wall brown, which was once common, decreased considerably over this period, whilst the gatekeeper became well established. Other species frequently recorded included small white, green-veined white and orange tip, all of which laid eggs on cruciferous plants such as charlock, hoary cress , hedge mustard and garlic mustard. The most notable species in the woodland area was the purple hairstreak, associated with both evergreen and Turkey oaks. Speckled wood was also well established, having recently expanded its range across London. One of the commonest butterflies was the holly blue, which depends on both holly and ivy as host plants. It is perhaps the most closely adapted to life in the cemetery!

Freed (2001) looked in some detail at the significance of ivy for wildlife and found that it supports a remarkably large number of species. Because it flowers very late in the year it is an important source of nectar and pollen for invertebrates in the autumn and its highly nutritious berries provide food for birds well into the winter. It appears that its evergreen foliage is of value to a range of species, especially for nesting, roosting and hibernating. Freed listed 261 species associated with ivy, including several red data book invertebrates. At Kensal Green he found ten butterflies feeding on ivy flowers, the most frequent being holly blue, red admiral, small tortoiseshell, comma and speckled wood. Also recorded on ivy flowers were 66 species of moths, and 19 species of hoverflies, some of which were unusual species for inner London. Freed makes a strong plea for ivy to be retained as an important ecological component of the urban cemetery.

In several cemeteries attempts have been made to encourage butterflies by planting a variety of wild flowers and appropriate shrubs. During the 1980s at

FIG 73. Urban cemeteries provide the right mix of conditions for speckled wood butterflies.

Highgate two open areas were managed as meadows, and extensive wildflower planting was carried out along paths and rides. By 1993 a total of eighteen species of butterflies were recorded, sixteen of which were breeding, including holly blue, small copper, wall, green-veined white and comma. A survey at that time identified a total of 227 plant species in the cemetery. At Tower Hamlets too butterfly numbers benefited from glades created in the 1980s and at least fifteen species were breeding by the mid-1990s. These included holly blue, brimstone, orange tip and speckled wood. Bushes of buckthorn, planted specially to encourage the brimstone, were very successful. Other species recorded recently include the silver washed fritillary and small blue, both notable species for London.

Most of these cemeteries are significant as the only large pieces of woodland within extensive tracts of suburbia. Their bird populations are therefore particularly important. They generally have 20–30 breeding species many of which are birds of gardens and urban parks. However there are some that are characteristic of woodland, or woodland edge, which have a more restricted distribution in heavily built-up urban areas. These include chiffchaff, garden warbler, blackcap, goldcrest, treecreeper, nuthatch, great spotted woodpecker, green woodpecker, sparrowhawk, jay, tawny owl and stock dove. Before its recent decline the spotted flycatcher was a typical member of this group. Other species are now moving in. Old trees, which are full of holes, provide ideal nest sites for ring necked parakeets which now breed in many of the London cemeteries including Tower Hamlets. This has also become a regular wintering haunt of firecrests, which could well breed here before long. At Arnos Vale in Bristol buzzards have taken up residence, entertaining visitors with their courtship aerobatics in springtime.

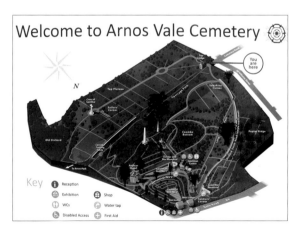

FIG 74. Arnos Vale is becoming a popular venue for many Bristolians.

Recent surveys of breeding birds at Arnos Vale produced 26 species, totalling some 300 pairs. By far the commonest is the wren, followed by robin, blackbird and woodpigeon which together make up 62 per cent of the total number of pairs. A further 25 per cent comprised blackcap, blue tit, great tit, dunnock, chiffchaff and goldcrest. The remaining 13 per cent included chaffinch, song thrush, magpie and greenfinch, also bullfinch, jay and stock dove. None of this latter group had more than ten pairs. A few species such as sparrowhawk and great spotted woodpecker nested in some years but not others.

It is no surprise that roe and muntjack deer are regularly seen in city cemeteries. The large extent and relative seclusion of these places is ideal for them, though the presence of roe deer in Glasgow's Necropolis in the centre of the city caused something of a stir. Foxes are resident in most, with plenty of ready-made holes for their earths. Badgers too have long established setts, or use cemeteries and burial grounds for foraging, in places such as Bath, Bristol and Brighton where there are large urban badger populations. Most of the early cemeteries have significant populations of bats, which roost in the old chapels and in subterranean vaults and tombs. Arnos Vale has a roost of lesser horseshoe bats and also supports noctule and pipistrelle bats. Highgate Old Cemetery hit the headlines in 2013 when ecologists surveying for bats found a population of the orb-weaver spider (*Meta bourneti*) living deep inside the vaults of the Egyptian Avenue. Also known as the cave spider, this species has a very limited distribution in Britain. Like its close relative which occupies conduits and vaults in Bath (see Chapter 1) it lives in total darkness, but spiderlings are known to venture out to colonise new subterranean haunts elsewhere.

Those managing these old Victorian cemeteries today are faced with an extraordinary range of problems. They may have acquired a cemetery for next to nothing, but some are finding that the ongoing costs are enormous. At Highgate the running costs for one year in 2005 were £263,000! But finance isn't the only problem. Nowhere is there a better example of conflicting interests than in these cemeteries. At one end of the spectrum are those who are primarily concerned with protection and preservation of the historic monuments. For them the ivy is an anathema, to be removed at whatever cost. Then there are those for whom the local cemetery is their refuge from the city, cut off from the rest of the world. Some walk their dogs, others simply sit in quiet contemplation. Yet others see it as a place where nature can thrive in the midst of urban life. For some that means leaving it alone, undisturbed. For others it means detailed plans for individual species, with trees to be felled and grassland to be managed. Reaching agreement between these disparate groups demands much patience and diplomacy.

When Southwark Council took responsibility for Nunhead Cemetery it decided to keep about 10 hectares as burial ground and designate the remainder as public open space and a nature reserve. Zoning was one way of dealing with potential conflicts (Archer *et al.*, 1989). One of the aims at Highgate Old Cemetery is to 'conserve the natural plant, animal and bird life in the cemetery and, as far as practical, of its surroundings.' For many years ecological management has been carried out in accordance with a conservation management plan. Some describe this as a policy of benign neglect. Although a huge amount of work has been done to maintain the most important monuments, and to diversify the flora, large parts of the cemetery have been left alone and are still as wild as ever.

A document published jointly by English Heritage and Natural England addresses all the issues involved in management of historic cemeteries. *Paradise Preserved* (White & Hodson, 2007) brings a fresh perspective to the problems and makes recommendations which help to set clear priorities. Most of the early Victorian cemeteries are listed as Landscapes of Special Historic Interest. *Paradise Preserved* recommends that they should all have a Conservation Management Plan that caters for species of particular note. Non-intervention or low-key management is recommended. In wildlife areas vegetation need not be cut so regularly as in other parts of the cemetery, although it is good practice to demarcate areas managed for wildlife so as to show that apparent neglect is intentional and managed. Grassland should be cut only once or twice a year to benefit wildflowers and insects. It is important to recognise the value of veteran trees as habitats for invertebrates and fungi. Dead or dying trees should be retained wherever it is safe to do so. These ideas will no doubt reach a receptive audience within the Friends groups and one can only hope that the interests of nature conservation will get a fair hearing.

Looking to the future it is likely that the next big change to affect these old Victorian cemeteries will be the loss of ash trees as a result of ash dieback, (*Chalara fraxinea*). This fungal disease only recently spread to Britain but there are fears that it could devastate ash woodlands. In view of the dominance of ash in cemeteries it is possible that it will dramatically alter these landscapes. But such an event would also offer opportunities to create a much greater diversity of habitats than has been possible hitherto. So far as the cemeteries are concerned it might even prove beneficial.

RAILWAYS

While some Victorians were engrossed in designing cemeteries engineers were promoting one of the most significant developments of the new industrial age, the railways. From a modest beginning in 1830, when there were only 100 miles of track, the network expanded rapidly to 10,000 miles by 1860, and by the early

1900s most towns and cities were connected to the national rail network. The legacy of this spate of development is still with us today. Most railways in urban areas still follow original routes of cuttings, tunnels and raised embankments, and much of the architecture of bridges, retaining walls and even stations date back to those early days. Indeed there are many towns where canals and railways now provide some of the oldest structures, apart that is from churches and long established features of historic town centres. The industrial archaeology of railway land provides the historical context for much of present-day urban ecology.

Although the railways have been with us for over 150 years, they have been subject to significant changes over this period. The way that line-sides have been managed has changed dramatically. In the first half of the twentieth century the vegetation was controlled by gangs of workmen who kept the embankments scrupulously free of woody growth. This was partly to avoid the risk of fires that occurred as a result of sparks from steam engines and the gangers themselves used burning to keep vegetation under control. It is clear from many photographs illustrating the 'age of steam' that embankments along suburban lines in the 1940s were predominantly grassland with scattered trees. But with the change to diesel and electric locomotives the frequency of fires diminished and track-side maintenance was carried out by machinery, such as flail-mowers mounted on special trains, and by the use of chemical herbicides. Scrub was no longer rigorously controlled except in the immediate vicinity of the track, or where trees posed a threat to the railway. As a result the landscape of the railways has changed from relatively open grassland communities to dense stands of scrub and even secondary woodland.

FIG 75. Over the past 50 years railsides have become dominated by secondary woodland of sycamore, horse chestnut and ash, providing green corridors like this one in the suburbs of Edinburgh.

Other changes relate to the surroundings of the railway land. Most towns and cities have grown significantly since the railways were built, so that long sections of line which now lie in the outer suburbs of big cities were once part of the rural scene. As a result some may have relict populations of species which colonised the banks from meadows and hayfields which have long since disappeared. Equally the same banks are now prone to colonisation from suburban gardens.

The rail network itself has suffered enormous changes. During the past fifty years a large number of branch lines were closed, particularly after the Beeching report of 1963. Some disused lines in urban areas have been retained as footpaths or cycle routes and others as nature reserves, providing green corridors through the urban fabric. Reduction in the carriage of freight had an even greater effect, with closure of several thousand urban sidings and marshalling yards, which then became potential development sites. But in the absence of development they were soon colonised by a particular kind of flower-rich 'wasteland' vegetation characterised by species such as wild mignonette, Oxford ragwort, great mullein and rosebay willowherb, which gave way in time to dense thickets of buddleia. Such areas were typical of derelict railway land. They became a regular feature of many towns and cities, especially in industrial areas, and formed a prominent element of 'urban commons' described so well by Oliver Gilbert (1989). Such is the value of these habitats within the urban scene that many have been protected as local nature reserves.

Rail travellers passing through urban areas today are faced by the squalid side of the city. All too often endless rows of back gardens are bounded by a scene of dilapidation, with broken fences, piles of refuse and garden rubbish thrown over onto the embankments. Graffiti covers walls and bridges. Buddleia grows out of the brickwork and dense thickets of Japanese knotweed cover the banks. It is a no-man's land that is wild and disorderly; out of control. Yet amongst all this a great variety of wildlife still manages to thrive.

What are the elements of railway land that give it a special quality? There are a number of components, providing a range of ecological conditions. Firstly there is the permanent way, which is the railway track plus the bed on which it lies. Traditionally this has been constructed from a layer of cinders, known as the cess, with coarser ballast of limestone, granite or even furnace slag on top to support the sleepers and rails. This is a very well drained structure that is kept free of vegetation by regular herbicide spraying. Despite this, localised patches are frequently colonised by plants such as field horsetail, lesser toadflax and bright yellow biting stonecrop where the herbicide has failed to penetrate. The cinder-bed of the cess is more prone to invasion by a variety of plants, including St John's wort, michaelmas daisy, herb-Robert, scarlet pimpernel, germander speedwell and procumbent pearlwort; together with mosses such as *Brium capillare* and *Funaria hygrometrica*. In general the permanent way of operational

FIG 76. Biting stonecrop is one of the first plants to colonise disused sidings.

lines has little wildlife value, though drainage channels along the edge of the cess may well support frogs and newts. Sidings and freight terminals tend to have a much greater range of plants as they are less frequently sprayed, common species being coltsfoot, evening primrose, rosebay willowherb, goldenrod, Canadian fleabane and increasingly Guernsey fleabane; together with incipient scrub development with bramble, bindweed, buddleia and old man's beard.

The vegetation of cuttings and embankments varies according to the nature of the soil or underlying rock. Since many railway lines are well over 100 years old there has been a long period available for succession to take place and in many places woodland now prevails with sycamore, horse chestnut and ash the dominant species. But local variations in soil bring contrasts and many cuttings and embankments still retain a patchwork of open grassland communities and scrub. A national study of railway land (Sargent, 1984) identified three main structural components of line-side vegetation. By far the commonest was coarse grassland dominated by false oat grass, with a wide range of variants. Next in abundance was bramble, followed by various kinds of scrub and secondary woodland. Although the study excluded urban areas it seems likely that the same components would prevail.

Along many urban railway lines patches of earlier vegetation still persist. Where railways were built across heathlands, which have subsequently been converted to suburbia, the railside banks are often covered in relict populations of bracken, gorse and broom, and woodland is dominated by birch and rowan. More commonly in urban areas is the tendency for embankments to become unofficial dumping grounds for all kinds of material from builder's rubble and unwanted topsoil, to garden rubbish and domestic waste. The banks become heavily enriched in nutrients which encourages colonisation by vigorous species such as bindweed, rosebay willowherb, great willowherb, Japanese knotweed, nettle and bramble. Gilbert (1989) comments that such species grow with a performance rarely achieved

FIG 77. Japanese knotweed is particularly invasive on railside land and may even occur on station platforms.

along rural stretches of line. Unwanted plants, dumped by gardeners, give rise to colourful drifts of lupin, goldenrod, everlasting pea, Michaelmas daisy and honesty, together with localised pockets of montbretia, daffodil, iris, geraniums and even sunflowers.

For many years I travelled daily into London by train along the line from Croydon to London Bridge, which passes through one of the finest stretches of rail-side habitat in the capital. The deep cutting from Forest Hill to New Cross Gate is nearly 4 km long and in places over 200 m wide, cutting a broad swathe through the densely built-up suburban landscape of Lewisham. Its banks support a mixture of secondary woodland, scrub, grassland and even reed beds, which provide a great variety of habitats. Safety fences alongside the track allow parts of the cutting to be managed as nature reserves, much used by local schools. As they pass through this rural enclave rail passengers could be forgiven for thinking that the borough of Lewisham is mostly countryside, until they suddenly emerge at New Cross Gate into a broad vista of central London, with towering office blocks of the city beyond the rooftops of Bermondsey.

The natural history of this cutting is well described in *Nature Conservation in Lewisham* (Archer & Yarham, 2000). The railway was built in the mid-nineteenth century along the route of a disused canal, which explains the presence of reed-beds. Brick waste was used in places to stabilise the steep slopes which had been cut through London Clay. This encouraged localised areas of acid and neutral grassland, but the majority of the cutting was colonised by woodland, dominated by sycamore and ash with an understory of hawthorn and elder. Other trees and shrubs include hazel, sessile oak, holly, wild cherry, suckering elms and dense thickets of blackthorn. In places old man's beard covers many of the trees and honeysuckle takes its place where soils are more acidic. The ground flora is dominated in places by dense growths of bramble and ivy, but more open areas have abundant cow parsley, pendulous sedge, Spanish bluebell and male

FIG 78. Broad-leaved everlasting pea commonly occurs on railway banks in suburbia.

fern, together with hedge woundwort, garlic mustard and wood avens. Giant hogweed dominates some of the woodland clearings. Wild garlic occurs in places, possibly a survivor from the ancient woodland of this part of London. Another notable species is the white-letter hairstreak butterfly which is dependent on elm trees and has recently made something of a come-back in areas with young elm suckers. Both species of stag beetle are also abundant in areas with older trees.

Pockets of open grassland have survived in places along the cutting where the banks are composed of clay. Some of these are typical of the rough grassland dominated by false oat-grass and cocksfoot that covers so many railway embankments. But others have a greater range of grasses, including Yorkshire fog and red fescue, together with a variety of flowering plants such as bird's-foot-trefoil, common and tufted vetches, red and white clovers, yarrow, common knapweed, autumn hawkbit, goat's beard, ox-eye daisy and cut-leaved cranesbill. These open areas are becoming colonised by more persistent species such as tansy, spear thistle, teasel, hogweed, Canadian goldenrod, rosebay willowherb and Michaelmas daisy. It is these open communities with their dense stands of naturalised species that give the railway banks their changing colours during the course of the year (Goode 1986). On more acid soils the grassland is dominated by red fescue, wavy hair-grass and common bent, together with sheep's sorrel and cat's ear.

The mixture of habitats in this cutting results in a variety of breeding birds. Secondary woodland and scrub supports tawny owl, blackcap, garden warbler, willow warbler and chiffchaff. Lesser-spotted woodpeckers were seen regularly in the 1990s as well as the commoner great-spotted. Sparrowhawks and kestrels regularly hunt along the cutting. Carrion crows and jays are resident. Bramble scrub provides habitat for both whitethroat and lesser whitethroat. The most obvious mammal is the fox, which can regularly be seen from the train, especially when there are cubs. Surveys at the Devonshire Road Nature Reserve found a large population of wood mice, but oddly a lack of shrews and voles. Slow worms and common lizards are abundant. Because these embankments were formed when the surrounding land was open countryside the grasslands of the cutting may now act as a refugium for invertebrate species that have survived from earlier times, including crickets and grasshoppers. Other more recent arrivals include Roesel's bush cricket which is now very abundant, and Jersey tiger moth which has recently become established locally.

Not every railway cutting has such a variety of wildlife, but most will have some of the habitats described and in total the amount of railway land in urban areas must be very considerable. The fact that the railways form corridors through the urban fabric also means that there are opportunities for mobile species to colonise new areas.

Retaining walls, bridges, stations and platforms together provide a range of habitats for urban colonists. Examples include ferns still growing under platforms where steam from the cylinders of steam engines created humid conditions that helped them to become established. Old railway architecture frequently supports good populations of ferns. Deptford station in London has an old carriage ramp leading down to the High Street that supports polypody, maidenhair spleenwort, male-fern, hart's tongue and bracken. In the Midlands the blue brick railway bridges support a similar assemblage, also including black spleenwort. But these are nothing compared with the luxuriant growths of ferns on stations and cuttings in wetter districts, notably the mid-Wales line at Barmouth and Aberystwith and the Highland line at Fort William.

Dilapidation brings its own particular range of species. In both Birmingham and London derelict railway buildings provided suitable habitat for both fox and black redstart. During the 1980s the old Broad Street station in the city of London, now demolished, had foxes living under a platform and black redstarts nesting in the wall (Goode, 1986). Old railway buildings seem to be particularly attractive to black redstarts. The older the better it seems. In Birmingham the dilapidated station at Snow Hill was the most favoured site from 1974–92. Other pairs nested on old station buildings at Leicester in 1974–5. Two broods were raised at the disused Swindon GWR works in 1979 and others nested at Clapham Junction station in 1986. More recent arrivals using station buildings include collared doves nesting under the station canopy at Newport and Bath.

Railway land also includes a number of triangles between the railway lines that have remained land-locked over the years and developed interesting habitats. Oliver Gilbert (1989) mentioned a triangle less than 2 km from the centre of Sheffield covered in heather moorland, and others in Nottingham colonised by wetland communities. One of the most impressive habitats of this kind is Potteric Carr on the edge of Doncaster where the main London to Edinburgh railway and local disused freight lines bisect what was once a much more extensive wetland. Famous as a place where bitterns used to breed, the wetland is now managed as a nature reserve by the Yorkshire Wildlife Trust and it is becoming famous again as

FIG 79. Some disused railways provide routes for linear parks; as at the Parkland Walk in Haringey.

a place to see wetland wildlife. There are other railway triangles that have turned to marshland in the Lea Valley adjacent to the Olympic Park in London. The small patch in Chiswick known as Gunnersbury Triangle was used as allotments in the 1940s but forty years later most of it had become colonised by birch and willow woodland and is now a London Wildlife Trust reserve (see Chapter 13).

Disused railway land has rather special qualities for wildlife. Old railway lines now converted to linear parks include the Parkland Walk in Haringey in London, the Harborne Line Walkway in Birmingham and the Linear Park in Bath (see Chapter 1). The Parkland Walk follows most of the disused branch line from Finsbury Park to Alexandra Palace which was closed in 1972. The campaign to turn it into a linear nature reserve is described in Chapter 13. The old railway line has become one of north London's most valuable green corridors, with a footpath and cycle track along the seven kilometre route. Most of the banks are now clothed in secondary woodland dominated by sycamore, ash, hawthorn, elder and horse chestnut, with some fine stands of birch in places. This has been augmented by planting of a range of native shrubs such as guelder rose, wayfaring tree, dogwood, blackthorn and spindle. A tree that is becoming well established is the holm oak, which probably owes its spread to jays carrying acorns from local gardens. Woodland edge plants include cow parsley, hogweed, hemlock, nettle, comfrey and green alkanet.

Until recently the old track bed still had plants of open ground such as common spotted orchid, small toadflax, common broomrape and meadow cranesbill. A notable rarity on some of the bridges is black spleenwort, which appears to be thriving in the absence of over zealous maintenance. Since it has been managed as a nature reserve about 340 species of plants and over 60 species of birds have been recorded. Tawny owls are resident and until recently spotted flycatchers were regular breeders. As well as garden birds chiffchaff and willow warbler occur and parakeets are now in residence. The variety of habitats supports over 20 species of butterflies, which surprisingly includes the silver-washed fritillary. Muntjack deer have been recorded.

The Harborne Line Walkway runs for nearly 4 km from Harborne in the outer suburbs of Birmingham through Chad Valley to Summerfield, just over 2 km from the city centre. It follows the line of the Birmingham to Harborne Railway, which closed in 1963. In his book of wildlife walks in Birmingham and the Black Country, Peter Shirley (1988) described it as just what you might expect for a linear path with many gardens adjoining, 'the vegetation is dominated by a few aggressive species typical of rich and disturbed soil. These included sycamore, Himalayan balsam, Canadian goldenrod, comfrey and rosebay willowherb.' He also found the fodder plant lucerne still growing near an old station site and noted the prominence of field scabious. Butterflies included meadow brown, wall and small skipper. A natural stream, the Chad Brook, runs alongside part of the route which was upgraded in 2009 and now incorporates a cycle way. Shirley felt that 'it is one of those places where you can easily forget that you are close to a major city centre'.

Also in Birmingham a wonderful example of a disused railway in the process of being colonised can be seen at Parkhead near Dudley. In places the old track is still intact with rails and sleepers but it is rapidly becoming colonised. Where the track bed is still open it is gradually becoming vegetated by plants such as ribwort plantain, hare's foot clover and lesser yellow trefoil. As grasses such as crested dog's tail and early hair grass become established other plants follow, such as wild mignonette, yarrow, bladder campion, mugwort, hawkweed oxtongue and even stinking hellebore which is growing in the centre of the railway tracks. Some of these prefer calcareous soils and it is likely that limestone ballast is present. Both common toadflax and pale toadflax are abundant, together with hybrids between the two, which seem to be a speciality of railway lands. Edges of the track are colonised by perforate St John's wort, with a number of nitrogen fixing legumes including red and white clover, hop-trefoil and bird's-foot trefoil. As you follow the track you soon find yourself forcing a way through thickets of grey and goat willow with fine stands of birch and patches of bramble with hawthorn and sycamore. Blackcap and whitethroat breed in the scrub. The old railway track

FIG 80. Woodland now covers the Parkhead Viaduct in Birmingham.

crosses Parkhead Viaduct which is now clothed in woodland. A similar wooded viaduct forms the centrepiece of Royate Hill nature reserve in Bristol.

Disused sidings and marshalling yards offer greater opportunities for a variety of species because the substrate tends to be more variable. In marshalling yards rails were often laid straight onto the cinder-bed of the cess, but this could well be mixed with a variety of other materials. A good example is the disused Feltham Marshalling Yard near Heathrow Airport, which has gradually been colonised by a remarkably large number of species since it became redundant in 1969. It is an extensive area, covering nearly twenty hectares, with a range of habitats from bare clinker and cinders with thin cover of moss and lichens, through open herb-rich communities to well established birch and sallow woodland. Initially the rate of colonisation by trees and shrubs was very slow. Lack of nutrients in the surface layers prevented the establishment of vigorous competitive species such as coarse grasses. Instead it encouraged a great variety of stress-tolerant species. The varied substrates, which include clinker, coal waste and chalk ballast also provided a range of conditions from acidic to calcareous, which explains why there is such a rich mixture of plants. Over 200 species of flowering plants have been recorded, including many naturalised species and a number of rarities. In ecological terms there is much similarity here with wasteland habitats described in the next chapter.

Although much of the site has now progressed to scrub and secondary woodland the surface is still disturbed in many places by motor-bike scramble riding so the early stages of colonisation are still being replicated. Bare surfaces are first covered in biting stonecrop, reflexed stonecrop and perforate St John's wort. As these primary colonisers became established another group of plants followed. These are the legumes which are crucial in fixing nitrogen. Red and white clover, bird's-foot-trefoil, hop trefoil, black medic, meadow vetchling and hare's foot clover are all abundant in the rather sparse grassland that persisted for many years. It is perhaps best referred to as a herb-rich patchwork, within which are at least fifteen different sorts of grass. Alongside these grasses and legumes are a number of characteristic species including common and pale toadflax, yarrow, centaury, chicory, common stork's-bill, sneezewort, fodder burnet and lesser broomrape, along with lucerne, melilot and common knapweed (Goode, 1986).

As the succession progressed a number of taller plants became established such as musk thistle, evening primrose, crow garlic, tansy, horseradish, dark mullein, sulphur cinquefoil, sainfoin and viper's bugloss. Japanese knotweed forms dense clumps in places and a variety of climbing plants are now well established, including everlasting pea, bindweed and old man's beard. In the more acidic areas gorse, broom and bracken prevail, with dwarf gorse in places. Among the alien shrubs bladder senna from southern Europe and Duke of

FIG 81. The disused Feltham Marshalling Yard in west London supports 200 species of flowering plants, including viper's bugloss ...

FIG 82. ... and great mullein ...

FIG 83. ... butterflies are also well represented with over 20 species including the small copper. (Paul Wilkins)

Argyll's tea plant from China are particularly characteristic of railway land. Although birch and sallow are the main components of the secondary woodland, other trees include sycamore, goat willow, elder and whitebeam, with dog rose and bramble in the clearings. Buddleia forms thickets in places, but is less dominant than on many of London's wasteland habitats. It seems that trees colonised this area rather more rapidly than on railway lands in more central parts of London where seed sources are more limited.

One area of sidings alongside Shakespeare Road in Lambeth which closed in the 1960s remained almost free of trees and developed a lichen-rich community and herb-rich grassland that persisted until the 1980s. Over 150 species of flowering plants were recorded, including eyebright, musk thistle, soapwort, bee orchid and hare's foot clover. Bare areas were colonised by mosses such as *Brachythecium rutablum, Bryum argentium, Dicranella heteromalla, Eurinchium praelongum* and *Polytrichum juniperinum.* In places a lichen community was well established, containing several species of *Cladonia* together with *Lecanora muralis, Lepraria incana* and *Peltigera polydactyla.* The unusual nature of these habitats was recognised by the London Wildlife Trust in 1986 when it mounted a campaign to protect the area from housing development and very nearly succeeded (see Chapter 13).

One of the most extraordinary patches of disused railway land is the area of sidings at Darnick Street in Glasgow which became colonised by bog plants (Dickson *et al.,* 2000). These sidings were last used in the late 1960s and

FIG 84. New Ferry Butterfly Park near Birkenhead: a small educational nature reserve on disused railway land managed by the Cheshire Wildlife Trust. (Artwork by Vicky Hose)

subsequently became partially flooded. The area was left unused for the next twenty years, during which time the acid and waterlogged conditions promoted the growth of bog plants, including six species of Sphagnum moss together with cottongrasses and sedges. But what was particularly striking was the abundance of round-leaved sundew, which not only grew on the Sphagnum moss but also on wooden sleepers and ballast. Large stands of common spotted orchid and northern marsh orchid also occurred. Drier parts of the site had their share of alien species, including Michaelmas-daisies, rhododendron and bushes of prickly heath, a shrub that is native to Chile.

A very attractive nature reserve has been created on disused sidings near Birkenhead. Known as the New Ferry Butterfly Park it is a flagship reserve of the Cheshire Wildlife Trust attracting several thousand visitors, including over 1,000 schoolchildren, per year. As well as being well used by local schools for ecological field work it is greatly appreciated by the local community who have fought several battles to stave off development. The reserve shows all stages in succession from bare ballast, through sparsely vegetated areas with bee orchids and vipers bugloss, to patches of secondary woodland. Open patches were stripped of vegetation in 1996 and 2004 to maintain the early successional stages. Hilary Ash has kept detailed records of the way the site has changed, and has also successfully introduced plants to encourage a greater variety of butterflies: for example, alder buckthorn for the brimstone butterfly. It provides a remarkable demonstration of what can be achieved on a relatively small site.

CHAPTER 5

Post-industrial Habitats and 'Urban Commons'

THE DISCOVERY IN 1954 of orchids growing on an old waste tip in Bolton in the heartland of Lancashire's cotton industry was one of those special events that brought much delight to local botanists, and paved the way for a host of studies of the plant communities of industrial wastelands. Roy Lancaster (2007) describes graphically how it came about. At a local primary school in Bolton the children had been asked to bring wild flowers for an exhibition. One brought a jam jar full of wild orchids, including the fragrant orchid which had never before been recorded in the area. One can imagine the excitement amongst local botanists who wanted to know where they had been found. 'Down at tip' was the response. So in July 1954 a group of enthusiasts went to investigate. The place, known locally as Nob End, was an old waste tip from a Victorian chemical works that produced washing soda for the cotton industry. Some 100,000 cubic metres of highly caustic sludge of calcium sulphide and quicklime (calcium hydroxide), was dumped over an extended period during the nineteenth century resulting in a mound of chemical waste that filled a loop of the River Croal to a depth of about ten metres. Since tipping ceased in 1885 the surface layers gradually ameliorated through weathering and the extremely alkaline waste was eventually colonised by a sparse cover of vegetation. The thin surface layer of soil now has a pH of 7.7, which is comparable with long established limestone grassland.

Botanists from Bolton were amazed by what they found. Not only were there spectacular stands of fragrant orchids but there were other species typical of calcareous grassland, such as fairy flax, yellow-wort, common centaury, carline thistle and blue fleabane. Subsequent visits revealed a great variety of orchids, including pyramidal, southern marsh, early marsh, northern marsh

FIG 85. A Victorian chemical waste tip at Nob End in Bolton, Greater Manchester.

FIG 86. Marsh helleborine at Nob End.

and common spotted, together with marsh helleborine, twayblade and broad-leaved helleborine. Other notable species include lesser broomrape, and adder's tongue fern. The flora also includes some naturalised species such as the North American blue-eyed grass (*Sisyrinchium montanum*).

The presence of this island of calcicolous plants among the predominantly acidic habitats of south Lancashire posed some interesting questions. Where did these plants come from and what were the ecological processes leading to their successful colonisation? It was not long before researchers got their teeth into the issues. By 1978 a number of post-industrial sites supporting orchid populations, particularly marsh orchids, had been discovered elsewhere in northwest England. Lee and Greenwood (1976) recognised that many of the unusual species found on calcareous waste sites have very tiny seeds that can be carried great distances by wind. This could well be the explanation. The nearest source was most likely to be the dune-slack vegetation of the Lancashire and Welsh coastline, which support rich communities of orchids. Given the prevailing wind the Ainsdale sand dunes near Southport were the most likely source of the orchids at Nob End, even though they are over 40 km from Bolton.

We don't know exactly when they started to colonise the tip, but it is unlikely that local botanists would have missed them if they been there for very long, especially since their members included the Rev. Charles Shaw, known to many as the Weed King, who spent a great deal of his time poking about unlikely spots in search of aliens. It seems much more likely that gradual amelioration of the surface layers of the tip had reached a critical point when colonisation became possible. Orchid seeds had been blowing across Lancashire for years when conditions at Nob End suddenly became favourable for their germination and magnificent colonies of orchids appeared as if by magic.

There were of course earlier studies of the vegetation that develops spontaneously on derelict land. Most famous was the work of Sir Edward Salisbury on the flora of bombed areas in London during World War II in which he emphasised the importance of windborne seeds for the success of the pioneer colonists (Salisbury, 1943). After the war the London Natural History Society (LNHS) made the most of the short 'window of opportunity' that still existed to study the process of colonisation (Bevan, 2008). Annual monitoring of bombsites by members of the Society provided a detailed picture of the changes as succession progressed. Reports of the *City Bombed Site Survey* (Wrighton, 1948; Jones, 1958) make excellent reading and provide a fine example of the way that amateur natural history studies can contribute to our understanding of ecology.

During the 1970s and 1980s a number of British ecologists began to delve into the factors influencing plant communities on urban wasteland. Notable among these were Professor Tony Bradshaw at Liverpool University, Dr Oliver Gilbert in Landscape Architecture at Sheffield University and Dr Hilary Ash who worked with Bradshaw in Liverpool. Elsewhere in Europe others had been engaged in similar studies for some time. Among these the most outstanding was Professor Herbert Sukopp, Director of the Institute of Ecology at the Technical University in Berlin, who had made urban ecology his life's work. The work of these and others at this time provided the basis for much of our subsequent understanding of urban vegetation dynamics.

But let us return to the orchid covered tips of Lancashire. The growing interest in such places was not confined to understanding their ecology. The fact that a number of regionally rare and localised species had become established on industrial waste dumps led some to suggest that these unlikely places might actually have significance for nature conservation. Others went even further, advocating that industrial sites could provide exciting possibilities for deliberate creation of habitats of high wildlife value (Greenwood & Gemmell, 1978). The tip at Nob End became something of a *cause célèbre*, with much debate about the implications for industrial spoil heaps elsewhere. Bolton's botanists eventually won the day for their local patch when it was notified as an SSSI in 1988 and it now forms part of Moses Gate Country Park. The very considerable influence of post-industrial sites on the development of urban nature conservation is explored in later chapters.

POST-INDUSTRIAL ECOLOGY

Nob End may seem a rather extreme example of a post-industrial habitat, but it illustrates a number of features and processes that are fundamental to the ecology of such sites. Virtually all post-industrial sites and urban wastelands exhibit these features. They can be summarised as follows:

- The site is entirely man-made.
- It was created relatively recently.
- The nature of the substrate is crucially important.
- It is deficient in plant nutrients, especially nitrogen.
- Vegetation succession is influenced by provenance of seeds.
- Timescale of succession is determined by the nature of the substrate.
- Nutrient deficiency creates stress conditions, so high diversity of species.

The most obvious feature is the fact that the site is entirely the result of human activity. Compared with semi-natural habitats in the surrounding landscape, it originated relatively recently. This applies to all post-industrial habitats and to the majority of other urban wastelands. Such habitats develop on a wide range of artificial substrates. These are superimposed on the pre-existing natural landscape, which now only rarely has any influence on their ecological development. Many habitats of this kind are ephemeral. Depending on the vicissitudes of urban development they may exist for only ten or twenty years, whilst others may survive for much longer periods. The timescale of their development is critical in determining their ecological character.

The nature of the substrate is crucially important. Most post-industrial habitats do not have anything resembling soil in the normal sense that we know it. In the case of Nob End the material was initially extremely caustic and it took many decades before the surface layers ameliorated sufficiently for colonisation by plants to occur. Even then the levels of plant nutrients available, especially nitrogen, were extremely limited. Not all post-industrial habitats are as extreme as that, but the majority have skeletal soils that lack organic content, simply because there has been insufficient time for such material to accumulate. These soils are likely to present severe constraints for potential colonisers because of their physical and chemical composition. Most have some degree of nutrient deficiency, which has a direct effect on the process of colonisation and subsequent succession. Absence of organic material means that such substrates lack the ability to hold water in the surface layers making them extremely inhospitable for colonising seedlings.

Post-industrial and wasteland substrates include a huge variety of different materials. Brick rubble resulting from demolition of buildings, together with solid foundations of the buildings themselves, still covers large areas of many towns and cities, forming much of what is nowadays referred to as brownfield land. This material is often composed almost entirely of mineral particles, varying from the size of sand-grains up to much larger pieces of rubble including brick fragments, cobbles, broken paving slabs, lumps of concrete and kerbstones. Such conditions are often freely draining and the surface layers can be very hot and dry. In its raw state brick rubble has a severe deficiency in available nitrogen, but levels of other nutrients are generally sufficient for plant growth. Some brownfield sites may have high levels of calcium resulting from mortar, cement, plaster and other components of demolition waste. Moderate levels of calcium will help to maintain pH in the region of 6.5 to 8 which assists nitrogen fixation, but some demolition waste contains higher levels of calcium which can be inimical to plant growth. Under such circumstances initial colonisation will be slow while the substrate ameliorates through leaching and even then only those species capable of withstanding high levels of pH will be successful.

Some of these substrates pose more problems than others. Ash (1983) investigated the natural colonisation of waste deposits from various industries in Lancashire. These ranged from acidic colliery waste, with a pH of 3 to 5, through to highly alkaline wastes from the Leblanc process, such as the tip at Nob End. Each had its own particular set of ecological conditions and some of these were extremely demanding. Colliery tips are some of the most extreme. High levels of sulphur in the coal can create very acid conditions, but these tips are also severely deficient in nutrients, especially nitrogen and phosphate, and being freely draining they suffer from lack of water and have extreme temperatures. Acidic colliery waste could only be colonised by plants capable of withstanding these extreme conditions. At the other end of the scale the highly alkaline residues from the Leblanc process were initially totally inimical to plant growth and only after a long period of amelioration were surface conditions suitable for colonisation. Not surprisingly these various substrates gave rise to very different

FIG 87. Pineapple weed ...

... Coltsfoot ...

... and Hare's-foot clover: some of the pioneer colonisers of urban wastelands.

types of vegetation. In contrast to the calcicolous plants that flourished at Nob End, acidic colliery tips were often colonised by a range of species associated with heaths and moors, of which there was a ready source of material close at hand on the acidic sandstones and shales of the Lancashire hills.

It was not just a question of where the colonising plants came from, but rather why other species didn't make it. Hilary Ash investigated a range of seemingly appropriate plant species which did not have long distance dispersal mechanisms, to see whether they would survive on these industrial waste tips if artificially transplanted. Several species from calcareous grassland were successfully established on alkaline chemical waste and species from acidic heathland on colliery shale. She proved conclusively that provenance and dispersal mechanisms are critical factors in the composition of post-industrial vegetation (Ash *et al.*, 1994).

The colonisation of acid colliery waste may follow several different courses after the initial stages (Ash, 1991). Early colonisers tend to be perennial grasses such as bent and Yorkshire fog, together with hawkweed, rosebay willowherb and coltsfoot. Although birch and willow may become established at this stage they do not grow well and the dominant vegetation becomes grassland with scrub. It may well take 50 years to reach this stage. Thereafter it might progress slowly to birch and willow woodland, possibly with oak becoming dominant in time if local seed sources are available. Or, more often, it may develop into acid grassland dominated by mat grass and wavy hair grass, or possibly purple moor grass. Sometimes it develops into heathland with heather, crowberry and wavy hair grass. Examples of all these variations have been described from Lancashire and the West Midlands.

But what happens in inner city wastelands? The first real clues came from the surveys of London's bomb-sites carried out by the LNHS from 1947 to 1955. Cripplegate, an area just north of St Paul's was chosen for detailed studies (Wrighton, 1948; Jones, 1958). This part of the City had been utterly devastated by incendiary raids in 1940–41 and few buildings were left standing. Sixteen permanent quadrats and transects were laid out to record changes in the flora over the years, and detailed botanical maps were drawn each year for the whole Cripplegate area. One of the quadrats clearly demonstrated the steady spread of perennial plants such as mugwort, perennial wall rocket and bracken at the expense of annuals, such as common orache and fat hen that had been important early colonisers. However, some initial colonisers, particularly rosebay willowherb and Oxford ragwort, became firmly established and persisted for much longer. Because of its profusion rosebay willowherb became symbolic of the areas blighted by the blitz. Long after the war huge areas of bombed out buildings were

FIG **88.** The vegetation of this derelict site by Vauxhall Bridge in the 1980s was typical of London's bomb-sites, covered in rosebay willowherb and Canadian goldenrod.

still ablaze with a continuous swathe of red fireweed. Other species were also remarkably successful. In one part of Cripplegate a large area of rubble-filled basements was covered by an extensive colony of perennial wall rocket, to the exclusion of most other plants. The most constant species throughout the whole of Cripplegate were dandelion, spear thistle, creeping thistle, Canadian fleabane, chickweed, perennial rye-grass and annual meadow-grass. The studies revealed a total of 153 species of plants over the period 1947–9. By 1952–5 the list had grown to 342 species of flowering plants and ferns (Jones, 1958).

It is now generally recognised that plant succession on urban wasteland can be divided into four phases. An initial stage of primary colonisation, dominated mainly by annuals distributed by windborne seeds, is often followed by a lengthy period of mature wasteland vegetation. This is characterised at first by a great variety of species, particularly tall herbs, most of which are perennials and often include a large numbers of exotic species. Colonisation is often patchy with much bare ground still exposed and the vegetation forms an intricate mosaic of different elements. With time this community gives way to closed herb-rich grassland, often with open patches dominated by bryophytes and residual clumps of tall herbs. Eventually the characteristic open wasteland community is colonised by scrub or secondary woodland, by which time much of the botanical diversity has declined.

Hilary Ash found great variations in the timescale of succession on different substrates. Pulverised fuel ash (PFA) from power stations may allow fairly rapid succession to mature birch and willow woodland within 30 to 40 years, compared with 100 years needed to establish woodland of oak, birch and willow on acidic colliery shale. Alkali wastes from the Leblanc process have taken up to 70 years for initial colonisers to become established and possibly 100 years for

FIG 89. Bladder senna, a naturalised species from Europe, is commonly found on disused railway land and areas of dereliction. (David Bevan)

formation of closed grassland with hawthorn scrub. The timescale for succession to mature woodland on such sites is still unknown (Ash, 1991).

Oliver Gilbert (1989) studied many inner city wasteland sites in Sheffield and described the vegetation succession in considerable detail. He showed that primary colonisation, which he referred to as the Oxford ragwort phase, could last for up to 3–6 years. The first plant colonists were those capable of withstanding severe drought and nitrogen deficiency. It is no surprise to find that the initial vegetation was patchy and composed of plants found naturally in stressed environments. Oxford ragwort is perhaps the best known example. A native of the volcanic ash slopes of Mount Etna in Sicily it has become one of the most successful colonists of urban rubble. Other frequent early colonists include low growing grasses such as rat's-tail fescue which has deep roots that gather moisture from deep down and narrow leaves preventing water loss. Frequent too are annuals such as groundsel, knotgrass, pineapple weed, shepherd's-purse, spear-leaved orache and fat hen. Gilbert points out that many early colonisers belong to genera that were widespread during the late-glacial period immediately after retreat of the ice sheets when newly exposed mineral ground provided similar stressed conditions for the first colonists.

The initial phase of colonisation in Sheffield was followed by establishment of an open community dominated by a wide variety of tall herbs typical of more mature wasteland. It was these tall herb communities with their rich assemblage of species including many aliens that led Gilbert to coin the term 'Urban Commons'. After 8 to 10 years these 'flowery meadows' gradually became dominated by grassland, but still contained scattered clumps of tall herbs. An early phase of colonisation by trees with windborne seeds such as birch, willows and buddleia was held in check by the thickness of the herbaceous sward. At the grassland stage scattered clumps of Japanese knotweed became established. Brambles became prominent on many sites after only 5 to 10 years. In time such sites tended to be colonised by a variety of trees with larger seeds which were able to germinate despite the grass sward, but this of course depended on there being such trees in the vicinity. Typical species include ash, sycamore, laburnum, rowan, hawthorn, elder and apple, together with shrubs such as broom and Duke of Argyll's tea-plant, and others of garden origin such as currant and gooseberry. Many of these trees bear berries or fruits that are attractive to birds and the seeds are spread by this means. Gilbert suggested that the succession may take 40 years to reach the stage of mature secondary woodland and described small copses in the centres of Birmingham and Newcastle that have strange mixtures of native and cultivated species which originated by this process (Gilbert, 1983, 1989).

Colonisation of Sheffield's urban wastelands demonstrated the importance in the first year of plants with windborne seeds. One particular plot cleared in January 1984 was colonised by 41 species by August. Of these the most abundant were American willowherb, annual meadow grass, buddleia, coltsfoot, goat willow, groundsel, knotgrass, Oxford ragwort, rosebay willowherb and perennial rye-grass. All were established from seed and seven were dispersed by wind. About half of all the species had windborne seeds. Many of these plants produce vast numbers of seeds. A young plant of rosebay willowherb may yield 80,000 seeds in a single season. Canadian fleabane can produce 120,000. There is no shortage of seeds in the urban environment. Gilbert found that a large proportion of the initial colonisers in Sheffield were annuals or biennials. By 20 months they represented 40 per cent of the vegetation. Several of the dominant species were aliens. Whilst Oxford ragwort dominated in the first year it was replaced by rosebay willowherb by the second. By this time white clover and dandelion were well established together with a variety of tall herbs, notably mugwort, wormwood, tall melilot and weld. The abundance of both buddleia and goat willow shows that woody species can become established even during initial stages of colonisation.

The process of colonisation and succession in any particular locality will depend on availability of seeds or other propagules. Most inner city wastelands become colonised by species already established in the vicinity. However the process owes a great deal to chance circumstances in the early stages. In particular the establishment of perennial herbs often involves a 'founder effect' whereby certain species once established gain an advantage over other potential colonisers. In effect these early colonisers inhibit others from becoming established. This is just one of a number of possible processes that may determine the course of succession. Other species, such as clovers and vetches, facilitate succession through their ability to fix nitrogen in root nodules. Species that would otherwise be precluded by lack of sufficient nitrogen are enabled to move in by the presence of these legumes. Crucial ecological factors on urban wastelands are the virtual absence of organic material and relatively low levels of plant nutrients. This facilitates species capable of tolerating stress conditions and inhibits the development of dense stands of vigorous plants such as nettles and coarse grasses that thrive on rich organic soil. As a result many urban wastelands support a remarkable variety of species, particularly during the tall-herb phase, and there is often a substantial proportion of alien species.

A TOUR OF BRITAIN'S WASTELANDS

A few examples may help to illustrate the nature of such places. Gilbert (1989) provides a detailed picture of the tall-herb stage on Sheffield's wastelands where many of the most prominent species are naturalised aliens. Rosebay willowherb is particularly abundant, together with Michaelmas daisy, fennel, goat's rue, lupin, feverfew, Chinese mugwort, Russian comfrey and garden escapes such as Jacob's ladder and columbine. Goat's rue is particularly abundant on derelict industrial sites around Sheffield with swathes of it covering the hillsides and railway embankments. Among the many native species some are particularly noticeable, including wormwood, mugwort, tansy, ox-eye daisy, great willowherb, common mallow and red clover. Damp patches may be dominated by stands of hemp agrimony or Himalayan balsam, and drier areas by hardheads, yarrow and cat's ear.

In his account of waste ground in the centre of Glasgow, Dickson (1991) described an area adjacent to High Street that had become typical of many inner-city wastelands. There were stretches of redundant cobbles, exposed walls of former cellars and other remains of totally derelict buildings. Much of the area had been used as a goods yard until the late 1960s, and there were still railway lines and the remains of a signal box. By the late 1980s parts were used as a car park and others were being developed for housing. Dickson recorded 115 species of which 43 were annuals, 59 perennials and 13 were shrubs or trees. The vegetation was on the verge of turning into woodland. Some areas, which had previously been covered in dense buddleia scrub, had already been cleared in preparation for new developments. Only 18 alien species were recorded which may well reflect the late stage in succession. When I visited it in 2007 there were piles of fresh rubble covered in prickly sow-thistle and attractive mixtures of mullein, great willowherb or 'codlins and cream', mugwort, perforate St John's wort, coltsfoot and rosebay willowherb. Tall stands of giant hogweed had invaded less disturbed corners and around the edges of the site buddleia, broom, goat willow, birch, sycamore and Swedish whitebeam formed a belt of scrub and secondary woodland. Bushes were covered in a rampaging growth of large bindweed and the derelict signal box was invaded by buddleia. Despite being only a stone's throw from the city centre willow warblers, swallows and bullfinch were very much in evidence.

The Greater London Council included a review of urban wastelands in the first volume of a Nature Conservation Strategy for London (GLC, 1986). By that time virtually all the bomb-sites from World War II had been built over and the wasteland scene had shifted to London's docklands where numerous wharves and goods depots now lay redundant. In most places the industrial fabric was still intact with acres of cobblestones and disused buildings providing the focus for colonisation. A number of old wharves were found to be particularly rich botanically. All supported a rich wasteland flora with species such as prickly lettuce, black horehound, buddleia, melilots and rockets. Other typical plants were flax, wild parsnip, cornflower, thornapple, deadly nightshade and Scotch thistle. More notable were warty cabbage, London rocket, Guernsey fleabane, giant hogweed, bladder-senna and treacle mustard. The great variety of plants on these old wharves was most attractive, added to which were the bollards, capstans, rusting cranes and railway lines of the old docks. Although most of these sites have since been built over, the range of plants is still typical of wasteland habitats within the post-industrial sectors of east London.

One of the most floristically rich of London's wastelands in recent times was Gargoyle Wharf, a five hectare patch by the side of the Thames next to Wandsworth Bridge. The land had a long history of industrial use, including a petrol storage depot and whisky distillery, before falling into disuse in the late 1980s after which it was left for several years. When examined by botanists in 1996 a total of 333 species of flowering plants were recorded. Only five of these were listed as abundant and a further 34 as frequent. Another 87 were recorded as occasional, leaving all the remaining 207 species as very infrequent scattered individuals. The five species that were abundant were soft brome, hawkweed oxtongue, buddleia, beaked hawksbeard and hoary mustard, the last three of which were naturalised aliens. Those noted as frequent were a mixture of early colonisers, tall herbs, legumes and some woody species. Most of these were native species with a few aliens, notably Oxford ragwort, ribbed melilot and rosebay willowherb. Native species included eleven species of grasses, together with common toadflax, ribwort plantain, yarrow and a range of clovers and vetches. Brambles, dog rose and poplar were all recorded as frequent.

The vast majority of species found on this site were listed as occasional
to rare, but it was the unusually large number of such species that made it so
exceptional. It was an extraordinary experience to find a great variety of different
plants within the space of a few yards, and a very different mixture a few steps
further on. Over 40 per cent of the species were naturalised aliens. Notable
among these were Guernsey fleabane, a South American species which has spread
enormously in the London area since it was discovered in the docklands in
1984; tree of heaven which originated in southern Europe, but is now becoming
a dominant species on waste-ground in many northern cities; larkspur and
snow-in-summer from the Mediterranean; shrubby scorpion-vetch also from
the Mediterranean, which is naturalised in only a few places on the south
coast; Japanese quince; robin's plantain from north America; and finally treacle
mustard and goat's rue, both from Europe. The list could go on and on. There
were 137 species of naturalised aliens growing on this site. This small selection
provides some indication of the variety of plants involved. Why there were so
many is still not known, but it seems that material from many different sources
was tipped on the site over the years, resulting in a great variety of substrates and
an equally varied mixture of seed sources. It was even suggested that some of the
spoil originated from Channel Tunnel excavations.

Because of its unusually rich flora efforts were made by conservationists to
protect Gargoyle Wharf from development. In July 1996 the London Ecology
Committee was informed that the site might merit designation as a Site of
Metropolitan Importance for Nature Conservation. Shortly afterwards all the
vegetation was bulldozed from the site. The area remained undeveloped for
several years but in 2000 the go-ahead was given for a new housing scheme.

A very different kind of post-industrial habitat is found on Rowley Hills in
Birmingham where centuries of quarrying have left a varied landscape. The hills
form a prominent feature in the western suburbs of the city between the M5
motorway and Dudley. Igneous rock, mainly dolerite known locally as Rowley
Rag, was extracted from a series of quarries some of which were subsequently
used for landfill. The whole area has gradually become re-vegetated and the
hillsides are now covered in coarse grassland and scattered scrub. But there is
a great mixture of plants including some early ruderals. Others like mullein,
mugwort, weld, lucerne, bladder campion, musk-mallow and bee orchid are more
typical of mature wasteland. Some of the hotter south-facing slopes have lower
growing communities with fine leaved grasses and legumes such as hare's-foot
clover and lesser yellow trefoil, together with plants of garden origin, including
tall mouse-ear hawkweed and reflexed stonecrop. Grassland habitats still support
skylarks, and both whitethroat and bullfinch occur in areas of scrub. Not far away,

FIG 90. Southern marsh orchids at Canvey Wick in Essex, an oil refinery that was never built.

within sight of Dudley Castle, old tips of furnace slag and casting sand have created extremely arid conditions now colonised by a most unusual assemblage of plants including hoary-mustard, bee orchid, wall rocket, blue fleabane, common cudweed and purple cranesbill, together with thyme-leaved sandwort and even sea buckthorn. A spectacular feature is the abundance of rose campion. Swathes of this bright red flower cover the tips in June.

The most extraordinary 'post-industrial' site in Britain must be Canvey Wick in Essex. This is the site of an oil refinery that was never used. The area was originally grazing marsh, which was covered with dredgings of sand and gravel from the Thames to a depth of 2 or 3 m before construction started in the 1960s. Much of the infrastructure was built, including over twenty huge storage tanks and a long jetty out into the Thames Estuary, together with drainage ditches, roads, lamp-posts and all the necessary services. The site covers some 90 hectares along the bank of the Thames on the south side of Canvey Island. For various reasons the refinery was never brought into use and after the tanks were dismantled the land was left abandoned. Fifty years later it now supports a wide range of habitats including herb-rich grassland and scrub, as well as a peculiar mixture of plants that have colonised different elements of the infrastructure. This includes the asphalt bases of the oil storage tanks, each 50 m across, various roads and concrete bases of buildings, and the network of drainage ditches. It all makes for an extremely heterogeneous site.

The succession has reached the stage where much of the area is covered by herb-rich grassland with a great variety of perennials. Typical wasteland species include black horehound, bristly ox-tongue, lucerne, mugwort, prickly lettuce, ribbed melilot, teasel, ox-eye daisy and evening primrose. Broad-leaved everlasting pea, rose campion and snow-in-summer are all very conspicuous. Orchids are particularly abundant including southern marsh, common spotted,

FIG 91. Rose campion is one of the most conspicuous plants at Canvey Wick in June.

pyramidal and bee orchids. Other notable species include narrow-leaved bird's-foot trefoil, yellow-wort, common centaury, figwort, hoary whitlow-grass, fodder-vetch, sainfoin, hairy vetchling, ploughman's spikenard and hoary mullein. Bladder senna and buddleia are both well established and there are extensive areas of scrub and secondary woodland of willow, hawthorn and blackthorn. The large circular bases of asphalt are all being invaded from the edges by carpets of moss which provide the basis for other plants to become established. Biting stonecrop is one of the first to arrive with wild carrot and rose campion quickly following. In places common reed grows through the asphalt from below. During June and July the whole site is a magnificent blaze of colours.

The site has good populations of adder, grass snake, common lizard and water vole, but it is the invertebrate fauna that is particularly outstanding. Investigations by the invertebrate conservation organisation Buglife have demonstrated that a number of sites around the Thames Estuary support a high diversity of invertebrates, including many nationally rare species. As a result the East Thames Corridor is now recognised as being nationally important for invertebrates. Canvey Wick is the most significant of these sites and was designated as an SSSI in 2005. Bees, wasps, beetles, flies and bugs are particularly well represented, plus a number of rare spiders. The insects include four priority species listed in the UK Biodiversity Action Plan and more than a hundred that are nationally scarce or threatened. Thirty of these are Red Data Book species. SSSI designation was based on this nationally important assemblage of invertebrates and the presence of a large population of the shrill carder bee (*Bombus sylvarum*), an extremely scarce and declining species associated mainly with herb-rich grassland. Other notable species include the marbled-white butterfly and scarce-emerald damselfly.

Canvey Wick is now managed as a rather unusual nature reserve. Surrounded by residential and commercial developments it clearly demonstrates the value

FIG 92. The shrill carder bee: a national rarity that occurs at Canvey Wick. (Steven Falk/Buglife)

of brownfield land for wildlife. A brochure published in 2005 by English Nature (now Natural England) described it as: 'a community wildlife space that will protect the special wildlife interest of the site and actively involve local people in its management.'

There are other post-industrial habitats that deserve mention. In the central lowlands of Scotland some of the remaining colliery spoil tips around Glasgow, and 'bings' from the oil-shale industry in West Lothian, now support a number of unusual plants. In his delightful book on *Wild Plants of Glasgow*, Dickson (1991) described some of the typical plants of colliery tips, including viper's bugloss and great mullein, also alien species such as weld or dyer's rocket, and grand-toothed hawkweed, an incomer from the mountains of central Europe. More notable was the presence of three species of helleborine on two of the tips. One of these was the common broad-leaved helleborine, but the other two were most unusual. These were Young's helleborine and narrow-lipped helleborine, neither of which were recorded elsewhere in Scotland. The discovery of these two exceptional orchids on colliery tips was the highlight of the Glasgow botanical surveys in the 1980s. It reinforces the point that orchids have a remarkable ability to find such places.

FIG 93. Post-industrial habitats have many origins: hemlock water-dropwort survives amongst discarded tyres on the banks of the River Lea in east London.

The distinctive red mounds of the oil-shale bings in West Lothian, which pepper the industrial landscape around Broxburn and Livingston, have their own particular plant specialities, including alpine and stag's-horn club-mosses, common wintergreen, and again a suite of orchids, the most notable being early-purple and greater-butterfly orchids. These bings are also noted for the presence of several nationally scarce species of lichens and mosses. Several are now managed as nature reserves by the Scottish Wildlife Trust.

No account of post-industrial habitats is complete without reference to pulverised fuel ash (PFA) from coal-fired power stations. Over the past fifty years it has been one of the commonest industrial wastes deposited in or near urban areas. The ash is normally deposited as semi-liquid silt, often in disused gravel pits or opencast quarries. When first tipped it has a pH of about 8 to 9 or even higher and is deficient in both nitrogen and calcium. Initial conditions favour salt-tolerant plants that are found naturally at the landward end of saltmarshes. These early colonisers also need to be able to withstand high levels of boron found in PFA. But after 10 to 15 years of leaching the ash beds become colonised rapidly by a mosaic of grassland with marshy pools, often with patches of willow scrub. Open areas of sparse grassland, dominated by Yorkshire fog, field horsetail, rosebay willowherb and coltsfoot, contain extensive stands of orchids, including early and southern marsh orchids and marsh helleborine. Willow scrub may become well established within 20 years of tipping, followed by birch and willow woodland (Gemmell, 1982). Solidified PFA frequently has extensive bare areas of ash that provide suitable conditions for mining bees and other burrowing invertebrates.

The ash always includes a proportion of hollow particles that float, which coalesce to form floating islands when PFA is deposited in deep water. Spinning spinnies may seem rather far-fetched but that is what they are. These circular islands, covered in birch and sometimes willow, drift around the site blown by the wind! In 1991 at Welbeck landfill near Wakefield there were 22 such islands, the largest 35 m across (Shaw, 1994). A number of power stations run by the Central Electricity Generating Board, in the East Midlands and Yorkshire, pioneered the use of industrial sites as educational nature reserves in the 1970s. Several had spectacular orchid populations. A number of PFA tips have been protected as nature reserves specifically to encourage orchids, but this particular phase of the succession tends to be lost very quickly as trees become dominant.

SO WHAT'S SO SPECIAL ABOUT WASTELANDS?

The places that I have described illustrate one of the key issues in post-industrial ecology. Every site is different. Admittedly there are broad categories of land use such as demolition sites, various kinds of quarries and industrial waste tips, flooded sand and gravel pits, disused wharves, dock basins and waterworks, as well as many habitats associated with disused canals and railways. But the range of variables affecting any individual site is enormous owing to the particular circumstances of its history. By their very nature wasteland sites are prone to disturbance. They often have a great mixture of materials dumped at different times. Similarly piecemeal excavation frequently affects different parts of a site, exposing a variety of substrates. The effect of this is to produce a patchwork of plant communities at various stages in the succession. But there are also ecological factors that result in variations even on areas with similar substrates. Founder effects and the changing nature of source material for colonisation and succession strongly influence the way a particular site develops. Added to which there is the very significant contribution made by alien species which introduce yet another dimension to the overall diversity.

Having examined a great many wasteland sites I can only say that the botanical palette is remarkably large. It is possible to list the characteristic species that occur most frequently. Excluding the grasses I find that there are about one hundred of these. They feature strongly in the places that I have described. Naturalised aliens represent 40 per cent of this list. Some individual sites show a similar proportion. Of the 333 species recorded on Gargoyle Wharf 41 per cent were naturalised aliens. The detailed plant communities of urban wastelands are remarkably diverse and there is always the possibility that something totally unfamiliar will turn up. The intimate mixture of native and alien species is quite unlike any semi-natural vegetation occurring in Britain. It sets these habitats apart from the norm. The phrase 'ecological recombination' has been coined for this kind of mixture. It is perhaps best developed in post-industrial habitats and urban wasteland but, as you will gather from earlier chapters, it is in varying degrees a feature of many urban situations.

The fact that post-industrial habitats contain a high proportion of naturalised aliens should come as no surprise. These places are essentially artificial habitats where ecological conditions are very unusual. As I have explained they can be exceedingly hot and dry and they also suffer from stress conditions owing to nutrient deficiency. Many of the naturalised aliens that are particularly successful in colonising these habitats come from hotter climatic regions and they are capable of surviving in highly stressed conditions. It is perhaps more surprising that so many of our native British species manage to accommodate to the rigours of urban wastelands.

As a general rule the proportion of naturalised aliens tends to be highest in those parts of the urban environment that have been most intensely modified and then allowed to fall into decay and dereliction. So areas of rubble and dereliction, older, heavily built-up areas of the inner city and even unmanaged patches adjacent to residential areas have a greater proportion of aliens than most other urban habitats. Conversely more natural areas such as old woodlands or meadows caught within the urban scene generally support fewer aliens. Where they do occur it tends to be in disturbed ground. Those that manage to persist are either strongly invasive species such as Japanese knotweed or Himalayan balsam, or those with a ready source of supply, such as garden plants colonising neighbouring areas of woodland.

Provenance is crucial. Docklands have long provided some of the best places to hunt for alien plants. Since Victorian times local natural history societies in our major ports have regularly arranged field visits to the environs of the local docks and it still goes on today. I well remember visits to Hull Docks in the 1960s with members of the Hull Scientific and Field Naturalists Club, led with great enthusiasm by the indomitable Eva Crackles. She was one of that rather special breed of botanist who take great delight in discovering unusual aliens and I was fortunate indeed to have her as my botany teacher at school. Hull Docks were

FIG 94. Lupins on waste ground in Wolverhampton.

well known for their rich assemblage of exotic plants. About 150 species were recorded last century (Wilmore, 2000). Bristol docks were even more impressive. These were the hot spots where strange species, associated with trade in exotic foodstuffs, first became established. A report of the Botanical Exchange Club (Sandwith, 1933) lists 717 alien species growing in the docks, mostly from the Mediterranean region of Europe. Many species were ephemeral but a few became established and still occur on wastelands near the docks, including beggarticks, eastern rocket, hoary mustard and Austrian yellow-cress. Nowadays far fewer aliens are introduced in this way owing to higher standards of hygiene in food processing and more rigorous use of herbicides on the docks (Myles, 2000). Instead we have an increasing number of alien plants spreading from domestic gardens and allotments and, as we have seen, many of these are now turning up on urban wastelands.

Post-industrial landscapes are not the most popular places. They have an image of blight and decay. Many are securely fenced for reasons of safety. Some are indeed dangerous. In the 1980s I visited parts of the old Woolwich Arsenal near Greenwich, which covered a large area right next to the new town of Thamesmead. Numerous remains of blast-proof buildings that had been used for manufacture and storage of high-explosive shells were surrounded by

FIG 95. Trooper's Hill in Bristol, once a centre of coalmining and copper smelting, now a Local Nature Reserve with extensive areas of bell heather.

thick earthen banks covered in dense elder scrub and nettles. Ferns grew in the damp recesses of the workshops and grassy roofs and paths were covered in a rich array of wasteland flowers. Drainage ditches had a large population of water voles and the extensive scrubland supported whitethroat, lesser whitethroat, blackcap and garden warbler.

The Greater London Council, which owned the area, had plans to make it a country park and nature reserve, incorporating elements of the old arsenal as a blend of industrial archaeology and ecology. The place was even recognised at that time as a Site of Metropolitan Importance for Nature Conservation. The extraordinary profusion of elder and nettles was probably due to high concentrations of nitrogen in the soil, a by-product of making explosives. That in itself was not a problem, but there were other more insidious products. The arsenal was found to be heavily contaminated. In places layers of blue and green were clearly visible in the soil. Fascinating though it was, it proved impossible to allow public access and it has remained securely fenced ever since, with periodic visits by ecologists to monitor water voles and other wildlife.

An interesting parallel, though very much larger, is the disused Rocky Mountain Arsenal at Denver, Colorado which is situated right on the doorstep of the city. A vast area of 47 square miles was protected as a buffer zone for the arsenal which produced chemical weapons, nerve gas and pesticides. Areas around the factory are said to be some of the most heavily contaminated places in the USA. But most of the buffer zone is uncontaminated and after the arsenal ceased operations in 1982 the prairie ecosystem recovered spectacularly, supporting large populations of deer and up to 40,000 prairie dogs. Predators did well with numerous burrowing owls, ferruginous hawks, bald eagles and even coyotes. It has since become a popular safari park. During the first year of wildlife tours in 1988 more than 1,500 people took the double-decker London bus to see the wildlife. The danger from chemical contamination required people to stay on the bus and the whole place is surrounded by a secure fence nearly 50 km long.

Corrugated iron fencing surrounds most vacant plots in London. My job as an ecologist with the GLC frequently required me to visit such places to do ecological surveys. The first step was to find the holes created by local children, or perhaps by other less desirable users. When Ken Livingstone took part in the BBC's *Natural World* programme we visited a derelict building with a flooded basement full of newts. The rattling of corrugated iron as we made our entry made good radio. The programme even made it onto the BBC's annual 'pick of the year'. But not all post-industrial sites are barricaded off. Many of the places I have described are now managed as country parks or nature reserves and there are plenty more, including the aptly named Mucky Mountain near St Helens in Lancashire, Trooper's Hill in Bristol and Bow Creek Ecology Park on a peninsula in the River Lea in London's East End. But you don't have to make a trip to one of these specially protected places. Wander around any old industrial town or city and you will find vacant spaces full of weeds. They are the very essence of urban ecology.

BROWNFIELD INVERTEBRATES

These places are also alive with a great variety of invertebrate life. We have already seen that some post-industrial sites, such as Canvey Wick, support important assemblages of invertebrates with many nationally rare species. But even the most ordinary patch of wasteland with the usual mixture of bare ground and tall herbs will attract many species. There are several reasons for this. Lack of management is crucial. Many invertebrates over-winter in plant stems, leaves or seedheads. Many use specific plants such as the persistent heads of cocksfoot and wild carrot, or the hollow stems of umbellifers. The absence of mowing, grazing or general tidying up enables these species to survive from year to year. The abundance of flowers throughout summer and early autumn provides a significant source of nectar and pollen. Open herb-rich habitats that persist for many years as a result of environmental stress can be particularly important. Equally the range of habitats from open ground through to patches of scrub offers opportunities for a great variety of species. Bare ground provides ideal conditions for species such as mining bees and other burrowing insects. Some degree of disturbance can be an advantage. Paths worn by walkers and cyclists can be sufficient. Finally there is warmth. Many insects and spiders benefit from the warm, dry conditions. South-facing slopes and banks are particularly important

FIG 96. The streaked bombardier beetle (*Brachinus sclopeta*) is only found on brownfield habitats in the UK. (Craig Slawson)

as they provide hot, sunny situations. This makes it possible for species on the northern edge of their range in Europe to gain a foothold in Britain. Many nationally rare species fall into this category (Buglife, 2009).

Some of the most noticeable groups are hoverflies, bees, wasps, beetles, butterflies and day-flying moths. There are of course regional differences in the distribution of species. Many of the following are widely distributed, but some are absent from northern Britain. Butterflies such as small tortoiseshell, peacock, red admiral and comma are attracted to the flowers of buddleia. Bird's-foot trefoil and clovers on bare rubble can attract common blue, brown argus and grizzled skipper, whilst more acid substrates with sorrel and hawkweed may have large numbers of small copper and dingy skipper. As grasses become more dominant meadow brown can become abundant, together with small skipper, Essex skipper, large skipper and even marbled white. During periodic invasions painted lady butterflies seem particularly attracted to derelict urban areas where large numbers feed on ox-eye daisies. Day flying moths such as six spot burnet, burnet companion and even latticed heath may be found on herb-rich areas, and caterpillars of cinnabar moth can be abundant on ragwort and coltsfoot.

FIG 97. The six spot burnet moth is one of the commonest day-flying moths; seen here on common knapweed.

In sunny conditions plants such as Michaelmas daisy, Canadian goldenrod, wild carrot, yarrow, feverfew, thistles and tansy all attract a great variety of invertebrates including beetles, shield bugs and especially hoverflies and parasitic wasps. Bees are particularly abundant, especially the common carder bee (*Bombus pascuorum*). Nationally rare species such as the shrill carder bee (*Bombus sylvarum*) and brown-banded carder bee (*Bombus humulis*) may be abundant on some sites. The solitary bee (*Colletes daviesana*) frequently occurs on tansy and scentless mayweed. Hogweed soldier beetles and the very attractive thick-thighed flower beetle can be abundant. A variety of hoverflies are attracted to the flowers, two of the commonest being (*Helophilus pendulus*) and the drone fly (*Eristalis tenax*). Ichneumons, which are parasitic on other insects particularly butterflies and moths, are also frequently seen on flower heads. Hawthorn shield bugs are particularly common on wastelands where there is some scrub. Mature wasteland with herb-rich grassland supports several species of crickets and grasshoppers. The common field grasshopper is often abundant and as scrub develops so speckled bush crickets increase. One of the specialities of wasteland habitats is Roesel's bush cricket which has recently spread from Essex to colonise many southern towns and cities. Among the many spiders one of the commonest is

FIG 98. The distinguished jumping spider (*Sitticus distinguendus*): one of the rarest and most striking species of post-industrial habitats. (Peter Harvey)

Drassodes lapidosus, but there are other more spectacular species, such as the extremely rare distinguished jumping spider (above) and the wasp spider – an incomer from Europe that has become well established on urban wasteland and rough unmanaged grassland in recent years.

Since the mid-1990s it became apparent that post-industrial habitats have considerable significance for populations of rare and scarce invertebrates, but there was a lack of comprehensive surveys to back this up. However, a systematic investigation of the invertebrate fauna of brownfield sites in the Thames Gateway was carried out by Buglife stimulated by the substantial threat to many sites in this area. From 2005 to 2008 a large number of sites were mapped, surveyed and evaluated in terms of their value for invertebrates. Over five thousand hectares of brownfield land were assessed and six thousand invertebrate species recorded, of which a significant proportion were of conservation concern. Several species are found nowhere else in the UK. Fourteen of these were listed in the National Biodiversity Action Plan. The national importance of key brownfield sites for invertebrates is dealt with further in Chapter 14.

CHAPTER 6

A Legacy of New Wetlands

T HE VAST MAJORITY OF WETLANDS in urban areas have originated through human activities. Reservoirs, water-works and sewage farms were built for specific purposes but they have all been utilised by wildlife in varying degrees. Others are the legacy of extractive industries such as gravel pits, opencast quarries and subsidence flashes. A few lakes, marshes and bogs that have more natural origins have managed to survive, but much modified by urban influences. A remarkable number of these urban wetlands are now protected as nature reserves, often with a strong emphasis on birds. In many cases local natural history organisations have played a key role in protecting individual sites, very often working with industry and supported by local authorities. This chapter describes a selection of such places. They provide some of the richest and perhaps least expected habitats of towns and cities. We start in Scotland with those of more natural origins.

DUDDINGSTON LOCH AND POSSIL MARSH

Stand on top of Arthur's Seat in Edinburgh and you have a fine view of the city spread out below. To the north is the Palace of Holyrood with the Royal Mile and Castle beyond, but on the south side, nestling at the foot of the crags, is Duddingston Loch and the marshland known as Bawsinch. This is one of the most natural freshwater lakes in any town or city in the UK. It has long been protected within private land and there are records of swans being kept there in 1680. Over the centuries it has been popular for skating and was the place where curling first started. In 1923 the Loch and surrounding marshland was donated to the nation and became part of the Royal Park of Holyrood. So it might have remained had it not been for Viscount Peel who was responsible for Royal

FIG 99. Duddingston Loch and Bawsinch Fen in Edinburgh: the view from Arthur's Seat.

Parks at that time. Having been impressed by the success of bird sanctuaries in London's Royal Parks, he decided to investigate the possibility of doing the same in Scotland, with the result that Duddingston Loch was established as a bird sanctuary in 1925.

The early history of the sanctuary is well described by Professor James Richie in a special supplement to *Scottish Birds* (Ritchie, 1961). Public access was restricted to the northern shore of the loch. Voluntary bird recorders were appointed, together with a warden during the nesting season to protect birds and eggs from trespassers. Hides were built and nest-boxes installed. In the early days less than twenty species were recorded as breeding. By 1961 this had risen to just over fifty and it had become well known as a wintering area for waterfowl with up to 1500 pochard and 600 tufted duck. For a time the loch was a local centre for bird ringing, concentrating on waterfowl. It was designated an SSSI in 1953 as part of Holyrood Park. Both the loch and the adjacent reedbeds and fen woodland are now managed as a nature reserve by the Scottish Wildlife Trust.

The loch is nowhere more than three metres deep and has a fine natural gradation from open water to fringing reedswamp and fen with substantial areas of willow and alder woodland. A number of uncommon plants occur, including several that are rare in a Scottish context, notably nodding bur marigold, greater spearwort, fennel, lesser water plantain and fool's watercress. Breeding birds include great crested and little grebes, a colony of 30 to 40 pairs of herons, and small numbers of pochard, tufted duck, water rail and coot. Winter visitors include teal and goldeneye, together with up to 200 black headed gulls and smaller numbers of common gulls. Bitterns are seen with increasing frequency in winter and otters are well established.

Glasgow has its own very special piece of wetland called Possil Marsh. It lies on the northern edge of the city bounded by industrial estates and the Forth and Clyde Canal on one side, and a large cemetery on the other. A small loch surrounded by marsh, fen and willow scrub occupies a shallow basin, not unlike Duddingston, and you could well believe that the whole place is equally natural. But in the early 1800s much of the area now covered by marsh was occupied by ironstone mines. It seems that mining subsidence has been partially responsible for the present nature of the wetland. Dickson (1991) describes it as an extensive fen with stands of great reedmace, bulrush, bogbean and bottle sedge, together with greater spearwort, marsh cinquefoil and common cottongrass. Sir William Hooker who was Professor of Botany at Glasgow University before he became Director of Kew Gardens in 1841 commented that, 'Every Glasgow Naturalist is baptised in Possil Marsh'. It was certainly well known to botanists for the remarkable number of rarities that once grew there, including bog plants like round-leaved sundew and bog asphodel. That habitat has long since gone.

The marsh was also much appreciated by ornithologists for the variety of waterfowl and other wetland birds. As a result it was acquired as a bird sanctuary in 1930 by the Scottish Wild Birds Sanctuaries Trust and so joined Duddingston as one of Scotland's first nature reserves. It was scheduled as an SSSI in 1954 and was given to the Scottish Wildlife Trust in 1982. Since then it has been managed as an urban nature reserve, catering for people from the Glasgow area. The reserve has open access to a circular walk around the perimeter. Breeding birds include water rail, grasshopper warbler and reed bunting, together with stonechat and occasional whinchat. Nesting waterfowl suffer from predation by mink. An urban nature reserve in Glasgow brings its own set of problems. A hide built for birdwatching had to be dismantled as it was being used by poachers and there are still problems of lurchers chasing roe deer in the marsh.

WIGAN FLASHES

Further south in Lancashire, within a few minutes walk from the town centre of Wigan along the Leeds and Liverpool Canal, you find yourself in an extensive landscape of lakes and reedbeds known as the Wigan Flashes. These wetlands originated as subsidence flashes following coalmining, which started on a large scale after the Leeds and Liverpool Canal was linked to Manchester in 1820. Large numbers of pits were opened and the Wigan coalfield became one of the most productive in Lancashire. In the early 1900s it was a landscape peppered with pitheads and mounds of colliery spoil, separated by ponds and marshes that arose as the worked-out areas gradually collapsed. The canal and railways also suffered from subsidence and had to be raised on high embankments. Some of the flashes were filled with colliery spoil and new industries moved in, including a power station which produced its own brand of industrial waste in the form of PFA.

But all that has now changed. The last deep mine closed in 1962 and the power station was demolished in 1989. Natural colonisation and large-scale reclamation works have resulted in a new landscape in which hardly any vestiges of industry survive. The flashes cover about 250 hectares, with extensive areas of open water and reedbeds, together with fen, rough grassland and a mixture of wet woodland. They have become one of the most significant new wetlands in northwest England. Most of the area is designated as a Local Nature Reserve (LNR) and part as SSSI. The nature reserve is particularly significant for its winter water-bird populations, which include large numbers of tufted duck, coot, pochard, goldeneye, gadwall and great crested grebe. Bittern is also recorded regularly in winter. Breeding birds include reed bunting, willow tit, reed warbler, sedge warbler, common tern and water rail. The area is an important feeding ground for bats, with large numbers of noctule and Daubenton's bats.

Wigan Flashes are accessible to large numbers of people. One estimate suggests that six million people live within 20 minutes drive! Over 100,000 people visit every year. The flashes are managed by the Lancashire Wildlife Trust in partnership with Wigan Council. They form the centrepiece of the Greenheart Regional Park.

FAIRBURN INGS, SWILLINGTON AND THE DEARNE VALLEY

Across the Pennines in Yorkshire the coalfields provide similar areas that were once entirely dominated by mining but are now becoming known for the very fine wetland habitats that resulted either from subsidence or from open-cast mining. The Lower Aire Valley within a few kilometres of Leeds has a number of examples, the most notable being the group of subsidence flashes known as Fairburn Ings. Another area of newly created wetlands lies in the Dearne Valley near Barnsley which is one of only twelve sites included in the national scheme of Nature Improvement Areas.

Fairburn Ings has been known to Yorkshire's ornithologists since the late 1940s. Bob Dickens who was a teacher in nearby Castleford was one of these. He championed the place from the day he settled nearby and in 1957 along with others he persuaded the West Riding County Council and National Coal Board to designate it as a Local Nature Reserve. Dickens later became President of the Yorkshire Naturalist's Union and worked closely with the RSPB, which might explain the fact that in 1968 management of the reserve passed to the RSPB in conjunction with the County Council. In 1984 the site was recognised as an SSSI. The lakes and smaller water bodies owe their existence to mining subsidence and there are also areas of marsh and wet pasture dissected by dykes. The reserve is bordered on one side by industrial and urban landscapes. Yet it manages to sustain a remarkable variety of wildlife. It attracts large numbers of birds and is particularly noted for its wintering wildfowl. Gadwall, mallard and shoveler regularly exceed 1 per cent of national populations and at times there are over 100 whooper swans. It is said that over 75 bird species breed within the SSSI. A great variety of migrants have also been recorded. Local birdwatchers are proud of the fact that Fairburn Ings holds the record for the highest number of species seen at an inland site in the UK (274). The waterways and wetlands support a variety of aquatic and fenland plants including bur-reed, both species of bur-marigold, golden dock, water violet and tubular water-dropwort. For many years Fairburn Ings has provided a model of what is possible within post-industrial landscapes. It demonstrates very clearly that high quality habitats can become established through natural processes. It has also taken a lead in promoting environmental education. Further up the Aire Valley is Swillington Ings and the St Aidans site which is on the verge of becoming another major nature reserve as I write. Annual reports of local bird recorders at Swillington Ings provide an excellent summary of the natural history and an insight into local politics.

In the South Yorkshire Coalfield near Barnsley a series of wetlands has become established, some through subsidence and others through re-landscaping of colliery land. One of these is the Old Moor nature reserve in the Dearne Valley which was once a derelict marshalling yard and coal storage area for local collieries. Re-landscaped after the pit closures it was opened as a wetland reserve in 1998. Since 2003 it has been managed for Barnsley Metropolitan Borough Council by the RSPB. There are other nature reserves in the Dearne Valley at Gypsy Marsh and Wombwell Ings which are being managed as nature reserves in much the same way as those in the Aire Valley. But the new Nature Improvement Area for the Dearne Valley aims to link these and create a 1300 hectare core of high quality wetland and woodland habitat with a buffer zone of nearly 3000 hectares of reclaimed industrial land and other open land that will be enhanced for wildlife conservation. This is an example of the 'bigger, better and joined-up' approach to nature conservation advocated by the Lawton Report *Making Space for Nature* (2010). In other words, this is the landscape-scale approach, which could have a significant effect if applied to post-industrial landscapes more widely.

ATTENBOROUGH LAKES

What is probably the most spectacular gravel pit nature reserves in the UK lies
only 7 km from the centre of Nottingham between the outer suburbs of Beeston
and Long Eaton. The landscape of five large lakes, together with associated
wetlands and wet woodland, is the result of nearly forty years of sand and gravel
extraction. In the 1960s there were plans for the flooded gravel pits to be filled
with fly ash from a local power station and then restored to agriculture. But
local residents and naturalists campaigned successfully for the gravel pits to be
retained as a nature reserve. The reserve is sandwiched between the River Trent
and the main railway line from Nottingham to the Midlands. It is managed by
the Nottinghamshire Wildlife Trust in partnership with the owners Cemex and
supported by the local borough council of Broxtowe. The reserve was established
in 1966 and opened by Sir David Attenborough. It gained SSSI status in 1982
and an award winning nature centre was opened in 2005. Gravel extraction still
continues on adjacent land. New areas are added to the reserve as extraction
ceases, the most recent being in 2010. The reserve currently covers 145 hectares.

The lakes and associated wetlands are exceptionally rich in aquatic and
emergent plants. Shallow margins have an assemblage of floating and submerged

FIG 100. Attenborough Lakes, Nottingham: the award-winning nature centre.
(Nottinghamshire Wildlife Trust)

FIG 101. Attenborough Lakes: reedbeds with common reed and bulrush, and wooded edges composed of willow and alder. (Nottinghamshire Wildlife Trust)

aquatic plants including lesser pondweed, fennel pondweed, fan-leaved water-crowfoot, common stonewort and the nationally scarce short-leaved water-starwort. Sheltered bays and inlets have been colonised by a diverse range of emergent swamp and fen vegetation which includes purple-loosestrife, flowering-rush, marsh thistle, fine-leaved water-dropwort and marsh stitchwort. Other areas are dominated by a variety of emergent species forming dense stands, such as common reed, greater pond sedge, bulrush, reed canary-grass, reed sweet-grass and common club-rush. Large areas have been colonised by willow carr dominated by grey willow, common osier and sallow.

The very varied local topography, with many islands and shallow bays, promotes dense vegetation cover providing ideal nesting habitat for birds. These include great crested grebe, little grebe, tufted duck, gadwall, mute swan, sedge and reed warblers. Cetti's warblers have gradually increased since they first colonised the reserve in 2008. Open sandy areas on islands and spits provide suitable conditions for little ringed plover to nest (see Chapter 8) and there is a large colony of common terns. Old quarry faces provide ideal nest sites for kingfisher and support a large colony of sandmartins, which also use an artificial bank. A remarkably accessible heronry with about forty pairs provides spectacular views for visitors, and some fifty pairs of cormorants nest on the reserve. As with many gravel pits substantial numbers of Canada and greylag geese are resident, with up to 200 of each.

The lakes are particularly important for wintering water birds especially shoveler and great crested grebe, and increasingly for bitterns which are becoming a regular winter attraction. Small parties of whooper and Bewick's swans drop in at times. As with other wetlands of this kind a great variety of migrants can be seen throughout the year. One of the least expected was a squacco heron that appeared in November 2011 attracting hundreds of twitchers from all over the country. But it is the easy accessibility of the reserve for people living in and around Nottingham that gives it special importance. For them it provides a distinctly different kind of landscape from the usual country park and offers opportunities to see less common wildlife close at hand. The visitor centre attracts 250,000 people every year and the total number visiting the reserve, which has open access, could be half a million. Well over half are from the local area.

Attenborough Nature Reserve is a particularly good example of what can be achieved by careful design and good long-term management. Flooded gravel pits provide an extremely valuable new wildlife habitat, resulting directly from the most widespread extractive industry in the UK. An estimate by the RSPB in 1993 suggested that 15,000 hectares of flooded pits had been produced historically in the UK and up to 500 hectares of new lakes were being added each year. The value of these areas for water birds is considerable. They support over 30 per cent of the UK breeding population of tufted duck, Canada goose and great crested grebe as well as 25 per cent of the wintering population of gadwall and pochard. The total number of waterbirds dependent on gravel pits for breeding was 33,000, or one fifth of the UK total (Andrews & Kinsman, 1990). A very large number of these flooded gravel pits are associated with towns and cities throughout the UK. Many are long established and may have had little direct management. Others have been intensively managed as nature reserves. A remarkably large number have been given SSSI or LNR status. We have come a long way since Pamela and Jeffrey Harrison published their small booklet describing the Gravel Pit Nature Reserve at Sevenoaks in Kent. This was a pioneer venture working with the gravel company to landscape the area for waterfowl after gravel extraction ceased. The immense potential of such areas in the urban context is now widely appreciated. The practical manual published by the RSPB in 1993 referred to above provides detailed guidance on the restoration of gravel pits for wildlife and it has now become common practice for such areas to be managed for nature conservation, sometimes in conjunction with local sailing clubs and angling associations.

DOXEY MARSHES

From Nottingham we move across the north Midlands to Stafford where we find an extraordinary wetland right on the doorstep of the County Town. Doxey Marshes cover a large part of the floodplain of the River Sow reaching almost into the centre of the city. They are completely surrounded by housing, business parks, light industry and transport routes. The west coast mainline railway crosses the marshes and the M6 motorway forms the northern boundary. Historically the land was low-lying damp pasture and grazing marsh, and drier parts are still grazed by cattle. Much of the area has, however, been affected by subsidence caused by extraction of brine from the underlying Keuper salt beds. This resulted in a series of shallow pools or flashes producing a patchwork of wetland habitats including open water, marsh, fen and reedswamp. Although extraction ceased over thirty years ago some parts still appear to be subsiding. The whole area of marshes, totalling 124 hectares, is managed as an open-access nature reserve by the Staffordshire Wildlife Trust. It was designated as an SSSI in 1977.

The marshes are an important habitat for breeding and wintering birds. Regular breeding species include up to twenty pairs of lapwing, and smaller numbers of redshank and snipe, the latter being particularly significant in view of the recent decline in its numbers. Other notable breeding species include

FIG 102. Doxey marshes, Stafford: popular for both bird-watching and pond-dipping.

FIG 103. Families of mute swans are always a popular attraction.

great crested grebe, tufted duck, shoveler, reed and sedge warbler and water rail. Kingfisher, teal, little grebe and grasshopper warbler occur in small numbers. Marsh harriers have become annual visitors. In late summer large swallow roosts occur on the reserve when several thousand birds congregate prior to migrating. Wintering species include up to 1,000 Canada geese and several hundred lapwing and snipe, golden plover and teal, together with wigeon, jack snipe and small numbers of goosander and bittern. The marshes attract

FIG 104. Doxey Marshes extend almost to the centre of Stafford.

a great variety of migrants and are becoming well known as one of the best birdwatching sites in the West Midlands.

The area is also notable for its mammals with significant numbers of otter, harvest mouse and water shrew being recorded. A good range of marsh plants occur. There are extensive beds of reed sweet grass and common reed. Fen communities contain skullcap, great willowherb, water dock, marsh pennywort, marsh marigold and lesser water parsnip. Public walkways allow access to most of the marshes and there are public hides overlooking some of the flashes, and scrapes that have been constructed to encourage waders. As with other wetlands described in this chapter the presence of such a large area of wild habitat so close to the city centre is truly remarkable.

RADIPOLE LAKE AND LODMOOR

The south-coast town of Weymouth in Dorset boasts two large wetland nature reserves, Radipole Lake which extends right into the middle of the town, and Lodmoor which lies within the eastern suburbs. Radipole Lake was formed in

FIG 105. Radipole Lake in Weymouth, Dorset: aerial view of the nature reserve in the middle of the town. (David Wooton/RSPB)

FIG 106. Extensive reed beds support marsh harriers and bearded tits close to Weymouth town centre.

the 1920s when a bridge and dam was built across the River Wey and sluices were installed so that the river was no longer tidal. Since then the lake, which covers 87 hectares, changed from a saline, tidal estuary to a freshwater reed-dominated lake. The area has been managed as a nature reserve by the RSPB since 1975. The entrance to the reserve lies only a five-minute walk from the railway station in the town centre, from where the wetland habitats extend northwards for over one kilometre. Like so many wetland reserves the footpaths are carried on raised walkways through the reeds with higher viewing platforms in places from which it is possible to see over the reedbeds. Famous as one of the first places in Britain to be colonised by Cetti's warbler in the 1960s the reserve also supports a resident population of bearded tits. Marsh harriers started breeding in 2009 and small numbers of bitterns regularly winter here. As in other places in southern England most of them are from continental Europe. Breeding birds include large numbers of reed warblers, along with kingfisher, great crested grebe, water rail and occasional pairs of garganey ducks. Water voles and otters breed on the reserve and noctule bats are frequently recorded.

Lodmoor is rather different with a substantial area of saltmarsh and brackish pools immediately behind the sea wall, backed by another extensive reedbed which also has nesting marsh harriers and bearded tits, as well as Cetti's and reed warblers. Lodmoor is particularly noted for the winter flocks of up to 300 pochard, together with many waders that congregate on the brackish pools in autumn and winter. Black tailed godwits are particularly abundant, but owing to its coastal location the reserve attracts a great variety of migrant birds despite being virtually surrounded by the suburbs of Weymouth. Water pipits are a winter speciality. A breeding colony of about seventy common terns provides quite a spectacle in the summer and there are breeding oystercatchers and ringed plovers. Large green bush crickets and slow worms may be seen along the paths.

RAINHAM MARSHES

Our tour of wetlands brings us finally to London where we start with Rainham Marshes which was referred to briefly in Chapter 3 as one of London's few remaining areas of Thames-side grazing marsh. But the area has a complex history that produced a great mixture of habitats. In the late 1800s the whole of the north side of the Thames, from Rainham to Purfleet was uninterrupted grazing marsh. Both ends of the marshes were used as rifle ranges by the army from early last century, and by the 1950s industrial development had spread onto the western end. Over the period 1967–87 silt lagoons were constructed on a large

FIG 107. Rainham Marshes, Essex: aerial view of RSPB Reserve. (Rolf Williams/RSPB)

central section of the marshes by the Port of London Authority to take dredgings from the Thames. Other parts were used as small-scale domestic refuse tips. A large area adjacent to the river then became a major landfill site that has dominated the landscape for the past thirty or more years. Today the high-speed channel tunnel rail link, together with the new elevated A13 trunk road, form the landward boundary of the marshes. Despite all this a broad swathe of open marshland remains. It is extensive enough to have its own characteristic wild landscape and must be one of the most outstanding wildlife sites in the capital. The RSPB bought the majority of the site from the MOD in 2000 and leases other parts from Havering Council. This is all now managed as a wetland nature reserve. Most of the site is an SSSI. The adjacent landfill site will eventually be converted into a country park alongside the Thames.

The grazing marshes with their wet meadows and drainage ditches support many uncommon species. Notable plants include marsh dock, golden dock, brackish water-crowfoot and divided sedge. Invertebrates include the scarce emerald damselfly and saltmarsh spider (*Baryphyma duffeyi*), along with a great variety of water beetles and brackish water snails. There are also a thriving populations of water voles and grass snakes. Drier areas support a large

FIG 108. Lapwings are regular visitors at Rainham Marshes. (Andy Hay/RSPB)

population of the very localised bumblebee (*Bombus humilis*), a UK BAP priority species. But it is the birds which capture most attention from naturalists. Rainham Marshes have long been known to London's birdwatchers as one of the best places to see winter visitors such as short-eared owl and hen harrier, but in recent years small numbers of penduline tits and serins have become a regular feature. In 2005 there were up to ten penduline tits wintering here, almost certainly one of the consequences of climate change. During winter months proximity to the river brings substantial numbers of waders including over 1,000 dunlin and lapwing and several hundred black tailed godwits and golden plover, with smaller numbers of curlew, grey plovers and turnstone. The reserve also attracts up to 1,000 wigeon and over 3,000 teal, together with pintail, water rail and snipe. Merlin and marsh harrier are also frequently seen.

Breeding birds are equally impressive. There are significant numbers of lapwing, redshank, reed bunting, little grebe, meadow pipit and skylark, whilst shoveler, tufted duck, gadwall, grasshopper warbler, water rail, Cetti's warbler and barn owl all breed regularly. Avocets have attempted to breed and there have been numerous visits from other marshland birds which could become established, including bearded tit, little egret and spoonbill. A pair of marsh harriers has been in residence since 2012. Erection of over 5 km of fences to keep out foxes has resulted in much greater fledging success for ground nesting waders such as lapwing and redshank.

LONDON'S WATER SUPPLY RESERVOIRS

Many large reservoirs have been constructed in and around London to supply drinking water for the capital. The earliest were those at Walthamstow in the Lea Valley built in the mid- to late 1800s, whilst most of the others were built during the first half of the twentieth century. A string of nine large reservoirs lying in the Thames Valley in west London, stretches from Island Barn Reservoir near Bushy Park to Datchet Reservoir on the edge of Slough. The largest is Queen Mary Reservoir, built in 1931, which is nearly 3 km in extent. Wraysbury and Staines Reservoirs near Heathrow are also very extensive. For passengers landing at Heathrow Airport a large part of the landscape appears to be water. Similarly 10 km of the Lea Valley from Tottenham out to the M25 is occupied by five huge reservoirs. The change in London's landscape through the building of all these reservoirs was immense. Over 1,200 hectares of concrete lined reservoirs were created which provided an important new habitat for waterfowl and other wetland birds.

These reservoirs have become some of the most popular places for London's bird watchers. Thames Water issues permits and the dedicated band of birders who regularly record the numbers of waterfowl and other birds on and around the reservoirs has resulted in a very considerable body of data on population fluctuations and on visible migration. Many of the reservoirs have been scheduled as SSSIs and the two main groups in southwest London and the Lea Valley were designated as Special Protection Areas (SPA) under the EU Habitats Directive in 2000. Staines Reservoir built in 1901 is one of the best known for its birds and was the first to gain recognition as an SSSI in 1955.

Walthamstow, already a bird sanctuary in the 1920s, gained SSSI status in 1986, largely because of the very large heronry with more than 100 pairs nesting on wooded islands. This heronry is still one of the five largest in the country. It is also notable as one of the first urban breeding sites for little egret in the UK, with ten pairs in 2011 (Woodward & Arnold, 2012). Cormorants also nest in large numbers, with 360 pairs in 2004. Walthamstow is unlike most of the other reservoirs in having softer banks with emergent vegetation that provides a greater range of habitat, contrasting with the stark concrete edges of so many others. The range of breeding species is accordingly greater with great-crested grebe, pochard, tufted duck, shoveler, Canada goose and coot, together with both reed and sedge warbler and yellow wagtail. It is particularly important as a late summer moulting site for tufted duck and holds nationally important numbers of shoveler and tufted duck in winter. The large cormorant roost

FIG 109. Goldeneye, one of the regular wintering species on London's reservoirs. (Paul Wilkins)

on the islands adds to its value. Chingford reservoirs nearby have similar
winter populations of waterfowl, also including goldeneye and goosander
which concentrate in the flood relief channel. Here the late summer refuge for
moulting birds includes large numbers of great-crested grebes. Winter gull
roosts regularly hold 70,000 birds including black-headed, common, lesser
black-backed and herring gulls.

The large reservoirs in the Thames Valley are particularly important for
their winter duck populations, especially gadwall, shoveler, tufted duck, pochard,
goosander and goldeneye, together with cormorant and great crested grebe.
Gadwall and shoveler reach internationally important numbers. Again large
numbers of gulls roost on the reservoirs in winter. Kempton Park Reservoirs,
which lie immediately north of the racecourse in the west London suburbs of
Hampton and Feltham, provide an unusual habitat. The two reservoirs cover
about 25 hectares and have been redundant since 1980. The eastern one has
been actively managed as a nature reserve by Thames Water since 1996 under a
planning agreement with the local authority. Water levels have been maintained
at low levels, with large areas of mud exposed at times. Substantial works have
been carried out to create refuge islands, deep-water channels and reed beds. The
site has SSSI status primarily because of the number of wintering gadwall, but it

is also important for its breeding birds which include lapwing, redshank, ringed plover and little ringed plover. Avocets nested here in 1996, which was notable not only as one of the first successful inland breeding pairs but the first to nest in an urban setting. As might be expected the wetland habitats attract a wide range of passage migrants. Temminck's stint, spotted crake and red-necked phalarope are some of the notable species recorded. These reservoirs are feeding areas for noctule, serotine, Daubenton's and pipistrelle bats (Pape, 1990).

London's reservoirs provide endless delight for birdwatchers, many of whom adopt particular reservoirs as their local patch. Whilst the large concentrations of water birds are an important part of the picture, it is the chance of the unexpected that brings most excitement. Staines is one of the most outstanding sites. A selection from the highlights for 2009 (Innes, 2012) provides the flavour of what is involved:

> *Large concentrations of water birds included 457 pochard and 234 shoveler in January, 60 goldeneye in March, 700 tufted duck in July, and 500 coot and 72 great-crested grebes in August. Individual great northern divers occurred thoughout winter months, as late as May, and there were nine black-necked grebes by the end of February. Migrant waders including avocet, little ringed plover and black-tailed godwit started to appear in March, when there were also eight smew and ten little gulls. A group of five velvet scoters arrived one day in April and that month there were up to fifty little gulls, one purple heron, a kittiwake and an osprey. Swifts arrived in large numbers by the end of the month. Wader passage continued in May with greenshank, turnstones and six avocets, but the highlight of the month was a white-winged black tern. An influx of up to 24 of the more normal black terns also occurred. Parties of whimbrel were notable in July and August, together with a great variety of other waders, the odd marsh harrier and yet another white-winged black tern. September was notable for the presence of a Leach's petrel blown in from the Atlantic, and there was a gannet in October. A short-eared owl in November was less surprising as up to six regularly winter on the nearby Staines Moor, but a marsh harrier in December was out of the ordinary.*

You can see the attraction for birdwatchers, but what is extraordinary is that all this happened within a mile or two of Heathrow Airport! London is fortunate to have so many large reservoirs but some of the smaller ones nearer to central London also prove attractive to local birdwatchers. Lonsdale Road Reservoir in Barnes and Stoke Newington Reservoir in Hackney are good examples: the London Wildlife Trust is currently developing a major new nature reserve at Stoke Newington. There are similar examples in most big cities and they all have a similar tale to tell.

BRENT RESERVOIR

Finally we come to Brent Reservoir, also known as the Welsh Harp, which is a very different kind of habitat from the concrete-sided lakes previously described. Built in 1835 to supply water for the Regents Canal in London this shallow reservoir lies in the valley of the River Brent next to Edgeware Road and the North Circular, surrounded by business parks and suburban housing. For the past sixty years it has been cherished by local naturalists and is now one of the most delightful wildlife habitats in the capital. Although much of the reservoir is intensively used for sailing the shallower northern arms provide a gradation from open water through fen and reedswamp to fringing woodland of willow and alder. Together with surrounding areas of rough grassland and parkland the site covers 100 hectares. Parts were designated as an SSSI in 1950 and there is a Joint Consultative Committee led by local boroughs that includes representatives from the Welsh Harp Conservation Group. One of the earliest day field centres in London has provided facilities for school parties since the 1970s.

FIG 110. Brent Reservoir, London: The northern arm with Canada geese, black-headed gulls and coot.

FIG 111. Brent Reservoir and surrounding habitats. Whilst the main reservoir is used for sailing, the northern and eastern arms provide sanctuary for a great variety of water birds.

The Conservation Group was formed in 1972 to organise opposition to a housing scheme that would have destroyed key areas of the site. Since 1980 it has been involved in a long-term programme of conservation management that continues today. This has involved large-scale redesign of the reedswamp and willow carr. A range of new habitats has been created to provide refuge areas for water birds during sailing activities on the main water body and to diversify wetland habitats for wildlife other than birds. Dr Leo Batten has been one of the key figures in making it all happen, not only developing plans for habitat enhancement and provision of public hides, but also successfully arguing the case for conservation with the many conflicting interests. One of his most successful innovations was the provision of nesting rafts for common terns; another the installation of oil traps on inflow streams. (Batten, 1972; & Batten et al., 2002)

Even in the 1850s the reservoir was known to attract a variety of unusual birds and records from 1860 suggest that 72 species were known to breed. The total number of regular breeding species is now 51 of which 12 are new additions to the list over the past 50 years. The reservoir is particularly notable for the large number of breeding pairs of great crested grebe (see Chapter 8). Other breeding birds include reed and sedge warblers, reed bunting, water rail and common terns, whilst overgrown hedges and scrub support whitethroat, lesser whitethroat and blackcap. In winter the reservoir supports nationally significant numbers of shoveler and gadwall, together with large numbers of tufted duck, coot and snipe. Bittern and bearded tit occur sporadically. Like Staines the reservoir has a core of regular and committed observers who delight in finding something new. Many migratory species are recorded and the total species list stood at 243 in 2002.

Insects recorded include eight Red Data Book species and over sixty nationally notable species including the longhorn beetle (*Phyoecia cylindrica*) and the chimney-sweeper moth. Butterflies include the white-letter hairstreak. A recent coloniser is the ruddy darter dragonfly. Some of the more notable plants are flowering rush, fringed water lily, greater spearwort, marsh woundwort, great burnet and golden dock.

In his foreword to *Birds of Brent Reservoir* (Batten *et al.*, 2002) Bill Oddie said that 'Brent Reservoir might just be the ideal local patch'. It is certainly well frequented by many London naturalists and much loved by local residents.

CHAPTER 7

Parks, Squares and Gardens

E VERY TOWN AND CITY has its parks and gardens that are enormously
important in providing a wealth of habitats amongst the brick, stone,
concrete and glass that dominates so much of our lives. Look across
the landscape of any city and you will see trees rising above the buildings. Some
are the tops of street trees but the majority are growing in gardens. In outer 'leafy
suburbs' trees may seem to form a continuous canopy. From a good vantage
point it can look as if the whole city is wooded. Inner areas are less fortunate but
the amount of green can still be very significant. Here and there clumps of long-

FIG 112. Trees in private gardens in Edinburgh give the impression of a wooded city.

established trees rise above the rest marking some of the older parks, city squares and even botanical gardens. These trees provide a living record of the changing landscape of the city.

This chapter is devoted to the places that have traditionally provided links with nature within the town environment. They are places where horticulture, landscape design and gardening hold sway; places with soil, lawns, specimen trees and compost heaps, as well as floral displays and shrubberies. Some of our largest parks have more affinity with areas of encapsulated countryside described earlier. The tiniest may serve as nature gardens or even city farms. There is a huge array of possibilities from domestic gardens and allotments to the most elaborate parkland landscape or botanical garden. Each has its own particular suite of wildlife, which depends on the specific habitats that it contains and also on the degree of urbanisation of its surroundings. We start with some of our largest parks, with groves of ancient oaks and herds of deer, and end with a fairly average suburban garden in which more than 2,500 species have been recorded.

ANCIENT PARKS: SUTTON AND RICHMOND.

Sutton Park lies within the Birmingham conurbation only 11 km from the city centre and totally surrounded by built up areas. At 900 hectares it is the second largest urban park in the UK and also one of the oldest. In the twelfth century it formed part of an extensive area of woodland and heath known as Sutton Chase. The park was established by Royal Charter in 1528 when land was enclosed for the benefit of the people of Sutton Coldfield who were allowed to graze stock and hunt within the park. For several centuries it was maintained as a deer park with open heathland and woodland. As surrounding areas became heavily industrialised in the nineteenth century the park was subject to a range of recreational uses, including golf courses and two racecourses. More facilities for entertainment were constructed after the railway came in 1862 (Trueman *et al.*, 2013).

Despite this the area has retained much of its wild character. It was designated an SSSI in 1987 and became a National Nature Reserve in 1997. It must rank as one of the most extensive tracts of semi-natural habitat in any urban area. Higher ground is dominated by birch and bracken, with heather, western gorse, cowberry and acidic grassland on the slopes. But it is the valley bottoms with their wet heath and patches of bog that are particularly unusual, especially in an urban context. Cross-leafed heath, purple moor grass and cotton grass cover wetter parts and a remarkable number of bog plants still survive,

including butterwort, round-leafed sundew, marsh pennywort, bog pimpernel
and cranberry, along with patches of Sphagnum moss. Breeding birds still
include skylark, meadow pipit, grasshopper warbler and yellowhammer. As in
other heathlands close to large urban areas a number of species have declined
dramatically over the past fifty years and now no longer breed. Nightjars were
the first to go in the 1960s. More recently redstarts and tree pipits followed and
both stonechat and redpoll are now much reduced in numbers. But Sutton Park
remains a remarkably wild tract of country within the industrial landscape of the
West Midlands.

Richmond Park in London provides an even greater contrast. Its wild vistas
are without parallel in the capital. Nowhere else is there such a sense of untamed
wilderness, heightened by the multitude of ancient oaks and herds of deer that
roam at will throughout the park. Over 3 km across and covering 955 hectares,
this is by far the largest open space in London. It was enclosed in 1637 by
Charles I, for use as a royal deer park. The King's act provoked fierce opposition
from local commoners, which led him to provide a number of gates and ladder
stiles along the 13-mile boundary wall to allow commoners rights to continue.
Public access to the whole park was granted in the twentieth century. For over
300 years it was under the control of successive Rangers appointed by the Crown,
until 1910 when the Commissioners of Works became responsible for the Royal
Parks. Throughout its history the landscape has changed considerably. Extensive
tracts of oak woodland were cleared during the 1700s to create more open heath,
but many oaks dating from before the enclosure still remain and these ancient

FIG 113. Richmond Park in London: a long established deer park with ancient trees.

trees give the park a special quality. Other trees were planted as avenues and plantations. Oaks and sweet chestnuts along the Queen's Ride were planted in the 1700s and new woodlands such as the Isabella Plantation were planted in the mid-1800s. The famous woodland garden with its water features and displays of azaleas was a more recent creation of the 1950s.

Management of the deer has always been the primary concern. When the park was first enclosed there were about 1,500 fallow deer and 200 red deer. Numbers are now much reduced with about 300 of each. Groups grazing by the roadside, or lying lazily beneath the trees are a familiar sight for visitors and commuters alike. In autumn the rut brings a different spectacle when red deer stags engage in battle to defend their hinds. The roars of the stags can be heard far across the park, despite the noise of jumbo jets passing low overhead on their way to Heathrow.

The outstanding ecological feature of the park is the exceptionally rich invertebrate fauna associated with the large number of ancient oaks. There are over a thousand of these trees, nearly half of which were there before the park was enclosed. Some are thought to be over 800 years old. Like the old pollards at Epping Forest referred to earlier these trees contain a large amount of dead wood supporting a great variety of specialist invertebrates. Over two hundred species of beetles have been recorded in Richmond Park, including many that are nationally rare. Thirty four are listed in the *Red Data Book* of endangered species. Some are restricted to a limited number of places where ancient trees are found, such as Windsor Great Park and the New Forest. Some of the same 'Royal Beetles' found at Epping are also found in Richmond Park. Several are restricted to specific individual trees. One tiny beetle, *Cryptophagus confusus*, is known from only two trees at Windsor and one at Richmond. Another tiny click-beetle, *Ampedus cardinalis,* is almost entirely restricted to Richmond Park. It lives in the rotten heartwood of old oaks, feeding on the larvae of other invertebrates. The hairy fungus beetle (*Mycetophagus piceus*) feeds on the mycelium of the sulphur polypore fungus deep in the decaying trunk. Because of these important invertebrate populations the park was scheduled as an SSSI in 1992 and became London's second National Nature Reserve in 2000. It is also a Special Area of Conservation under the European Habitats Directive on account of the thriving population of stag beetles. The ancient trees also support an extremely diverse fungal flora. Over fifty species of birds regularly breed in the park, including heron, mandarin duck, hobby, kestrel, sparrowhawk and stock dove, together with all three woodpeckers, tawny and little owls, ring-necked parakeet and large numbers of jackdaws nesting in the hollow trees (Archer & Curson, 1993).

ROYAL PARKS IN CENTRAL LONDON

Early morning in St James's Park can be a magical experience. One May morning, I crossed Birdcage Walk at six o'clock, with hardly a car in sight, to find a remarkably peaceful scene. Large groups of greylag and Canada geese were still roosting on the grassy slopes where they had spent the night, and a flock of fifty coot stood tightly packed alongside feral pigeons soaking up the early morning sun on the banks of the lake. Great crested grebes were displaying out on the water and a variety of ducks, including pochard and tufted ducks, as well as more exotic birds from the waterfowl collection, gathered under the bridge expecting food. A great spotted woodpecker called from the trees on Duck Island and I heard the wavering trill of a dabchick just as Big Ben struck the quarter. Reed warblers sang from the narrow fringe of reeds near the Buckingham Palace end of the lake where a heron stalked about in the shallows. Song thrushes and a blackcap were singing and the harsh calls of jays and magpies announced the presence of a sparrowhawk. It wasn't the only predator. Carrion crows and herring gulls were also on the look out for easy pickings. A family of newly hatched 'cootlets' looked particularly vulnerable. Grey squirrels were looking for food too. Anyone who stopped was regarded as a potential source of peanuts. They would even climb up your trousers if you gave them half a chance! By half-past six, there was a steady stream of people crossing the park on their way to work … and half an hour later the surrounding roads were full of traffic as London came to life.

FIG 114. St James's Park, Westminster: one of the most popular parks in central London.

The park is an extraordinary oasis right in the heart of London. It was created by Henry VIII in 1530 as a deer park and pleasure garden, but appears to have become rather moribund during the Commonwealth. With restoration of the monarchy in 1660 Charles II launched into an ambitious scheme to revitalise the park, constructing a long canal for his waterfowl collection and providing aviaries alongside Birdcage Walk. In 1665 he built one of the earliest duck decoys in the country, worked by a Royal Decoyman. Both Samuel Pepys and John Evelyn took a great interest in these developments. Evelyn provides a graphic account of a visit to the park in February 1665:

> *The park was at this time stored with numerous flocks of several sorts of ordinary and extraordinary wild fowle, breeding about the decoy, which for being near so great a city and among such a concourse of souldiers and people, is a singular and diverting thing.*

He was particularly impressed by a crane fitted with a wooden leg made by a soldier, and the pelicans which had been presented by the Russian Ambassador which he described as, 'a melancholy waterfowl, between a stork and a swan'.

The park was opened to the public in 1660 and has remained so ever since, providing a place for people to stroll in a quiet green environment, away from the city streets. The lake was re-designed by John Nash in the nineteenth century and the collection of 'ornamental' waterfowl persists to this day. Pelicans still provide one of the greatest attractions, but they also cause indignation for visitors when one of them catches a pigeon, or even worse a whole flotilla of ducklings in one scoop! The collection includes a great variety of exotic and native ducks and geese all of which can be seen at close quarters near the park restaurant. Small troops of red-breasted, bar-headed, Hawaiian and snow geese are particularly attractive. The ducks include native eider, smew, shoveler and shelduck, as well as exotic species such as whistling ducks, mandarin, hooded merganser, Cape teal and white headed duck. Moorhen and coot are both resident on the lake. In 2010 there were six pairs of moorhen and thirty pairs of coot. A count in September recorded 172 coot and in December there were 84 moorhens. Every winter they are joined by large numbers of wintering birds, particularly black-headed gulls, pochard, tufted duck and the occasional cormorant and heron.

The spectacle of so many water-birds just across the road from Downing Street is a constant source of wonder and astonishment for foreign visitors to London. For some it is the high point of their trip. It is all the more amazing given the vast number of people who visit the park, and the fact that it is also used daily for ceremonial occasions. Much of its success is due to the landscape design which allows hundreds of people to walk around the lake without

FIG 115. Winter in St James's Park, when large numbers of black-headed gulls compete with resident waterfowl for food.

disturbing the birds. The key element is the narrow border of grass surrounding the lake, which makes it into a veritable outdoor aviary where people can look but cannot go. A low fence alongside the path is all that is needed. In one or two places the path runs immediately along the edge of the lake. This is where you can feed the birds. Many gather on the path, waiting for food. Some of the larger geese will tug impatiently at your clothes. Coot dash hither and thither. On occasions pelicans sit on the park benches. Moorhens pick their way quietly among the other water-birds and in recent years herons have joined the throng. Black-headed gulls are some of the most voracious feeders. They line up along the railings of the bridge where some will take food from your hand. It is said that when the park was closed to the public during World War II these gulls deserted the park within three days.

For many years the park has attracted people who take great delight in feeding the birds. Every day of the week there is a regular procession of devoted individuals who come from all parts of London and some from much further afield. Some spend so much time in the park that they can recognise individual wild birds, and this has led some to specialise in taming particular species. Until the late 1980s one of their favourite places was by the bridge over the lake where, given a handful of grain, you could guarantee to have a clutch of house sparrows feeding in your hand. Now, in the absence of sparrows, they have to make do with

FIG 116. John Jones, known to his friends as 'JJ', feeds a jay with almonds.

feral pigeons, tits, gulls and squirrels, although one man has perfected the art of feeding jays. John Jones, known appropriately as 'JJ', comes by tube from the East End every morning. The jays see him coming as he enters the park and one or two whistles have them sitting in nearby trees. He has a bag of almonds with him, which jays particularly like. One of the birds swoops in to catch a nut thrown in the air. Another snatches it from his hand in flight. But one bird has become sufficiently tame to land on his hand where it stuffs several nuts into its throat before flying off. I don't know of any other place where jays have become so tame.

Another person who spent a lot of time both taming and studying the birds was Audley Gosling. In the 1980s he tamed the woodpigeons in St James's Park. By feeding them regularly and gradually getting them to come closer he eventually had them eating out of his hands. For some time he was the envy of all the other 'bird feeders'. Now these birds will come to anyone for food. Gosling also tamed a carrion crow that got to know him so well that it would spot him in a crowd and swoop down onto his arm to be fed. He also took a particular interest in the black-headed gulls that spend the winter in London's parks. During the 1980s there were about 600 at mid-winter in St James's Park. Some of these were ringed as young birds in breeding colonies around the Baltic. Gosling perfected the art of identifying individual birds by reading ring numbers with binoculars and kept a detailed record of the dates when they arrived and left. He found that individual birds return to the same London park each year in July or August. One bird spent every winter feeding just outside the restaurant in St James's Park. Another consistently spent the first few months there and then moved to Regents Park after Christmas. Most of these birds leave for their breeding grounds by the end of March (Gosling, 1986).

The most spectacular example of birds becoming tame can be seen every day in Regents Park. Herons first nested on an island in the lake in 1968. Since then

FIG 117. Herons in Regents Park have become remarkably tame as a result of regular feeding.

the heronry has grown steadily. During the 1980s there were only about ten pairs nesting. Now there are nearly thirty pairs and the birds have become remarkably tame. There is one place in the park where herons gather at particular times every day. They stand by a footpath near Clarence Gate waiting to be fed. Two ladies feed them at different times. At ten o'clock one of them arrives bringing bags bulging with food and the herons gather in a circle around her. She has names for all of them. 'Eddy' is adept at catching thin strips of cheese thrown to him. They each take their turn. Feeding time doesn't take long, after which the birds presumably return to a more normal diet. Another lady who comes to feed the moorhens and coot complained that, 'there are far too many herons'.

Bird life in the central London parks has changed enormously over the years. The naturalist W. H. Hudson was acutely aware of the diminishing range of species during the 1890s and his book *Birds in London* (1898) was written with the express purpose of encouraging people, especially park managers, to take action to promote bird-life in the parks. He argued that many species were being lost solely through the indifference of park authorities and that the abundance and variety of wild birds in different parks depended on the degree of protection and encouragement they received, in particular by providing them with islands and shrubberies required for successful breeding. Hudson suggested a variety of species that might easily be catered for, including grebes, coots and moorhens as well as robin, dunnock, mistle thrush, great tit, wren and nuthatch. He went on to suggest a number of summer visitors that could be encouraged to breed in the parks, including blackcap, chiffchaff and reed warbler. His suggestion that 'it would be a good plan to construct an artificial bank or rockery, with breeding holes for kingfishers, on an island in a suitable place, like Battersea Park', was way ahead of its time. His vision was to restore all aspects of bird-life, including kestrel, sparrow hawk, tawny owl, carrion crow, jackdaw, magpie and jay. At that time none of these were breeding in central London. His final words were a plea for all the parks, even in the central parts of London, to provide sanctuaries where birds could thrive.

Hudson's vision became a reality twenty years later when the Office of Works responsible for the Royal Parks set up a Committee on Bird Sanctuaries in Royal Parks to advise on the most appropriate sites for such sanctuaries. Areas were set aside in Hyde Park, Kensington Gardens and Richmond Park. Official observers were appointed and the Committee published annual reports on the *Birds of Royal Parks in London* from 1928–38 and for a number of years after the war. Many of their suggestions for improving parks as habitats for birds are just as relevant today. One of the most valuable was a detailed list of trees and shrubs of value to birds which was proposed as a means of bringing greater diversity to the copses and shrubberies. They also recommended that lake margins be planted with sedges and reeds. But the greatest legacy of this Committee was the positive attitude towards nature that was instilled within the management of the Royal Parks, a tradition that still continues today. It has certainly been very successful.

The birds of the central Royal Parks have been the subject of detailed studies for well over a hundred years. Max Nicholson's records for 1924–6 in Kensington Gardens and Hyde Park (Nicholson, 1995) provide a remarkable benchmark for subsequent surveys. At that time there were only nineteen breeding species. By 1947 there were twenty five and by 1995 the total was thirty seven species (Sanderson, 1995). Additions since then (including ring-necked parakeet) mean that today there are more than twice the number recorded in the 1920s. Very few species have been lost, jackdaw and house sparrow being the most notable examples. Nicholson also counted the total number of birds of all species early in November and December 1925 and similar counts have been done periodically since 1948. The most dramatic change over this period was the decline in numbers of house sparrows from 2,603 in 1925 to zero in 2005 (see Chapter 11). These autumn counts also show a steady rise in the overall number of species recorded in the park from 26 to 48 over the same period. The dedicated naturalists of the London Natural History Society have played a crucial role in organising these surveys and the results have been published in annual *London Bird Reports* (Sanderson, 2005) and in periodic reviews such as the New Naturalist special volume on *The Birds of the London Area Since 1900* (LNHS, 1957).

Over fifty species of birds now breed regularly in one or more of the central Royal Parks, including many species that Hudson suggested might be re-instated. Water-birds have been particularly successful. They include great-crested and little grebes, heron, greylag, Canada and Egyptian geese, shelduck, mandarin, gadwall, pochard and tufted duck. A thriving colony of red-crested pochard at Regents Park could well spread to other central parks. The ancient trees of

Kensington gardens support both green and great spotted woodpeckers and treecreeper, as well as tawny and little owls. Kestrels are becoming less common and sparrowhawks are increasing. Stock doves are well established in Regents Park where warblers include chiffchaff, reed warbler and blackcap. The latter is rapidly becoming the commonest warbler in many towns and cities. The increasing number of species in the London parks is partly due to colonisation by naturalised species, especially geese and ducks, and also ring-necked parakeets which can now be seen daily in all the central parks (see Chapter 9). Improvement of the habitats has resulted in many other notable species turning up, including two bearded tits foraging in the newly created reedbeds along the Serpentine in Hyde Park in January 2013. Hudson would have been delighted.

The Royal Parks have their share of other unintended incomers that have now become part of the local food chain. One of these is the Turkish crayfish which has become established since the 1970s in a number of water bodies in London, including the Regents Canal, ponds on Hampstead Heath and the Serpentine in Hyde Park. Apart from anglers and restaurateurs most people would be unaware of its presence, but during the winter of 2005–6 herons and lesser black-backed gulls were observed feeding on crayfish. The following summer there was a more dramatic episode when a period of unusually hot weather resulted in oxygen levels in the Serpentine being seriously depleted. Large numbers of crayfish struggled to the bank where they were snapped up by gulls and crows. Later great crested grebes were frequently observed catching crayfish for themselves and their young (Wiltshire et al., 2006). Oxygen depletion during hot weather is a regular problem faced by park managers. The lake at St James's Park has a system for circulating and aerating the water, but this still does not prevent periodic outbreaks of botulism *Clostridium botulinum* (type C) which can devastate waterfowl populations. After one such outbreak at St James's Park in 2009 very few of the exotic and ornamental waterfowl survived.

MUNICIPAL PARKS

The local town park is so familiar to most urban dwellers that we may not appreciate its origins at the height of the industrial revolution. The rapid expansion of towns and cities during the nineteenth century created appallingly overcrowded conditions for many people. The worst effects of industrialisation produced abject squalor in many places, with serious implications for public health. Widespread cholera epidemics and chronic pollution of both air and water led Parliament to take action to improve the life of city dwellers. Town councils were required to provide clean water, discharge sewage and provide

FIG 118. Brandon Hill in Bristol has all the features of a town park, but part is managed as a nature reserve by the Avon Wildlife Trust.

parks and open spaces for the populace. A Select Committee was set up in 1833 'to consider the best means of securing open spaces in the immediate vicinity of populous towns … to promote the health and comfort of the inhabitants'. So it was that a multitude of parks were created. One that had already proved successful was the Royal Victoria Park in Bath where local business leaders hit on the idea of making a public park to counter pressure for new housing schemes. With much public support the park was opened in 1830, and named after the 11 year old Princess Victoria. At first managed privately, grazed by Freemen of the City, it was taken over by the City Council in 1921.

Birkenhead Park, across the Mersey from Liverpool, was the first to be publicly funded. Conceived as part of the overall plan for this rapidly growing new town it was designed by Joseph Paxton in 1843 and opened in 1847. Though small in scale the landscape was modelled on the great aristocratic parks created by 'Capability' Brown and his successor Humphry Repton in the eighteenth century. Rolling vistas with clumps of trees and a lake with islands was the essence of this newly created landscape. At the same time J. C. Loudon, famed for his cemeteries, had great influence. He had advocated the need for publicly owned parks as early as 1803 and actively promoted herbaceous borders and the 'gardenesque' style incorporating a great variety of exotic trees and shrubs. Together these ideas provided a pattern for urban parks throughout the land. But Birkenhead Park has a rather special place in the history of urban parks because it was here that Frederick Law Olmsted gained some of his inspiration for Central Park in New York when he visited it in 1850. He wrote about the strong influence of Birkenhead Park, commenting,

> *five minutes of admiration, and a few more spent studying the manner in which art had been employed to obtain from nature so much beauty, and I was ready to admit that in Democratic America there was nothing to be thought of as comparable with this People's Garden.*

Meanwhile other parks were getting underway. A public petition to Queen Victoria signed by 30,000 people led to the creation of Victoria Park in the East End of London. It was seen as their equivalent to Regent's Park. So keen were people to have their own piece of open space that 25,000 people invaded the new park before it was even finished. That was on Good Friday 1846. Considerably greater numbers were there on Easter Monday, making the most of the opportunity to swim in the lakes. The design included a tree-lined drive encircling the park with a series of lakes for boating, swimming, model boats and ornamental waterfowl, together with lawns, sports pitches and pavilions, a bandstand, tea house and impressive gardens where the brilliance and intricacy of the carpet bedding was famous. It was the very essence of a Victorian park; a place for the people. The model was repeated with local variations in almost every town and city in the land.

How far a town park caters for wildlife will depend on the range of habitats that it offers and the intensity of horticultural management to which it is subjected. So where there is a good variety of habitats, especially extensive shrubberies, ponds and lakes, long established old trees and herb-rich grassland the diversity of species will be considerable. The more naturalistic the landscape, especially where there are gradations between habitats such as woodland, meadow and lake, the greater the degree of diversity. Much will depend on the original design and age of the park. Despite their intensive recreational use the very best of our urban parks can be as good as many local nature reserves in the diversity of wildlife that they support. But they have to be managed sensitively to achieve this. Even the most formal parks with heavily manicured lawns, flowerbeds and ornamental trees can still attract a variety of invertebrates and a number of common garden birds. Lawns invariably provide feeding areas for blackbirds and, depending on the degree of disturbance, may also attract mistle thrush and pied wagtail. Larger expanses of grass, particularly sports pitches, attract roosting flocks of Canada geese, greylags and gulls; especially common and black headed gulls. They also provide important feeding grounds for starlings. In coastal towns such as Weston Super Mare oystercatchers gather at high tide on lawns along the esplanade.

Even in the most heavily used park there will always be odd corners where wild plants such as foxglove, alkanet and cow parsley manage to become established and scarcer species such as cuckooflower, bee orchid and broomrape turn up to surprise us. One such patch in Battersea Park originated as the ash dump from the miniature steam railway. But after being left to its own devises it turned into a mini nature reserve with a small amphitheatre of herb-rich meadow surrounded by a fringe of hornbeam, suckering elms and ash trees. During the 1980s it was well used for field studies by local schools. This tiny patch supported 17 species of butterfly, including speckled wood and common

FIG 119. The grey squirrel, which was introduced from North America, is popular with visitors but not with park managers owing to the damage done to trees.

blue, but also the much more notable purple hairstreak and white letter hairstreak. Unintended pockets of this kind occur in many urban parks. Sometimes their ecological features are appreciated by park managers and they may even become Local Nature Reserves. Others suffer from antisocial activities that may result in them being sanitised; probably through conversion to the official townscape of mown grass and lollipop trees. Much depends on the policies of local managers (Goode, 1986).

But parks are there primarily for people to enjoy. Wildlife comes as an extra and may not always be welcomed. Canada geese roosting on the picnic tables, or congregating at the water's edge where mothers take toddlers to feed the ducks, pose problems for those in charge. But the immediacy of wildlife in parks can be an advantage. Where else can you feed a wild bird or squirrel by hand, or watch the antics of water birds at such close quarters? The tameness of such species is a special feature of many town parks and for local residents it provides their most regular contact with nature.

Over the past thirty years deliberate attempts have been made in many places to change the way that parks are managed, by creating new habitats such as hay meadows, native woodlands, ponds and different kinds of wetlands. Some parks have been completely redesigned to create a more naturalistic landscape instead of the formal landscape inherited from Victorian times. Some of the most striking changes have been achieved in parks where streams which were previously culverted are now restored to more natural conditions. These changes have been immensely popular with local people who now take delight in seeing kingfishers, herons and dragonflies in a place that was previously a drab expanse of grass (see Chapter 15).

The Victorian enthusiasm for planting specimen trees means that many of our older parks now provide ideal conditions for hole-nesting birds, including green and great spotted woodpeckers, nuthatch, treecreeper, jackdaw, tawny owl and even little owl. In recent years ring-necked parakeets and mandarin ducks have joined this assemblage in the London area. Exotic conifers such as Douglas fir and Wellingtonia provide nest sites for sparrowhawk. Carrion crow and magpie breed in many parks and jays occur frequently where there are patches of woodland. Blackcap and chiffchaff are the only warblers likely to occur, and then only where wooded patches with dense shrubberies are protected from disturbance by dogs.

CITY SQUARES

City squares have a more restricted range of breeding birds but they demonstrate very clearly what is possible through sensitive landscape design. The great squares of London's West End such as Berkeley Square and Belgrave Square have equivalents in many other cities, such as Queen Square in Bristol and St James's in Bath. They were created as formal gardens as part of the grand design of fashionable new residential districts in the eighteenth and nineteenth centuries. Some were laid out with intricate patterns of parterres with box hedges and topiary. Others provided extensive lawns with geometric patterns of gravel walks. Most were private gardens, surrounded by fences and only accessible to keyholders. Many still are, but their landscapes have changed out of all recognition. One legacy we do have is the trees, especially the huge plane trees that now dominate some of these squares. Those in Berkeley Square were planted in 1789 and there are trees of similar stature in Lincoln's Inn Fields. In both of these the trees are set in great expanses of grass. Other squares have much more varied landscapes and, given their situation, they support a remarkable diversity of breeding birds.

FIG 120. Belgrave Square, one of the largest of London's squares, has about 20 breeding species of birds.

One of the most impressive is Belgrave Square where the gardens cover about two hectares, forming a large island surrounded by very busy roads. Like many other squares in Belgravia these gardens are private and access is limited to local residents or office workers. One such was Dr Leo Batten who worked in the headquarters of the Nature Conservancy Council when it was based in the square. From 1978 to 1980 he carried out regular surveys of breeding birds in the gardens that provided a remarkable sanctuary that was little disturbed. Over the three years there was an average of 33 pairs of birds, of 14 different species (Goode 1986). At that time the gardens consisted of a broad outer belt of mature trees and extensive shrubberies, with a patch of grassland and a tennis court in the centre. Dense shrubberies with glades were perfect for blackbirds, dunnocks, robins and song thrush and the trees provided nest sites for greenfinch, goldfinch, woodpigeon and crow. Blackbirds were most numerous with up to nine pairs, closely followed by dunnocks with up to eight. Woodpigeon, song thrush, greenfinch and blue tit had two to five pairs each. Another eight species had only one or two pairs each. These were great tit, robin, carrion crow, feral pigeon, mistle thrush, goldfinch, wren and, the highlight, a pair of spotted flycatchers that bred each year. I remember the day when Leo announced at tea to everyone's amazement that flycatchers were breeding just across the road. For most of us navigating the square meant dodging the traffic rather than seeking out birds.

Subsequent studies have demonstrated the influence of vegetation structure on bird populations. In the City of Westminster it was found that squares could support up to about twenty breeding species, but many fell far short of that (Hewlett *et al.*, 1995). Squares were divided into four types and the species of birds found during the breeding season were listed for each category. The four types exhibited an increasing range of ecological complexity, matched by increasing numbers of breeding species:

1. predominantly open paved surfaces with planters and street trees (3 species)
2. squares with lawns, flower beds and mature trees, mainly London plane (up to 7 species)
3. as for 2. with the addition of shrubberies and a greater variety of mature trees (up to 12 species)
4. Squares with a complex layered structure akin to woodland where the tree canopy, understory and shrub layer provide a great variety of ecological conditions (up to 19 species).

Hard paved surfaces such as Trafalgar Square attracted little other than feral pigeons, though at that time both house sparrow and starling were recorded. Squares with lawns, flower-beds and mature trees, such as London plane, also had blackbird, blue tit, woodpigeon and carrion crow (e.g. Soho Square). The addition of shrubberies, as at Embankment Gardens, attracted a number of common garden birds, including robin, wren, dunnock, great tit and magpie. Squares with the greatest vegetation structure such as Belgrave Square, Eccleston Square and Portman Square attracted another seven species, namely song thrush, mistle thrush, greenfinch, goldfinch, jay, long-tailed tit and even blackcap. By the time this study was done flycatchers were no longer breeding in central London, but other species had moved in, including long-tailed tit, magpie, jay and blackcap. Since then ring-necked parakeets and greater spotted woodpeckers have nested in some of the larger squares. Mallard ducks have also nested successfully, giving rise to many stories of their journeys, with a string of ducklings in tow, through streets full of traffic to get to the nearest pond or lake.

GARDENS

As with parks let us start with one of the largest examples, Buckingham Palace Gardens in the heart of London. The gardens cover sixteen hectares, with extensive lawns and a peripheral area of shrubberies, herbaceous borders, an ornamental lake and even a strip of woodland. We are fortunate to have a detailed account of the fauna and flora resulting from a survey organised by the London Natural History Society in the late 1990s at the invitation of the Head Gardener, Mark Lane. In collaboration with taxonomists from the Natural History Museum and Kew Gardens, together with its own experts, the LNHS was able to provide a remarkably good inventory of a wide range of groups (Plant, 1999, 2001). Over one hundred taxonomists were involved in what became the most intensive investigation of any area in London. The few groups left out were relatively insignificant in terms of the overall ecology. The main survey took place during 1996–7 with additional work on some groups in subsequent years.

There had been earlier surveys in the 1950s and 1960s of particular groups of species, including birds and moths, which provided some information on recent changes. Changes in bird populations in the gardens closely mirrored gains and losses in the much larger Royal Parks over the same period. Breeding birds totalled thirty species, which is comparable with large city squares but with an additional nine species dependent on wetland habitats associated with the lake. A more recent report lists forty-one species that have nested in the gardens since 1995 (Sanderson, 2013). Newcomers since 2000 include dabchick, Egyptian goose, gadwall, red-crested pochard, ring-necked parakeet and blackcap. Although the number of breeding species in the 1990s was similar to nearby Royal Parks the density of pairs was up to four times higher, which is probably due to the secluded nature of the gardens. Compared with public parks the Palace gardens are subject to relatively little disturbance, apart from the thousands of people attending Royal garden parties during the summer months.

The LNHS survey recorded a total of 322 species of flowering plants growing wild, including several notable species such as marsh pennywort, adder's tongue fern and chamomile, a nationally scarce plant, abundant in the lawn, which is possibly a survivor from old meadowland. Patches of disturbed ground supported alien species including golden hedge parsley and a Russian form of giant hogweed. Together with those recorded in earlier surveys the list of flowering plants seen since 1950 totals 431. Mycologists found 700 species of fungi, the highlights of their forays being two species new to science. A surprisingly large number of slime moulds were also found; 68 species representing 20 per cent of the 356 recorded in Britain. Most of these were on tree bark.

The number of lichens recorded was particularly significant. A previous survey, thirty years earlier, recorded only two species, both of which were tolerant of high levels of atmospheric sulphur dioxide prevalent at that time. The recent survey recorded 39 species, including several which are particularly sensitive to SO_2 pollution (for example: *Evernia prunastri, Parmelia caperata, P. subaurifera* and *Ramalina farinacea*). This is just one example of the re-colonisation of central London by lichens since the level of SO_2 decreased after the Clean Air Act of 1956. Ambient levels declined from 450 µg m^3 in 1962 to less than 30 µg m^3 in the late 1990s. The presence of *Parmelia caperata* is particularly notable as it had not been recorded in the London area for 200 years.

The survey identified more than 2,160 species of insects and 207 other invertebrates of which 112 were spiders. Lepidoptera had been particularly intensively investigated, yielding 640 species. Trapping over forty years revealed

FIG 121. A private garden in Sheringham, Norfolk excellent for both wildlife and traditional garden features. Old oak trees add to the biodiversity.

that 25 per cent of the total species-list of UK butterflies and moths had visited the gardens. Of these the butterflies totalled 22 species, including thriving populations of speckled wood and holly blue, together with common blue, comma and brimstone, and many commoner species. Of the other insects beetles totalled 287 species and various groups of flies 827 species.

The number of species recorded may appear surprising in view of the garden's position in the middle of London. But this is a common misconception. The garden has a great variety of habitats and there has been a long period of sympathetic management. A survey of this kind using the skills of a wide range of specialists can be expected to produce a large species list. Indeed it is likely that many more species would be identified if some more difficult taxonomic groups were included. But the LNHS survey provides a good illustration of the range of species that can be found by a large team of taxonomists over a relatively limited period.

Most domestic gardens are a great deal smaller, but in aggregate they have a considerable influence on the wildlife of towns and cities. They are by far the most extensive of any single category of urban land use. In a number of cities that have been examined (Edinburgh, Belfast, Cardiff, Oxford and Leicester) they account for around 25 per cent of the urban area. In some towns they cover up to 50 per cent. In Greater London the figure is 19 per cent, covering a total area of 304 km². So how many gardens are there in the UK? Estimates suggest that 87 per cent of households or 22.7 million homes have domestic gardens. The average size of a garden is 190 m², which means that the total land area of gardens is about 4,330 km², an area greater than the county of Suffolk (Davies *et al.*, 2009).

In ecological terms most domestic gardens form part of a continuum. Each garden is a separate entity in terms of ownership and management, but it is just one element in a much larger landscape of urban or suburban gardens. Together they provide an extremely heterogeneous habitat which supports a remarkable diversity of species. Individual gardens vary in size from small courtyards in heavily built-up areas to extensive grounds of detached houses in outer suburbs where gardens may exceed 0.5 hectares. Between these two extremes lie the majority of urban and suburban gardens, which range from relatively small gardens, often only 100 m², along the backs of terraced housing, to larger plots associated with semi-detached properties which may vary from 200 to 1,000 m². Suburban residential developments of the Victorian period and those of the inter-war years tend to have larger gardens than later periods and new housing schemes over the past thirty years are characterised by smaller gardens irrespective of the type of property. The size and age of gardens influences the ecology, in that older and larger gardens have more mature trees and may even support narrow

FIG 122. Reduced levels of predation by domestic cats on allotments may explain the presence of slow worms, which are particularly attracted to compost heaps.

belts of secondary woodland along boundaries at the bottom of gardens. These larger gardens have a greater diversity of bird species associated with the mature trees (Dawson & Gittings, 1990). In ecological terms it is perhaps appropriate to include allotments as part of the garden environment, though their management is directed more specifically at food production rather than amenity and there may be greater use of chemical herbicides and pesticides. Whilst allotments exhibit many of the same species as gardens they provide a habitat that is often less affected by predation from domestic cats. This could well explain the frequent occurence of slow worms which tend to be associated with compost heaps.

In 1989 Gilbert pointed out that with a few notable exceptions, gardens have been ignored by ecologists and that 'the ecology of gardens is an exciting field

FIG 123. With the widespread use of peanut feeders great spotted woodpeckers have become common visitors to gardens.

where pioneering studies have still to be made'. One of the notable exceptions is Jennifer Owen's thirty-year study of her rather ordinary suburban garden in Leicester which is rapidly becoming recognised as one of the most significant long term ecological studies anywhere in the country (Owen, 1991, 2010). Her garden covers 741 m^2 and incorporates all the elements of a conventional suburban garden, with lawn, flowerbeds, herbaceous borders, rockeries, vegetable patches, a variety of trees and shrubs, fruit bushes, pond, compost heap, glasshouse and paved areas. The vegetation is neat, attractive and productive and does not differ markedly from neighbouring gardens. No special wildlife areas were created and in no sense is it a wilderness. However, every effort was made to enhance the garden as a whole as a wildlife habitat through subtle use of horticultural management. Examples include: growing an abundance of plants with flowers attractive to insects for as much of the year as possible; maintaining a high diversity of plant species to promote maximum feeding opportunities for invertebrates; delaying pruning and clearing of dead plant material until winter; planting a variety of berry-bearing shrubs to provide food for birds; and not using any chemical pesticides.

For thirty years Owen recorded many groups of organisms in her garden, monitoring changes on an annual basis. She used a number of standard techniques for trapping insects and other invertebrates and over the years recorded a total of 2,673 species, comprising 474 plants, 1,997 insects, 138 other invertebrates and 64 vertebrates, of which 54 were birds. Of the flowering plants 75 per cent were cultivated and 25 per cent arrived spontaneously. Nearly 60 per cent were alien species and 40 per cent native. The number of species recorded in different taxonomic groups are shown in Table 1. This may seem a remarkably large number of species for a suburban garden but it is still only

TABLE 1. Numbers of species of plants and animals recorded in Jennifer Owen's garden. (After Owen, 2010, with permission of the Royal Horticultural Society.)

All plants	474	Lacewings & allies	23
Native flowering plants	170	Butterflies	23
Flatworms	3	Macro-moths	282
Snails and slugs	17	Micro-moths	93
Earthworms	5	Caddisflies	5
Leeches	1	Hoverflies	94
Woodlice	8	Other flies	51
Centipedes	7	Sawflies	91
Millipedes	5	Ichneumons	533
False scorpions	1	Other parasitic wasps	24
Harvestmen	11	Ants	2
Spiders	80	Wasps	62
Dragonflies	7	Bees	59
Grasshoppers and crickets	4	Beetles	442
		Amphibians	3
Earwigs	1	Birds	54
Psocids	18	Mammals	7
Bugs	183	**Total**	**2,673**

part of the picture. As with the study of Buckingham Palace Garden, Owen's work depended on specialist taxonomists being available to deal with difficult groups. Several animal groups that were intensively investigated had a significant proportion of the total number of species in the UK, with 20–25 per cent for bees, wasps and ichneumons (parasitic wasps), over 30 per cent for butterflies, macro-moths and hoverflies, and over 50 per cent for ladybirds. If other taxonomically difficult groups were examined in similar detail Owen expects that the total number of species in her garden could exceed 8,000. She does not consider her garden to be unusual in the richness of its animal life:

> There is every reason to suppose that the majority of gardens have an equally varied fauna. In other words, the diverse and abundant animal life of my garden is that of gardens in general.

As might be expected the study threw up several species that were new to Britain and a small number that were previously undescribed. But Owen's study is more than just an inventory. She provides a remarkable picture of the life histories of garden organisms and the intricate and varied food webs involved. Over half the insect species are either predators or parasitoids (parasites that eventually kill their host) dependent on other species in the garden, and many insect groups capable of flight, such as bees, butterflies and moths, visit to feed on pollen or nectar. A large proportion of these complete their life histories in the garden. Of the 94 species of hoverflies 50 can be regarded as part of the resident fauna of the garden, the remainder being only casual or chance visitors. The majority of invertebrates that cannot fly are clearly residents and are totally dependent on the garden as their habitat.

But how typical is this single garden? In 2000 a research group at Sheffield University set out to investigate the ecology of Sheffield's gardens. *BUGS* (or, Biodiversity in Urban Gardens in Sheffield) led by Gaston and Thompson, and involving many others, was the first detailed study of a wide range of urban gardens. They had three objectives: to investigate the resources that domestic gardens provide for biodiversity; to find out which factors are most important in influencing biodiversity; and thirdly to find ways in which gardens can be manipulated to enhance native biodiversity (Thompson *et al.*, 2003). They estimated that the city contained 175,000 domestic gardens, covering about 3,000 hectares. These contained 25,000 ponds, 360,000 trees and 45,000 nest boxes for birds.

The team chose 61 gardens for detailed examination, representing a wide range of conditions in the city. Like Owen they used a series of standardised trapping methods. Over a two year period they caught 40,000 individual

FIG 124. Insects in the author's garden: a red-headed cardinal beetle (left) that emerged from a rotten tree stump; scarlet tiger-moth caterpillar (below left) feeding on comfrey; the day-flying scarlet tiger-moth (below right) is becoming much more common in gardens in southern England.

invertebrates, most of which were allocated to family groups with about 700 identified to species level. The object was not to seek out unusual or spectacular features of garden wildlife but rather to gain an overall picture of the biodiversity and how it related to particular features of the gardens. Even so a number of nationally rare species of beetles, bugs, snails and flies turned up. The overall number of plants identified was 1,176 species, of which the majority were aliens. The gardens were also sampled on a consistent basis using metre-square quadrats, which revealed 438 species, of which 33 per cent were native British species. The other 67 per cent were alien plants from many parts of the world now grown in gardens. The great variety of aliens reflects the fact that some 14,000 species (and many other varieties) are now available to gardeners from British nurseries. Seventeen of the twenty plants most frequently encountered in the gardens were native weeds, of which the commonest were broad-leaved willowherb, wood avens, columbine, dandelion, red fescue and creeping buttercup. However, the study suggests that a large number of the invertebrate herbivores found do not differentiate between native and alien species, and that traditionally managed gardens support a considerable diversity of wildlife.

These findings support Owen's suggestion that 'private gardens taken together might reasonably be described as the UK's most important nature reserve'. It has been suggested that some declining species once common in

FIG 125. Wall lizards are extending their range along the south coast of England, where they now occur in suburban gardens (above left). The Bowls Club at Boscombe in Bournemouth has them living in the walls (Tim Bernhard). Providing food for birds in the garden can result in nice surprises, like this fieldfare (above right), a winter visitor from northern Europe. (Paul Wilkins)

traditionally managed, low intensity farmland are now more abundant in urban areas, particularly in domestic gardens. For some bird species gardens support a significant fraction of the total UK population (Chamberlain *et al.*, 2009).

Apart from these detailed studies there are a number of books describing the natural history of gardens, as well as a growing literature on wildlife gardening referred to in Chapter 15. The New Naturalist series already includes a volume devoted to garden natural history (Buczacki, 2007) and Michael Chinery has produced several popular accounts that cover the multitude of species to be found (Chinery, 1977, 2007). For the interested gardener the latter provide a good starting point for getting to grips with the species. For those who wish to study a particular group such as butterflies, hoverflies or ladybirds, all of which are well represented in gardens, there are specialist websites to assist. With the rapid development of taxonomic information on the internet it becomes possible to identify more difficult species with remarkable ease; as for example a small beetle that emerged from a tree stump in my garden that turned out to be the red-headed cardinal beetle. Similarly I found that caterpillars on my comfrey plants were those of the scarlet tiger moth, a species that has become much more common in gardens in recent years. Use of the internet by non-specialists to assist identification is dealt with more fully in Chapter 15, which also includes details of popular schemes to encourage participation in garden bird surveys.

PART TWO

Colonisers and Specialists

FIG 126. The colonisation of towns and cities by peregrine falcons has been one of the most dramatic changes in British wildlife in recent years. This is the male of the pair nesting on St John's church in Bath, which has mated with its mother. (Hamish Smith)

CHAPTER 8

Birds As New Urban Colonisers

INTRODUCTION

IT IS CLEAR FROM DESCRIPTIONS OF the habitats of towns and cities that urban areas are subject to continuous change. Our brief excursion around the city of Bath demonstrated a large number of species that have arrived relatively recently, and which are now firmly established as part of the urban scene. The host of alien species, especially plants and insects, associated with post-industrial habitats is even more striking. This and the next chapter are concerned with birds that have colonised urban areas, especially over the past fifty years. There are many reasons why particular species have been successful and it is worth considering some of the processes involved before looking in more detail at individual species.

Appearance of a new species in Britain may be the result of a long-term gradual spread or in some cases a rapid expansion of its range. One of the most dramatic examples is the collared dove which first colonised towns along the east coast of England in the 1950s, having spread across Europe from the Balkans and Turkey since the 1930s in one of the most rapid range expansions of any European bird in recent times. These early colonisers were initially restricted to ports with grain silos where they found an abundant supply of food, but they quickly spread to suburban parks and gardens and are now found in towns and cities throughout the UK, though generally absent from city centres. What triggered the sudden and massive expansion of their range is still not fully understood, but it seems that their very high reproductive capacity was a factor, together with availability of suitable habitat in urban areas; a niche that was not already occupied.

Some of these new colonisers have taken advantage of opportunities presented by the urban environment. It is difficult to know what causes some individuals to take the plunge and move into town, like roof nesting gulls and

FIG 127. Collared dove: a newcomer in the 1950s but now well established in the suburbs of many towns and cities. (Paul Wilkins)

peregrine falcons. However, once a species breeds successfully in an urban area the behaviour can spread quickly as young birds colonise places with which they are familiar, i.e. other towns and cities. Some that manage to nest amongst bricks and mortar, like kittiwakes on the Tyne Bridge in Newcastle and black guillemots in Bangor harbour, are still regarded as oddities, yet they are as much a part of urban colonisation as more widespread species.

Other species may be influenced by major environmental factors such as climate change. Several species have expanded their range northwards in Europe over the past thirty years and are now steadily colonising Britain. The range expansion of the little egret has been by far the most spectacular. Since the first pair bred in 1996 in Dorset numbers have increased enormously. The recent BTO Atlas (Balmer *et al.*, 2013) shows confirmed breeding in more than 160 10-km squares in England, Wales and Ireland and a much wider winter distribution. This bird is now in the process of establishing breeding colonies on urban wetlands. There are at least five breeding sites in and around London, and probably others elsewhere. Others, like the Mediterranean gull, winter in substantial numbers and there are now over 1,000 breeding pairs in Britain. They are likewise poised to become an urban breeding species. Other species showing a similar trend, but in smaller numbers, include the firecrest, bittern and penduline tit, all of which are now regularly wintering in Britain.

FIG 128. The Jay has taken advantage of the lack of persecution and is now commonly seen in urban parks and gardens.

Many of the birds that have recently become established in towns and cities were introduced by human activities. A few, like the red kite, were deliberate introductions that have proved successful. Others were introduced unintentionally when they escaped from captivity. Ruddy duck, Canada goose, ring-necked parakeet, mandarin duck and Egyptian goose are good examples. Some have become particularly successful and present a range of ecological problems in urban areas.

Improvements in the physical environment, especially air and water quality, have also resulted in particular species moving back into town (Cramp, 1975). Examples are the house martin, which re-colonised central London during the 1980s. Cormorants too have become a common sight fishing on the Thames and other urban rivers and canals that were too heavily polluted to support fish populations in the 1950s. Other influences may be less direct, but nevertheless have profound consequences. Changes in public attitudes account for many species becoming established. No longer is it acceptable to shoot the gulls from London Bridge as happened in Victorian times. Wildlife legislation now protects many species and has considerable public support. As mentioned earlier, game management has gradually declined and the greater tolerance of predators and scavengers has meant that species that were previously heavily controlled are now some of the commonest in urban areas. Crows, magpies and jays, held in check by gamekeepers until the 1960s, have now colonised most towns and cities. Birds of prey have also benefited from such changes. The extensive feeding of garden birds and encouragement of wildlife in public open spaces and parks has also resulted in a greater variety of species. It is noticeable that many birds, not just the ducks, have become much tamer in public parks than in the countryside, including species such as crow, jay, heron and wood pigeon, all of which have learnt to take food from people who feed them regularly. Provision of artificial nesting sites for owls, kestrels and even peregrines ensures that such species can exist in heavily built up areas. Public concern affects other groups too. The popularity of bat boxes, together with greater public appreciation of the requirements of bats, is helping to stem depletion of their populations.

Finally there has over the past thirty years been a significant increase in the amount of land in towns and cities managed as nature reserves. Important habitats are being protected and new habitats created. The emphasis on important local species and habitats in Local Biodiversity Action Plans helps to ensure that action is taken to provide the right conditions for critical species. All these strands play a part in encouraging new species to colonise towns and cities.

In discussing new urban colonisers I have concentrated first on particular groups of birds, notably waterfowl and birds of prey. The next chapter considers a selection of other opportunistic species, including roof nesting gulls, parakeets and others that have become urban birds.

WETLAND BIRDS AND WATERFOWL

The variety of birds associated with urban wetlands has increased substantially over the past fifty years. Introductions resulting from escapes of ducks and geese from waterfowl collections have been particularly significant. Some species were encouraged to colonise urban areas by provision of nesting rafts. Others, especially fish eaters, have increased due to improvements in water quality. An overall increase in bird populations has also been encouraged by the large number of artificial water bodies associated with urban areas, including reservoirs, gravel pits, sewage works, filter beds and canals, as well as more traditional ornamental park lakes. All these provide significant habitats for birds.

Two species illustrate the kinds of influences affecting urban bird populations rather well. These are the great crested grebe and little ringed plover, both of which grew in numbers during the twentieth century but their details are rather different. The first is a remarkable story of recovery and re-colonisation after being brought to the brink of extinction in Britain during the Victorian period when thousands were shot for the millincry trade. The second tells of rapid natural colonisation by a species that spread across Europe and found a suitable habitat in sand and gravel pits that proliferated during the period of urban reconstruction after World War II. In both cases there has been a close relationship between human actions and the bird's success.

The plight of the great crested grebe during the mid-nineteenth century was a key factor in promoting legislation for the protection of birds and also led to the formation of the Royal Society for the Protection of Birds. Vast numbers of skins were being imported every year to cater for the burgeoning trade in women's fashion accessories. The use of feathers had become a major industry supporting the fashion houses of Europe and the USA. 'Grebe fur' adorned hats and shoulder capes and the long plumes of little egrets and elegant head-dresses of grebes were some of the most desirable fashion items. In Britain most grebe skins came from Europe until about 1855 when suppliers turned their attention to British birds. In three years the population was virtually exterminated with possibly as few as thirty-two pairs surviving by 1860. Water company reservoirs protected from shooting, and privately owncd lakes on large estates provided crucial sanctuaries for the remaining birds. But whilst this was happening opposition to the slaughter was growing and a series of Bird Protection Acts were passed between 1870 and 1880, the last of which provided full protection during the breeding season. The subsequent recovery of great crested grebes has been one of the best documented of any native species. By 1900 the total British population had grown to around 300 pairs and a comprehensive census in 1931 showed a total of over 1,200 pairs. By the time the next full survey was done in 1965 the population had risen dramatically to 4,500 birds. Much of this expansion took place after the 1940s. Since then the population has continued to grow, with estimates of 7,000 birds in 1975 and 8,000 by 1990.

Whilst the initial recovery resulted from greater legal protection and changing attitudes towards the killing of wild birds, the massive expansion in the latter half of the twentieth century was primarily due to the creation of vast numbers of new wetlands in the form of flooded gravel pits and water supply reservoirs, particularly in the Midlands and southeast England. Gravel pits provided ideal conditions for breeding as they have an abundance of emergent vegetation around the margins and provide suitable habitat for fishing. Angling clubs stocked many of these new waters with fish and generally tolerated the presence of grebes which readily colonised the new habitats. With the pressure for post-war reconstruction many gravel pits were situated close to or even within urban areas and so it was that great crested grebes have become a familiar sight in many country parks and on lakes and ponds now surrounded by the built environment.

FIG 129. Great crested grebe: a familiar sight on many urban water bodies. (Mark Coller)

Colonisation of urban areas has been a feature of their recent expansion and London provides a dramatic illustration. In 1900 breeding was known from only three localities within the area recorded by the London Natural History Society, but by the time the first full census was done in 1931 there were 68 pairs at 22 sites with a total of well over 200 birds. By 1972 the number of breeding pairs had risen to 90 and ten years later it reached 193. After that numbers grew more slowly to a maximum of 238 pairs in 1990. Growth in numbers was accompanied by a gradual spread from the outer edges of London towards the centre.

In the 1930s breeding pairs were mainly restricted to the outer fringes of the London area in Surrey and Essex. The proliferation of gravel pits in the 1950s was a key factor. They soon supported half the breeding pairs of grebes. The first atlas of London's breeding birds (1968–72) showed strong concentrations around the periphery of London from Weybridge to the Colne Valley in the west, along the Lea Valley in the north and the Darent Valley in the south. In all these areas the birds were almost entirely dependent on gravel pits for breeding. Within Greater London breeding was still patchy with records from only 32 'tetrads' (2 × 2 km). However, the gradual inward colonisation had reached inner London, with breeding at both Hyde Park and Regents Park in 1972 (Montier, 1977).

By the time the next atlas was produced (1988–94) the number of tetrads where breeding was recorded within Greater London had more than doubled. Grebes were now nesting on a large number of ornamental lakes and ponds in parks and open spaces throughout the capital. Some shallow reservoirs also provided opportunities for nesting. Brent Reservoir (see Chapter 6) had the highest recorded density of breeding pairs in the UK, with fifty pairs nesting in 1991. Since then several new areas have been colonised in inner London including Battersea Park, St James's Park, Buckingham Palace Gardens, Greenland Dock and Canada Water (Hewlett, 2002). The larger London reservoirs such as Staines, Queen Mary and Queen Elizabeth II can each attract up to 200 grebes, especially during the winter but also on occasions in late summer when birds gather after breeding. Figures for 2009 suggest that the maximum number of grebes in the London area varied from 500 birds during the breeding season to 700 during winter months when the London reservoirs attract birds from further north.

So from a city devoid of grebes in the late 1800s London now supports hundreds of these birds. It is even possible to pause for a moment on the bridge in St James's Park and watch their extraordinary courtship rituals, or maybe see the young carried on their parent's backs, all at close quarters and to the accompaniment of Big Ben.

The little ringed plover may not have quite the same popular appeal, but its place in the annals of ornithology is assured as one of only a handful of species that naturally colonised the UK during the twentieth century. It had extended its range across Western Europe during the early 1900s and was first recorded nesting in Britain at Tring Reservoir in 1938. This is a bird that prefers shingle banks and sandy edges of lakes and rivers unlike its larger relative the ringed plover which prefers coastal habitats. So it was not altogether surprising that the next breeding site to be discovered in 1944 was in an area of gravel diggings in the Thames Valley near Heathrow Airport. The next few years provided great excitement for London's birdwatchers as they charted the progress of this new colonist. Nesting was recorded at several gravel pits and also in the gravelly beds of new reservoirs under construction in the Lea Valley and near Heathrow Airport. By 1953 about 18 pairs were present in the London area, nearly all of them associated with gravel workings. More remarkable was a pair that occupied a small patch of stony ground at the end of the runway at Heathrow. Their preference for gravel beds associated with freshwater meant that active gravel workings provided ideal conditions for breeding, so long as they could survive the continuous disturbance from bulldozers, diggers and other machinery. But survive they did and London's naturalists noted that they had an astonishing disregard for human disturbance. They also found that the birds quickly adapted to new circumstances, moving from disused gravel workings as they became overgrown and finding newly exposed gravel beds in active workings elsewhere.

FIG 130. Colonisation of the UK by the little ringed plover in the 1940s onwards was largely due to suitable habitats being created by the proliferation of wet gravel workings. (Mark Coller)

By the mid-1950s little ringed plovers had spread throughout eastern England from Hampshire to Yorkshire, capitalising on the proliferation of gravel pits associated with growth of major towns and cities. In the West Midlands numbers grew from a few isolated pairs in the mid-1950s to 57 pairs at 34 sites by 1984 when the BTO carried out a detailed census. This national count suggested a population of 800–1,000 pairs in Britain. They occupied a wide range of man-made habitats including reservoirs, sewage works, filter beds, waste dumps, quarries and disused colliery complexes, with gravel pits still providing the majority of nest sites. This mix of artificial habitats, including many post-industrial sites, accounted for over 90 per cent of breeding records, with only 3 per cent nesting in natural habitats. Their spread has continued, reaching Wales, Cumbria and Scotland by the 1990s.

Although the little ringed plover is unlikely to ever become particularly common it has established itself as one of the characteristic birds of post-industrial landscapes. Given the right conditions it may even nest in the heart of the built environment. One pair nested on a factory roof in King's Lynn, and in 1984 two pairs caused local excitement when they nested in disused filterbeds at Lea Bridge Road, only a short walk from Hackney High Street in London. Over the past ten years several pairs have nested regularly on specially constructed gravel islands at the London Wetland Centre (Chapter 16) where their courtship displays and song-flight can be observed from the hides.

Some of the most obvious new arrivals on the urban scene are waterfowl, especially Canada and greylag geese. Whilst the Canada goose, as its name suggests, is an incomer from North America, the greylag is a native British species restricted in a truly wild state to the west of Scotland. Both of these have now become well established with breeding populations in many towns and cities, originating either from accidental escapes from waterfowl collections, or from deliberate introductions. The Canada goose has long been kept in private collections in Europe. It was said to be breeding in considerable numbers at Versailles at the time of Louis XIV (1643–1715) and a number of observers recorded it in the royal wildfowl collection at St James's Park including John Evelyn in 1665. There is evidence that these geese became popular with landed gentry during the 1700s. In 1785 Latham wrote, 'they are thought a great ornament to the pieces of water in many gentlemen's seats, where they are very familiar and breed freely' (Lever, 1997). By 1900 they were widely distributed on such estates and a few pairs were known to breed in the wild.

The Canada goose was added to the British list as an introduction in 1938. In 1953 the total feral population was estimated to be about 3–4,000 birds and a further census in 1967–9 found over 10,000 birds. The majority occupied rural locations, with many small sub-populations based on particular water bodies often associated with country estates. But signs of things to come were evident on Merseyside even in 1953 where a colony using the lake at Knowsley Park as a breeding site spent winter months in the municipal parks of Liverpool. Gravel pits and reservoirs were increasingly used for breeding and the proliferation of these new man-made water bodies partly explains the huge increase in numbers of geese. But this was also due to a translocation programme carried out mainly by the Wildfowlers Association (WAGBI) which resulted in hundreds of young birds being moved to new areas during the 1950s and 1960s. Many new colonies were established including some in urban areas. These were just the beginnings of a massive growth in the national population and with that came the remarkably rapid colonisation of towns and cities.

The process is well documented in the case of London (Baker, 1985, 1992). In the 1930s the nearest breeding colony was at Gatton Park near Redhill, twenty miles from central London. Here numbers grew from 36 birds in 1930 to about 200 in 1938, by which time estate workers were regularly destroying eggs to control the growing numbers of birds. Owing to military activity during the war the geese ceased to breed, and prior to the 1950s there were only occasional sightings of Canada geese in the London area. In 1955 seventeen free flying birds

from estates in Leicestershire and Yorkshire were released by the Wildfowl Trust
in Hyde Park. Some of these birds were later transferred to Regents Park and
Hampton Court. By 1963 Baker estimates that 25 to 30 pairs were breeding at
14 sites in the London Area, with over 30 goslings produced. Expansion continued
rapidly and by 1973 there were over 100 breeding pairs at some 60 sites. Ten years
later a detailed survey was undertaken by the LNHS which found a total of nearly
300 pairs breeding at just over 100 sites and producing 1,251 goslings. In addition
there were about 1,500 non-breeding birds.

Six main habitats where breeding occurred were identified in the 1983 survey,
see Table 2. The largest numbers were breeding on banks and islands in flooded
sand and gravel pits, closely followed by those on lakes or ponds in parks. At
this time relatively few were recorded on reservoirs. The total number of Canada
geese in the London area ranged from about 3,400 (including goslings) in
summer 1983, to 2,550 the following winter.

TABLE 2. Canada goose breeding sites in London area 1983 (after Baker, 1985).

Type of site	Number of sites	Number of pairs	Goslings
Lakes or ponds in parks	41	90	369
Gravel or sand pits	30	106	502
Reservoirs	6	48	181
Ponds on commons, golf courses, and farmland	14	23	82
Sewage works	2	6	19
River Thames	10	25	98
Total	103	298	1,251

Another national census in 1991 demonstrated a substantial growth of the
population in London. Just over 5,000 birds were recorded in Greater London,
compared with only 1,500 in the equivalent area in 1983. This suggests an
annual growth rate of nearly 16 per cent, compared with the national figure
of 8.3 per cent for the same period. The dramatic spread in London is well
illustrated by comparison of the distribution maps of the two atlas periods
1968–72 and 1988–94. Over this twenty-year period evidence of breeding increased

FIG 131. The Canada goose is the most numerous species of goose in urban areas with large flocks occurring in both country parks and inner cities.

from 56 to 287 tetrads (Hewlett, 2002). Breeding pairs had spread across the whole of London, and some previously unoccupied sites, such as Walthamstow Reservoirs in the Lea Valley, now supported some of the largest concentrations in the country, with over 1100 birds. The total national population continued to rise, reaching 64,000 by 1991 and 82,000 in 1999.

Farmers had been calling for control measures since the 1960s when Canada geese first started to cause agricultural damage, but by the 1980s it was clear that they were also becoming a problem in many urban areas. In London flocks of several hundred birds moved around the central London parks where they caused extensive damage to amenity grassland as well as eutrophication of ponds and lakes. One of the biggest problems was the fouling of paths and grassy areas close to ponds, which still presents potential health hazards today. Large numbers also took to roosting on picnic tables in some parks such as Battersea Park where the tables had to be cleaned every morning. There were stories too of geese injuring small children feeding the ducks. As a result some local authorities, such as Wandsworth Council, embarked on control measures in the late 1980s, including licensed egg-pricking, in an attempt to reduce the numbers.

With the population still growing the Government set up a Canada Goose Working Group, led by what was then the Department of Environment, to review potential problems and possible control measures. In addition to the effects on parks and open spaces, other potential problems were impacts on a variety of

FIG 132. Canada geese with young near Gas Street Basin in Birmingham city centre.

other aquatic species and the possibility of collision with aircraft. Air strikes were thought to be a real possibility as large numbers of geese had become established on water bodies around Heathrow Airport. The Group produced a booklet on methods of controlling numbers of geese and a national scheme got underway. Every year during the period 1991–95 about 200 adult birds were killed and 4,000–10,000 eggs destroyed, all under license by the DoE (Cabot, 2009). Adult geese were mostly shot on farmland. Public opinion was firmly against the killing of geese in urban areas. Indeed many local residents enjoyed seeing the geese and were opposed to any form of control.

In London the London Ecology Unit convened annual meetings throughout the 1990s involving local authorities, Royal Parks, Thames Water, British Waterways and London Wildlife Trust to review the position and try to reach agreement on possible control measures. It soon became clear that any action needed to be co-ordinated throughout the capital and that there was little to be gained from localised control. However, agreement could not be reached. At a meeting in 1994 there was a wide divergence of opinion on whether action was necessary. A report to the London Ecology Committee said, 'There seems little hope of a consensus for co-ordinated control in the short term.' In the meantime some park managers were creating new landscapes around their lakes, with low fences and taller vegetation along the water's edge that avoided much of the goose damage. This, together with regular pricking of eggs, has to some extent reduced the rate of population growth.

Canada geese are now the most familiar species of goose seen in urban areas. Individual pairs with goslings, or large groups of full-grown geese can be seen in many towns and cities. They are just as likely to be seen on city-centre canals in Manchester or Birmingham as on larger ponds and lakes. New water bodies designed as amenity areas in country parks, and well-vegetated islands in town parks and along large rivers all provide attractive habitats for breeding. At other times of year large flocks may congregate on reservoirs, or in open spaces such as parks and school playing-fields, which the birds use for both roosting and feeding.

Greylag geese were slower to become established as urban birds but their story is much the same. Apart from native stock in northern Scotland most of the greylag geese in Britain originated from reintroductions from the 1950s onwards. Initially their numbers did not grow so quickly as Canada geese and the vast majority are still found in rural areas. The national population reached about 22,000 by 1989 and topped 30,000 by the year 2000. Small parties can be seen in many towns and cities. In the West Midlands such flocks occur at many gravel pits, lakes or reservoirs across the region, where they commonly consort with Canada geese. Colonisation began when birds were first introduced in the 1960s to Packington Park, a country estate a few miles east of Birmingham Airport.

FIG 133. Greylag and Canada geese with other waterfowl in St James's Park.

From here birds gradually spread, but numbers remained limited until the 1990s when a substantial increase occurred and by 2005 the regional total had reached 700 birds. London too showed slow initial colonisation. One of the key sources was the feral flock at Sevenoaks Gravel Pit Nature Reserve where 38 birds were introduced between 1961 and 1966. By 1974 numbers had grown to over 100 birds. Another feral flock at St James's Park was 28 strong in 1981, building up to 66 birds by 1986. This flock gradually increased in size over the years and is known to move around the central Royal Parks. In 2009 the highest count was 402 greylags in Hyde Park. It appears that numbers are now increasing rather more rapidly than hitherto, despite attempts to control them by egg-pricking. Pairs tend to nest in isolation and in thicker cover than Canada geese, making effective control difficult to achieve.

For many people skeins of Canada geese and greylags moving through the urban landscape provide an enjoyable wildlife spectacle. They are probably the only species of geese that are regularly encountered by the public. In many places they are remarkably tame and where they are accustomed to people feeding them they will regularly tug at your clothing for food. Early morning in St James's Park would not be the same without the large number of geese roosting on grassland beneath the trees. It looks very much as if they are here to stay.

One species that is not here to stay is the ruddy duck. Again this was introduced from North America and became firmly established in Britain after young birds escaped from the wildfowl collection at Slimbridge in the 1950s. They were remarkably successful and like the geese became a familiar sight on many artificial water bodies such as gravel pits and reservoirs, particularly in the English Midlands. By 1991 the population had grown to over 3,400 birds. However, their increasing numbers elsewhere in Europe posed a threat through hybridisation to the Spanish population of the closely related white-headed duck, a globally threatened species. International pressure resulted in the British Government commencing action in 2003 to eradicate ruddy ducks from Britain over a period of five to seven years. By 2007 the national population had been reduced by about 2000 birds. Whether it will ever prove possible to completely eradicate ruddy ducks from Europe remains to be seen. The case illustrates very clearly how unforeseen consequences of introductions can pose serious ecological problems.

Another species of introduced waterfowl that has successfully colonised urban areas is the mandarin duck. This very attractive duck, which is native to China, Korea and Japan, has been kept in waterfowl collections in many countries over the past 250 years. Sir Matthew Decker, a director of the East India Company, first brought it to Britain in about 1745 and kept a flock in his garden at Richmond. It seems likely that most of those now breeding in the wild in and

FIG 134. There are now substantial populations of mandarin ducks in some urban areas.

around London originated from a collection at Cobham in Surrey in the 1930s. From here they spread into the surrounding countryside where they found ideal breeding habitats along the river valleys of the Wey and Mole and around Virginia Water and Windsor Great Park, where they nest in hollow trees. They particularly favour places where old trees grow beside rivers or lakes, or where there are secluded ponds in ancient woodland.

Over the past fifty years the feral population in Britain has grown substantially and it is now thought that there could be over 7,000 birds. But it is only in London and the Home counties that substantial numbers have colonised the urban environment. During the 1970s they were still restricted to southwestern fringes of London, but by 1990 had spread to many wooded lakes and ponds in several of the outer boroughs, including Richmond, Bromley and Enfield. In 1999 a survey of Epping Forest found a total of up to twenty pairs. Mandarins may suffer from a shortage of suitable nest holes and will readily use nest boxes. People with gardens backing on to rivers may be lucky enough to attract them and may even find more than one pair in the same box. Numbers are always difficult to assess because of the secretive nature of this duck, but there is no doubt that it has now become firmly established in London, even breeding in small numbers in some of the inner London parks.

FIG 135. Egyptian geese breed on park lakes in central London.

Yet another introduced species showing early signs of colonising towns and cities is the Egyptian goose. Recent estimates suggest a total British population of 2,500 to 3,000 birds, almost all of which are restricted to rural East Anglia, but in recent years increasing numbers have bred in London and locally in the East Midlands. This is another tree-nesting species, which finds wood pasture or common land with old trees particularly suitable. In London it has bred successfully at Bushy Park and Hampstead Heath and increasingly in central London parks including Clapham Common, Hyde Park and St James's Park.

An unusual example of an alien species that almost became naturalised was the small colony of American black-crowned night herons that became established in Edinburgh during the 1950s (Lever, 1977). It seems the Zoo acquired three pairs in 1936 which bred in captivity and by 1950 there were some twenty birds. That year some escaped through a hole in the aviary roof but remained in the confines of the Zoo. The following year it was decided to let all the birds fly freely. The birds set up a breeding colony in trees around the Zoo, but made excursions elsewhere in Edinburgh to feed. Small parties would fly out in the evening to feed along the Gogar Burn on the edge of the city, returning by morning to roost in their rookery. By 1975 the population had risen to 40–50 birds by which time they were a well-known ornithological feature of the city. It is said that the colony gradually declined after birds were recaptured when new legislation made it illegal to release non-native species to the wild.

Other ways of encouraging wetland birds in urban areas include the provision of artificial nesting rafts to attract common terns in places such as reservoirs, disused docks, canals and other waterways. Such rafts have been in place at Brent Reservoir in London since the early 1980s and terns have nested every year since 1983. The colony has gradually grown in numbers, reaching 44 pairs in 2000. As well as fishing on the reservoir these terns fish along the River Brent and Grand Union Canal and on ponds at Hampstead Heath (Batten, 2002). Others nest on rafts in the old Rotherhithe Docks and on dock basins immediately adjacent to the financial centre at Canary Wharf. The effectiveness of rafts even in intensely built-up areas has long been demonstrated. One of the best examples was the construction of rafts on a lagoon at the huge steel works at Shotton next to the Dee Estuary in 1970. It was hoped they would provide nesting sites for about a dozen pairs of common terns, but the following year about 150 pairs nested in the midst of this centre of heavy industry.

BIRDS OF PREY

Birds of prey bring a wilder and sometimes spectacular side of nature into towns and cities and we are fortunate that trends over the past fifty years have led to an increase in the number and diversity of these birds. The general decline in game management in post-war years, together with increased tolerance of predators have been major factors. Other positive influences have been the dramatic recovery of predators from the effects of organochlorine insecticides of the 1960s, and the effectiveness of national legislation to protect these species. Undoubtedly some have benefited from increased public interest in birds. Though not always welcome, the sparrowhawk has capitalised on increased availability of prey resulting from extensive feeding of garden birds in urban areas. Some species have gained from the provision of artificial nest boxes on buildings, whilst others like the red kite are now becoming a common sight in some towns and cities following major re-introduction schemes. Together these factors have resulted in one of the most remarkable changes in urban ecology of the past half century.

Living near the centre of Bath, I am frequently alerted to buzzards circling overhead by the frantic yelps of rooftop herring gulls, and on several occasions have witnessed courtship displays of buzzards over the city. But they have not always been here. There was a period when buzzards were virtually exterminated from most of Britain in the interests of game preservation. After more than a hundred years of persecution they were restricted by 1915 to the southwest peninsula of England, and the uplands of Wales, Cumbria and western Scotland; with a few pairs surviving elsewhere in isolated pockets, such as the New Forest. But after the rapid decline in game management precipitated by World War I birds gradually started to spread from their upland strongholds. It was a slow process. By 1945 ornithologists in Bath reported that the nearest breeding birds were in the Mendips, Quantocks and Exmoor. But it was not long before they recolonised woodlands around Bath and Bristol and their very noticeable eastward spread across lowland England has been one of the most successful recoveries achieved by any bird species in the post-war years. Their ability to colonise woodlands of towns and cities has been particularly striking.

By the 1990s buzzards reached the North Downs and Chilterns and there has been a steady increase in their numbers in London since 2000. They can now be seen even in the centre of the city, where I watched one drifting lazily over Horseguards Parade in September 2007. That autumn over 50 were recorded in different parts of the capital. Observations made daily since 1999 at the Wetland Centre in Barnes demonstrate these changes rather well. None was seen during the first two years, but since then their frequency gradually increased with birds seen in five months of the year by 2004. In 2005 two or three birds were seen on some days, rising to six or seven individuals on some days by 2007–8. By then they were seen in eight months of the year. Although improved vigilance by recorders might account for some of these figures, the overall trend is clear (Bullock, 2009). One pair has already nested in the London Borough of Kingston and we can look forward to buzzards becoming established as breeding birds in other well-wooded outer boroughs. The recent spread of the buzzard has resulted in colonisation of other cities, notably Belfast. During the 1960s the nearest breeding pairs were on the north Antrim coast, but by the 1990s they had spread across the Province and are now seen regularly in Belfast where some even frequent landfill sites. They breed above Carr's Glen and in Redburn Country Park.

Every year there are numerous records of harriers, kites, ospreys and honey buzzards seen over London as they pass through on migration. But those that make their home in the city bring a special sense of wildness. In 1898, W. H. Hudson predicted that 'It is exceedingly improbable that any of the raptoral species which formally inhabited London – peregrine falcon, kestrel and kite – will ever return.' On all three birds Hudson got it wrong. Kestrels re-established themselves in central London after an absence of 50 years when a pair nested at the old St Paul's school in Hammersmith in 1931. Peregrines have made a spectacular come-back since 2000 and the red kite is on the verge of breeding in Greater London, though admittedly this is the result of the extremely successful reintroduction programme during the 1990s in Oxfordshire.

FIG 136. Although still present in many towns and cities the number of kestrels has declined in recent years. (Paul Wilkins)

In post-war years kestrels quickly colonised central London, making use of bombed buildings for nesting and finding plenty of territory for hunting in the newly vegetated bombsites. By the late 1950s they became the dominant avian predator across the capital, having already become established in the urban environment elsewhere in the UK. Many small towns still support a pair or two nesting somewhere in the urban fabric. They are able to penetrate to the heart of the city through their use of prominent municipal buildings, church steeples, and even window ledges on high-rise offices for nest sites. In the older industrial cities derelict buildings provide suitable sites and they also benefit from an ample supply of urban wasteland for hunting. These post-industrial landscapes with their high populations of voles in the rough grasslands provide ideal conditions for kestrels. In 2007 a pair nested on concrete supports under Spaghetti Junction in Birmingham where the patchwork of open wasteland between the motorways is a perfect hunting ground. Another pair nested on the old signal box at Snow Hill Station. Elsewhere in Birmingham numerous kestrels still nest on commercial or industrial buildings, but they are also found in the city centre on the Art Gallery and Museum. In Edinburgh a pair regularly nested on the cliffs below the castle during the 1970s. One year they brought their young off the nest in the middle of an open-air musical performance in Princes Street Gardens. The strident 'kek kek kek' of the young birds taking their first flights all but drowned out the music!

In the 1980s kestrels could regularly be seen catching house sparrows in central London (Goode, 1986). They would fly alongside a building and pick them off the window ledges. At that time sparrows were abundant and the kestrel was one of their main predators, with over 100 pairs nesting in the capital. Since then there has been a significant growth in London's urban sparrowhawk population

FIG 137. Sparrowhawk numbers have increased substantially and they commonly hunt in suburban gardens. This one has caught a collared dove. (Elizabeth Allen)

and now you are more likely to see these birds, rather than the kestrel, hunting in central London parks. Over the same period sparrow populations have plummeted. Whether the increased number of sparrowhawks has played a part in the national decline of the sparrow is not yet known, but it is a possible factor (see Chapter 11).

Records from the London Wetland Centre, since 1999, show that the sparrowhawk has gradually overtaken the kestrel as the most frequently recorded predator. It is now seen almost every day and its hunting behaviour at the Centre shows how adaptable these birds are to different conditions. When snipe or other small waders are feeding or resting by the side of pools some sparrowhawks have taken to stalking them on the ground. They fly in very low and land a little way off behind rushes or other low vegetation. From here they creep between the tussocks, suddenly pouncing forward to catch one of the birds. Better known is the sparrowhawk's skill in catching small birds at garden feeders and bird tables, which is now well documented. As well as tits, robins and thrushes they are just as likely to take wood pigeons and collared doves. It is clear that these birds have become remarkably well adapted to urban life.

Another bird of prey that has shown a marked increase in recent years is the hobby. Since the 1980s its breeding population in Britain has grown significantly, almost certainly in response to climate change. So instead of being restricted to scattered heaths and downland in southeast England it has spread northwards, colonising a wider range of countryside, including farmland with copses and small woodlands. In expanding its range it has also colonised some suburban areas, especially in the Bournemouth conurbation and in London. When the first atlas of breeding birds in the London area was produced (Montier, 1977) the hobby was extremely scarce. Only five breeding pairs were recorded during

1968–72 within 20 miles of St Paul's, this being the LNHS recording area. None of these were within Greater London. However, by the time surveys were carried out for the second atlas in 1988–94 they had spread all around the capital, with 84 confirmed breeding records, of which 20 were in Greater London. The first pair to nest in inner London was in 2002. During late summer hobbys are seen almost daily at the Wetland Centre where they feed on dragonflies and young sand martins.

The red kite has also become well established as an urban bird in some parts of the country following reintroductions which started in 1989. Although at one time a common scavenger in towns and cities, kites were persecuted relentlessly and became extinct in England in 1871. In view of their falling numbers across Europe, the UK Joint Nature Conservation Committee promoted a major programme of reintroductions in several locations from the Chilterns to northern Scotland. Most of these were in rural areas. However, the most recent introductions were made in semi-urban landscapes, in Gateshead and on the outskirts of Aberdeen.

The first reintroduction near Stokenchurch in the Chilterns between 1989 and 1993 was remarkably successful and it was not long before birds started to appear in the towns and villages of Berkshire and Oxfordshire where they soon became accustomed to feeding in gardens. The birds can be seen lazily quartering the suburbs of Reading and Didcot, and the population is gradually expanding westwards along the M4 corridor towards Bristol and Bath, and eastwards into London. Monitoring of this population shows a higher density of nests, and larger broods, close to sources of artificial feeding. In the Chiltern area it was found that large numbers of people feed the birds in their gardens, with the result that kites are now becoming strongly associated with towns and villages. So common is the practice of feeding that Natural England issued an information note on the effects of feeding kites, with guidance on best practice. In some small suburban gardens 20 or 30 birds will arrive as soon as food is put out and larger gatherings may occur in places where food is provided at a regular time. At Icknield Community College in Watlington, not far from the place where kites were released, they soon learnt that food was to be had at break time as pupils went outside to eat their lunch. The *Daily Telegraph* reported that 'red kites come and swarm round everyone when they are eating, and snatch their sandwiches; one boy even had to have a tetanus jab.' It seems the kites are behaving much as they have ever done in urban surroundings.

The more recent reintroduction in 2004 at Gateshead in the northeast of England has exceeded all expectations. The original target was to have 15 breeding pairs by 2012, but after only three years there were 25 pairs, which raised

22 young. Three pairs nested within 900 m of each other, one just 450 m from a big housing estate. One local resident was able to watch a pair building a nest and incubating eggs in a tree close to her garden. Others nest in trees next to a local supermarket. These birds have plenty of material to decorate their nests, as is their habit. Examples include an England football fan's flag, a pair of men's briefs, some socks, a cuddly toy and a glove. The red kites of Gateshead have achieved a special status locally. There is even the 'kite bus' direct from Newcastle Central Station to some of the best vantage points to see the birds, one of which is the Black Horse public house car park, at Barlow village. It seems that people who might have been totally unaware of kites a few years ago are thrilled to see them and proud to have them on the doorstep.

By 2011 the RSPB estimated that there were at least 2,000 pairs of red kites breeding in the UK. By then the original Chiltern population had grown to over 800 pairs and they have since spread to Wiltshire, Hampshire and Sussex. They are spreading relentlessly. It will not be long before they are breeding again in London town.

Peregrine Falcon

Of all the recent changes in birds of prey the colonisation of towns and cities by peregrine falcons has been most spectacular and deserves special mention. The gradual re-colonisation of areas previously occupied by peregrines, following their massive decline resulting from pesticides in the 1950s and 1960s, has been well documented (Ratcliffe, 1994). By 1990 the population was restored to its pre-pesticide level with most available nest sites occupied in rural locations. Some birds then took to nesting in quarries in parts of the country where they had never occurred before, whilst a few started to occupy prominent buildings in towns and cities. With the secrecy surrounding the location of peregrine nests at that time we shall probably never know for certain which were the first of these urban pioneers, but it seems that Swansea and Exeter are the most likely locations. Birds were resident if not breeding in both places during the late 1980s and a pair took up residence on the Avon Gorge in Bristol in 1990. The Swansea pair bred successfully in 1994 rearing four young, but these were later found dead at the foot of the Guildhall clock tower apparently poisoned. Another brood was poisoned in 1996, this time from a nest on the Telecom Tower. Meanwhile the birds in Exeter had been occupying St Michael's church for nearly ten years, by the time they first nested in 1997. The following year an artificial nest platform was put up on a tower block in Brighton with immediate success, two young being raised. According to published records this was also the first year that peregrines nested successfully in London, producing four young on the Spillars Millenium Mills in the Royal

Docks. By 2000 the stage was set for the peregrine to colonise the towns and cities of southern England and nowhere has it been more successful than in London.

I well remember the thrill of seeing the birds nesting on Battersea Power Station in the spring of 2000 and from that time on the birds could be seen on a number of buildings in central London, including Kings Reach Tower by Blackfriars Bridge, which happened to house the offices of *Country Life* magazine. On one occasion in 2002 I witnessed a pair of peregrines displaying at rooftop height along Caxton Street at a time when they appeared to be prospecting possible breeding sites around the Foreign Office. By 2003 as well as Battersea there was one other confirmed breeding pair (though unsuccessful) in central London, and others in Croydon, Barking and the Isle of Dogs. Until 2004 all this was happening with little public knowledge, but that year a pair nested on the University of Westminster's building just south of Regents Park. A public viewing point was set up in the park, complete with telescope and for the first time Londoners could experience at first hand the thrill of seeing the birds displaying at the nest. This pair later moved to nest at the Barbican and has since been seen outside the nesting season roosting on Tate Modern.

In London the peregrines have gone from strength to strength. In 2007 there were at least seven pairs breeding and birds were frequently seen hunting along the Thames in central London. By then they were breeding in many towns and cities, including Aberdeen, Bristol, Bath, Canterbury, Chichester, Derby, Manchester, Coventry, Taunton, Plymouth, Worcester and Cardiff, in addition to those in Exeter, Swansea and Brighton. In 2002 the BTO reviewed peregrine numbers in the UK and identified 62 pairs breeding on man-made structures, including church-spires, offices, bridges, pylons and even on a watchtower at Filton Airport in Bristol (Crick *et al.*, 2003). Not all of these were in the urban environment, but it demonstrated a willingness for the bird to move away from its traditional nest sites of cliff ledges to utilise man-made structures in a wide variety of situations. The erection of nest boxes or platforms on prominent buildings has certainly assisted their spread into urban areas. A nest box erected on Chichester Cathedral in the spring of 2001 was immediately occupied, though breeding that first year was unsuccessful. However, they have bred every year since then, rearing 18 young by 2007. In Bath peregrines were in residence on St John's church in the late 1990s and first bred in 2006 after a nest box was erected. In Derby and Manchester nest platforms resulted in immediate breeding success in 2006 and 2007 respectively. But not all the recent colonisation is due to nest boxes. In Cardiff peregrines moved in after ravens vacated their nest on County Hall in 2006. The ravens are said to have moved to alternative accommodation on Cardiff University the following year.

FIG 138. A female peregrine on its favourite plucking-post in Bath.

As the peregrine became established in cities it was soon realised that here was an opportunity for people to see this spectacular bird as part of daily life. No longer did one have to make a special trip to the Wye Valley to watch peregrines at the nest. For many people it was suddenly possible to see them on their own doorstep. A web-cam was set up on Chichester Cathedral in 2001 and the RSPB has organised similar public viewing facilities in Manchester, Derby, Exeter and London. The watch point in Regents Park from 2 to 11 June 2004 attracted nearly 2,000 people. The following year it was extended to three weeks, attracting 6,750 people. When this pair then moved to Tate Modern as a roosting site outside the breeding season this provided the ideal opportunity for the RSPB to set up a public viewing site in central London, which attracted 40,000 people. In Manchester a big screen was erected in Piccadilly Square for the public to see what was happening at the nearby nest site.

One of my greatest pleasures is to walk down to see how the birds are doing in my home town of Bath. There is a seat by the riverside opposite the church which seems purpose-built for peregrine watching. Sitting here with a telescope trained on the birds has resulted in endless conversations with complete strangers who are captivated and thrilled by seeing the bird in close up, often for the first time. 'Oh, wow!' is the standard response, and frequently people say, 'That's made my day'. It is said we are a nation of gardeners, but at times like this we seem to be a nation of naturalists. One lady commented that she had enjoyed watching kestrels nesting on her window ledge in London. It turned out that she was the wife of a Beefeater and lived in the Tower of London.

The story of the Bath peregrines is worth recounting as it illustrates the hazards of living in the city. Although peregrines were resident during the autumn and winter on St John's Church in the late 1990s, they went elsewhere to breed. At that time there was no suitable ledge for them to nest on the church, but in the winter of 2004 Andy Grant of the local group of the Hawk and Owl Trust put up a box in the hope that they would nest. The following year the birds still nested elsewhere, but in 2006 they used the new nest box and produced four young. They have nested on the church every year since then. Almost every year the young peregrines suffer some kind of mishap after their first flight. In 2007 they produced two young, one of which ended up amongst the traffic in Manvers Street after its first flight. The following year two chicks were fledged and left the nest during a gale. One of them had to be rescued from a local garden. It was put on the roof of Georgian flats adjacent to the church where it was mobbed by the resident herring gulls. Its mother coaxed it back to the church by flying very slowly across the street. Eventually, after several attempts by its mother, it followed and reached the relative safety of the church steeple. The other fledgling was grounded somewhere for a week before it reappeared on the church in an exhausted state. Amazingly both birds survived. In 2009 one young was produced, which suffered a similar experience to those of 2008. After its first flight it was rescued from the shrubberies of a local domestic garden and put on the rooftops

FIG 139. Adult peregrines often sit for long periods after feeding and provide good views for spectators.

FIG 140. Permanent cameras fitted to nestboxes in Bath and Norwich allow progress to be monitored daily. (Hawk and Owl Trust)

where it was constantly attacked by herring gulls. This one was harried to such an extent that it ended up in the river, where it was rescued yet again and returned to the safety of its nesting box on the church. In 2011 one the young birds fell down a chimney. It was exceedingly lucky that it happened to be the house of local naturalists Alan and Gillian Barrett. Gillian was astonished to find the bird sitting in a rather dishevelled state on her desk, having fought its way out of the chimney which was blocked up with cardboard. Yet again the Hawk and Owl Trust looked after the bird before releasing it. The following year the first bird to fly became grounded in a garden and was put back on a roof. On its next flight it ended up swimming in the river, from where it was rescued by a wildlife cameraman. In 2012 an identical incident was filmed by the BBC *Springwatch* programme. Similar stories are told from other towns and cities where the hazards of urban life pose major problems for young birds. Nine lives may be for cats, but urban peregrines certainly benefit from the watchful eyes of many people.

The Bath peregrines have also revealed fascinating family dynamics. Every year, whilst still in the nest, young birds have been marked with distinctive blue numbered rings. In 2008 after the adults mated the male bird disappeared, and the

FIG 141. Young birds being ringed in 2008. (Ian Sparrowhawk)

mother had to cope alone. But whilst she was sitting on eggs an immature male bird from the previous year started to help out by bringing food for her. Three young hatched but one was lost from the nest as a tiny chick. The immature male continued to bring food and also took over baby-sitting duties whilst the mother went off hunting. When he first took charge he assumed an air of great self-importance, mixed with doubts as to whether he should really be there. As soon as the mother bird came back he was off like a shot. Later that year he moulted into full adult plumage, a year before normal and the following year (2009) he mated with his mother! They became the established pair, raising young each year. In 2012 an immature male from the previous year was still around and he took his turn in incubating the eggs. As it happens the BBC had set up a camera at the nest for the *Springwatch* programme, and we all saw his rather clumsy attempts at incubation. On one occasion there was something of a stand off when the adult male returned and the younger bird refused to get off the eggs. Involvement of immature birds in this way is not well documented and the detailed history of individual pairs may well become better known with so many observers in urban areas. *Springwatch* certainly put the Bath peregrines on the map.

In parallel with all the publicity of web-cams and public viewing, others were quietly investigating the diet of urban peregrines, with some surprising results. Ed Drewitt and others arranged for prey remains to be collected for analysis in Bristol, Bath and Exeter. Information about the diet of urban peregrines had previously been fragmentary, with the assumption that they would feed predominantly on urban bird species, especially pigeons (Ratcliffe, 1993). In fact they found that their diet is very diverse, including many species associated with non-urban habitats, and particularly interesting is the fact that these urban peregrines are regularly hunting by night (Drewitt & Dixon, 2008). A total of 98

FIG 142. Young in the nest.
Their first flight has proved
hazardous for many birds.

species were recorded out of 5,275 prey remains identified. Of these feral pigeons were the most significant comprising 42 per cent of prey by frequency and 63 per cent by weight. Next most frequent were starlings at 9 per cent, collared doves 4 per cent, redwings 4 per cent, greenfinch 4 per cent and teal 2 per cent. In summer the proportion of starlings rose with over half of them juveniles. Swifts and collared doves were both an important part of the diet in summer, whilst in winter the most frequent prey apart from feral pigeon were blackbirds, redwing and teal. But there were also a number of species which are most likely to have been caught at night. These include quail, little grebe, black-necked grebe, water rail, corncrake, moorhen, common snipe, jack snipe and woodcock. Some of these were taken in substantial numbers, notably 46 woodcock and 71 snipe during winter months in Bath. Drewitt has subsequently reviewed the status of urban peregrines in the UK and elsewhere (Drewitt, 2014).

There is substantial evidence of peregrines feeding at night from elsewhere in Europe and north America, and it would seem that the birds are taking advantage of a new set of conditions presented by the urban environment. The first direct evidence came from a web-cam on Derby Cathedral which recorded a peregrine leaving its perch in the middle of the night and returning a couple of minutes later with a woodcock, still alive but not for long. Together with the fact that feral pigeons are the mainstay of their diet, this new capacity to hunt by the lights of the city makes these truly urban birds. Indeed it can be argued that they are demonstrating successful evolution, gaining a distinct advantage from urbanisation. It will not be long before they are breeding in every major town and city in the country.

CHAPTER 9

A Motley Selection of Opportunists

ROOF NESTING GULLS

W E TEND TO ASSOCIATE HERRING gulls with the seaside. Their ringing calls bring back memories of holidays at Whitby and Teignmouth. But today one is just as likely to hear them in towns and cities far from the sea, where they have taken up residence and are doing remarkably well. When I lived in the centre of Bath I was all too aware of the herring gulls and lesser black-backed gulls, large numbers of which now live in the city. On Thursday mornings I was woken early by their determined attacks on refuse bags, the contents of which were spread about the pavements. Many birds are resident throughout the year but their territorial behaviour increases in April and vociferous displays are not restricted to the rooftops where they nest, but often take place amidst traffic and tourists on the streets of the city. For those working in shops and offices the constant noise from the gulls can become a nuisance and the birds have learnt that there are easy pickings from outdoor tables of cafes and restaurants, even snatching food directly from people's hands. Their presence does not fit well with the genteel image of Bath.

There are now 1,100 pairs nesting in the city and the birds get on with their life, treating chimneys and roofs as an extended colony. Whilst the city provides ideal conditions for breeding, the birds are largely dependent on landfill sites for their main food supply and so they make daily journeys to and from these places throughout the year. Huge strings of gulls can be seen leaving the city in the morning and returning in late afternoon and evening.

Bath is just one of many towns and cities which have been colonised by gulls over the past 50 years. Prior to the 1940s nesting on roofs in Britain was a rare

FIG 143. Gulls on their territory among chimneypots and rooftops.

occurrence worthy of note in local natural history journals. Early records include
herring gulls nesting on a roof at Port Isaac in Cornwall and on an old mill
at Gulval near Penzance in 1910. They were also recorded nesting at Budleigh
Salterton in 1923 and Torquay in 1928. Colonies started at Newquay in Cornwall
in 1926 and Dover in 1936.

By the 1940s herring gulls were colonising many coastal towns in the
southwest of England and the rapid spread of this new habit during the 1950s and
1960s was described by Parslow (1967). It was during this time that the first inland
breeding colonies of herring gulls in urban areas were recorded, with 45 pairs in
Merthyr Tydfil in 1958 and the start of another colony at Gloucester in 1967. When
Operation Seafarer, the first national survey of seabirds, was carried out in 1969–70
members of the Seabird Group decided to make special efforts to include roof-
nesting gulls in the survey. The results were described by Stanley Cramp (1971)
who readily admitted that the numbers of birds were likely to be underestimated
for several reasons, especially the problems of counting birds in urban areas. Over
1,300 pairs of herring gull and lesser black-backed gull were found to be nesting
on buildings in over 50 urban locations from southwest England to the north of
Scotland. Most of these were in coastal towns, exceptions being Merthyr Tydfil,
Carmarthen, London and Kilmarnock. Herring gulls totalled between 1,252 and

1,365 pairs. This included an estimate of 225 nests for the largest colony at Dover. At that time the next largest colonies were Newquay (189 pairs), Culdrose (100–150), Hastings (106), Newport (100) and St Ives in Cornwall with over 100 pairs. Cramp concluded that there had been a remarkable and almost uninterrupted growth, both in the number of colonies and their average size over the period 1940 to 1970. The habit began in southwest England spreading in the 1930s to Kent and later to eastern England, Wales and Scotland. Lesser black-backed gulls were rather slower to adopt the habit of nesting on buildings with the first known example in south Wales in 1945–6. The number of colonies increased gradually to five by 1969–70. These held a total of 62 pairs, mostly in south Wales but with a small colony in Gloucester and one pair in Hastings.

By 1976 a further survey showed that numbers of roof nesting gulls had doubled to 3,291 pairs (mostly herring gulls) and the number of urban locations had also dramatically increased (Monaghan & Coulson, 1977). Urban colonies grew substantially during the 1980s. In Bristol the colony which was first established in 1972 increased from about 100 pairs in 1980 to about 1,000 pairs by the early 1990s (Rock, 2005). By 1994 national surveys showed a ten-fold increase since 1970 with a conservative estimate of 13,591 pairs. These comprised 11,047 pairs of herring gulls in 188 places and 2,544 pairs of lesser black-backed gulls in 84 colonies. The majority of sites supported fewer than 50 pairs. At this time it was estimated that there could be as many as 20,000 pairs in the UK (Raven & Coulson, 1997).

The next national survey in 2000 recorded over 30,000 pairs nesting on rooftops (Mitchell *et al.*, 2004). Rock pointed out that many inland colonies were missed and he suggested that the national total could have been over 100,000 pairs by 2004 (Rock, 2005). In 2012 the 41 colonies in the Severn Estuary Region held 19,000 pairs. Some of the largest were Bristol (2,500 pairs), Gloucester (2,900 pairs) and Cardiff with 3,300 pairs. Recent estimates (2012) in Bath suggest that there are 790 pairs of lesser black-backed gulls and 310 pairs of herring gulls. Using the lowest estimate of breeding success Rock predicts that there will be 1,700 pairs by 2020.

So from the relatively small numbers recorded by Cramp in 1969 there has been a huge and continuing increase in the number of urban gulls and new colonies continue to be formed.

What seems to have happened is that the birds are benefiting from a number of factors. Compared with more natural colonies on cliffs, islands and sand dunes, the gulls nesting on rooftops are relatively safe from predators and each pair is capable of raising two or three young every year. This results in an average increase in population size of 13–25 per cent per annum. It is salutary to note that a colony of only 20 breeding pairs can produce between 150 and 200 young

FIG 144. Young gulls on rooftops are relatively safe from predators, including other gulls, compared with coastal colonies.

birds over five years. The life expectancy of adult gulls is 10–15 years. Many live for 20 years, the oldest known individual being 35, and with each pair producing 2 or 3 young every year it is easy to see how these gull populations have grown so quickly. This high reproductive rate is, however, only partially responsible for their success. The other major factor is food supply. Inland breeding colonies are thought to be largely dependent on landfill sites for the majority of their food. Rock has suggested that the Clean Air Act 1956 was a critical factor in allowing development of these colonies. This legislation prohibited the burning of rubbish on landfill sites and instead required the dumped material to be covered with a layer of inert material at the end of each day. In practice this suddenly led to vast quantities of food becoming available to the gulls.

Urban gulls are also opportunistic in obtaining food within the towns and cities where they breed. As well as systematically attacking black plastic rubbish bags put out for collection they keep a close eye on any source of food. Birds at St Ives in Cornwall have become so used to taking food from visitors that they will snatch ice creams out of their hands with impunity. In Aberdeen a herring gull was filmed walking into a shop, taking a packet of cheese Doritos from the display, then calmly walking outside where it ripped it open and consumed the contents. The bird first raided the shop early in July 2007 and soon became a regular. Nicknamed Sam, he became so popular that locals started paying for his crisps. The shopkeeper Mr Nagarajan said:

> *He's got it down to a fine art. He waits until there are no customers around and I'm standing by the till. Then he raids the place, but for some reason he only takes one kind of crisp packet. He's becoming a bit of a celebrity. Seagulls are not usually that popular, but Sam is a star because he's so funny.*

Herring gulls are certainly not popular at the outdoor restaurants in Bristol docks where they make a habit of landing on the tables. In London the resident herring gulls regularly patrol the lake in St James's Park during summer months on the look out for newly fledged ducklings of tufted duck and pochard. I have witnessed them taking these ducklings on many occasions. Once I watched a gull sidle quietly up to a group of feral pigeons happily sunning themselves, then it made a dash into their midst and grabbed one. An easy meal!

Most urban gulls nest in commercial areas on the relatively flat roofs of industrial and warehousing sites rather than in residential areas. One of the largest single concentrations is on a factory roof at Butetown in Cardiff where 110 pairs of mainly lesser black-backed gulls nested in 2004. This large, gently sloping roof of asbestos supports abundant lichen and moss growth and provides conditions that most closely resemble those of the sand dunes favoured by these birds in more natural circumstances (Rock, 2005). But in Bath many of the birds nest on the chimneystacks of Georgian houses placing their nests securely between the chimney pots, or at the highest point in the gutter that runs alongside the roof parapet. Large numbers also nest on the roofs of terraced

FIG 145. Pavements are covered in rubbish as gulls tear into bin bags. One bird can make a lot of mess.

houses in Cardiff and Cheltenham. In London, where the numbers have so far remained relatively small, pairs have chosen imposing buildings, such as the stands at Lords cricket ground and the roof of County Hall at Westminster. I was working in County Hall in 1983 when a pair nested there and as the resident ecologist I was called to the Director General's office when one of the young birds fell down the chimney into his fireplace!

One of the great differences between natural colonies and those of urban areas is that many urban birds remain attached to the colony throughout the year. In his New Naturalist treatise on the herring gull Niko Tinbergen describes vividly the spring day on which the gulls return to their sand-dune breeding grounds which have remained empty for the rest of the year. He goes on to describe the territorial behaviour which precedes courtship and nesting (Tinbergen, 1953). It seems that this behaviour is somewhat reduced in urban populations, particularly in residential areas. In Bath many birds remain throughout the year keeping station on their chosen nest site, but large numbers of lesser black-backed gulls still leave for wintering grounds in Portugul and North Africa. In spring their courtship displays and mating generally take place on the rooftops, but there are times when small parties of birds gather noisily on the street and this may be the equivalent of the 'clubs' described by Tinbergen

for the sand-dune birds. Mating takes place in April or May generally three weeks earlier than coastal cliff nesting birds. Young birds are fed on the rooftops until they are able to fly and their incessant calls are a feature of life during June and July. Their initial flight from the rooftop is a risky business with a fair chance of ending up amongst the traffic down below. During the 1990s a pair of herring gulls nested for several years on the chimney stacks of shops in Camden High Street in London and several of their young ended up being rescued when they landed in the street amongst the cars and buses.

The problems caused by urban gulls are of five kinds: noise, mess from their droppings, blockages from nest material, attacks on rubbish bags and aggression.

FIG 146. A young gull that falls to street level rarely survives.

FIG 147. Their strident calls reverberate around the streets.

They are certainly noisy, especially during the breeding season, when their strident calls can be particularly annoying in the hours after dawn. The mess from their droppings not only causes damage to stonework, but people and cars in the streets below may well be spattered. These droppings can be costly to remove from stonework. Nest material may well be carried by rainwater into drainpipes, which then get blocked. In Bath this has caused costly damage to buildings as water accumulates on rooftops and gets into the walls.

Aggression tends to be more localised, but where it occurs it can be a real problem. If people invade their space gulls will normally give warning cries before resorting to more aggressive tactics. The warning 'gag-gag-gag' is frequently heard when the birds have young. However, there are plenty of instances of birds which have taken things further and become a danger to people passing nearby as they swoop down and clout them on the head with their feet. BBC news reported in 2005 that residents of Pontcanna, a suburb of Cardiff, were forced to carry umbrellas to deter low flying attacks from gulls when chicks had hatched on nearby roofs. In April 2008 local press in Kirkintilloch reported residents saying they were too frightened to step

FIG 148. After a warning call has failed a gull will attack an intruder.

outside their front doors for fear of being attacked by seagulls. They claimed that, 'vicious birds were dive-bombing pedestrians and pets, ripping open rubbish bags and covering the area in droppings. You have to be on the lookout for droppings – ready to duck when they are in flight.' There are endless examples of such behaviour, especially when chicks are newly hatched, and it is at this time that public complaints are most vociferous.

Attacks on rubbish bags are all too common in Bath not only in residential areas, but also in the city centre. Rubbish bags are put out overnight for collection next morning. In the summer months the birds have ample time in the early morning to get at the bags and frequently leave refuse spread all over the pavements. It seems that this is a common problem. In Kirkintilloch it was reported that, 'noise begins at 3 a.m. – they rip open the bags on the street leaving rubbish everywhere'. In Bath, new gull-proof bags have been issued to residents and commercial firms, which appear to be having the desired effect.

Where there are large numbers of gulls, particularly in residential areas and town centres, public feelings can become quite heated and there are demands that something should be done about the birds. In most places where gulls are well established local councils have responded by trying a variety of ways to reduce their numbers. Guidance notes have been issued explaining the problem and recommending appropriate action. They include using models of owls and other predators; use of alarm calls; flying hawks to scare the birds; using netting and spikes to prevent access to nest sites; putting oil on the eggs to prevent them from hatching; or substituting artificial eggs in the nests. Such activities vary from the completely useless to a few which do have some value.

Once a large colony has become established there is little one can do to reduce the number of adult gulls. Although some licences were issued in the past to cull adult gulls (because of possible risks to public health) this provoked such intense public reaction that plans were quickly dropped. It seems unlikely that any local council would now consider such action. In any case it would be difficult to achieve an effective cull, as both shooting and poisoning are out of the question in urban areas. We are left then with finding ways of reducing the breeding success of gulls in an attempt to hold the population in check. Most of the activities undertaken by pest control firms are aimed at doing just this.

The use of model owls and eagles on the roof is quite useless. The gulls ignore them and may well nest right next to them. Use of the gull's own alarm calls may cause some short-term reaction but has no long-term effect as the birds grow used to hearing such calls. Netting to prevent access to roofs, and use of spikes to prevent them from using specific locations between chimneys can have some limited value, especially in residential areas where gulls are a particular

FIG 149. Harris hawks are used to displace gulls during incubation

problem. The flying of hawks certainly disturbs the birds for the period concerned. Most of the adult birds fly up from the rooftops whilst the hawk is being flown. But they quickly settle down again afterwards. Unless the hawk is flown every day for extended periods it seems unlikely that it would have an effect on the success of the colony. Egg oiling and use of artificial eggs are useful, both in reducing breeding success and in reducing noise from breeding birds.

Dipping the eggs in oil prevents them from developing further and encourages the adults to incubate the eggs for longer than the normal period of one month. They then abandon breeding for that year. So this is an effective way of reducing breeding success. As it happens it also reduces the amount of noise. Although there is a fair amount of noise during courtship, incubation is a relatively quiet period. The birds are noisiest once the chicks have hatched. This is also the time when

FIG 150. Oiling the eggs or replacing them with artificial eggs will reduce nesting success

most aggression occurs towards people as the birds endeavour to protect their young. So oiling the eggs to prevent them from hatching reduces the noise levels considerably. Replacing the eggs with artificial ones does exactly the same job. In Bath the council has carried out systematic oiling of eggs for a number of years and its policies have been copied by other councils elsewhere. For a while the Council offered to match-fund efforts by local residents associations to carry out oiling of eggs, and this was proving effective in some residential areas. There is even some evidence that in specific localities where oiling has been carried out over several years the birds started to move elsewhere. But unless this is done across a whole city the birds will simply move to new areas nearby. It doesn't solve the problem.

The issue has become so contentious in Bath that the Council has organised public meetings to take people's views and to promote new initiatives to reduce the impact of gulls. The local MP Don Foster also raised the matter in Parliament in 2009 suggesting that the grounds for issuing a general license be broadened to include nuisance and damage to property. He has also pointed out that current control measures are not working and that we need to find a solution that can be applied in all the cities affected. At a recent scrutiny session in Bath much time was devoted to finding ways of reducing the availability of food within the city. That is certainly an important issue that needs to be addressed. Having refuse strewn about the pavements every day is unsightly and squalid. But solving that problem will not reduce the numbers of gulls. It is likely that such food represents only a small fraction of a gull's diet. I suspect that we will continue to be faced with a steadily rising number of urban gulls so long as ample food is available to them at landfill sites. Even with the most rigorous and concerted action to remove their nests and stop them breeding, it seems likely that large numbers of birds are going to be around for some time to come.

KITTIWAKE

Of all our British gulls the kittiwake is most deserving of being called a seagull as it spends most of the year foraging out in the Atlantic well away from land. It therefore comes as something of a surprise to find these oceanic birds coming to nest by the River Tyne in the centre of Newcastle. Yet small colonies of kittiwakes have existed in coastal towns and cities of northeast England and Scotland for many years. They first started to make use of man-made structures when a small colony was established on the harbour wall at Granton near Edinburgh in 1931 and at Dunbar in 1934. By 1969 there were 410 pairs in seven urban colonies the

FIG 151. Kittiwakes nesting on the Tyne Bridge in Newcastle.

largest of which, Dunbar, held 163 nests. Others were located along the Tyne, at Lowestoft in Suffolk, and a small colony at Thurso in Caithness. At that time most were on warehouses and similar buildings with birds nesting on window ledges. Some were on piers or sea walls. All were in coastal towns except for those 16 km up the Tyne at Newcastle and Gateshead (Cramp, 1971).

Some of these colonies on warehouses along the Tyne have been in existence since 1949 and one at North Shields was the subject of detailed studies over 30 years which found that breeding success closely matched the vicissitudes of the North Sea herring fishery. The most famous of these Tyneside colonies occupied the ledges of a giant grain warehouse known as Baltic Flour Mills where the birds became firmly established in the 1960s. However, they were displaced when the building was converted into an art gallery in the late 1990s. As compensation Gateshead Council erected an artificial nest platform on the riverside at Baltic Square in 1998. This Kittiwake Tower was an immediate success and is arguably the most unusual Local Nature Reserve in the country. In 2001 the Tower was moved half a mile downstream to a permanent location at Saltmeadows where some 100 young were fledged in 2002. By 2007 the colony had grown to 130 nests.

Many of the birds displaced from the Baltic Flour Mill found a new home on the Tyne Bridge where two pairs first nested in 1997. The next few years saw a rapid expansion of this colony with 13 nests in 1998, 39 in 1999, 82 in 2000 and 160 by 2002. Since then the numbers have levelled off at about 150 pairs. I visited the colony in early June 2007 when many young birds had just hatched. The characteristic 'kittiwaic' calls, together with the strong smell of guano, which covered the pavement below the bridge, immediately brought back memories of the great seabird colonies of Bempton cliffs in Yorkshire. Most of the nests were on metal supports beneath the bridge but some birds used stone ledges on the buttresses, and an overflow colony was developing on the window ledges of an adjacent solicitor's office. It is an extraordinary place for these birds to be nesting, surrounded by roads and buildings, yet they appeared to be doing well.

The kittiwake is one of our most attractive gulls with its pure white head, dark eye and bright yellow bill. It is quite distinct from other similar sized gulls, and is easily recognisable. There are regular records of kittiwakes being seen in London along the Thames and at some of the reservoirs. But as an urban breeding bird it has yet to spread from its stronghold in the northeast.

BLACK GUILLEMOT

Like kittiwakes the black guillemot has established breeding colonies in a few coastal towns where its presence comes as something of a surprise, not least because the birds in such places tend to be remarkably tame. A few nest in harbour walls at Portpatrick in Wigtownshire, but the largest colony is at Bangor in County Down on the southern shore of Belfast Lough. Here they have been known since 1911 when they were first found nesting in the old pier. The colony was later described by Edward Armstrong in *Birds of the Grey Wind* (1946), when there were no more than about six pairs.

Julian Greenwood kept records of the colony since 1985 when seven pairs nested successfully on the North Pier and another two pairs attempted to nest with less success on the South Pier (Greenwood, 2010). In 1987 work began on building a new marina and Greenwood managed to get work stopped until young birds had fledged. This led to a re-examination of the plans to see whether nest boxes could be incorporated which would be suitable for the guillemots. In 1989 the architects installed 27 nest boxes under the new central pier of the marina, together with several other plastic tubes elsewhere. Some of these were occupied immediately, and the colony has grown substantially since that time. Today about 30 pairs nest annually in the harbour, amidst the hustle and bustle of a busy yacht marina and commercial fishing jetty. Birds are not easily scared off, but have become accustomed to a high level of human activity and can often be approached to within 2 m.

FIG 152. Black guillemots nest in the harbour wall at Bangor, Co. Down. (Julian Greenwood)

This may be explained by the fact that the birds are around the harbour for much of the year. After the young have fledged towards the end of July the adults leave for a couple of months, but they come back again from October onwards to take possession of preferred nest chambers which they occupy throughout the winter. Most birds stay faithful to their nest hole from year to year. Even in winter plumage they sit tight in their nest chambers, securing a place for the coming season.

Breeding success is comparable to that of birds in more natural conditions. Of 563 breeding attempts between 1985 and 2009 a total of 557 young were fledged, making the average for the whole colony one young per pair. Those nesting in the older holes in the North Pier have achieved 1.3 young per pair, which is the same as birds nesting on sea cliffs of Shetland. Some predation has been observed, particularly from herring gulls which have occasionally been seen taking young birds and even adults out of the nest holes.

The increased population of guillemots at Bangor has been due largely to the installation of purpose built nest boxes which have been very successful. Similar provision has since been made in the new harbour wall at Glenarm, County Antrim, and wooden nest boxes have been provided for guillemots on Strangford Lough. Perhaps the most unusual example of a black guillemot nest site was on one of the ferries plying between the islands in Shetland!

BLACK REDSTART

The black redstart is a relative newcomer to the UK as a breeding species and the fact that it chooses to inhabit some of the most run down urban environments gives it a rather special status. Although there are generally less than 100 breeding pairs in the UK most of these occur in areas of urban dereliction and decay, and it has become something of a flagship species for urban biodiversity. The story of its colonisation in London was described in detail by Fitter (1945) who referred to it as 'quite the most remarkable in the annals of London ornithology in the past half century'.

Originally a bird of mountainous regions of southern Europe the black redstart gradually spread northwards reaching Jutland in the second half of the nineteenth century and Scandinavia in the 1940s. As it spread the bird adapted to man-made conditions, frequently using buildings instead of cliffs for nest sites and song posts and obtaining a ready supply of insects which it found in urban wastelands. Throughout much of Europe it is now well established as a bird of towns and villages.

Not long after the first breeding record for the UK on the Sussex coast in 1923, a pair was found nesting in London on the Palace of Engineering at Wembley. This was in 1926 when the building lay unused a year after the Wembley Exhibition. The birds nested on a ledge 18 feet (5.5 m) from the ground above the main doors. In fact three pairs nested on the building every year from 1926 to 1941. Other records at this time were sporadic. A cock bird took up territory on the Natural History Museum in 1927 and a pair was recorded breeding in a shed at Woolwich Arsenal in 1933. In 1936 Max Nicholson heard a male singing from high buildings near Marsham Street in Westminster, and another pair occupied Senate House in Bloomsbury in 1939. The first confirmed breeding in inner London was from the precincts of Westminster Abbey where a pair raised two broods in 1940. By that time at least four other males held territory in central London (LNHS, 1964). One wonders how many other pairs there were in London at this time in the more inaccessible gas works and power stations. Elsewhere in the country the bird was known to nest in Cornwall in 1929, Cambridge in 1936 and was well established in Dover by 1940 (Fitter, 1965).

By 1940 the scene was set for black redstarts to colonise London, and German bombing raids, which laid much of central London to waste, undoubtedly helped. The landscape of bombsites was almost exactly what the bird required in terms of insect-rich habitat with plenty of nest sites, and the population expanded accordingly. By 1942 there were 20 singing males in central London (Fitter, 1945).

FIG 153. Black redstart: a truly urban bird in the UK. (Jerzy Strzelecki)

For the next decade the species was particularly associated with bombsites in the capital and the population reached a peak of nearly 30 pairs by 1950. This period also marked the start of a gradual increase in the population in southeast England with strong populations in Cambridge and Dover.

Some birds reached Birmingham where they first bred at the University in 1943, but colonisation was slow and it was not until 1958 that a local population became established, again mainly associated with inner city bombsites and other derelict land. The old Snow Hill railway station, and Gas Street Basin on the Worcester and Birmingham Canal were particularly favoured locations. There was a further increase in the population during the 1960s and 1970s as land was cleared for redevelopment and birds moved out into neighbouring industrial areas. A peak of 34 pairs came during 1985–89 when the region's manufacturing base collapsed, leaving many large buildings empty and derelict (Harrison, 2005). Many of these sites have since been developed and numbers have subsequently declined. The Birmingham area now supports only 5 to 15 breeding pairs. A few pairs have bred on city centre buildings and industrial sites in other cities such as Norwich and Leicester and on sugar beet factories in East Anglia.

A survey in London during the 1960s (Meadows, 1970), found that although 7 pairs were still using the few remaining bomb-sites, the majority were associated with large industrial plants such as power stations (20 pairs), gas works

(18 pairs), other smaller industrial areas such as timber yards, railway sidings and Thames-side warehousing (11 pairs), and areas cleared for redevelopment (9 pairs). Since then numbers have varied from year to year with an average of 17 pairs for 1968–72 and 24 for 1988–98. Intensive searches revealed 31 pairs in 2000 and 20 in 2001. A notable feature of its distribution in London is the strong link with rivers, particularly the Thames and Lea. Meadows suggests that the birds are dependent on the chironomid midges abundant along these waterways.

National figures show a surge in numbers in 1969 which was maintained throughout the 1970s with fewer birds using coastal cliffs and bombsites, more often preferring modern industrial complexes. In 1977 a detailed UK survey revealed a minimum of 104 territory-holding males, with a broad spectrum of nesting places, ranging from derelict industrial sites to gas works, sewage farms, railway sheds, power stations and town centres (Morgan & Glue, 1981). Subsequent population estimates suggest that numbers in the UK peaked in 1988 at 118 pairs, falling to 82 in 1989 and 74 in 1990. In 2007 the Rare Breeding Birds Committee published national trends that showed a gradually declining population. However, the recent figures for London revealed by intensive surveys from 2000 onwards suggests that the species is still under-recorded. The main concentrations remain in London and Birmingham, with a scattering of birds in coastal towns of East Sussex, Kent, Essex and Suffolk.

FIG 154. The derelict Battersea Power Station: perfect habitat for the black redstart.

There seems no doubt that bomb-damage provided the initial stimulus for rapid growth of the UK population and that birds took advantage of economic recession in the 1970s and into the 1980s. It is also possible that the heat island effect of London and Birmingham was instrumental to some degree for a species on the edge of its range, making these cities more suitable than would otherwise be the case. Climate change may be expected to facilitate more rapid expansion in future years.

A number of notable buildings have provided nest sites including St Paul's Cathedral, Westminster Abbey, Senate House, the Natural History Museum

FIG 155. Part of a 'living roof' designed to encourage a greater variety of wildlife especially invertebrate species associated with brownfield land. (Fleur Timmer)

and Clare College Cambridge. During the 1980s, when the population was at its peak, birds were frequently seen in central London. One pair held territory on Clapham Junction railway station, the intermittent song being particularly hard to pick out between the frequent passage of trains. Another pair occupied the derelict Broad Street station in the City where the cock bird regularly sang from the roof. On the day that Margaret Thatcher announced the abolition of the Greater London Council a black redstart arrived on the roof of County Hall and sang lustily. As it happens it was nesting on the dilapidated Westminster tube station across the river, but it caused wry smiles amongst GLC staff when I told them it was a bird of derelict buildings (Goode, 1986). At the same time another pair occupied a derelict warehouse adjacent to the William Curtis Ecological Park at Tower Bridge. Long since demolished this site is now occupied by the glass dome of the Greater London Authority where there is no chance of them finding a nest hole today. One of the nicest stories concerns a pair that nested in a mobile crane in Lowestoft Harbour. The parent birds followed the crane around the harbour to feed their chicks, sometimes feeding them on the move (Cocker & Mabey, 2005).

The black redstart is listed as a schedule 1 species under the Wildlife and Countryside Act, making it an offence to disturb the bird during breeding. A pair which nested on the Millennium Dome during its construction almost brought the project to a halt! With the advent of the UK Biodiversity Strategy, local action plans have been drawn up for the black redstart in London, Birmingham and other towns and cities. In London the emphasis was placed on creating living-roofs on buildings to replicate the habitat conditions of urban wastelands. Known by some as 'black redstart roofs', architects are increasingly accepting these ideas and incorporating them into new developments (see also Chapter 16). This has been assisted by a web site: www.blackredstarts.org.uk.

RING-NECKED PARAKEET

Of all the recent additions to our urban fauna this must rank as the most incongruous. To see noisy flocks of bright green parrots in London's parks and woodlands, or in coastal towns of Kent and Sussex, comes as a surprise to many people. Visitors to Kew Gardens frequently report with some excitement that they have seen parrots in the trees, only to be told, 'Yes, they live here'. For people living close to one of the roosting sites there is cause for serious discontent. Even the smaller roosts with several hundred individuals are noisy affairs as the birds repeatedly shriek their shrill calls from the treetops. The fact that they often choose to roost in otherwise quiet suburbs makes their presence all the more unwelcome, particularly so when some of the larger roosts now contain many thousands of birds.

The ring-necked (or rose-ringed) parakeet is a native of southern Asia and northern Africa, but the UK population is thought to be derived from birds of Asian stock (Morgan, 1993). In the Indian sub-continent these birds inhabit a range of habitats including towns and villages, lightly wooded areas, orchards and farmland, as well as the rhododendron-covered Himalayan foothills of Nepal. Throughout their range they are considered to be a serious agricultural pest of fruit and grain. In towns and cities large numbers congregate around warehouses where they split open sacks to feed on grain; whilst in fields and orchards they congregate in hundreds when fruit or grain is ripe. Studies in India found that these parakeets could reduce crop yields of maize and sorghum by up to 70–80 per cent. The bird is remarkably successful. It is the most widely introduced species of parrot in the world, with naturalised populations in 35 countries on 5 continents. In Europe there are well-established populations in Germany, Belgium and the Netherlands as well as those in the UK.

These birds are widely kept as cage birds in the UK and it is probable that escapes from captivity were the initial source of the UK population. Some claim that these were from an aviary at Marlow where flocks were periodically allowed to fly freely around the grounds. Another possible source was an aviary at Syon Park damaged by fragments falling from an aircraft in the early 1970s. It is even suggested that some birds escaped from Shepperton Studios in 1951 after they had been used in the filming of *The African Queen*. There are many stories. Whatever the origin the bird has dramatically increased in numbers over the past forty years and is now well established as a breeding bird in the UK.

As long ago as the 1930s a few were living wild in gardens near Epping, but there is no evidence that they nested. Other sightings occurred from time to

FIG 156. Ring-necked parakeets have become frequent visitors to garden bird feeders.

time but it was not until the late 1960s that small groups of birds were seen in several London suburbs. The first breeding in London was confirmed in 1971 near Croydon, and at Claygate near Esher, but from the number of records at that time it seems likely that they had been nesting successfully for several years. The same year there was a flock of 22 in north London around Woodford Green and Higham Park near Walthamstow. A family party of parakeets was seen at Southfleet near Rochester in Kent in 1969, and two years later breeding was confirmed at Margate. Even then it was said to be spreading to the Medway towns from Gravesend. Parakeets also bred in Stockport, Greater Manchester, in 1976 (Lever, 1977). By 1981 the species achieved its first mention in the London Bird Report, with records from 24 locations in London. A total of 110 birds was recorded at a roost near Beckenham at the end of 1980.

In December 1983 it was officially accepted by the British Ornithologists Union as a naturalised species, with an estimated UK population of 500 to 1,000 birds, almost entirely confined to the London area and towns of north Kent. Small outlying populations were reported from Sussex and Dorset. The first national census of 1992 found up to 2000 birds. In London there were records of 700 birds in 1992 (LBR) with 150 pairs recorded as breeding. A count of all known roosts in 1996 produced a total of 1,508 birds (Pithon & Dytham, 1999). By 1998 the aggregate total of all peak winter roost counts in the London area reached

2,845 birds (Hewlett, 2002), yet only a year later there were 2,500 at one roost
alone. By the winter of 2001/2 the roost at Esher reached over 4,000 birds (Butler,
2002), and the UK population in 2002 was estimated to be over 6,000, with
breeding in at least five counties. On 24 August 2003, there were 6,918 birds at
Esher Rugby Club, a roost that held only 600 birds in 1994. Counts during winter
2003/4 gave a UK total of 10,000 birds (BTO, 2005). Since then the population has
grown considerably. Counts from six London roosts totalled 20,123 birds in 2010
(LBR). Since 2010 counts have been organised on a regular three monthly basis
at all the known roosts in order to obtain an accurate estimate of the population.
This was part of a PhD study at Imperial College London by Hannah Peck under
the title 'Project Parakeet'. It found a maximum figure of 30,869 birds in July
2010, including all large roosts in London and Ramsgate. So in less than 40 years
the population had grown from zero to over 30,000 birds (Project Parakeet, 2011).

Their spread has been equally spectacular. In the 1980s breeding in London was
restricted to very specific areas, especially along the Thames valley in west London
and in the southern suburbs from Carshalton to Sidcup extending in to Lewisham
and Greenwich. In the Thames valley birds were reported from Old Windsor
and Runnymede eastwards through Shepperton and extending into London as
far as Chiswick. A few were known to nest at Osterley Park, and Chiswick House
Grounds, with a concentration along the Thames around Brentford and Kew.
The more southerly birds were spread through the leafy suburbs of Croydon
and Bromley with breeding confirmed at Beddington, Park Langley, Scadbury
Park, Petts Wood, Foots Cray Meadow and possibly at Beckenham Place Park and
Greenwich Park. At that time there were no records of breeding in north London,
or in the centre of the city (Goode, 1986). In all these areas the birds favoured
mature or old trees for nest sites, hence the preference for park landscapes.

Since that time the birds have built up much larger populations in the
original areas and also spread widely throughout the metropolis. The bird is
now particularly well established in west London and the Thames valley with
large concentrations from Windsor and Wraysbury eastwards to Shepperton
and Hampton Court. Further into London many birds occur along the Thames
between Kingston and Kew, but also at Syon Park, Chiswick House grounds and
Ravenscourt Park. Richmond and Bushy Parks have substantial numbers nesting
in the ancient trees. Another concentration lies further south around Esher
and Claygate, and in old parklands along the Mole Valley, in the southwestern
fringes of London. Others are concentrated in a swathe from Sutton and Croydon
through Beckenham and Sidcup, to Greenwich and Bexley in southeast London.
Pairs at Epping Forest near Woodford in 1994 and Kenwood on Hampstead
Heath in 2000 were the first evidence of breeding in north London, since

when they have spread through the parks, woodlands and cemeteries around Hampstead Heath and Highgate northwards into Barnet, and northeastwards into Epping Forest. Movement into the East End has been relatively slow, but they reached Tower Hamlets Cemetery in 2009 where they have bred since 2010. The London Bird Report for 2008 recorded parakeets from 206 sites, with a marked spread northwards and eastwards into Hertfordshire and Essex.

Although parakeets were first seen in inner London at Battersea Park in 1986 they have only started to colonise central London parks and squares since 2000. A few pairs have bred in Kensington Gardens since 2000 and can now be seen regularly at the bird feeders not far from the Peter Pan statue. They were first reported in St James's Park in 2005 and Eaton Square in 2007, and are now seen frequently in both. It seems that it will not be long before these birds are a familiar sight in any London park.

Elsewhere parakeets are well established with substantial populations in towns of north Kent from Gravesend to Ramsgate. But they have also spread northwards, colonising Birmingham, Manchester, Liverpool and Sheffield (Balmer et al., 2013). Others occur on Tyneside and locally in central Scotland. Winter sightings show a wider distribution (see Chapter 15).

Assessing the total number of breeding pairs has inevitably resulted in underestimates with pairs scattered so widely, but the bird is much easier to count at its roosting sites which gather birds from a wide area. A detailed study in 2001–3 revealed that the population was increasing at an average annual rate of 25 per cent based on roost counts (Butler, 2003). Population models for Greater London suggested an even higher figure of 30 per cent per year, with a range expansion of 0.4 km per year. Reproductive rates were found to be higher than expected, with 1.9 fledglings per nest. By using telemetry to track male birds Butler also discovered that the males continue to roost communally throughout the nesting season, leaving the female on the nest. Comparison of the total numbers of birds at roosts before and during the nesting season thus provides a measure of the total breeding population.

Parakeets have adapted well to life in suburbia, where they have been assisted by the copious quantities of food provided for birds in private gardens. They regularly feed at bird tables and on peanut feeders, as well as taking fruit, especially cherries and plums, from gardens and orchards, and nuts of hazel and sweet chestnut. They are particularly partial to flower buds of trees, stripping trees of young buds in spring. The species seems able to withstand cold spells in winter, and probably benefits from the ameliorating effects of London's heat island. Interestingly the Monk Parakeet (*Myiopsitta monachus*), a native of South America, has become naturalised in Chicago, USA despite winter temperatures of –33°C.

FIG 157. There is concern that the presence of parakeets may prevent the effective use of feeders by other garden birds.

For nest sites parakeets use holes in old trees, many of which are old holes of green woodpecker. Suburban parks, cemeteries and large Victorian gardens are particularly favoured, as also are long-established parkland landscapes with ancient trees, and wooded riversides with old crack willows. Examples include a ginkgo tree in Beddington churchyard near Croydon; Kew Gardens where numerous pairs nest in a wide variety of exotic trees; Kensal Green Cemetery where several pairs use large old poplars; and the ancient oaks of Kenwood at Hampstead and Richmond Park provide many nest sites. Elsewhere, along the Thames they use willows, poplars and alders.

There has been a roost in Reigate in Surrey since the late 1980s when they used a tall fir tree in a garden close to the town centre. Since then the roost has moved eastwards through Redhill in a series of steps. Each time the birds have chosen prominent trees (of sycamore, lime or oak) about 1 or 2 km further east. For a time they roosted in trees by Redhill sports centre, later moving to trees around the pond in Frenches Road, and then moved again to East Surrey College. The roost totalled over 350 birds in 2005/6 made up of many small flocks of 10–40 birds. By January 2012 this same roost had grown to about 1,000 birds. One evening in spring 2005 many of the flocks heading for the roost stopped off at a small roadside horse-chestnut tree in a suburban crescent, the flowers of which were just opening. Flock after flock gathered in this small tree until it was filled with over a hundred birds. Within minutes the tree was decimated as the birds stripped all the flowers, dropping many flower buds to the ground. Whilst watching this I witnessed a sparrow hawk catch one of the parakeets, which caused the whole flock to take to the air screaming. Whilst on the subject of predators it is worth mentioning that peregrine falcons frequently catch parakeets, as evidenced by prey remains at the Citybank building in Lewisham town centre (Archer, pers. comm.).

Many of the roosts in the London area have remained in the same place since the 1980s and local residents have seen the numbers swell from only fifty to several thousand birds. Examples include Lewisham Crematorium, Hither Green Cemetery, Kew Gardens, Richmond Park, Osterley Park and Bushy Park. The long established roost in a row of poplar trees at Esher Rugby Club led to the ladies team being known as the Parakeets. The club may have missed the birds when this roost moved to the local sewage farm, but local residents were extremely relieved at the respite. Recently new locations have been favoured including the copse at Wormwood Scrubs open space, Perivale golf course, Mitcham Common, Stanwell by Heathrow Airport and West Ewell.

Times are changing. From being celebrated as a curious oddity during the initial years of its colonisation, the ring-necked parakeet is now regarded more cautiously. With over 30,000 birds, and the population still rising, questions are being asked as to whether it poses a threat to native species of birds. There is concern that parakeets have the capacity to out-compete native cavity-nesting species as they start nesting in late February before most native species start breeding. Birds that could be affected include jackdaw, stock dove, kestrel, starling, nuthatch and the larger woodpeckers. A study in Belgium found no evidence of native species being disadvantaged, except perhaps nuthatch, and Butler (2003) also concluded that there was no evidence at that time of any effect on native species, though he carefully qualified that by saying that the situation may well change. In view of the huge increase in numbers of parakeets there is also concern that native species may be disadvantaged by the presence of parakeets at bird tables and other garden feeding stations.

In view of its reputation as a serious agricultural pest in its native land there are good grounds for concern that it might prove to become a serious problem in the UK. So far, despite the large number of parakeets now present in the UK, there have been few instances of agricultural damage. However, one example illustrates the potential problems that could well arise in the future. Painshill Park Vineyard in Surrey reported up to 200 parakeets regularly visiting and eating the grape crop, resulting in a loss of crop and need for preventative control measures, costing an estimated £5,000 annually (FERA, 2009). Gardeners are also aware of parakeets taking fruit from trees, and sweet corn from allotments. An amusing article in the *Independent* newspaper by its science editor Michael McCarthy described his experience with parakeets. He is very familiar with the birds as he lives at the epicenter of their operations along the Thames near Kew and had considered them a pleasing addition to the local avifauna until June 2010 when a flock of parakeets descended on his cherry tree, with its fine crop of fruit. Over several days they stripped it bare, leaving not a single cherry. His verdict: 'I sense that after years of being Mr Popular in the bright green suit, for *Psittacula krameri* there may be trouble ahead.'

In fact trouble had already started. In January 2010 the government added the ring-necked parakeet to the list of species that can be legally killed without special permission (i.e. by a general license) if damage is being done. This means that it has been recognised as a potential pest species and this was the first step in providing measures for its control. 'About time too!' some would say, particularly those plagued day after day by the raucus cacophony of one of the larger roosts. But they will not be the ones to benefit from this change as it is intended primarily to prevent damage to crops or wild birds. Perhaps what we are witnessing is only the first stage of colonisation. The parakeet may have started as an urban bird in the UK, but as its population continues to grow a bigger question will be whether it will extend its range into rural areas, as it has in other naturalised populations in Europe (Butler, 2003). If it does then there is a very real likelihood that it will become a significant agricultural pest. Urban life may have provided easy pickings and encouraged rapid colonisation, but we have yet to see what is in store in the future.

PIED WAGTAIL

During the last century the pied wagtail has moved into towns and cities and is now a familiar sight, not only by ponds in town parks, but also in streets and shopping precincts. Normally inconspicuous, seen only one or two at a time, it is a bird that has nevertheless become well adapted to city living, utilising a very specific range of habitats. Short mown grass is one of these, so bowling greens and cricket pitches are very much favoured, and according to the BTO it is a regular visitor to 10 per cent of private gardens, especially those with large lawns. But equally it is at home on the hard surfaces of pavements and roadways amongst parked cars, or up on the rooftops. It is just as likely to be found around industrial sites such as cement factories and sewage farms. All these places have one thing in common, the availability of insects. Being one of our few resident insectivorous birds it has demonstrated a remarkable ability to make the most of the urban environment. Feeding on the local bowling green these birds make short sharp dashes hither and thither to catch flies and other insects. On rooftops they will follow the gutters, where they find a ready supply of flies and other small invertebrates. Car parks too provide rich pickings in the form of dead insects stuck to the cars. Wagtails have even been known to visit car-wash plants to collect the dead insects as they are washed away. Sewage farms make a favourite habitat in winter, where they benefit from a continued supply of insects resulting from the warm water and bacterial activity. Parties of birds are frequently seen in winter snapping flies along the concrete channels of old style sewage farms, or hawking from railings around the filterbeds.

Pied wagtails are renowned for nesting in odd places. Hersham sewage farm in London regularly supported ten to twenty pairs during the early 1960s where they nested in the clinker walls of the sprinklers, inside buildings, and even in abandoned cars (Parr, 1972). Others in strange places include a pair nesting in the retaining wall at South Kensington Underground station, two broods raised in a flower tub at Imperial College, and another successful nest on the engine of a tractor in daily use at Walton on Thames (Hewlett, 2002). At gravel pits one pair nested in the framework supporting a conveyor belt, another in a working excavator. The birds would wait whilst a lorry was filled with sand, and then quickly feed the young before the next lorry arrived. Horticultural greenhouses are a great attraction. At a nursery specialising in carnation growing near Woking the greenhouses always had wagtails flitting about inside. George Goldspink, who was in charge told me they were always there and took no notice when you went in. Quite a few pairs nested amongst the carnations. Boat yards and builder's yards are both favoured places, with lots of nooks and crannies for nests. In the village of Lympstone beside the Exe estuary a pair which feed along the tide-line caused much delight by nesting in a woodpile beside a house on the harbour front.

One feature which makes the pied wagtail truly an urban bird is its habit of roosting in large numbers in town centres, where particular trees are used year after year. Large communal roosts of wagtails have been known for over 100 years. Writing in 1902 Cornish tells of hundreds of wagtails roosting in the reeds of a pond at Golders Hill near Hampstead. But the first record of a truly urban roost was in the plane trees of O'Connell Street in Dublin, first known in 1929 and still in use seventy years later. The largest number of birds seen was 3,600 in 1950. In the 1990s numbers averaged about 750, but since then most of the trees have been removed and by 2003 only 100 birds remained.

FIG 158. Pied wagtail nest in a woodpile. (John Welton)

Several roosts were known in built up areas of London during the 1930s. One roost of 150 birds was in holly trees along Balham High Road. Another, in pollarded plane trees along the main London Road in Thornton Heath, was first commented on in 1937 and was still in use in 1950. Birds were tracked from their feeding grounds at Beddington sewage farm to this roost, which in September 1949 held nearly 300 birds (Homes, 1964).

During the late 1970s a study of London's wagtail roosts was carried out to try to assess the total number of pied wagtails wintering in the capital (Chandler, 1979). Ten roosts were found within Greater London including several in the city centre. One of these was in plane trees by St Stephens's church in Walbrook, in the heart of the City of London. Some 900 birds were congregated here in October 1978 and 500 the following January. Other roosts were in plane trees along Buckingham Palace Road and at Hammersmith Broadway. The largest gathering at that time was in laurel bushes outside the civic hall in Orpington that regularly held over 2,000 birds, with a peak of 4,300 in January 1977. The thick evergreen bushes offered good protection from the weather and maybe accounted for the size of this roost. Other more recent town centre roosts include shopping areas in the middle of Bath, Norwich and Wimbledon, the Maltings in Ely, and Redhill town centre in Surrey.

This last roost was one that I got to know particularly well. As dusk approached small flocks of wagtails could be seen converging on the town centre from all directions, where they gathered in large numbers on the rooftops of shops and offices. At this time they were very obvious, with their persistent 'chissick' calls coming from all the surrounding buildings. At times they would all take flight, but eventually they settled down and then, a few at a time, they dropped down into a small maple tree planted by the local civic society to brighten the town centre. As they gradually disappeared it was difficult to believe that up to 300 birds might be congregated together in the tree. But later in the autumn when it lost its leaves they were exposed to full view with light from the adjacent offices and street lamps. I was always surprised how few people noticed them as they walked by underneath. During periods of particularly cold weather the whole flock would move to warmer surroundings in nearby holly bushes (Goode, 1986).

It seems that this habit of roosting in town centres is a good means of finding a secure and warm roosting place. Certainly the temperature in amongst buildings will be significantly higher than in a rural reed bed. But wagtails are good at finding warm places. The secluded courtyards of hospitals, like Addenbrookes at Cambridge, provide ideal conditions. One of their favourite roosting sites in northeast London is on the boiler-house roof of Rye House Power station. In Birmingham large roosts of up to 1500 birds were found on the roof of a factory at Sparkhill and another on a building in Brierley Hill (Teagle, 1978). Foundries in the Black Country, the glass roof of the GPO in Leicester, Bacton Gas terminal in Suffolk and Cockenzie power station near Edinburgh have all provided roost sites.

Then there are the birds that have found heated glasshouses. In cold weather hundreds of wagtails have been observed perched in serried ranks along the heating pipes. Sheltered well from rain and wind this must be the ultimate in luxury. But it is not always safe. Cats have been known to get in, and in one place little owls are said to have wreaked havoc! One of the strangest roosting sites is on revolving arms of sprinklers at sewage treatment works, where the birds spend the night going round and round. But at least it is relatively warm.

CHAPTER 10

Badger and Fox

BADGER

EACH YEAR IN MAY a small graveyard in Bath becomes the centre of activity for badgers which have their sett under the tombstones. The graveyard is situated along a busy main road in a heavily built up part of the city. Yet I was told by the lady living next door that, 'there are 14 resident badgers and they regularly run along the churchyard wall', which bounds her garden. An inspection of the sett revealed about ten holes, one of which had a fresh mound of soil outside, about a metre high, with a scattering of human bones on top! When the badgers emerge at dusk the young ones can be heard racing round the gravel paths with much grunting and squealing. The graveyard itself has little habitat suitable for badgers to forage in, but the wrought iron gate is carefully designed with a hole for badgers to pass through on their nightly excursions. From their sanctuary in the burial ground they make excursions around the neighbourhood, foraging in adjacent gardens and over lawns and flowerbeds of a nearby park.

For badgers to exist in such a situation seems hardly likely, but Bath is riddled with badgers. Amazingly the local environmental record centre has nearly 100 records of badger setts in the city. They are by no means confined to the wooded slopes around the edges, but can occur almost anywhere in even the smallest patches of open land. Many occur in heavily built-up areas close to the centre, where they manage to exist in overgrown gardens, churchyards, allotments and around the edges of recreation areas. A large sett with several holes has even been constructed under the rockery in the Botanic Gardens and in the winter of 2008 one of these badgers was regularly seen at midday crossing Victoria Park to gather

FIG 159. Badger's sett in a churchyard in Bath.

vegetables in adjacent allotments. Others live on the steep slopes just below the Georgian buildings of Lansdown Crescent and Somerset Place. From here their nocturnal trips take them up the narrow mews between the houses and along the back lane to visit gardens where they are provided with food. Not far from here is a carefully constructed 'badger gate' in the stonework of a garden wall. It seems that badgers have been well established in the city for many years.

Bath may be unusual in the number of badgers that it supports, but it is not alone among British towns and cities in having a thriving population. Fitter attempted to assess the status of badgers in the London area in 1949, concluding that they were much more common around the capital than was generally supposed, particularly on the chalk hills in the south, and at Epping and Hainault Forests in the north. He found they were still present in Richmond Park, but others previously known from Kew Gardens and Hampstead Heath had disappeared. But it was notable that Fitter's records were mostly from more rural surroundings of London and he did not record any from truly urban areas (Fitter, 1949).

Teagle (1969) organised a more comprehensive study of London's badgers in a survey carried out by the London Natural History Society between 1959 and 1964. It was thought that a badger survey would be of interest to the newly formed Young Naturalists Section of the LNHS, which included Pat Morris and Derek Yaldon, both of whom went on to become specialists in mammal ecology. Nearly 300 setts were recorded, but Teagle states that the actual number was likely to be much greater. As with Fitter's assessment most were outside the truly urban limits of London. Whilst the vast majority were recorded in woodland, 20 were in grounds of institutions or in private gardens, and a few on railway embankments and in parkland. Richmond Park, Wimbledon Common and several open spaces in Croydon all supported badgers. Teagle also referred to a comment by Ernest

FIG 160. Churchyard badger-gate.

Neal that some badgers manage to survive even closer to the centre of the capital, but added, 'the less said about them the better'. He concluded that, 'as the badger is a less adaptable animal than the fox, it is unlikely to prove very successful as an urban colonist', though he quoted a number of instances where animals had been seen in central London, including one crossing Putney Bridge, one found dead in South Kensington and another observed by the police at three in the morning crossing Clapham High Street!

From a number of observations early last century Teagle concluded that whilst relatively scarce in 1900 the number of badgers had clearly increased and by the 1960s it had become quite numerous in some areas. Even at that time he found instances where people were feeding the local badgers, including a group of housewives in south London who let their neighbours know when the visitors arrived so that they could all enjoy the performance. The *Daily Mail* ran a story in 1962 about the vendors of a house in Weybridge expressing their hopes that the new owners would continue to feed the badgers that came regularly to their french windows.

During the early 1970s Dorothy Smith kept a diary of visits to her garden in Bath by badgers which had made their sett on a piece of undeveloped land little over half a mile from the city centre (Smith, 1974). *Brocky the Bathwick Badger* is a delightful book which gives an insight into the immense pleasure that badgers can give to urban residents. In his introduction Ernest Neal says,

> Many of our towns and cities now contain resident populations of badgers,
> the most usual cause of this phenomenon being the spread of urban areas into
> occupied badger country ... Where conditions have not become too intolerable
> badgers have adapted remarkably well and exploited the opportunities provided by
> the changed environment and enforced human associations.

Clearly changes were afoot and these early anecdotes illustrate the beginnings of what was to become a significant change in the lifestyle of badgers, especially after they became legally protected in 1973.

In the late 1970s Stephen Harris of Bristol University embarked on studies of urban badgers in Bristol, and as a prelude to this work he gathered information on the distribution of urban badgers in Britain by sending a questionnaire to environmental health officers, local naturalists and Mammal Society recorders. About 400 local authorities were contacted and, remarkably, 378 replied. The results suggested that at that time very few towns and cities had resident urban badger populations. The four places where badgers were reported to be most numerous were southwest London, Bristol, Bath and South Benfleet in Essex. It is notable that all of these were places where sizable patches of long established woodland occurred within the urban area. Badgers were also reported from Edinburgh, the Birmingham conurbation, Sussex coastal towns and some of the towns around London. Harris concluded that Bristol probably contained more badger setts than any other city in Britain (Harris, 1984). Since that time urban badgers appear to have become more widespread. Well established populations have been studied in Brighton, Hastings, Swindon and Yeovil, and Defra has received complaints about urban badgers from every region of England (Roper, 2010).

To find out exactly how many setts there were in Bristol Harris undertook a detailed survey in 1981–2 which covered about 130 km² including the city of Bristol, suburbs of Kingswood and Filton, Avonmouth Docks and the parkland and factory estates adjacent to the city. In addition, for two areas of Bristol where badgers were known to frequent gardens regularly, all the residents were contacted to request information on badger activity in their gardens. The survey revealed a total of 346 setts in three distinct parts of the city (Harris, 1984) and an estimated total population of 218 badgers (Harris & Cresswell, 1988). Within the three areas of the city occupied by badgers there was a mean density of 9.5 setts per km² which is comparable with that recorded in many rural areas. Harris concluded that most of the larger setts persisted as relicts in patches of land such as parkland and wasteland that had survived urban encroachment. Some of these setts were long established, but in other areas there was evidence of new setts being created in urban habitats such as gardens, factory sites and even under sheds and buildings.

Harris and others went on to study Bristol's badgers in greater depth and found a number of differences from rural populations in both behaviour and food preferences. Although different social groups could be recognised they varied substantially in size, and were inconsistent over time. Compared with

TABLE 3. Habitats from which the 346 badger setts in Bristol were recorded (Harris, 1984).

Habitat	Number of setts
Wooded banks, woodland	143
Wasteland, scrub, disused gardens	65
Gardens	42
Fields, sports grounds, paddocks	21
Rubbish tips	13
Golf courses	11
Disused quarries	11
Under sheds, buildings	11
Allotments	6
Hedgerows	6
Factory sites	4
Under walls	4
Railway banks	3
School grounds	2
Old drains	2
Ditches	1
Cemeteries	1
Total	**346**

rural badgers it was found that home ranges of different social groups overlapped more and territorial boundaries were not well defined. Instead of clearly marking the boundaries of their territory with dung pits or latrines these urban badgers had their latrines much closer to their setts. It was also found that compared to rural badgers the average time of emergence was an hour to an hour and a half later (Cresswell & Harris, 1988).

Harris suggests that the reason why these badgers didn't defend their territories to the same degree as their rural counterparts was probably due to the inherent lack of predictability of the urban environment. If you cannot predict with certainty the best feeding areas then there is no point in defending the boundaries of the territory. So the Bristol badgers resorted to simply defending the immediate neighbourhood of the sett. Also there was a lack of stability in the population owing to underlying variability of mortality rates, which led to fluctuations in the size of social groups and thus to the size of their territory.

But the most notable difference between these badgers and those in rural areas was in their diet. Faecal analysis showed that their food was enormously varied, and that the badgers ate different kinds of food at different times of year. In this respect their diet seemed very different from rural badgers, which were thought to be specialist earthworm feeders (Kruuk & Parish, 1981). In Bristol earthworms never exceeded 30 per cent of their diet and were only a supplement to other food sources. Most earthworms were eaten between December and May, and other invertebrates from April to July. Vertebrate prey was rare at all times but most common in May and June when young fledgling birds were available. Vegetables were eaten rarely, but most frequently in May and June when most damage occurred to garden crops. Fruit was of major importance from August to November amounting to 60 per cent of the diet at that time. Scavenged food, including scraps put on compost heaps and food put out specifically for the badgers, provided up to 40 per cent of their diet between December and May (Harris & Cresswell, 1988). It seems that much of the variability in behaviour throughout the year was due to the need for these urban badgers to exploit a wide range of food sources. Their average home range varied from only 10 ha in the winter to over 50 ha in the spring.

As part of his studies Harris (1984) attempted to assess the damage done by badgers, by sending questionnaires to householders. Out of nearly 1,600 returns he found that rifling dustbins (16 per cent) and breaking fences (10 per cent) were the two commonest causes of damage. Others included various digging activities, including holes dug in lawns, flower beds and compost heaps, also dung pits dug in the garden and fruit cages damaged. Damage to vegetables was suffered by nearly 20 per cent of households, with carrots by far the most popular crop taken. Although damage was a regular occurrence many householders regarded it as tolerable, and accepted that they could no longer grow crops such as carrots and strawberries. Predation on pets was negligible. Other more alarming damage, though fortunately infrequent, included digging up rockeries and drains and even digging under sheds. It seems that compared to the impact of urban foxes in

FIG 161. Badgers will take food wherever it is available, including refuse bins and compost heaps. (Paul Hobson/FLPA)

the same area, badgers presented more problems, especially as a result of digging and breaking fences.

But the problems recorded by Harris were as nothing compared with some of the more problematic badgers of today. Since the 1970s we have seen a spread in the occurrence of urban badgers and feeding has become popular in many places. I described a number of examples in London (Goode, 1986) where local badger populations were clearly dependent on artificial feeding. One lady in the south London suburb of Sanderstead put out syrup sandwiches every night for many years, and was rewarded by a regular troop of up to eight badgers enjoying the feast. But not everyone is so keen to have them in their garden. In July 1985, Mrs Cecily Horsham of Warlingham wrote to the *Croydon Advertiser* about her problems with badgers. It seems that for several years she had enjoyed seeing badgers on their nightly visits to her garden. Even when they started digging holes, which required her to spend a lot of time clearing up piles of rubble, she still did not consider them to be a nuisance until their activity was in danger of undermining her house. Although she took official advice on what to do nothing really worked. Even galvanised wire mesh fences sunk below ground level did not keep them out. Fortunately the main sett was situated in nearby woodland

FIG 162. Badgers are regular visitors to gardens in cities such as Bristol, Bath and Brighton. (Jeremy Early/FLPA)

and eventually the combined efforts of the local badger group and NCC were successful in making her garden badger proof. Her letter to the newspaper concludes:

> *The first act of cruelty to the badgers was perpetrated by the planning department when planning permission was granted to build houses on the fringe of the wood – cruelty to the badgers and unfairness to the unsuspecting house buyers.*

The scenario has been repeated many times since then, with numerous examples of badgers taking up residence in gardens when displaced by new urban developments. Every year brings new shock horror stories, like one reported in the *Daily Mail* in January 2009 about a family in Bournemouth whose garden was being ruined by badgers rooting up the lawn. 'Garden turned into mudbath but family powerless to stop badger invasion' ran the headline. Badgers were thought to have moved from a nearby area of open space that had recently been built on. The owners were precluded from putting up a fence because it would be too close to the sett, and the cost of closing the sett and relocating the badgers would be prohibitively expensive.

Recent work by Roper and colleagues in Brighton, Hastings, Swindon and Yeovil revealed a variety of locations for setts, including:

inaccessible corners of wasteland, a patch of scrub beside some allotments and an overgrown bank behind a terrace of houses. Others were in relatively quiet and untended parts of parks and cemeteries, some in private gardens, and others beneath buildings.

It has been suggested that supplementary feeding may result in artificially high populations of badgers in urban areas, but until recently there has been little evidence to support this. Cresswell considered that such feeding has a role in reducing cub mortality and can result in larger social groups, but whether it increases overall density was debatable. However, detailed investigations of a truly urban population in Brighton in an area of high-density housing and other mixed-use development, showed that group ranges were extremely small, averaging only 9.3 ha, and individual home ranges were even smaller at 4.9 ha (Davison *et al.*, 2008). These badgers had the highest population density ever recorded; about 33 adults per km². Roper (2010) attributes this to the presence of easily available food provided either intentionally or unintentionally by householders: 'Food is present in sufficient quantities that badgers do not need to venture far away from their setts in order to get enough to eat.' The range of one social group was essentially restricted to just two back gardens, immediately adjacent to the main sett, where the owners provided a regular and substantial supply of food.

Legislation to protect badgers was first introduced in 1973 and was mainly intended to protect the animals from badger baiting. Subsequent amendments resulted in the Protection of Badgers Act 1992, which is intended to protect badgers from the incidental effects of lawful activity as well as deliberate attempts to inflict injury or kill badgers.

Under the Act it is illegal to:

- wilfully kill, injure, take, possess or cruelly ill-treat a badger, or attempt to do so;
- interfere with a badger sett by damaging or destroying it;
- obstruct access to, or any entrance of, a badger sett;
- disturb a badger when it is occupying a sett.

A sett is defined as any structure or place which displays signs indicating current use by a badger. This can include culverts, pipes and holes under sheds, piles of boulders, old mines and quarries, etc. Under the 1992 Act any activity causing disturbance of badgers when they are occupying a sett is an offence

FIG 163. Badgers exploring bags of garden rubbish. (David Hosking/FLPA)

unless it is undertaken in accordance with the terms of a disturbance licence from Natural England.

When the Badger Act was first passed in 1973 the emphasis was mainly on preventing cruelty through illegal badger baiting and digging of badgers for 'sport'. One of the reasons why the Badger Protection Society was set up in 1979 was because there had been a spate of such digging around the south London suburbs and it was well known that badger baiting was still going on. Since that time badger protection groups have grown in number and there are now some 60 groups across the country, all of which are now members of the Badger Trust. The Trust campaigns for the protection of badgers and provides advice on badger problems. One of its most useful publications is a leaflet explaining what to do if you have badgers in your garden.

Although many badger groups also act as recorders for local record centres they are still reluctant to release information about the locations of badger setts in view of the continuing threat from those involved in badger baiting. However, some local groups have become rather more outgoing. The Northampton Badger Group recently launched a questionnaire survey to find out how many badgers there are in the town and what people think about having them in their garden. They found a surprising number of badgers living within the Borough boundaries, from the undeveloped fringes to within a mile of the town centre. One group of five setts was discovered in a small housing estate where some householders feed them, whilst others hate them because of the damage they do.

As a result of the Badger Protection Act 1992 there has been a huge change in the way that badgers are treated in relation to planning and urban development. Government guidance states that the presence of badgers, as with other protected species, is a *material consideration* when a local planning authority is considering a planning application. The factors that are considered to be relevant include: the likelihood of disturbing a badger sett, or adversely affecting badgers foraging territory, or links between them, or significantly increasing the likelihood of road or rail casualties amongst badger populations. In effect it has meant that for all planning proposals where badgers may be involved developers are required to undertake detailed surveys as part of the planning process, and to take expert advice with regard to any proposals which might result in disturbance of the badgers. Guidelines for developers issued shortly after the protection of setts came into effect still remain applicable today (English Nature, 1995).

So how are badgers fairing now in urban areas? Recent records from the Bristol Environmental Records Centre suggest that there has been little change since the 1980s. They have 336 sett records for the Unitary Authority area, whilst Harris had a total of 346 setts in much the same area. Elsewhere there may be a process of colonisation, as in the West Midlands where there is still much unused post-industrial land available. In the Cotswolds too badgers seem to be moving into small towns as the population has increased in surrounding rural areas (Cresswell, pers. comm.). London still has its local badgers near Wimbledon Common and Putney Heath (Drakeford & Sutcliffe, 2000) and they have recently returned to Kew Gardens. In Edinburgh there is a thriving population on Corstorphine Hill, and others are dotted round the city at Dreghorn, Mortonhall, Braid Hills and notably in the Royal Botanic Gardens where nine badgers were seen in 2008. Roper in his New Naturalist volume (2010) refers to the badger as a remarkably adaptable and resourceful animal. It has certainly proved to be so in towns and cities.

FOX

The colonisation of British towns and cities by foxes was one of the most dramatic changes in urban wildlife during the second half of the twentieth century. People are now so accustomed to seeing 'urban foxes' in their gardens and around the town it seems hard to believe that before World War II they were almost completely absent from towns and cities. The process of colonisation is well documented in the case of London. From records during the 1930s Fitter (1945) stated that the nearest genuinely wild foxes to the centre of London were found at Hampstead and Mill Hill to the north; Epping Forest and Walthamstow to the east; Elmstead Woods in the Kentish suburbs; and Purley, Wimbledon and Richmond Park in the south and west. All these are places where extensive tracts of woodland and other semi-natural habitat still survived in amongst the rapidly expanding outer suburbs. Fitter initially regarded occasional reports of foxes in inner London as almost certainly escapes from captivity, but by 1949 he accepted that some records could in fact refer to wild invaders from the outer areas. He was witnessing a critical stage in the colonisation of London.

Figures supplied by the Ministry of Agriculture Fisheries and Food (MAFF) for post-war years showed that foxes were present in the Kentish suburbs of London in surprisingly large numbers. Over the eight years from 1947 to 1954 a total of 1,250 foxes were shot. On one occasion 23 were killed on a single drive at Scadbury Park near Bromley. Not surprisingly it was huntsmen who first spotted what was happening. As early as 1949 one hunt secretary in Surrey commented that a fox 'likes to be as near London as he can get, with no aversion to being close to human habitation'. More detailed information came from the London Natural History Society which embarked on surveys of both badgers and foxes in 1959. The resulting review of the fox in the London suburbs (Teagle, 1967) provides a fascinating picture of the early stages of colonisation. From 1959 to 1965 the society collected all records of foxes within the built-up area of London resulting in a detailed map of their distribution. Foxes occupied a broad belt within the outer boroughs, especially around the east and south of London. It was clear that they had penetrated much further into London since Fitter's observations. However, densely built-up central areas were still largely unoccupied, except for scattered pockets where some had gained a foothold.

By the 1960s foxes were no longer restricted to woods and heaths. They had turned their attention to the affluent urban fringe. It seems clear that as the city spread its tentacles out across surrounding countryside foxes found themselves in a win-win situation. They were safe from the hunt and the large secluded gardens of the new leafy suburbs built during the 1930s provided an ideal habitat. Desirable residences for raising cubs were there in plenty, under almost every garden shed, and foxes were already beginning to use a wide range of other urban habitats within the outer boroughs. Teagle listed parks, cemeteries, hospital grounds, building sites, sewage farms and railway embankments, as well as large gardens. Occupation of the outer suburbs had provided the springboard for colonisation of the city.

Records collected during the 1960s provided a valuable snapshot, but it was difficult to appreciate the pace of change that was underway. Foxes had penetrated inwards as far as Greenwich Park and Blackheath, as well as Streatham, Dulwich and south Lambeth. There were also records from Heathrow,

FIG 164. Foxes are now well established in many towns and cities. (Jamie Hall/FLPA)

Feltham and Osterley Park. With hindsight it is clear from Teagle's report that colonisation of central London was already happening. One of the pioneers was a vixen that raised cubs on a bombsite near Stockwell tube station in 1958 and another was living in Hyde Park in 1963. Teagle's assertion that successful colonisation of the inner suburbs seemed unlikely was soon to be proved wrong. Over the next 20 years foxes spread rapidly across central London, adding derelict land, docklands, industrial estates, schools, railway stations and even densely built-up residential areas to the list of places successfully colonised.

In 1982 the London Wildlife Trust organised a phone-in count of foxes and were amazed by the response. Within one month over 2,000 sightings were reported, the peak time on *Foxline* being 3 a.m. By then foxes were living in the heart of the city. I remember one sitting on the pavement opposite the Old Vic Theatre one night. As people left the theatre it melted away into a buddleia patch behind some advertisement hoardings. Another pair raised cubs under a platform in the old Broad Street railway station (whilst it was still in use) five minutes' walk from the Bank of England. It may have been one of those that turned up one night in 1984 in the 'scenes of crimes' office at Snowshill police station near St Paul's Cathedral. The duty policeman locked it up and sent for the RSPCA who transported it to Epping Forest. It had a long walk home (Goode, 1986). Nowadays the police are so used to seeing foxes by night in central London they don't give them a second glance.

London was not unusual. By the 1960s there were reports of foxes from many towns and cities. Some local papers played on the novelty of foxes in town. Others warned that we were in danger of being over-run by packs of vermin roaming the streets. Myths were rife. It was a new phenomenon that required investigation. In the late 1970s researchers in Oxford produced a detailed map of urban fox distribution in England and Wales through responses from over 300 local RSPCA inspectors. Foxes were reported from about 150 towns. The proportion of towns with foxes varied in different parts of the country, with 75 per cent in southeast

England down to only 16 per cent in the north. Large conurbations were more inclined to support foxes than small towns (MacDonald & Newdick, 1982).

Some cities became a focus for detailed studies, notably Bristol and Oxford. Bristol has one of the most intensively studied fox populations in the world. Stephen Harris and a succession of colleagues at Bristol University started their work on the city's foxes in 1968 and their long-term study still continues today. Many residents were aware that foxes had been around since the early 1950s. The Bristol Natural History Society started to take an interest in 1967 with a 'Fox Rally' held on the Clifton Downs. Members drove round the city at night recording foxes. Harris investigated fox populations in two study areas, using the newly developing technique of radio tracking to identify the territories of different family groups. He also encouraged local residents and school children to provide details of active fox earths with cubs which enabled him to estimate the total number of foxes in the city. Harris has subsequently gone on to investigate almost every conceivable aspect of the life of urban foxes, and his long-term study areas have become an invaluable asset. In 1979 his work aroused considerable interest from the BBC Natural History Unit based in Bristol. Remote controlled cameras and infrared lighting were used to investigate a family of urban foxes, and the resulting series of live television programmes, *Foxwatch*, proved extremely popular (Harris & Baker, 2001).

In Oxford, David MacDonald started his quest to uncover and understand the social life of foxes in 1972, investigating not only the animals living in town but also those in nearby countryside and others in open fell country of the north Pennines. His book *Running With the Fox* (MacDonald, 1987) provides a most entertaining and revealing account of the life of urban foxes as well as the difficulties and challenges involved in studying a nocturnal animal that has an inbuilt capacity to avoid contact with people. For many years he kept a group of foxes captive to study their social behaviour. He too promoted a documentary film on urban foxes, entitled *The Night of the Fox*. Between them Harris and MacDonald have not only unravelled the ecology of urban foxes but they have also done much to promote greater public understanding of the issues involved.

What did these various studies find? They quickly dispelled one of the myths. There were no packs of foxes roaming the streets. Foxes live in small family groups of two or more adults that occupy a specific territory. In most social groups only one dominant vixen breeds each year. MacDonald reckons that others of lower rank are effectively sterilised by their subordinate status. So each group normally produces one litter of about four cubs each year. Harris found that in Bristol all the cubs were born at about the same time in mid-March. They emerge above ground four weeks later. So finding breeding earths in May when the cubs are most obvious provides a means of assessing the total number of fox families. Harris did this in two study areas of northwest Bristol in 1979 and 1980. He found 20 family groups in one area and 10 in the other, but foxes were not evenly distributed across the study areas. Their numbers varied from about two to nearly five family groups per km². By using a combination of the number of foxes sighted within the city as a whole, together with intensive field surveys of the study areas, he was able to produce a total of 211 family groups for the whole city. This gave an average of 1.82 family groups per km² (Harris & Baker, 2001).

Subsequent studies of other towns and cities have yielded average densities ranging from 0.2 families per km² in Wolverhampton, 1 family per km² in Bath, up to a maximum of 2.2 per km² in Cheltenham. In every case there were great variations in density across the urban area, but even in the areas of greatest density the number of family groups never exceeded 5 per km². Harris considered that this is probably the maximum density that can be supported in urban areas. In contrast to this few rural districts support more than one family group per km². In open fell country the density may be much lower with a single group occupying an area of 5–10 km².

By comparing local fox densities with variations in habitat in a number of cities Harris and Rayner (1986) found that foxes were most frequent in areas of low density owner-occupied housing and less frequent in more densely built-up residential areas or council estates, industrial areas and city centres. Harris commented that 'local electoral wards provide a good guide to the number of urban foxes in the area. Wards that vote Conservative will have foxes, those that vote Labour will have few or none.' Night-time radio tracking of foxes living in a residential area of Oxford showed that up to 30 per cent of their time was spent in gardens of detached housing that covered only 7 per cent of the area. They spent another 22 per cent of their time in gardens of semi-detached houses and a similar amount of time was spent in a variety of open spaces including golf-courses, parklands, school and church grounds and patches of scrub.

Having estimated the number of family groups Harris went on to produce a figure for the total number of foxes in Bristol. Detailed studies of local populations provided crucial figures on breeding success and sex ratios that were then extrapolated to the whole city. His calculation went something like this. Of the 211 breeding vixens about 10 per cent failed to produce a litter, so there were 190 breeding vixens. In addition there were 143 vixens that were non-breeding or failed to breed, giving a total number of 333 adult vixens. The adult male population was estimated to be 383, giving a total adult population of 716. A mean litter size of 4.72 cubs meant that 897 cubs were produced each year. So the total fox population in Bristol after cubs were born in April in the early 1980s was estimated to be 1,613 (Harris & Woollard, 1988).

It seems that numbers were relatively constant through the 1970s and 1980s, but in 1990 some areas experienced a sudden rapid increase. The number of foxes within the long-term study area almost doubled. This was largely due to an increased number of foxes in each group and partly to an increased number of groups. The change was thought to be due to an over-abundance of food being provided by householders. An even greater change occurred in 1994 when the population crashed dramatically after Bristol's foxes were infected with sarcoptic mange. Harris estimated that over 95 per cent of Bristol's foxes died within two years.

As a result of radio tracking, in both Bristol and Oxford, maps were produced to show the territories of different family or social groups. The size of a territory depended on the kinds of habitat it contained. The smallest, averaging 25 to 40 ha, were in residential suburbs with large gardens. This is the optimum habitat for urban foxes. In one case the territory was only nine hectares! In such circumstances the foxes appear to be heavily dependent on feeding by local residents. In less favourable areas, such as city centres, council housing estates and industrial areas, individual territories tend to be much larger, often exceeding one kilometre. This is because there are fewer easy pickings and the foxes have to range more widely for their food. Radio tracking also showed that urban foxes visit virtually every kind of habitat within their home range. MacDonald showed that many of Oxford's foxes lay up by day in secluded spots where they were relatively free from human disturbance. Although scrub and woodland made up only 5 per cent of the city some foxes spent up to 75 per cent of their time in such places. Others chose to sleep within the urban environment on garage roofs, warehouses and fire escapes. One spent the day up a pollarded willow tree near the park-and-ride bus stop. Many earths were in gardens, 25 per cent of them under garden sheds. Others were in a great variety of places, under houses, factories, schools and one in an air-raid shelter.

In the early 1990s Harris calculated the total number of urban foxes in the UK. Knowing the average fox density for different types of housing and linking this to local housing statistics for all major towns and cities he came up with a total of 33,000 urban foxes. Since then their numbers have been severely reduced in many places as a result of sarcoptic mange. As local fox populations were reduced to a fraction of what they had been, some family groups died out completely and neighbouring groups expanded their range into the vacant territory. Average territory size increased substantially and the number of foxes in each family group remained small. For a number of years population density remained low with less than two adults per km², compared with 30 adults per km² before the onset of mange. This appears to be one of the ways in which foxes can control the size of their population. Evidence that fox numbers are regulated by environmental factors and social behaviour of the animals themselves has helped to counter misguided arguments that, 'town foxes need to be controlled before they reach plague proportions' (Harris & Baker, 2001).

Population studies (prior to mange) show that life expectancy of urban foxes is very low. In Oxford, Bristol and London the average life expectancy was less than 18 months. In Bristol over half (63 per cent) the foxes died before they were one year old. An analysis of over 1,600 dead animals found that '52 per cent were less than one year old, 24 per cent one to two years old, 12 per cent two to three years old, 6 per cent three to four years old, 3 per cent four to five years old and only 3 per cent older than five'. So 75 per cent of foxes died by the age of two and 94 per cent before they were four. There is some evidence that dominant adult foxes live longer than subordinates, reaching an average of 4.5 years. The majority of urban foxes (63 per cent) are killed by road traffic. Such accidents also cause many injuries. One third of adult foxes are found to have suffered past fractures. Fights and diseases each amount to about 10 per cent of deaths and a variety of other causes include people digging with terriers or hunting with lurchers (Harris & Baker, 2001). Long-term studies show that, before the onset of mange, fox populations in Bristol were maintained at a fairly constant level. The number of cubs that survived each year approximately balanced the number of adults that died.

Among the many myths is the conviction that urban foxes depend on raiding rubbish bins. In fact their food is extraordinarily varied and if you see one in your garden it could well be after earthworms on the lawn or heading for the bird table rather than raiding the bin. MacDonald describes the great assortment of remains found in fox droppings including the hairs of mice and voles; claws, feathers, beaks and bones of birds; soil full of 'chaetae' of earthworms; blackberry pips and plum stones; together with fragments of plastic and silver paper that are vestiges of scavenged food. He examined nearly 2,000 fox droppings in Oxford. Here 36 per cent of the diet was 'scavenged' food, which included scraps put out on bird tables and food provided by residents specifically for foxes, as well as the remains of fish and chips and other fast food residues left on the street. Earthworms formed the next highest proportion of their diet at 21 per cent, followed by fruit, small mammals and birds at about 10 per cent each. Rabbits, poultry and insects made up the remaining 12 per cent. An analysis of stomach contents from about 1,500 dead foxes in Bristol and London produced a similar range of food sources. 'Scavenged' food was again most prevalent. As in Oxford this category included a variety of sources such as compost heaps and bird tables, as well as food put out purposely for foxes. What is clear is that foxes utilise a very wide range of food sources, making the most of what is available at any one time. In early summer they take fledgling blackbirds and other garden birds.

FIG 165. Families of foxes living in gardens can provide endless entertainment. (Terry Whittaker/FLPA)

Fruit is important in the autumn, especially blackberries and fallen apples. I once watched a fox plucking victoria plums from a tree by jumping until it could reach no more, leaving a grazing line as clear as if cut by a knife. In winter those living in central London catch feral pigeons and prey on waterfowl in the parks.

One of the great differences between town fox and country fox is the way that the 'townies' have become so accustomed to people that they seem totally unconcerned. Researchers tracking urban foxes by foot will tell you that some animals became so used to being followed that they would sit and wait for them to catch up! Particular individuals may be so used to seeing people that they become remarkably tame. This is often the case in private gardens where they are regularly fed. One vixen in Oxford would set off unusually early in the evening and scratch at doors asking for food, so beating others to it. In a poll of 4,000 households in Bristol 66 per cent said they liked seeing foxes and only a minority (8.5 per cent) disliked them. When mange hit the city's foxes people wanted to know how soon they would come back. They were missing something that had become part of their lives. I can well understand. We had foxes living in our suburban garden when I lived in Surrey. On one occasion we invited friends for a birthday celebration in mid-January and 'our' foxes were lying on the lawn or capering about throughout the proceedings. Friends never forgot the unique entertainment. Word spread and we had a phone call from someone who wanted to know where we had hired our party foxes.

FIG 166. Regular visitors to gardens can become remarkably tame. (Mike Waite)

There was entertainment too for 82,000 rugby fans at Twickenham who witnessed a fox sitting on the pitch whilst the band played the National Anthem before the England v. Scotland match in 2011. With the roars of the crowd it was soon eager to escape, but others can be remarkably blasé. One was living on a piece of waste ground when the new Mayor's Office was being built near Tower Bridge in 2002. With Ken Livingstone elected as Mayor it was not long before the local workforce dubbed the fox Red Ken. They would feed it sandwiches at lunchtime. Before long it took to visiting the nearby Hay's Wharf piazza in the middle of the day where it could find more up-market food. To everyone's amazement it would trot in, weaving its way between the tables and taking anything edible thrown its way. MacDonald tells of a male fox he called 'Unipart' that lived in a car factory in Oxford where it was adopted by the workforce. The fox spent much of the day sleeping on a blanket among a maze of pipes and wooden pallets with a continuous clamour of machinery all around. When night came he first visited all the places where workers left him scraps of food, then left for his nocturnal wanderings in Cowley. In contrast to that is the pair that once lived in the park-keeper's garden in St James's Park in London. At about ten o'clock one night I was walking past Horseguard's Parade when one of these foxes emerged from the park a few yards ahead and went across to the garden at the back of 10 Downing Street.

An Irish couple walking nearby were astonished to see it. 'Just fancy seeing that, and here of all places!' It was the highlight of their visit.

Not everyone is fond of having foxes about. In winter their night-time screams can be terrifying, and have resulted in many false alarms to the police. MacDonald's team in Oxford tried to assess the problems caused by urban foxes by circulating 14,000 households. About 3,500 replied, of which only 150 (4.3 per cent) reported nuisances. As well as disturbance by noise, the most numerous complaints were from people who kept livestock in their gardens. They had lost small numbers of chickens, ducks, pet rabbits and guinea pigs. Many residents admitted that the animals had not been firmly secured. There were also a few reports of cats killed by foxes, but where this was authenticated they were generally kittens. The consensus among wildlife experts and pest control officers is that foxes and cats generally coexist amicably and it is the fox that backs down first if there is a scrap. But there will always be some exceptions.

One of the dangers of encouraging foxes in residential areas is that some have become so used to our environment they will enter houses with impunity. This is cause for serious concern in view of recent attacks on babies and young children in the home. Since 2000 there have been seven incidents in the London area that have drawn attention to the problem. The cases are remarkably similar. A fox has entered a home through an open door or window and found babies or young children in bed. Some of the children have been bitten on the hands, arms or face and one was dragged out of its cot onto the floor. Fortunately there have been no fatalities so far, but the traumatic impact of such an attack, on both children and parents is considerable and it is not surprising that there has been much public concern. There was also a case where a woman was bitten on the ear by a fox whilst asleep in bed. The case of a four-week old baby dragged from his cot was covered extensively in the press and there were calls for a cull of London's foxes. The Mayor, Boris Johnson, said,

They may appear cuddly and romantic but foxes are also a pest and a menace, particularly in our cities. This must serve as a wake-up call to London's Borough Leaders who are responsible for pest control.

Meanwhile pest controllers dismissed the need for a cull, arguing that attacks by a fox inside a house are incredibly rare and that people should take adequate precautions if there are foxes in the vicinity. They should also ensure that there is no source of food in the garden to encourage them. As long as there are urban foxes there will be incidents of this kind and the arguments will continue.

CHAPTER 11

Pigeons, Sparrows and Swifts

T HERE IS EVIDENCE FROM EARLY civilisations that some birds have
been part of life in towns and cities ever since such places existed.
Feral pigeons in Mesopotamia in the Bronze Age, house sparrows
in ancient Egypt and swifts in ancient walls of Jerusalem demonstrate a long
association with human cultures. Each has a story to tell. But they are very
different stories, demonstrating the various ways in which species have become
adapted to urban development and the impacts of changing conditions, both
cultural and environmental.

TOWN PIGEON

The pigeon that scuttles under our feet in railway stations, parks and city
squares, and which is now so familiar in towns and cities throughout the world,
is the same species as the cliff-nesting rock dove from which it is derived. Our
town pigeons have a long history of association with humankind. It is probable
that domestication started during the Neolithic Period when rock doves lived
alongside cave dwelling people. When early farmers started growing cereals
in the fertile lands of Mesopotamia 10,000 years ago the birds benefited too.
Bronze-age artefacts from this area indicate that by 4500 BC the pigeon was
regarded as a sacred bird. Its almost magical ability to produce young throughout
the year led to an association with Astarte, the goddess of love and fertility.
Ancient Greeks and Romans linked it to Aphrodite and Venus. The pigeon's
fecundity also led to its widespread domestication. By 3000 BC it had been
domesticated in Egypt and must have been available in large numbers when

Rameses 3rd offered nearly 60,000 doves to the god Ammon at Thebes in about 1500 BC. The white variation of the pigeon, which occurs naturally on occasions, could easily be encouraged by selective breeding. This is the same bird that Noah released from the Ark and the white dove has been a symbol of love and peace down the centuries. Even today in times of conflict we talk of politicians as hawks or doves. But our association with the dove goes much further. Jean Hansell (2003) puts it well:

> no other bird has had such close links with man, nor been useful to him in so many ways. It has served him as symbol, sacrifice, source of food and, not least, as messenger, both sacred and secular. It is no ordinary bird.

This close relationship has taken many forms over several millennia, from enthusiastic breeding of ornamental varieties and widespread production of food through use of dovecots, to the use of pigeons as messengers carrying vital news, especially during conflicts, and more recently the development of pigeon racing as a major sport. In all of this the devotion of breeders and handlers and their care for the birds is striking.

FIG 167. The white dove, a symbol of love and peace, is the same bird as our urban pigeon. (Paul Wilkins)

But the same bird has another very different image. For many city dwellers and town councils the pigeon of today is a pariah, hated as a pest and scourge, a 'sky-rat' that needs to be removed. A huge industry has developed to control the number of urban pigeons. Yet there are others who love to feed them. Pigeons have a great attraction and are easily tamed to a degree that is not possible with most birds. Indeed it is likely that for many people who feed the pigeons in a city square it is the only kind of bird that they have ever touched. Some people get to know their local pigeons so well that they become fond of individual birds. The birds know the habits of their feeders equally well, gathering expectantly at the prescribed time and swooping down as soon as food appears. The pigeon has become a sociable opportunist which most of us take for granted and is now the commonest and most widespread bird of built-up areas throughout the world. Odd then that ornithologists have generally paid them little attention. Almost certainly this is due to the word feral, meaning that they are derived from domestic stock, which puts them in a different category from wild birds. But in an ecological sense they are just as much a part of the urban scene as any other. Indeed the town pigeon has become one of the most successful species on our increasingly urbanised planet.

Fitter (1945) pointed out that the 'London pigeon' is well adapted to living in the architectural canyons of the metropolis. Its lifestyle is not unlike that of wild rock doves that nest in nooks and crannies of sea cliffs and in the depths of caves, making forays onto cultivated land nearby to feed on cereals and seeds of agricultural weeds. Town pigeons treat high buildings as cliffs. Groups of birds nest colonially in roofs and towers, and in holes within the stonework. Ornate Victorian buildings are especially favoured, as are girders supporting bridges, but the variety of nest sites is enormous, including large institutional buildings, churches, railway stations, museums and hospitals. Whilst city-centres are their favoured terrain, industrial areas and docklands with factories and warehouses can attract large numbers. Some birds are even known to nest on the gantries of working cranes. Victorian suburbs also provide nest sites in houses with turrets and cupolas, helped by a degree of dilapidation (Simms, 1979).

Town pigeons gather on ledges and rooftops which allow them to keep an eye on areas where they are accustomed to finding food. They are essentially scavengers, making the most of every opportunity. In city centres they fly down to pavements and streets whenever anything edible is dropped. But they also know the places that are particularly productive, clustering around tables of outdoor cafés, park benches, overflowing litter bins and rubbish bags put out for collection. All these provide a dependable supply of scraps. The same applies under cover in railway stations and piazzas where many birds continue feeding

FIG 168. Wherever food is available pigeons will congregate.

late at night. Market days in town squares can attract sizable flocks when clearing up is underway. Larger numbers occur locally where birds rely on substantial amounts of food being continuously available, as at municipal rubbish tips (or landfill sites) where pigeons vie with gulls, crows and starlings for the pickings. Dockside grain silos are another regular source of food (as well as having an abundance of nest sites) and can support local populations of several thousand pigeons. But perhaps the most spectacular gatherings occur in places where it has become traditional to feed them. Major city squares have become famous for their pigeons such as San Marco's Square in Venice and, until recently, Trafalgar Square in London, of which more later.

Simms (1979) listed a great variety of food eaten by town pigeons, which may well be a clue to their success. As well as grain and other cereals they take the seeds of many wasteland plants such as treacle mustard, chickweed, shepherd's purse and knotweed. But it is the remains of our food that generally dominates. Domestic scraps include apple cores and cooked peas, but also a vast array of processed foods such as bacon, cheese, sausage, cold meats, chocolate and chips. Nowadays their diet is far more diverse, reflecting the international nature of fast food outlets. With chapattis, paninis, pizzas and tortilla wraps they have never had it so good.

FIG 169. Holes in masonry are one of their favourite nest sites.

The navigational ability of homing pigeons is well documented, but perhaps less well known is the ability of some adventurous individuals to find their way around the London Underground. They can be seen feeding on station platforms, even at the deepest levels of the tube system, and it seems they have been doing this for many years. In 1965 Simms witnessed a pigeon joining a Bakerloo Line train at Kilburn. It stayed on the train until Finchley Road where it hopped off and joined a small party of its mates on the platform. Some years later he recorded another foraging on the platform at Marble Arch station, far below ground. He assumed that it got there from the station entrance, having mastered the difficult flight down many steps with right-angle turns, through the booking hall and down a long escalator shaft. But perhaps like those at Finchley Road it had travelled there by train. In recent years I have often seen pigeons on District and Circle Line trains. These lines lie just below the surface in central London and pigeons are frequent passengers outside the rush hours when trains are relatively empty. In 2013 the BBC showed a clip of one boarding a train and travelling for several stations before getting off again. It seemed totally relaxed and habituated to its surroundings.

A number of studies have investigated ways of controlling urban pigeons, most notably in Basel, Switzerland, where despite a long campaign of shooting

FIG 170. Pigeons gather in the sunshine, seemingly unconcerned by the presence of a predatory gull. The gull struck a moment later.

and trapping that removed 100,000 birds over 25 years, the pigeon population was maintained at about 20,000 birds. Subsequently, by controlling the amount of feeding and restricting it to very specific areas, the population was significantly reduced. Another study at Salford Docks, where birds were dependent on spillage of cereals and animal feed, showed that although 9,000 birds were killed over three years the potential population of 2,600 birds was only halved. Control efforts were nullified by constant immigration, mainly by juveniles, so that in effect port authorities paid for the slaughter of pigeons from outside the docks. Attempts at control were shown to be both ineffective and costly and it was suggested that priority be given instead to removing the spillage which had enabled the population to survive (Murton et al., 1972).

Attempts to control the pigeons in Trafalgar Square became a major news story in 2000. Not long after Ken Livingstone had been elected as Mayor of London he announced plans to transform the square with a £25 million facelift, by closing the road along the north side next to the National Gallery and incorporating a new café within the square. He wanted to turn it into a cultural place for Londoners and visitors to enjoy and this would mean removing the pigeons. There was an immediate outcry. The pigeons of Trafalgar Square were one of the best-known features of the capital. Thousands of people enjoyed a trip to the square where there was a stall selling grain to feed the birds. So when the Mayor decided not to renew the license of the stall-holder there were instant demonstrations. Tony Banks MP raised the matter in Parliament saying that pigeons are part of the London scene, enjoyed by Londoners and visitors alike. The Mayor responded by pointing out the £100,000 annual cost of clearing

FIG 171. The author and his family feeding pigeons in Trafalgar Square in 1972.

pigeon droppings. By the following February the bird-food seller reached an out-of-court settlement and it was announced that there would be a phased withdrawal of feeding over a three-month period early in 2001.

But it was not to be. Objectors claimed that the Trafalgar Square birds were a special flock that had become accustomed to being fed. They argued that reducing the food over such a short period would result in at least a quarter of the birds starving to death and they quickly organised a campaign to save the pigeons. Volunteers were drafted in to spread up to 150 kg of seed in the square every day. The Mayor responded first with clappers and klaxons, then later with daily use of Harris hawks, all intended to scare the pigeons. Large vacuum cleaners were used to remove the grain spread by campaigners. Meetings were held with a newly formed Pigeon Alliance to try to resolve the problem but all to no avail and the saga dragged on into 2002. By then there were still over 4,000 pigeons in the square every day. In June that year the Evening Standard warned that the Mayor's Office had plans to cull the pigeons and in October protesters and animal-rights campaigners held a large public demonstration. Some members of the Pigeon Alliance had got wind of a possible agreement being negotiated, which they totally opposed; added to which the Mayor announced that he planned to bring in a byelaw to prohibit people from feeding the birds. At the height of these protests the square looked more like a battleground than the cultural place originally envisaged. Large numbers of protesters spread seed everywhere which was promptly set upon by big flocks of pigeons, closely followed by cleaning staff with brooms and hoovers. Some protesters tried to grab the brooms whilst others paraded round dangling dead pigeons that had been inadvertently caught in the vacuum cleaners. It was a macabre scene.

The impasse was broken in January 2003 when a peace deal was agreed with campaigners. Over a six-month period food was provided at 7 a.m. every day, starting with 180 kg per day but reducing by 1 kg each day. The health and wellbeing of the birds was monitored by an independent scientist. The Mayor was confident that this would reduce the bird numbers without causing them any harm. During this period it was clear that large numbers of birds were attracted to the square at 7 a.m. with significant flocks flying in from south of the Thames. By April feeding had been reduced to 100 kg per day and by mid-day there were only about 300 in the square. In July there was the grand opening of the revamped square which was notable for a distinct lack of pigeons. By the end of August early morning feeding was reduced to 66 kg and numbers had dropped to 2,400, with only 200 birds at noon. A report on the condition of the birds showed no significant change over eight months. At this time it was estimated that the square would be free of pigeons by the end of the year.

But yet again it was not to be. By now the Pigeon Alliance had a new title Save the Trafalgar Square Pigeons (STTSP). They managed to persuade the Mayor to extend the period of official early morning feeding and this continued for another two years. Some members remained convinced that insufficient food was being supplied. When the byelaw prohibiting any feeding of pigeons in the square came into force in November 2003 they quickly found a loophole by feeding birds on the upper terrace that had previously been a road. This was still under the jurisdiction of Westminster where the byelaw did not apply. Eventually the Mayor withdrew from the agreement in June 2006 because of the activities of these 'rogue feeders'. The following year the City of Westminster introduced a byelaw prohibiting feeding throughout the whole square and surrounding streets with fines of up to £500. Now the square is virtually devoid of pigeons most of the time. The Mayor achieved his ambition to make the square a place where people can enjoy cultural events, but it took a great deal longer than expected and even now there are visitors

PLEASE DO NOT FEED PIGEONS AND GULLS

By feeding these birds you cause
unnecessary mess and you encourage
GULLS to steal food from people and
children.

In the interests of Hygiene, Health & Safety

LET NATURE TAKE CARE

OF ITSELF

FIG 172. People are encouraged not to feed the birds.

who bewail the loss of the pigeons, which they regard as part of their heritage.

It has been suggested that the attempts to remove pigeons from Trafalgar Square and San Marco in Venice is symptomatic of our unwillingness to accept anything that does not conform to our mental picture of urban life. Pigeons lie at one end of the spectrum as outcasts like rats and other vermin that we have learnt to hate. It seems there is no place for them today, particularly in World Heritage Sites and other treasured places. But there is no doubt that they are immensely successful. Whilst it is possible, with great difficulty, to exclude them from specific locations, there will inevitably always be substantial populations of pigeons in urban areas.

HOUSE SPARROW

The house sparrow, which was at one time one of the commonest birds of towns and cities, has suffered a serious decline in many urban areas since the mid-1980s. The reduction in numbers in some of our major cities has been one of the most pronounced changes in urban wildlife in recent times. Dramatic losses which have occurred in London and elsewhere have resulted in the disappearance of sparrows from large parts of these cities and their distribution in other sectors has become patchy with severely reduced populations confined to localised areas. The loss of sparrows has raised much public concern. There have even been questions in Parliament and the *Independent* newspaper offered a prize of £5,000 to the person who could identify the cause. Though many theories have been put forward to explain the decline it seems we are, as yet, no nearer to finding the cause.

Sparrows have been a familiar sight around human habitations for thousands of years. They probably first developed their links with humans when grain was grown and settlements were first established. They were certainly well known in antiquity, with evidence from ancient Egypt, and classical Greece that the sparrow was not only a bird that everyone knew, but had already gained a reputation as a lecherous bird through its very public sexual exploits. The sparrow living in and

FIG 173. The pugnacious cockney sparrow has suffered a catastrophic decline in many towns and cities. (Paul Wilkins)

around our houses has been known by much the same name for 1,500 years since its Old English equivalent *sparwa* (Cocker & Mabey, 2005) and Linnaeus chose well when he gave it the Latin name *Passer domesticus*. Its cocky and pugnacious nature has given rise to a great many stories and there is much in literature that emphasises the close relationship between sparrows and humanity. Chaucer and Shakespeare both used sparrows to illustrate particular human traits and the Cockney Sparrow has been as much a part of towns and cities as we are ourselves. In his monumental work on British birds, Butler (1896) described the sparrow as the 'scavenger of the town and scourge of the country'. In Victorian times huge numbers of sparrows thrived in towns and cities, taking grain and seeds scattered from nosebags and in the dung of carriage and drey horses. In London it was described by Hudson (1898) as 'intimately known to every man, woman and child in the metropolis, even to the meanest gutter-child in the poorest districts'. He mentions how sparrows would gather daily in their thousands 'at some favourite meeting place in a park or square, known to Londoners as a sparrow's chapel'. In cereal-growing districts the sparrow became a serious pest, causing considerable damage during the few weeks before harvest, and gardeners are all too familiar with the damage done to early flowering crocuses, especially the yellow variety, as well as peas and beans.

When Max Nicholson (1995) first started to record the numbers of birds in London's parks in the 1920s he found thousands of sparrows. Records for 1924–26 showed that they were exceedingly common in Kensington Gardens and Hyde Park where they totalled twice the number of all other species combined. The number of sparrows recorded in 1925 was 2,603 and this provides a useful baseline for subsequent changes. This was at a time when vast numbers of sparrows also occurred in the surrounding countryside, feeding on grain and foraging on seed-heads of agricultural weeds. But the situation was changing fast. Motorised transport rapidly replaced horses and by 1948 the number of sparrows in the same parks had fallen to 885. When the status of birds in Inner London was reviewed by the LNHS (Homes, 1964) sparrow numbers in the parks had fallen to 642 and 11 years later the figure was 544. By 1995 the number had plummeted to 81 and only 8 were recorded in 2000 (Sanderson, 2001).

Hudson (1898) described his experience of workmen stopping off in the London parks to feed sparrows as they went home from work. Feeding of sparrows in the parks continued throughout the twentieth century. Fitter noted that it had become a commonplace activity in the 1940s and I found the practice still persisted in the 1980s. At that time it was possible to buy grain from stalls in Trafalgar Square and St James's park where feeding the pigeons and sparrows proved to be a great delight. There were many who came up to central London from the outskirts specially to feed the sparrows in St James's Park. The birds gathered in large flocks in bushes by the bridge. On one occasion I witnessed a young German girl standing with a handful of sparrows. She could not be dragged away by her parents, so enthralled was she to have these wild birds in her hand (Goode, 1986). These birds nested in the ornate lamp standards along the Mall and at that time, in the mid-1980s, there were up to 100 birds in the park. Now you don't see any.

For many of us sparrows have always been a daily feature. They were just part of life. My own recollection of childhood on the southern fringe of Manchester in the 1940s was that the house sparrow was the most familiar suburban bird perching up on the gutters chirping incessantly, having dust baths in the lane, or indulging in noisy skirmishes in the privet hedges where many birds would gather to witness the sexual exploits of a pair. Sparrows were both abundant and very obvious. So what has caused the dramatic decline?

The reduction started during the first half of the twentieth century. Numbers in the UK dropped substantially in the 1920s and 1930s as a result of the change from horse drawn transport to motorised vehicles. Depletion continued in the post-war period due to changes in farming practice that reduced the amount of grain available to farmland birds. A BTO report (Crick et al., 2002) estimated the

FIG 174. This was a common scene in the 1980s, but today there are no sparrows to be seen in St James's Park.

British breeding population to be between 12 and 15 million pairs in the early 1970s. Since then the overall population has declined by almost 60 per cent. Declines in farmland populations were already occurring in the mid-1970s when monitoring of house sparrows by the Common Bird Census first began. This was followed by a marked decline in farmland habitats during the late 1970s and early 1980s. In contrast the recent decline in towns and cities didn't start until the mid-1980s. Since then there has been a catastrophic decline in many urban areas, resulting in the virtual extinction of sparrow populations in the centres of large cities such as London, Edinburgh and Glasgow and a substantial reduction in city suburbs and in many smaller towns. The Breeding Birds Survey showed a decline of 59 per cent in the London region between 1994 and 2000, and monitoring of a small sample of London gardens showed a decline of 75 per cent between 1995 and 2002 (Baker, 2004).

Overall the populations in rural areas declined by about 47 per cent since the mid-1970s, whereas those in urban and suburban areas declined by 60 per cent. Figures for the late 1990s suggested a total UK population of approximately 6 million pairs, of which around 60 per cent occur in towns, villages and rural gardens, with about half of these in suburban areas. Densities are greatest in suburban and rural garden habitats. In 2002 the house sparrow was added to the Red List of endangered species of national conservation concern, because the Common Bird Census showed a 62 per cent decline in the 22-year period 1977–99.

From the late 1990s onwards there was a spate of accounts describing the decline. Denis Summers-Smith, who wrote the classic New Naturalist monograph on the *House Sparrow* in 1963, reviewed its status in 1999 and 2003, and also speculated on possible causes of its decline. Others swiftly followed, with the BTO report (Crick *et al.*, 2002, and the comprehensive review of Robinson *et al.*,

2005). Much has been made of the serious declines in some cities, notably London and Edinburgh, but it is clear that there has been great variability in the rate of decline in different urban areas. Prowse (2002) found decreases in London, Edinburgh, Hamburg and Dublin, but no clear trend in Manchester, and it seems that populations in smaller towns were declining to a lesser degree than in large cities (Summers-Smith, 2003). It was notable that urban populations in Wales were increasing significantly, whereas those of southeast England were decreasing significantly. The decline was not restricted to the UK, but was also happening in other parts of Europe, with reports from Scandinavia, the Netherlands, Belgium, Germany, Austria, Spain and Italy, though the scale of decline has not been equally severe everywhere. Summers-Smith referred to similar declines in North America and they have also occurred in Australia.

There is general agreement that the decline in numbers of sparrows in farmland habitats was due to changes in agricultural practices which reduced the amount of grain available to farmland birds in autumn and winter. The change from spring to autumn sowing of cereal crops was particularly significant. Sparrows also suffered as a result of stricter rules for farmers governing hygiene and the storage of seeds and grain. No such simple explanation can account for the catastrophic decline in urban areas. A disparate array of explanations has been offered including:

- increased predation by cats, magpies or sparrowhawks;
- increased competition with feral pigeons and possibly urban gulls;
- a reduction in the number of nest sites due to improvements to buildings;
- the possibility of disease;
- the suitability of food provided at garden feeders;
- loss of habitats, including brownfield sites and garden shrubs and hedgerows;
- effects of airborne chemical pollution from motor vehicles on invertebrate food supplies;
- and even the possible effects of mobile phones!

Some of these explanations would directly affect both adult and juvenile birds whilst others would affect only the survival rates of juveniles, but this would in time reduce the overall population. Research by the BTO showed that the decline of sparrows in farmland during the 1970s was brought about by a reduction in survival rates of first year birds in a habitat that was becoming increasingly hostile. Sparrow populations of arable farmland are now lower than in any other habitat type. In looking for the cause of reductions in urban areas the population dynamics need to be understood.

Summers-Smith (1963) pointed out that nestlings are dependant on invertebrate food, principally insects, including beetles, bugs, aphids, scale insects, a variety of flies (especially craneflies and house flies) and caterpillars of moths. Kate Vincent's study of sparrow populations, along an urban-suburban-rural gradient in Leicester (2005), suggested that availability of invertebrate food, was crucial to the survival of nestlings during their first week after hatching. Vincent found that the annual productivity of fledged young in Leicester was 16–25 per cent lower than that found in a farmland population in Oxfordshire. The main cause of this lower productivity was starvation of chicks, usually during the first five to six days after hatching, during June and July. She suggested that the abundance of invertebrate prey in suburban and rural garden habitats determines the quantity and quality of chicks raised to fledging. The combined effects of relatively high rates of chick starvation and low body masses at fledging (and consequently low post-fledging survival) in suburban localities were large enough to result in rapid population declines. Her study was followed by suggestions that a reduction in invertebrate populations might be due to the effects of increased levels of air pollution from nitrogen oxide, or additives to lead-free petrol such as methyl tertiary butyl ether (MTBE). However Prowse (2002) argued that other urban birds which depend on aphid populations have not suffered similar declines and it is difficult to see why the sparrow alone should be affected. The one thing that is clear is that nestling success appears to be a key issue.

But other factors may be important. Evidence from Bristol suggests that the present distribution of surviving colonies of sparrows seems to be correlated with areas of greatest social deprivation. A survey linked to city electoral wards in 2000–1 showed that sparrows were largely absent from the wealthy suburbs and most abundant in the post-war overspill housing estates. A survey in London showed similar results. The London Biodiversity Partnership's public survey *Where Have All the Sparrows Gone?* (RSPB, 2002) demonstrated that the decline was not evenly distributed throughout the capital. Although they had almost disappeared from central London, sparrows were still present in the outer suburbs, with the greatest density occurring in east London and relatively few in the west. Summers-Smith (2003) also noted that sparrows were doing best in socially deprived areas. There were reports too that sparrows had become a rarity in West Berlin, but remained relatively common in the former East Berlin. These observations suggest that more prosperous areas no longer provide suitable conditions for sparrows. Houses are better maintained with fewer nest sites available and the surrounding urban landscapes tend to be heavily manicured. In contrast, in socially deprived areas not only is there more likelihood of

FIG 175. One of the few places in central Bath where sparrows still survive. Local residents provide live meal-worms; bushes and hedges provide cover.

dilapidation and therefore available nest sites, but there is also a greater degree of unkempt vegetation, including patches of urban wasteland, which will be important in providing a source of invertebrate food. The continued presence of privet hedges may also be significant.

Another feature of sparrow populations of inner urban areas is that they appear to have changed their habits. Those that still persist tend to be restricted to distinct local colonies. Cock birds spend less time up on the rooftops and gutters and most of their chirping is done from the depths of bushes such as *Pyrocantha* and *Cotoneaster*. Such behaviour is well displayed in the courtyards among the Georgian buildings of Bath where small populations persist in some and not in others. The birds appear to prefer those with plenty of cover. I have investigated the distribution of sparrows in these courtyards since 2007. For some years sparrows had virtually disappeared, but in one of the courtyards near the Circus a small population of sparrows has become established and grown. Since 2010 other courtyards and gardens nearby have been recolonised, having been devoid of sparrows since 2007. All the areas where sparrows occur have an abundance of cover in the form of ivy, roses and viginia creeper. Other courtyards and gardens in the vicinity which do not have such cover are still devoid of sparrows. Whilst investigating sparrow numbers in the first courtyard I discovered that one local resident was feeding birds with live meal-worms, at the rate of 500 g per week. The courtyard also has a number of holes in the walls which are used for nesting. So it seems that a small population in this part of Bath is being sustained by very local circumstances. Such observations, although anecdotal, give weight to the view expressed by Robinson and others at the BTO (2005) that: 'Understanding fine-scale variation in urban habitat distribution is likely to be key in fathoming the mystery of the fate of the urban house sparrow.'

The change of habits and dependence on cover seems to be a widespread feature. A survey in London suggested that the surviving populations of sparrows are found where privet hedges still remain around front gardens, where these have not been removed to make way for parking cars. Here again there is a link with social issues, but there is also a possible link with predation. Over the past thirty years the sparrowhawk has become well established in many urban areas where it was practically unknown before 1980. It is now the commonest predatory bird in central London. In view of this it is possible that sparrows have adopted new strategies to avoid predation.

This is not just conjecture on my part. A recent study supports the possibility that increased numbers of urban sparrowhawks may have played a part in the recent decline of sparrows. The spread of sparrowhawks into towns and cities is well documented and has occurred over much the same period as the recent dramatic decline in sparrows. But the precise timing of sparrowhawk spread has differed in various parts of the country. Bell *et al.* (2010) analysed the relationship between timing of sparrowhawk spread and sparrow decline using data on the occurrence of both species at garden feeding stations. One outcome of the modelling indicated that house sparrow numbers were generally stable or increasing prior to recolonisation by sparrowhawks, but declined continuously afterwards. They also found a significantly greater decrease in sparrow numbers

FIG 176. Sparrows have changed their habits, hiding in shrubberies rather than sitting in the open. (Paul Wilkins)

FIG 177. Increasing numbers of sparrowhawks may have played a part in the demise of the house sparrow. (Paul Wilkins)

when sparrowhawks were present. They argued that predation by sparrowhawks may be sufficient to explain the decline in sparrows and also suggested that the long period over which sparrow populations existed with little pressure from predators made them especially vulnerable when urban habitats were colonised by sparrowhawks.

To complicate matters it is also possible that the increased numbers of sparrowhawks could have influenced sparrow behaviour and their physiology. MacLeod *et al.* (2006) found that sparrows do not acquire sufficient additional fat reserves to avoid the risk of starvation in winter, but instead are responding to the risk of predation by maintaining a lower than expected body weight so that they are better able to escape from predators. In effect they are balancing one risk against another, but reducing the risk of predation may heighten the susceptibility of the species to population decline as a consequence of starvation.

In trying to understand what has happened to sparrows in urban areas one needs to realise that numbers have been falling for a very long time and the population that still survived in the 1980s, though familiar to many of us, was only a small fraction of what it had been 100 years earlier. It may be that no single factor is responsible for the dramatic decline that has occurred recently. But equally it is possible that numbers in urban areas had dropped to such a critical level that they became more susceptible to changing conditions. Under such circumstances increasing numbers of sparrowhawks, or lack of invertebrate food supplies could become critical. When numbers fall to zero over large areas it is natural for people to be concerned, even though the main reduction had occurred long before.

Nor should we forget that another common urban bird, the starling, has suffered a similar though less catastrophic decline in urban areas in recent years. Numbers in the UK have declined by 50 per cent during 1995 to 2010 and the starling now has a very patchy distribution in many towns and cities where

FIG 178. The aerobatics of starlings gathering to roost on Brighton Pier provide an impressive wildlife spectacle.

it was once widespread and abundant. A comprehensive review by the BTO (Crick *et al.*, 2002) failed to explain the reduction in urban starling numbers. Detailed studies in urban areas have found that where they are still breeding productivity is undiminished, which suggests that wider influences are involved. Like the sparrow the cause is still unknown. Although the huge inner-city night time roosts of starlings in London, Birmingham and Manchester have mostly disappeared since the 1980s, some still roost on bridges over the Thames and there are impressively large roosts on sea-side piers at Brighton and Aberystwyth.

SWIFTS

If there is one bird that is attuned to town and city life it is the swift. It may not spend long with us, just three months to get its offspring fledged, and then it is off again. But every year in early May there are city dwellers who await the coming of the swifts with eager anticipation. This is the bird of summer skies when screaming flocks play silly-season tag around the steeples, chimney pots and clocks. Not only are they part of our lives, but their arrival also brings reassurance that all's well with the wider world. Ted Hughes put it well in his poem 'The Swifts':

They've made it again,
Which means the globe's still working, the Creation's
Still waking refreshed, our summer's
Still all to come—
And here they are, here they are again ...

Swifts are special in a number of ways. They have the distinction of living their lives entirely airborne, apart from the time when they make their nests. Everything is done in the sky: feeding, courting, gathering nest material and sometimes even mating. What is more surprising is their ability to sleep and roost on the wing. They are special too in that virtually the whole population of swifts in Britain breed in buildings and other man-made structures. The eaves of old houses and church towers are specially favoured. Sometimes large colonies depend on individual buildings, or old walls, which have been occupied for many years. The Wailing Wall in Jerusalem is thought to be the oldest known site of a colony. Ancient city walls of Siena in Italy have supported colonies of swifts for several hundred years. But given the opportunity, they will readily take to modern buildings, just as long as there are suitable holes for them to nest in. Some manage without buildings. A few used the nest holes of sand martins in a gravel pit near Preston, and others were found nesting in the disused copper mines at Coniston. But these are the exceptions, for the swift is essentially an urban bird.

Swifts are special too for their place in British ornithology. Those nesting in the tower above the University Museum of Science in Oxford were studied in great depth by David and Elizabeth Lack who untangled many of the mysteries of their lives. *Swifts in a Tower* (Lack, 1956) is a beautiful example of what can be achieved by patient observation and is one of the classics of ornithological literature. The colony was studied over 10 years during which time it grew from 16 to nearly 40 pairs. The birds nested in specially constructed nest boxes with glass windows, fixed inside ventilator holes in the tower. The boxes were reached by climbing ladders to observation platforms high up in the tower, set up especially for the study. There the Lacks sat for hours on end, recording in meticulous detail the daily lives of the birds.

The first birds generally arrive back from Africa in late April. In London the average date of first arrivals from the early 1930s to 1950 was 27 April. Since 2000 the equivalent date has been 10 April (London Bird Reports). Either they are getting here earlier, or there are more hawk-eyed birdwatchers on the lookout for them. During their first weeks in Britain they can be seen in large numbers feeding over lakes, reservoirs and gravel pits near to the areas where they breed. London reservoirs are famous for such concentrations, with 1,000 birds feeding over

FIG 179. Swift returning to the nest with its throat pouch bulging with food. (David and Jackie Moreton)

Staines Reservoir on 28 April 2005; and 2,000 birds were recorded on one occasion at Chichester's gravel pits. For me the crucial day is the 9 May, as for many years that was the date when they first appeared over the rooftops where I lived. I well remember one year when I was walking to the station early on that morning and saw the new arrivals circling forlornly around the jib of a crane. Sadly it was in the process of demolishing the old Co-op store in which they had bred for many years.

In Oxford it was found that birds of a pair rarely arrive back together, but may be separated by several days, or even weeks. Individual pairs used the same nest box in subsequent years, but there was a good deal of fighting for possession. The same nest material was used from year to year, being gradually added to throughout the season. All this material was collected on the wing, including dead grass, flower petals, numerous wind-blown seeds like dandelion with a pappus of hairs, winged seeds, bud sheaths, cocoons, lots of feathers, bits of paper and even a bus ticket. On one occasion several nests were suddenly adorned with bright red poppy petals. One pair incorporated a live cabbage white butterfly into their nest. Lack comments that during the war swifts in Denmark and Italy constructed their nests from shreds of tinfoil dropped by the RAF to confuse enemy radar!

Although mating generally took place in the nest boxes, Lack also records instances of mating on the wing, a phenomenon first described by Gilbert White (1789). Eggs are generally laid in the third or fourth week of May. One of the notable discoveries made during the Oxford study was that the length of time for

FIG 180. Swift's nest under the eaves. (Roger Wilmhurst/FLPA)

both incubation and fledging varied enormously according to the weather. The fledging period was particularly influenced by weather conditions, and could be extended by up to three weeks in response to periods of cold and rainy weather. Such a range of variability is quite unusual for a small bird, but it is the swift's means of survival in Britain's uncertain climate. As an aerial feeder the swift is badly affected by cold wet weather when airborne insects are no longer available. Without doubt its most significant adaptation to this way of life, is the ability of its fledglings to reduce their metabolism and remain torpid for long periods if no food is available. Under such conditions even tiny nestlings survive for up to two days without food, and well-grown birds may survive for many days or even weeks, using a store of fat under their skin produced when food is plentiful.

Parents carry food back to the nest in a large bulge below the beak, which is full of small insects and spiders packed into the throat and stuck together with saliva. The number and variety of species is extraordinary. The swift probably eats more species of animal than any other British bird. Lack found over 400 species in only 12 meals analysed. These were mainly flies and bugs (particularly aphids), but also included many hymenoptera, beetles and spiders, and at certain times mayflies, small dragonflies and moths. Each meal contained 300 to 1,000 insects and spiders, and it was found that one swift might bring as many as 42 meals a day to the nestlings, representing 20,000 insects caught in one day!

For its size the young swift spends a long time in the nest (from five to eight weeks), as compared, for example, with the blackbird whose fledging period is only two weeks. The difference is that blackbird chicks are fed by their parents for some time after they leave the nest. But the moment a young swift leaves its nest it is totally independent and has to fend for itself. It sets off immediately to make its own way south, with the adults leaving a few days later, and it may not set foot on the ground again for several years, when it first starts to breed.

On the 7 August one year, I witnessed the departure of the swifts as they passed over the North Downs. The evening sky was full of swifts wheeling in great circles, drifting south. I watched this spectacle for over an hour during which time many hundreds of birds passed over.

During the time they spend with us swifts will sometimes gather in substantial numbers on warm still evenings when they rise together into the sky, to 'roost'. Early in the season before eggs are laid all the birds may participate, later it is just the non-breeding birds. During such an ascent they may rise to heights of 1,000 to 2,000 m. There the birds bunch together and their flight is very different from normal, with relatively slow wing beats alternating with a few seconds of gliding. It is suggested that aerial roosting is achieved by switching off one half of their brain, and keeping one eye open at any one time! The precise nature of such gatherings is still one of the great mysteries of swift behaviour.

What is known with certainty is that swifts will travel for great distances, often hundreds of kilometres, around storms or depressions to avoid the rain. Such movements, involving thousands of birds, are particularly pronounced around the southeastern sector of approaching depressions where they fly into the wind and possibly take advantage of concentrations of airborne insects along the edge of a warm front. On one occasion 25,000 birds were seen flying south along the Lincolnshire coast, as they made their way round a strong depression crossing the UK.

Trying to assess the number of swifts breeding in the UK is notoriously difficult. It is known that they disappeared from the industrial townscapes of the Midlands, northern England and even central London during the worst periods of air pollution. Nelson (1907) quotes Thomas Allis who wrote in 1844 that 'a few pairs still breed in the vicinity of Halifax, but they have totally abandoned the streets where there were formerly considerable numbers'. Chislett (1952) noted their return to the manufacturing districts of Yorkshire as industry declined and air quality improved and, also in the 1950s, they were nesting abundantly in the heart of manufacturing towns of Lancashire. In London swifts have gradually spread back towards the centre after about 1960. Prior to that the inner breeding limit had not changed much in 50 years (Homes, 1964). Gooders detected the first clear signs of re-colonisation in 1973, and by the time of the second breeding bird atlas (Hewlett, 2002) swifts were recorded throughout inner London, though confirmed breeding records were still scarce.

FIG 181. My local colony; several pairs of swifts nest under the eaves of this house, which has just the right kind of holes.

In 1949 the LNHS carried out a census of swifts nesting in west London. Four sample areas were examined in detail, representing inner London, the inner and outer suburbs and the rural fringe. No breeding was detected in inner London. The highest density, 24 confirmed nests per 1,000 acres (and up to 40 probable nests), was found in the inner suburbs. In outer suburbs density was about half that. Some of the fringe villages had densities similar to outer suburbs, but others had no swifts at all. It was suggested that they were most abundant in areas near water, where there is an abundance of flying insects (Homes, 1964), and it is now known that nesting swifts catch most of their food locally.

During the 1980s and 1990s most assessments assumed the UK swift population was relatively stable. However, since 2000 a number of surveys suggest that there has been a substantial decline in numbers (Mayer, 2004). One of these was in Sussex, where a 24–33 per cent decline was recorded over the period 1968 to 2000. These declines have since been substantiated by the BTO breeding bird survey, which showed a reduction in the UK of 26 per cent between 1995 and 2006. Over the same period in Scotland the reduction was 42 per cent. Other counts suggest that the decline has been more serious, with a UK decline of 41 per cent recorded for 1994–2007 (BTO Website). This has led to the swift being placed on the 'amber list', comprising species that are cause for concern.

It is suggested that the reduction is largely due to loss of breeding sites, particularly through refurbishment and re-roofing of older buildings and the fact that many new buildings are made of materials that don't have suitable cavities. Certainly the glass and metal construction of many modern high-rise buildings does not offer much opportunity for swifts. Over the past ten years several initiatives have been taken to raise public awareness about what is happening and try to ensure that nesting sites are available. The first of these was Concern for Swifts, followed by its counterpart in Scotland in 2002. At about the same time

FIG 182. New building materials offer fewer opportunities for swifts to find cavities for nesting. This view of central Liverpool shows the contrast between old and new.

Edward Mayer set up a web-based advisory service called London's Swifts which soon spread its wings to provide advice in various parts of Europe. It has since joined forces with other groups to form Swift Conservation. There are also groups running local action plans for swifts in many towns and cities, including a very active group in Ely which has a website showing successful action in local churches. In Crewe a 1930s housing estate has been designated as a Site of Biological Importance for the large colony of swifts nesting in the roofs of the houses.

There is now a range of swift-bricks and nesting boxes available, which can be incorporated into new buildings or added to existing ones. Swift bricks are standard

FIG 183. One of the many kinds of nesting chamber or swift-brick which can be built in to new buildings. (Swift Conservation)

sized breezeblocks, with a hole leading to an internal nesting chamber. One of the advantages, when promoting their use, is that the nest is entirely self-contained and there is no danger of any mess in the building. The only external sign is a small hole in the wall. Such bricks need to be placed quite high, preferably above 5 m, on the shaded side of a building, where there are clear flight lines with no obstructions from trees or wires. A variety of designs of nest boxes are also available, which can be fitted under the eaves of both domestic and commercial buildings.

The widespread adoption of such boxes might be just what is needed to reverse the current decline in numbers. Advice provided to businesses and other organisations by Swift Conservation, has led to a significant shift in attitudes of architects and developers. Examples of successful schemes over recent years include several in Camden and Islington where the boroughs have promoted nest boxes or swift bricks in new developments. Nest boxes were fitted under the eaves of new apartments associated with Arsenal's Emirates Stadium, and a major new community housing development at Swiss Cottage, designed by architect Terry Farrell, incorporates a series of Schwegler swift bricks. Swift boxes were also built into a new town hall extension on Euston Road. Elsewhere, nest boxes made by schoolchildren at Mudchute City Farm were fitted behind the rooftop louvres of Canada Tower at Canary Wharf. In Glossop the Derbyshire Wildlife Trust became concerned for a large colony of swifts nesting in the walls of Wrens Nest Mill when the building was to be converted into apartments. London's Swifts advised on how existing nest holes, where the pointing had crumbled, could be maintained as part of the renovation. Swift bricks have recently been incorporated in New Scotland Yard and in the Olympic Village. In 2011 South Cambridgeshire District Council won the Best Practice Award from the Institute of Ecology and Environmental Management for a village project called Saving the Fulbourn Swifts which involved incorporating nesting chambers in a large number of newly-built houses. These various schemes have been welcomed by the development industry and all the indications are that this type of work will grow.

One particularly enthusiastic swift lover, Dick Newell, has constructed a condominium for swifts on his house. He has also designed swift towers on poles with a cluster of nesting boxes at the top. These can be erected in any open spaces, on roundabouts, or in commercial business parks. This is hardly a new idea as swift towers, or 'dovecots for swifts', were built long ago in Tuscany, but for a very different reason. There they were a source of food, the young swifts being considered a great delicacy! Hopefully swift towers will catch on and provide nesting sites that the swifts can rely on in the future.

PART THREE

Urban Nature Conservation

FIG 184. A black-tailed skimmer dragonfly at Crane Park Island, a nature reserve run by the London Wildlife Trust in the Borough of Richmond upon Thames. This species has shown a strong northward expansion of its UK range as a result of newly created wetlands and in response to climate change.

CHAPTER 12

A New Philosophy

T HE EMERGENCE OF A DISTINCTIVE and influential movement to protect nature in towns and cities was one of the most significant developments in nature conservation in Britain in the past forty years. It was slow in getting off the ground when compared with more traditional approaches to conservation. With hindsight it is easy to see why. When the Nature Conservancy was set up in 1949 there was a great sense of urgency to ensure that the most important wildlife areas were protected under the new legislation. Their selection was based on a scientific approach with the aim of including the best examples of natural habitats throughout the country. This approach served well to protect the gems of Britain's wildlife, but it also set the priorities for the conservation movement for the next thirty years. The newly emerging county wildlife trusts were imbued with the same urgency to protect key sites in the face of rapid changes in the countryside resulting from agricultural intensification, drainage and afforestation. Finding and protecting the best remaining examples of habitats such as bog, heath, ancient woodland or coastal marsh was the order of the day and conservation was firmly rooted in the protection of these key sites in the countryside. If nature occurred in towns and cities the leading conservation bodies showed little interest and it was certainly not on their agenda for protection. The cynic might say there was nothing sufficiently rare to warrant the attention of conservationists.

There are profound differences between this traditional key site approach and the dynamics of urban nature conservation as it is practised today. In the urban scene the emphasis is on the value of nature to people in their local surroundings, where common and ordinary species tend to prevail. The kinds of habitats involved are often quite unassuming. Private gardens, overgrown cemeteries and abandoned railway sidings may provide the best, or only, opportunities for nature in densely built-up areas. These are the typical building blocks of urban conservation, rather than the ancient woods and marshes of the countryside. A further distinction is the role of habitat creation, which has enormous potential throughout the urban fabric. Underpinning the whole approach is the importance of nature at a local level. Urban nature conservation is firmly rooted in support from local communities and individuals who value their contact with the natural world in the place where they live.

So how did this new approach come about, and where should we start in tracing its origins? Most appropriate perhaps are the writers Richard Jefferies and W. H. Hudson. Both enjoyed daily contact with nature in Victorian London and we can still share their experiences and enthusiasm. Jefferies took particular delight in the ordinary, whether pigeons in Trafalgar Square or a trout in the Hogsmill stream near his home in Surbiton. For pure enjoyment of nature his descriptions of London are still unrivalled (Jefferies, 1889). W. H. Hudson brought the talents of a life-long naturalist to the streets and parks of London and was one of the first to explore the detailed workings of London's natural history. He also had strong views on how things could be improved; in particular the fact that bird populations could be enhanced by sensitive management of parks (described in Chapter 7). Hudson's book *Birds in London* (1898) provides powerful arguments for urban nature and his legacy is still with us.

At the time when they were writing, the rapid growth of London and other cities had led to numerous battles to protect much loved landscapes from being swallowed up by the tide of urban development. Disputes affecting Hampstead Heath and Epping Forest in London were repeated in many other towns and cities where local people fought to save the commons. Clifton Downs in Bristol, Platt Fields in Manchester and the Town Moor in Newcastle were all under threat. The battles to protect common lands were described earlier (see Chapter 3). One of the most significant achievements was the setting up of the Commons Preservation Society, which had a crucial role in protecting many of the open spaces that are so valued today.

This period was remarkable for the way people organised themselves in their desire to protect their local environment. They were not the first to do so. Local residents fought to keep Leicester Fields in London as long ago as 1630. They survive today as Leicester Square. Other battles were fought in the mid-nineteenth century when Octavia Hill, later active in founding the National Trust, campaigned for the disued burial grounds in the City of London to be protected as open spaces. As a result the Metropolitan Public Gardens Association was formed which managed to protect nearly 500 churchyards as tiny parks or gardens. They remain one of London's precious assets.

The fight to protect open spaces still continues today, but there is an important difference. Appreciation of the natural world and the role of ecology have taken on

FIG 185. *London's Natural History* by Richard Fitter: a splendid analysis of the way nature responds to the workings of a big city.

a much greater significance. No longer is it just a matter of protecting open spaces and their landscapes. Nature itself is valued by many town and city dwellers. Britain's long tradition of natural history investigation has paved the way for greater awareness and understanding of nature in the urban environment. This was beautifully illustrated by Richard Fitter in his classic New Naturalist volume on *London's Natural History* (1945) which demonstrates so clearly how wildlife responds and accommodates to the many and varied activities in a great city. His analysis was only made possible by the wealth of information published over the years in the Journal of the London Natural History Society and its precursors.

Many local natural history societies sprang up during the Victorian period when there was an enormous growth of interest in the subject, particularly in industrial towns and cities. Natural history societies started in Liverpool, Manchester and Bristol during the 1860s and their field excursions attracted hundreds of participants. Manchester had 550 people attending one such gathering. The transactions of these societies are full of the accounts of field meetings to favoured localities, including some venues that were far from salubrious. A visit to the Birkenhead docks in 1908 by members of the Liverpool Botanical Society to record alien plants is a typical example. Such excursions continue in many places today. These societies were instrumental in organising the first systematic recording of Britain's natural history, and because many were based on cities they built up a wealth of information about nature within urban areas. Most records were collected by amateur naturalists specialising in particular groups of organisms, and indeed the majority of these societies are still organised this way. It was not until the second half of the twentieth century that ecological studies became established which cut across taxonomic boundaries.

During the immediate post-war period some natural history societies led the way in recommending places that should become nature reserves in urban areas. London was ahead of its time, possibly because a number of members of the London Natural History Society (LNHS), notably Richard Fitter and Max Nicholson, were directly involved in the national Wildlife Conservation Special Committee that gave rise to the Nature Conservancy as a government agency. It was a time when much thought was being given to nature conservation and the LNHS produced a map (Castell, 1947) showing 120 sites recommended by the society for protection as nature reserves. These were within twenty miles of St Paul's, the LNHS recording area, but it is striking that most were outside the boundary of Greater London, in what has since become London's Green Belt.

Following this the LNHS organised a London Conservation Committee, which became the focus for conservation issues in the capital over the next thirty years. During the 1950s, under the chairmanship of Cynthia Longfield it recommended a large number of sites for designation as SSSIs, but there was no way of protecting the vast majority of sites that were identified. To celebrate 'European Conservation Year' in 1970 the Society arranged a special programme of conservation activities, ably organised by Pearl Small who was to chair the Conservation Committee throughout most of the following decade. At that time the Committee consisted of twenty people from a wide range of bodies who provided advice on key issues. In 1972, for example, they played a prominent part in the successful campaign to save Staines Moor near Heathrow Airport from the threat of gravel extraction (Bevan, 1993). But the Committee stopped short of taking direct responsibility for acquisition or management of nature reserves. One reason was that naturalists were far more interested in recording things than protecting them, but more significantly none of the organisations involved were equipped to do that job.

With the emergence of County Naturalists' Trusts long established societies such as the Yorkshire Naturalists' Union, and its equivalent in Lincolnshire, found themselves working in parallel with these new bodies. Natural history societies retained much of the taxonomic expertise whilst County Trusts took responsibility for acquiring and managing nature reserves. As the new Trusts gained strength traditional natural history societies became progressively less influential in the realm of conservation. But sadly it was a long time before any of the County Trusts took an interest in urban issues.

It was not until the early 1970s that an appreciation of the value of nature in towns and cities began to find its way into the professional arena of those engaged in urban design and planning. As is so often the case with new innovations the catalyst seems to have been cross fertilisation of ideas between disciplines. Much of the stimulus at that time came from landscape designers working within the built environment, who could see the value of working with nature. Notable amongst these was Nan Fairbrother whose much-acclaimed

FIG 186. Richard Mabey's *The Unofficial Countryside* highlighted the wildlife value of derelict and unused land like this patch of abandoned fields in suburbia.

treatise *New Lives, New Landscapes* (1970) provided a farsighted model for urban planning and design. Another was Ian McHarg's *Design with Nature* (1969), which pioneered the benefits to be gained from using ecological approaches in landscape design. The boundless capacity of nature to thrive in forgotten corners of cities was exposed dramatically by Richard Mabey a few years later when he coined the phrase 'unofficial countryside' to describe the array of man-made habitats such as industrial wasteland, cemeteries, railway sides and flooded gravel pits that characterise many cities (Mabey, 1973).

Where Richard Fitter had led the way others quickly followed. John Kieran's *Natural History of New York City* (1959) is a remarkable celebration of the rich variety of wildlife in what must be one of the most densely built-up cities in the world. Kieran combined the talents of a journalist, writing on the *New York Times* and *Herald Tribune*, with a deep and lasting fascination with natural history. He had links with key specialists in the American Museum of Natural History and New York Botanical Garden and having lived in New York all his life he was able to bring together over 50 years of personal study and enjoyment of wildlife in what he called 'a book for sidewalk naturalists everywhere'. We can share his exhilaration as, on one occasion, he describes how he stood transfixed watching a migrating flock of snow geese pass over the skyscrapers of Manhattan. His book is full of such anecdotes, but also provides a comprehensive account of the species to be found including details of obscure, as well as more popular, groups. It is a journalist's perspective, but as an all-round naturalist he had a remarkable story to tell. Like Fitter's book on London, Kieran's treatment of New York opened up a whole new world for residents of the great metropolis.

It may seem a small step from cataloguing these new-found riches to taking action to encourage and protect them. But in America policies on wildlife conservation were largely determined by the hunting lobby. Non-game biology was itself a poor relation within the wildlife conservation movement, and protection of urban wildlife was unheard of. So the changes that occurred over the next ten years came as something of a surprise. If there was one catalyst in the ecological community it was Ray Dasmann who was one of the first in the USA to advocate the value of urban wildlife. In a speech in Maryland in 1966 he pointed out that city people were becoming divorced from the land and had little experience of the natural world. Arguing that wildlife managers in the States were too closely linked with hunting and game preserves, he urged naturalists to concentrate on the cities instead of the forests.

They should work with regional planners, landscape architects and others respon-sible for the urban environment, to make towns and cities into places where each person's everyday experience could be enriched by contact with nature.

Coming from one of the leading international figures in nature conservation this was a revelation. His ideas soon caught on. A national conference on 'Man and Nature in the City' held in Washington DC in 1968 set things moving and in 1973 a National Institute for Urban Wildlife was established in the USA. One of its primary functions was to make the results of research in urban ecology more readily available to those responsible for city management, so one of its first publications was a detailed report on planning for wildlife in cities. By the end of the 1970s several major cities had started to take wildlife seriously, including New York, which was one of the first to develop an urban wildlife programme funded by the city. This was the start of a significant new approach in which wildlife was valued in its own right.

Things were happening elsewhere in Europe too. Research on urban ecology was already underway at universities in Berlin and Warsaw, where many different aspects were investigated in great depth. Professor Herbert Sukopp established the Institute of Ecology at the Technical University in Berlin, initially concentrating largely on botany and vegetation, with a strong emphasis on the phytosociology of urban areas, but later encompassing almost all aspects of urban ecology. Dr Luniak and colleagues in Poland concentrated mainly on animal ecology. These two centres effectively led the way in urban ecological studies in Europe. The City of West Berlin had a very significant role in the development of urban nature conservation. During the 1970s nature conservation programmes were promoted in several states in the Federal Republic of Germany. West Berlin was included as a city-state. Isolated as an island in East Germany it was required to include nature conservation alongside other land uses within the confined boundaries of the city. Habitat mapping was carried out for the whole city and an extremely detailed strategic plan for nature conservation was adopted in 1979 (Henke & Sukopp, 1986). Not only was Berlin the first city to have such a plan, but it was also supported by an immense amount of ecological information. No other city has been subject to the same degree of investigation and the studies carried out over the years have provided major advances in our understanding of urban ecology. The Institute of Ecology became a world leader in the ecological management of cities.

In the Netherlands much work was underway to promote new ecological landscapes as part of post-war reconstruction of towns and cities (Ruff, 1979). School nature gardens, city farms, nature parks and more extensive naturalistic landscapes were all introduced in an attempt to create more liveable communities, where people could have direct links with nature in their local neighbourhood. These were to have a major influence on the way urban wildlife conservation developed in the UK.

The possibilities were not lost on ecologically minded landscape designers and the first detailed consideration of the issues in the UK came in 1974. Stimulated by the American conference of 1968, landscape architects in Manchester promoted a national conference on 'Nature in Cities'. Ian Laurie deserves the credit for making this happen. He brought people together for the first time from all the different disciplines concerned with the natural environment of cities. His aim was to focus on the role of nature in the design and development of urban open spaces. In addition to detailed aspects of urban ecology and natural history, the meeting considered ways of encouraging wildlife through better planning and design of greenspace. Also, for the first time, social issues were addressed, especially people's needs in relation to the natural environment (Laurie, 1975, 1979).

NATURE IN THE BLACK COUNTRY

By the late 1970s cracks were appearing in the strictly scientific rationale for conservation. The turning point came when several elements came together to demonstrate the importance of urban ecology. Brian Davis of the Institute of Terrestrial Ecology published a seminal review of wildlife in urban and industrial areas (1976), in which he argued that man-made habitats had considerable importance for wildlife conservation. Many regional staff of the government agency, the Nature Conservancy Council (NCC), working in urban areas were already well aware of their importance, but were hamstrung by the official line which gave little support to protecting areas of this kind. However, the team working in the English Midlands were more adventurous. At that time the Regional Officer was John Thompson who had been involved with ecological restoration in a number of towns including Stoke, Telford and Warrington. He was aware that urban areas could hold unsuspected riches and encouraged a more sympathetic approach. So when the new West Midlands Metropolitan Authority asked the NCC for advice on the nature conservation content of its forthcoming County Structure Plan he responded positively. He encouraged his deputy George Barker, who was already well versed in urban wildlife issues, to get on with it. Barker was more than willing to challenge the accepted wisdom and leapt at the opportunity. The Metropolitan Authority wanted to know which places ought to be protected and Barker was well aware that there was a dearth of information. Apart from a few SSSIs virtually nothing was known about the relative merits of places that might be valuable and he realised that there was a need for a thorough survey. So in 1974 he commissioned a systematic survey of wildlife in the predominantly urban landscape of Birmingham and the adjoining Black Country.

This was the first survey of its kind anywhere in the country. Bunny Teagle, an experienced urban naturalist who had previously worked in London, was charged with the task and spent much of 1975 delving into the countless places where nature flourished amidst the urban sprawl of Birmingham. He was greatly assisted by many local naturalists with detailed knowledge of particular places, and others who specialised in some of the less well-known plant and animal

FIG 187. Bunny Teagle, author of the influential report *The Endless Village*.

FIG 188. Post-industrial landscapes featured strongly in *The Endless Village*: Rowley Hills were quarried for dolerite and now support species-rich grassland.

groups such as spiders and other invertebrates. Teagle also made good use of the media and was rewarded by a tremendous public response to his requests for information published in the Birmingham Evening Mail and broadcast on the BBC programme *The Living World*. Hundreds of letters were received as a result of these appeals, providing a wealth of information on the wildlife of suburban gardens.

Teagle's report *The Endless Village*, published in September 1978, has a special place in the history of nature conservation. It demonstrated beyond doubt the wealth of wildlife to be found in a surprising variety of artificial habitats from the formal landscapes of parks, gardens and playing fields to the wilder areas of industrial dereliction. He points out that:

in the Black Country the conurbation embraces hundreds of acres of derelict industrial land where grassland, scrub, woodland, marsh and open water cover the scars of mining and quarrying, often creating a pleasant semi-rural landscape.

FIG 189. Bumble Hole: a high quality section of the Black Country canal network.

These habitats were found to contain a great variety of species, some of which were rare or declining in the wider countryside.

It was not just the evidence provided about urban nature that made this report so important. The very fact that the NCC commissioned it was crucial. The primary object of the survey was 'to obtain information on the fauna and flora of the conurbation so that the NCC would be better able to advise planners on matters concerning wildlife and wildlife habitats'. It didn't stop there. George Barker used the report as a vehicle to promote a new approach to conserving urban nature. The proposals for future action written by Barker and Teagle, which form the final chapter, would nowadays be called a policy or strategy for urban nature conservation. They recognised the need to protect the best remaining habitats, and to improve and enhance wildlife throughout the urban landscape in places like parks and cemeteries. They also advocated making the most of opportunities during restoration of derelict land to ensure that places are created for a variety of wildlife. The need for research was recognised, especially in relation to the complex inter-relationships between native species and the numerous alien species characteristic of urban wastelands. Over-riding all this they felt there was a need to interest people in their local wildlife heritage, recognising that such an approach would have benefits for people as well as nature.

The Endless Village was an important document. It not only destroyed the myth of the urban wildlife desert, which had persisted for so long in nature conservation circles, but also laid the foundations for urban nature conservation in the UK. In his foreword to the report Bob Boote, the NCC's Director General, announced that it formed the first part of a national project on nature conservation in urban areas, 'to show that wildlife is a vital part of the urban environment and of the renewal of inner-cities'. *The Endless Village* virtually changed the rules overnight.

This new dedication to the urban scene had not been without its difficulties. In the early days of the survey Barker had found himself reprimanded by higher authorities for spending money on what was regarded as an irrelevancy. However, attitudes changed sharply when Denis Howell, who was then government Minister responsible for the NCC's affairs, let drop how pleased he was to see the NCC doing something useful for his constituents of Birmingham (Smallheath). It was he who first encouraged the NCC to engage with the government's new thrust on urban regeneration and Bob Boote was not slow to see the opportunities. The widespread media interest following the book's publication took everyone by surprise. Maybe it was the catchy title, or the fact that it read more like an Edwardian naturalist's perambulations than an official government

FIG 190. George Barker (right) provided crucial leadership for nature conservation in towns and cities from the 1970s onwards. Seen here in a park in Poznań in 1987 with Polish ecologists Maciej Luniak and Tadeusz Mizera.

document. Whatever the reason it sounded a chord and led to a host of media coverage including light-hearted references on BBC Radio Four's satirical programme *Week Ending* and it even made it into *Punch*. So popular was it that the NCC had to reprint it before the end of the year.

The significance of *The Endless Village* is such that it was recently the subject of a detailed follow-up (Shirley, 2007) which explores the changes that have occurred since the 1970s. *The Endless Village Revisited* provides fascinating insights into the subsequent progress of urban nature conservation and the historical background provided by George Barker in the Preface is particularly illuminating.

DEVELOPING A NATIONAL STRATEGY

Although Teagle's report had the greatest impact when it hit the conservation world, another vital part of this new national project had already emerged from the NCC's headquarters in Belgrave Square. This was a report on *Nature Conservation in Urban Areas* by Lyndis Cole. In the summer of 1977 Boote found himself with time to think about the future and he jotted down the first draft of a policy paper on urban conservation. In the autumn he met with Max Nicholson and Lyndis Cole of Land Use Consultants (LUC) to discuss the details of what he liked to call 'the new thrust'. They were both heavily involved in the new ecological park near Tower Bridge which was Max's brainchild. Lyndis Cole was particularly well placed to advise. She was one of the few specialists on ecological design within the landscape profession, and had a strong interest in urban nature. Both were also involved in bringing an ecological approach to a major land reclamation project in Stoke on

FIG 191. As a previous Director General of the Nature Conservancy Max Nicholson's vision and influence provided a powerful stimulus in getting urban wildlife conservation underway in the UK. (Portrait by Mike Woodman with permission of British Trust for Ornithology)

Trent, a key element of which was the Central Forest Park that was designed and implemented by LUC. Bob Boote was very familiar with the transformation that had been achieved as he had started his career in the Staffordshire planning offices and knew at first hand the areas of industrial dereliction once described as 'original hell'.

The result was that NCC commissioned Land Use Consultants to review the potential for urban wildlife conservation in the UK. It was intended that this would provide the basis for a policy statement akin to the influential report on Nature Conservation and Agriculture, which NCC had just published. Whilst the contract was for a period of only six months, the brief was all embracing. As well as requiring a broad-brush appraisal of the wildlife resources of urban areas in the UK, it included the development of a strategy for their protection, to be accomplished through the planning and management of urban areas. If that was not enough the report was also to include examples of techniques for the enhancement of sites and for the creation of new habitats; plus a review of opportunities for environmental education and community involvement. One suspects the hand of Nicholson in all this.

Lyndis Cole rose to the challenge. Whilst her appraisal of the range of wildlife habitats found in urban areas remains one of the best summaries in the literature, it was her recommendations for action that were particularly significant. She laid the ground rules for protection of wildlife sites in urban areas, arguing that they should be assessed not only in terms of their intrinsic value for conservation, but also their value for recreation and environmental education. Her report explained in detail how a strategy for conservation could be implemented through the planning process and working with parks managers. However, the paucity of local authority ecologists working in urban areas meant that there was an urgent need to bring trained ecologists into the cities. Problems still existed with the County Trusts. Even those that included large urban centres were not interested, or didn't have the capacity to deal with urban sites, although Cole found that some natural history societies, such as the LNHS in London, were able to contribute valuable data and information.

Cole's report also set the scene for a new breed of landscape ecologist, by proposing a set of detailed techniques for enhancing existing open spaces and creating exciting new habitats. This was based on her personal knowledge of the new ecological landscapes of the Netherlands referred to earlier. She pointed up the need for a radical change in the management of urban green space and provided plenty of ideas on how this could be achieved. One of her key recommendations was that the NCC should create a new assistant regional officer post for each large conurbation with a specific brief for the urban environment, arguing that the experience gained by these urban specialists would help the NCC to build up its own expertise in urban conservation issues, which was essential if it was to offer leadership in this field.

Two other issues, environmental education and community involvement, should be mentioned because some of the ideas developed in this report were widely accepted as the urban conservation movement got underway. Cole had direct experience of developing opportunities for environmental education in the inner city and provided examples of simple projects that made the most of local conditions, like investigating the weed flora of vacant plots, or creating a butterfly garden in the school yard. They are just as relevant today. Although a few local educational nature reserves and nature trails already existed, this was the first attempt by a national agency to look systematically at what was needed to cater for schools in urban areas and how it could be achieved. Some of the proposals were particularly timely, and it is not surprising that the concept of 'Community Environmental Centres' at borough or district level became a reality in many towns and cities over the next decade.

One of the clear messages from this report was that it couldn't all be done by official agencies and that much of the enthusiasm and know-how would have to emanate from the bottom up, from voluntary bodies and local groups. This was a major departure for the NCC, at that time a top down organisation that still found difficulty liaising with national NGOs, never mind tenants associations. Recognition of the role of local groups was therefore a major step forward, but they were to become rather more significant than anyone realised. No one could then have predicted the radical new movement of urban wildlife trusts that emerged over the next few years.

Although the report by LUC never hit the headlines it was extremely influential behind the scenes. The NCC went on to commission further reports on social issues, one of which was a review by Barbara Mostyn (1979) of the personal benefits and satisfaction that could be gained from participation in urban wildlife projects. By then the NCC had accumulated a wealth of material to support its case for this new field of activity and it published a brief discussion paper entitled *Nature Conservation in Urban Areas: Challenge and Opportunity*, in which it set out the arguments for a new urban programme and the ways of achieving it (NCC, 1979; Cole, 1980). Virtually all of this was based directly on the LUC report. The NCC went ahead and appointed urban officers in four major conurbations, Greater London, West Midlands, Liverpool and Glasgow. It also produced wall charts and other material to encourage greater public interest in urban wildlife. By 1979 so much progress had been made that, for the first time, the subject merited a whole chapter in the NCC's Annual Report (NCC, 1980).

CREATING NEW HABITATS

Whilst policies and strategies were being developed at the national level, activities of a very different kind were beginning to happen on the ground in towns and cities up and down the country. Local people were taking it into their own hands to bring nature back into the city in all sorts of odd corners, often on tiny scraps of land that had been left unused for years. This sudden burgeoning of activity in the late 1970s took many forms. It had as much to do with promoting community gardens and city farms as with concern for nature. Often spearheaded by a few individuals who wanted to make a difference to their local neighbourhood, it was the beginning of a movement that was to become a major feature of urban nature conservation during the next decade. Meanwhile Gardens near Paddington, Mudchute City Farm in the Isle of Dogs and Phoenix Garden hidden away behind Charing Cross Road were some of those in London that caught the spirit of the time. All had a strong social emphasis as places transformed from wasteland to become much treasured by the local community. Most included some elements of nature whether a tiny pond, a butterfly garden or just a patch of buddleia and bramble.

As well as these grassroots community projects a number of others with a strong ecological base were getting underway that showed what could really be achieved in the middle of big cities. The Rural Preservation Association in Liverpool, and Ecological Parks Trust in London were two of the prime movers. In both cases it was a few inspired individuals who made it all happen. The Rural Preservation Association started life in 1975 when Grant Luscombe and two friends, who had recently graduated from Liverpool University, decided to have a go at setting up a new organisation to tackle the debilitating effects of run-down inner-city landscapes. From the outset they were strongly wedded to an ecological and community approach to the landscaping of these areas. Working with local people they developed imaginative solutions for several small wasteland sites and also improved the forlorn streets of Toxteth by providing everyone with a tub to put by their front door. Geraniums, hydrangeas and clematis were soon blooming in Toxteth.

The organisation went from strength to strength and soon became one of the leading players in the naturalistic approach to urban landscape design. In 1979 it launched its Greensight project transforming derelict areas into a new kind of urban landscape where patches of heather or bracken, and spinnies of birch provided a backdrop for more formal open spaces. The work was done by a combination of the design team together with a youth employment project, local volunteers and schools. Luscombe recognised that 'public education was needed to overcome the inbuilt prejudices and cynicism which had arisen from years of neglecting the urban landscape' and he encouraged local people and schools to be actively involved in the new schemes to have a better chance of success.

Not far away a group of landscape designers were putting their knowledge of ecological approaches to real effect in the development of Warrington New Town. Demolition of the derelict Royal Ordnance Factory had resulted in a featureless expanse of 400 ha which was to be developed for new housing. Here Bob Tregay, Duncan Moffatt and others embarked on a massive scheme to create a matrix of new woodlands and meadows, within which the new housing would be built. Their approach was to create a naturalistic landscape using native trees, which proved remarkably effective. The ideas of ecological design were beginning to take effect.

Back in London one tiny project made a huge impact. Creation of the William Curtis Ecological Park on a tiny piece of disused land right next to Tower Bridge was a stroke of genius. It came about because Max Nicholson was involved with planning for the Queen's Silver Jubilee celebrations in 1977. One of the themes was to find positive uses for patches of derelict land in central London. The bit next to Tower Bridge was in a prime position and Nicholson suggested that it should be an ecological park. I suspect that no one on that committee had the slightest idea what he had in mind. He just told them to wait and see.

The place was being used as a lorry park, on land that had recently been a derelict warehouse. Nicholson's aim was to transform this patch of industrial dereliction into a new kind of park where city people could experience nature on their doorstep and, in particular to provide local schools with a place for their environmental studies. The Silver Jubilee Committee provided a grant of £4,000 and Lyndis Cole was told to get on with it.

FIG 192. The William Curtis Ecological Park paved the way for similar parks in many other towns and cities. (David Hope)

In producing her plan for the new park in November 1976, Cole was much influenced by the Heemparken which had been so successful in Dutch cities. These were small parks or mini nature reserves designed to replicate on a small scale the natural habitats of the Netherlands. Accordingly she aimed to produce a variety of microhabitats including a pond and marsh, osier beds, thickets of native trees and shrubs, flower rich meadows, and even sand-dune vegetation. There were twenty different habitats crammed into the one-hectare plot! Where the basement of buildings remained, willows and buddleia were allowed to thrive and areas of rubble were produced to encourage a variety of wasteland species.

To many who heard of it, the idea that a bare expanse of hardcore could be rapidly transformed into a rich mosaic of mini-ecosystems in which hundreds of species of native plant and animal species could flourish sounded unbelievable. Yet that is what was achieved over a period of months. Cole used great ingenuity with the limited resources available and the design was based on ecological principles. This meant finding suitable substrates and avoiding use of inappropriate nutrient-rich topsoil, which was achieved by the simple expedient of opening the site as an inner-city subsoil dump. That way 350 lorry loads of subsoil were obtained over three weeks for virtually nothing. Volunteers from the Conservation Corps and the Bermondsey Boys and Girls Brigade carried out all the landscaping and tree planting, with nearly 1,000 trees donated by conservation organisations. Completed over about six months, just in time for the Silver Jubilee celebrations, the park was an instant success with the local community. It was not long before it was booked solid by local schools every day.

The park was named after William Curtis the eighteenth-century botanist famous for producing the first flora of London, and one of the pioneers of London's natural history (Curtis, 1771). The new park became something of a pioneer too. It was remarkably successful, not only in catering for local school

FIG 193. Aerial view of the William Curtis Ecological Park

children who would otherwise have had little or no contact with nature, but also by providing a model for nature parks elsewhere in the country. The William Curtis Ecological Park closed in 1985, when the land was handed back to its owners, but the Ecological Parks Trust that was set up to run it went on to become one of the leading players in this field.

So, by the end of the 1970s, the stage was set for a host of new initiatives in urban nature conservation. Although the NCC provided support and encouragement, I think it is fair to say that government departments were slow to appreciate the significance of what was happening. They were not alone. County Naturalists' Trusts were equally unaware, or chose to ignore the signs. But it was here that the first rumblings of change became apparent. At the annual conference of the Royal Society for Nature Conservation (RSNC) in 1979 a number of speakers, including John Davidson of the Countryside Commission, argued that county trusts must start to address urban issues. Some even warned that if they continued to be a cosy club that ignored the places where most people live they would be sidelined. The next few years were to prove them right.

CHAPTER 13

The 1980s: Time for Action

THE 1980S SAW A SURGE of activity in towns and cities throughout the country promoting urban nature conservation. It was a time when enthusiasm for this new approach was translated into action in many different ways and by widely different sectors, involving both voluntary and official agencies. The result was seen in several quite different strands of activity, all linked by a common philosophy.

At one level there was a grass-roots movement of local people fighting to protect places that were valued in their local neighbourhood. Others were involved in setting up urban wildlife groups, or new wildlife trusts for urban areas, challenging the established orthodoxy of the county naturalists trusts. Within the voluntary sector other new bodies emerged, devoted specifically to urban ecology and conservation. The Trust for Urban Ecology in London, Landlife in Liverpool and the Centre for Urban Ecology and Urban Wildlife Group in Birmingham all played their part in developing a new philosophy. Much of this was supported by government schemes to promote work experience for the unemployed, resulting in a combination of social and environmental objectives. At the same time in London and the new Metropolitan Counties, such as Merseyside, Manchester and the West Midlands, policies and programmes were adopted to deal specifically with conservation of nature in the urban environment. In parallel some landscape architects became enthused with these new ideas, and promoted ecological principles in landscape design, particularly in relation to green spaces in towns and cities. All of this was supported by a plethora of conferences and publications promoting the newly developing ideas of urban conservation.

LOCAL CAMPAIGNS

One of the first local battles took place in the suburbs of north London when a disused railway line in Haringey was bought by the local council for housing. The railway, about six miles long, was a branch line from Finsbury Park to Alexandra Palace. The line had been closed to passengers since 1954 but was still used for some freight traffic until eventually closed in 1972. By then the line sides had become wooded and the bridges and stations were well vegetated. Local people were adamant that it was of greater value as a natural asset and made a counter proposal for the line to become a linear park and nature reserve. An association was formed to protect the line, and when a public inquiry was held in 1978 the 'Friends' presented evidence with details of the birds, plants and insects found along the route, making a strong case for its retention. The Inspector found in their favour and recommended that it should become a linear nature park. The local Council accepted this decision and the Parkland Walk was opened in 1982. Since then some 340 species of plants and over 60 species of birds have been recorded. The range of habitats provides a variety of conditions supporting over 20 species of butterflies, including the silver-washed fritillary. It is used daily by hundreds of people for informal recreation and was designated in 1990 as a statutory Local Nature Reserve. This was the first case to be contested primarily on the basis of its value for nature conservation and it paved the way for many others during the 1980s.

FIG 194. The Parkland Walk, Haringey in 2010.

Gunnersbury Triangle was the one that really hit the headlines, and in doing so changed the rules for urban nature conservation. This small triangle of woodland between the railway lines at Chiswick in west London became a *cause célèbre* during the early 1980s when local people fought to protect the site from development. As with so many cases of this kind the first that people knew something was afoot was when local resident Anne Mayo saw that birch trees had been felled to provide access for drilling machinery. The trees were on a piece of land that had remained undisturbed for many years, landlocked between the railway tracks. Some years earlier one edge of the triangle had been developed for warehouses and offices, and now it looked as if there may be plans for the rest of the site. Ann Mayo made enquiries at the local planning office in Hounslow and found that this was indeed the case. Although no official planning application had been made, there were suggestions that the site be developed for warehousing and initial investigations were underway. Following urgent discussions with council officers, a tree preservation order was served on the owners British Rail to prevent any further destruction of the woodland. But in her discussions Anne Mayo also found that the site was designated for development in the local plan and it became clear that council planning officers fully expected the warehouse development to go ahead. The idea that nature conservation arguments might be taken seriously was not given a moment's thought.

This all started in December 1981. Over the next few months Anne Mayo was busy organising a local campaign to save the triangle. She succeeded in making the place famous by talking about it on radio and television, particularly on John Craven's *Newsround* (a BBC news programme for children), and she gained a great deal of local support for her ideas. By now some local councillors were questioning whether development should go ahead and it became a hot issue in Hounslow Council. I found myself involved in July 1982 when Alfred King, the leader of the council, came to see me at County Hall shortly after I joined the Greater London Council as its first ecologist. He was concerned that if the council turned down an application they would be faced with costs if they lost a public inquiry. So he asked me for a second opinion on the triangle's ecological value and I soon found myself on a site visit in the company of Anne Mayo. As it happened she was delighted to be able to visit the site officially as she and her associates in the recently formed Chiswick Wildlife Group had been unable to obtain such permission.

I didn't have to be inside the Triangle long to be convinced that a good case could be made for its protection. The woodland had a remarkably natural feel about it, with fine open stands of birch and thickets of willow interspersed with open glades that provided ideal habitat for butterflies. Although only 2.5 ha in

FIG 195. Aerial view of Gunnersbury Triangle.

extent it contained a variety of habitats and there was plenty of wildlife interest to make a good local nature reserve. The presence of willow warblers, blackcaps and redpolls, and the natural character of the woodland, distinguished it from the local parks and other green areas in that part of London. Indeed it soon became apparent that its natural character was its most valuable feature.

I had no difficulty in supporting the Chiswick Wildlife Group, which had by then produced a booklet outlining the features of the site and suggesting that it should become a nature reserve. The group gained a huge amount of popular support for its proposals, so it was no surprise to find councillors taking their suggestions very seriously and some were keen to negotiate directly with British Rail. So followed a series of meetings with the owners and developers, but all to no avail. Despite a great deal of pressure from the borough, several public meetings and a major public outcry against the development, British Rail decided to go ahead and a formal planning application was made early in 1983.

In view of the support that I had given, the borough asked whether I would act on its behalf as an expert witness at a public inquiry if it turned down the application. Even at that stage planning officers were not convinced that they had firm grounds for refusal of planning permission. However, it was refused and a public inquiry followed in July 1983.

The public inquiry on Gunnersbury Triangle was a turning point for urban nature conservation because it brought the whole philosophy into the public arena for the first time. It was significant in a number of ways.

FIG 196. Gunnersbury Triangle has a remarkably tranquil atmosphere, despite the trains running alongside.

For a start the triangle was not recognised in any way as a site of nature conservation value. At that time in London the only places that had any protection in planning terms were the few Sites of Special Scientific Interest notified by the Nature Conservancy Council. The triangle was way below the quality required for SSSI status. Worse still, it had been identified as land suitable for industrial development in the local Borough Plan which determined priorities for planning purposes. For those accustomed to traditional nature conservation arguments there seemed to be little chance of success.

But the arguments at this inquiry did not rely on traditional approaches. The strength of local opinion and the value of the place to local people mattered far more than the detailed factual evidence regarding the wildlife content of the site. It was argued by the developers that the triangle had no significant nature conservation value as it did not meet any of the nationally recognised criteria. In their view it was too small, contained no rare habitats or species, and lacked both diversity and long-established habitats. In short it had none of the features that, in traditional nature conservation terms, would make it a place worth conserving. But this inquiry was to demonstrate that the criteria used nationally to assess whether a site should become an SSSI or nature reserve, were largely irrelevant in the urban context. Instead the argument centred on the value of the triangle to local people. Two factors were paramount. The triangle was the only sizable piece of natural habitat for miles around, and it was surrounded by a large number of people. The fact that it was the only place where people in this part of London could experience a relatively natural habitat at first hand became the crucial argument.

The Chiswick Wildlife Group made a powerful case for the triangle to become a nature reserve for local residents and to provide facilities for environmental education for local schools. There was substantial support for this from local teachers and from Hounslow's science advisor, who had visited the site with me. He felt that it provided a strong feeling of being in the country surrounded by the natural world. He regarded this as an important experience for city children and argued that the triangle would be of value not only for ecological field studies, but also for geography, local history and art. He was impressed by the range of habitats and felt that a great deal of biological field work could be accommodated, including studies of food chains, vegetation succession and the natural history of woodlands. He emphasised that there was a shortage of areas locally for field studies in a relatively natural environment and was convinced that the triangle had considerable potential for such use.

For me the highlight of the inquiry was the evening session held in Chiswick Town Hall, attended by over 200 local residents, many of whom spoke with feeling about the value of having a piece of nature in their midst. One elderly lady talked about the enormous pleasure she gained from seeing the birch trees swaying in the wind. With her arms swaying like the trees she described what she saw from her window and was given a great ovation, for she expressed beautifully what so many wanted to say. After which the Inspector reminded everyone, yet again, that this was a public inquiry and there shall be no applause!

Three weeks after the inquiry the Inspector announced his decision. He considered 'that the local ecological significance of this site is so great that planning permission should not be granted' and the appeal was dismissed. He went on to say:

> Many of those who live in the area clearly regard the site as being of ecological importance, as well as being a valuable amenity feature. The strength of local feeling manifests itself in the petition of over 3,000 signatures, the large number of letters written in response to the application and this appeal, a well attended evening session of the inquiry and most importantly, the careful and empirical studies carried out by the Chiswick Wildlife Group, whose evidence and report impressed me greatly.

The land was subsequently bought from British Rail by the Borough of Hounslow, with the help of a grant from the Greater London Council of £58,000 (under powers for the creation of Local Nature Reserves in the National Parks and Access to the Countryside Act of 1949) and the Chiswick Wildlife Group took over management of the nature reserve in March 1985. It very quickly became enormously popular with local people, attracting up to 200 people on its open days during the first two years, when it was also used by 35 school groups. They soon had plans for 20 visits a month. The triangle was designated a statutory Local Nature Reserve in 1987 and remains one of London Wildlife Trust's key nature reserves.

FIG 197. The Triangle became a statutory Local Nature Reserve in 1987.

In London there followed a succession of public inquiries where nature conservation was the main issue. During the period 1982 to 1988, 16 out of 22 such inquiries were decided in favour of conservation. Some places were examples of semi-natural habitats of considerable nature conservation value, like Crayford Marshes one of the last remaining stretches of grazing marsh in London. Similarly there was Sydenham Hill Woods, the nearest survivor of ancient woodland to the centre of London. A vigorous and successful campaign was mounted to save Walthamstow Marshes which became known as 'the fen in the city'. But others were more like Gunnersbury Triangle; they were relatively insignificant ecologically. One of these was a patch of wet alder wood called Wilderness Island on the River Wandle at Hackbridge in the London suburbs of Sutton. Another was an area of unused land at the back of Halsbury Road in Ealing, where there was a proposal to build houses. Following an inquiry in 1989 the Inspector dismissed the appeal and this extract from her decision letter gets right to the heart of urban nature conservation:

> My opinion is that although the appeal site may posses few if any very rare species, or unusual habitats, its real value is not to be assessed in those very specialist terms. I consider its true value lies in the social, educational and environmental contribution it makes to the lives of people living in the area. The virtue of the appeal site is that it is immediately adjacent to large residential areas and is potentially accessible to all members of those communities. The habitats ... offer opportunities for the urban dweller to experience, learn and appreciate flora and fauna which they might otherwise not encounter.

Not all these campaigns succeeded. A small area of disused railway sidings alongside Shakespeare Road in Brixton hit the headlines in 1985 when a colony of

FIG 198. Local people formed Action Groups to save important wildlife sites, like the filter beds in Hackney which became part of the Lea Valley Park.

bee orchids was found. Further investigations revealed an unusual assemblage of plants including communities rich in lichens and mosses (see Chapter 4). When it became known that British Rail had plans to sell off the land for housing the London Wildlife Trust mounted a campaign to protect the area as a nature reserve. As in other places the Trust gained huge support from local people. The Borough of Lambeth refused planning permission for housing and a public inquiry was held in 1987. Like others at this time the result was a decision by the Government Inspector in favour of nature conservation. The local borough proposed to buy the land by compulsory purchase to establish a nature reserve. Conservationists thought they had won the battle until the Secretary of State for the Environment, Nicholas Ridley overturned his Inspector's decision and refused to allow the borough to buy the site. It was clear that Ridley favoured economic development over protection of a nature reserve, and had scant regard for local public opinion. His lack of enthusiasm for nature conservation later manifested itself more seriously at the national level when he proposed the break up of the Nature Conservancy Council and a sell-off of National Nature Reserves (Marren, 2002).

London was not the only place where such battles were being fought. In Bristol the newly formed Avon Wildlife Trust successfully challenged City Council plans for housing on part of Brandon Hill in the centre of the city, and subsequently

converted the area into a colourful wildflower meadow. It has since become one
of the Trust's best-known nature reserves. But one of the most influential battles
was in Birmingham, where a tiny patch of wooded bog achieved a special place in
the history of urban nature conservation. This is Moseley Bog, a strange mixture
of wet woodland and marsh, with abandoned Victorian gardens now colonised by
wood horsetail and remnants of a derelict millpond where Sphagnum moss and
marsh cinquefoil still thrive. For local people who know it well it is a rather special
secret place. It certainly influenced J. R. R. Tolkien who lived nearby as a boy, and
could well have provided inspiration for the enchanted valleys of Withywindle and
Rivendell in *The Lord of the Rings*.

Only three miles from the city centre, the bog lies hidden behind suburban
houses in the valley of the Coldbath Brook. It was once part of a heathland called
Great Common, which explains the past occurrence of rarities such as grass of
Parnassus, bog pimpernel and red rattle, and the presence today of royal fern.
The brook was turned into a millstream in the eighteenth century, with a pool to
feed Sarehole Mill, which was still working in 1919. The old pool, now the site of
the bog, became dilapidated and overgrown and the streamsides and old gardens
gradually became colonised by secondary woodland. So it was in 1978 when
Teagle included a short description in *The Endless Village*. He was particularly
impressed by the extraordinary abundance of wood horsetail, 'one of the last
things one would expect in suburban Birmingham'.

In the spring of 1980 students from a local school were on one of their regular
visits to record the wildlife of the area when they found surveyors measuring up
for a housing scheme. Local residents soon got to hear and were up in arms when
they discovered a plan to build over twenty houses, some of which would almost
certainly disrupt the spring-line that feeds the bog. They mounted a spontaneous
protest. The enthusiasm of those involved comes over very clearly in an article
by Joy Fifer and Lyn Roberts in the first Newsletter of the newly formed West
Midlands Urban Wildlife Group. When they started the 'Save our Bog' campaign
they had no idea how many people knew or cared about Moseley Bog. But the
first meeting attracted over 200 people and within a month they had collected
12,500 signatures for a petition presented to the city council. Joy Fifer said:
'little did we know what we were letting ourselves in for, but never have I done
anything so worth while ... Moseley Bog has touched people's hearts.'

It is said that when a council official was taken to visit the site he found a
small boy up a tree who asked, 'Are you the man who's come to save the bog?'
No doubt powerful arguments were presented regarding the fate of locally
endangered species, but it was local campaigners who carried the day. The bog
was notified as a Site of Special Scientific Interest (SSSI) in 1980 but the campaign

leaflet said: 'We all need to have the experience of being in a wilderness ... the site is more than an SSSI. It's magic!' David Nicholson-Lord (1987) pointed out that the story of Moseley Bog was a parable about riches found where they are least expected, in one's own backyard.

It was several years before the issue was settled, with a reduced number of houses being allowed which didn't affect the bog, and the site itself was bought by Birmingham City Council which later designated it as a Local Nature Reserve (LNR). It was also recognised by the Council as a Site of Importance for Nature Conservation in the strategic plan and is now leased by the Council to the Wildlife Trust. An adjacent area previously known as the Dell, created by infilling part of the brook to make football pitches, was subsequently planted with 10,000 trees to create a woodland known as Joy's Wood as a tribute to Joy Fifer. A boardwalk was constructed to allow safe access through the wet woodland and the whole site now forms part of the Shire Country Park which recognises the association with J. R. R. Tolkien.

In 2000 Joy Fifer received a Moseley Millennium Hero Award for her services to the local community. In a special edition of the *Moseley Bog Paper* she paid tribute to those who had supported the campaign, pointing out that it was not confined to local residents but also involved a number of professionals including Chris Baines and Jeremy Purseglove who provided scientific knowledge which enabled the local team to develop reasoned arguments. She also mentions George Barker, 'who was one of the first people to see the potential of the site. It was he who brought together the management committee of the bog and pushed for the site to be designated as an LNR.' The Moseley Bog campaign owes much to a heightened public awareness of wildlife in Birmingham and the Black Country following publication of the *Endless Village* only two years before. But the campaign itself also provided an opportunity to put George Barker's vision into practice, by building strong links between local people and professional ecologists. Moseley Bog provided a model that was to be repeated throughout the country

The success of these local campaigns highlights the radical nature of urban nature conservation. Something very significant was happening during the 1980s. In almost every respect urban conservation involved quite different approaches from what had gone before. The kinds of sites involved were often very different from those traditionally rated highly by conservationists. Derelict and disused industrial land, abandoned railway yards, overgrown Victorian cemeteries and colliery spoil tips were newcomers to the conservation world. In many cases their habitats were relatively new, often having developed within the past 50–100 years. Nor were they particularly rich in rare or unusual species, except perhaps the aliens which added novelty to their character. Indeed many were quite ordinary and unassuming, lacking any of the qualities that would give them high conservation importance. But these places had a special value for the people who lived near them. For urban dwellers they provided their only opportunity for contact with the natural world, and that gave them a very special significance which was reflected by the strength of public opinion exhibited when treasured sites were threatened. It was this social value, given formal recognition for the first time by Inspectors at public inquiries, that brought a whole new dimension to the nature conservation debate, and that is why these inquiries were so significant.

URBAN WILDLIFE GROUPS

The rise of new groups dealing with urban nature conservation was another key development during the early 1980s. New initiatives in the West Midlands, Merseyside and London paved the way and then it all happened very quickly, with new groups springing up all around the country.

In the West Midlands the seeds were sown with publication of *The Endless Village* in 1978. Shortly after that Council members of NCC took a trip to the West Midlands where they visited a disused sand and gravel working called Queslett Quarry near Walsall. This was one of the outstanding sites featured in the book, with a wide range of habitats including large breeding colonies of sand martins. But at the time that planning permission had been given for gravel working, it was specified that the after-use should be as a landfill site. The time had now come for the site to be filled. Bob Boote, the NCC's Director General, argued that it should be retained in entirety as a nature reserve, but became rather less enthusiastic when told that it would cost £3 million. However, the visit sparked a debate amongst local conservationists. One of those involved was Pete Byfield from Birmingham Friends of the Earth (FoE) who was impressed by the work of Landlife in Liverpool and advocated the need for a pro-active group in Birmingham. Another was Chris Baines, at that time a local landscape architect, who argued that NCC and the county wildlife trusts were not pulling their weight in urban areas. They felt that things needed shaking up. Inspired by a conference led by FoE, they brought together a small group of like-minded individuals to bring pressure on planners and others in the West Midlands for natural areas to be protected.

These were the beginnings of the West Midlands Urban Wildlife Group, which was launched in July 1980 less than two months after Moseley Bog first hit the headlines. Initially this was a small group of local naturalists, ecologists, planners, community workers, teachers and landscape designers. But fighting for the protection of threatened wildlife sites quickly transformed it into a popular local movement with a substantial membership. By 1984 the group had 350 full members, 3,000 life supporters, and up to eighty staff funded by the Manpower Services Commission. This new body was dealing with up to 100 planning cases a year, assisting local community groups and drawing up alternative proposals that were more beneficial to wildlife (Nicholson-Lord, 1987). As its influence grew the organisation broadened its activities as a national Urban Wildlife Group assisting others to develop similar solutions in other towns and cities.

Its success in Birmingham and the Black Country caused some of the leading members of the Worcester Wildlife Trust to become alarmed that this new upstart might be poaching members from the established nature conservation trusts. Baines argued strongly, and rightly as it turned out, that the urban group was attracting entirely new people, and that existing county trusts need not worry. But worry they did, and the antagonism between the newly developing urban groups and established county trusts rumbled on for at least ten years. Some would say it still persists.

Formation of the London Wildlife Trust went through similar problems, though here the situation was rather different. For many years the London Natural History Society had taken the lead in keeping an eye on conservation matters in the capital in view of the fact that the surrounding county trusts took little interest in London issues. The LNHS had in fact been extraordinarily good at recording and documenting London's wildlife and it was they rather than the county trusts who were most threatened by the emergence of the newly formed LWT. It was launched in the spring of 1981 at a weekend conference on Nature in London. The organisers made sure they had the right supporting cast. As well as senior figures from the London scene it was attended by Franklyn Perring from the Royal Society for Nature Conservation (RSNC) representing the county trusts, John Davidson of the Countryside Commission and Chris Baines from the West Midlands, who had by now become a leading figure in the urban conservation movement. The LWT quickly established itself as a major force in London. Within six years it had 16 permanent staff, a team of 40 employed from Manpower Services funding, and a membership of 5,500. If there was still any acrimony with existing wildlife trusts it was more to do with the style adopted by the new organisation, which in its early days promoted an overtly radical image. Two other new urban trusts were established at this time in Avon and Cleveland by an amicable splitting off from their local county trusts.

By the mid-1980s urban wildlife groups were established in many large towns and cities including Reading, Nottingham, Plymouth, Glasgow, Norwich, Leeds, Sheffield, Leicester, Manchester and the Lothians. Some, like Leeds, Sheffield and Norwich, were independent of the local county trust, and indeed were formed as a reaction to the rural bias of these bodies (Smyth, 1987). One of the most successful was the Leicester City Wildlife Project run by Phil Lomax and David Nicholls, which described itself as the urban arm of the Leicester and Rutland Trust for Nature Conservation. In 1985 it had a membership of 3,500, plus 40 staff assisted by several hundred volunteers, and was undertaking an extraordinary array of activities. These included a comprehensive ecological survey of all the open land in Leicester (amounting to 1,600 sites); giving advice on conservation to planners and land managers; managing some of the best examples of the city's wildlife habitats; creating new nature areas; and running campaigns and public events. Much of the work was funded through the government's Manpower Services scheme designed to provide training and work experience for the unemployed. It was a time of enormous energy and enthusiasm when those involved were carried forward by the zeal of a crusade. Despite its success there were still some members of the Leicester and Rutland Trust who felt that the urban project was inappropriate and might somehow damage the image of the trust.

In 1985 an umbrella organisation called the Fairbrother Group was established, named after Nan Fairbrother author of *New Lives New Landscapes* one of the seminal works on urban landscapes, and soon this became formalised as the Association of Urban Wildlife Groups. By 1987 there were over 80 groups and the RSNC provided an urban co-ordinator, with a steering group whose membership was largely determined by the Fairbrother Group. Urban wildlife groups have since grown from strength to strength and are now firmly established as a major part of the wildlife trust partnership.

URBAN PLANNING

Equally important at this time was the role played by the Metropolitan Counties. Indeed some would say they were the real catalysts. Each of these new counties was required to include policies for nature conservation in its so-called Structure Plan. I mentioned earlier that it was a request from the West Midlands County for details of nature conservation sites that led the NCC to commission the survey of the Black Country that resulted in publication of *The Endless Village*. The West Midlands was not alone in finding a dearth of information when it started the job. All the metropolitan counties were in the same position. Because sites in urban areas had been disregarded previously by the NCC and the county wildlife trusts, there was little information available and the metropolitan counties had to set about gathering information on important sites. They also needed to adopt policies for nature conservation that could withstand the pressures from development.

FIG 199. Nature Conservation Strategies were produced for most large towns and cities.

The first urban nature conservation strategy in the UK was produced for Liverpool and its fringes by the Urban Wildlife Unit of Landlife in 1983. It was commissioned by the NCC as part of a series of research reports on urban ecology. At the heart of this document was the concept of 'people as a part of nature rather than apart from nature'. Others quickly followed. The West Midlands Strategy (1984) again placed considerable emphasis on the value of wildlife to local people. It included a map showing wildlife reservoirs, open-space corridors, links and stepping stones, all of which were intended to protect areas of significance. It also identified Wildlife Action Areas in densely built-up districts lacking accessible wildlife habitats, suggesting that wherever possible existing habitats must be improved and new habitats created to improve access for the public. The strategy for Greater Manchester (1986), which won the Conservation Foundation Environment Award, was a beautifully produced slim volume setting out a series of policies for 'protection, development and enjoyment of wildlife resources in the county'. It did not attempt to identify important sites for nature conservation, but created a policy framework for the district councils to follow. Tyne and Wear, working closely with the NCC, produced a more comprehensive strategy identifying all the important wildlife sites. It was way ahead of its time in its emphasis on implementation through all sectors of the community, and in the detailed suggestions for creating new wildlife habitats (NCC, 1988).

In 1982 the Greater London Council (GLC) decided to bring ecology into planning. Audrey Lees had recently become the controller of planning, having moved from Merseyside where, as Chief Planner, she was used to the services of an ecological team. She had not been in London long when a contentious environmental issue arose at her weekly meeting with chief officers. Her suggestion that 'we had better ask the ecologist' was met with blank looks, and someone had the temerity to ask, 'do we have one?' Which resulted in the swift instruction: 'Well we had better get one!' So it came about that I was shortly appointed as London's first ecologist, soon to be supported by a team of ecologists, which brought a totally new dimension to the planning process. We had three main functions: to develop strategic policies for ecology and nature conservation; provide an ecological database for the whole of London; and provide ecological advice on planning issues and on the management of council-owned land. In addition we soon found ourselves involved in creating ecology parks and nature centres, and establishing a London Ecology Centre, as well as organising grants for environmental organisations. One of the team was called a 'community liaison ecologist', probably the first such job title in the UK, which emphasises the importance placed on links with local people.

At that time the Greater London Development Plan, which provided the strategic framework for planning in the capital, didn't mention either ecology or nature conservation, which meant that London boroughs were free to ignore such topics in their local plans. The first step, therefore, was to produce a set of policies for ecology and nature conservation suitable for local planning. These were to be incorporated in revisions of the London Plan currently underway. The most important of these policies was a requirement for local plans to identify sites of nature conservation value, and for ecological considerations to be taken into account in considering proposed new developments. Others recognised the need to encourage greater ecological diversity by appropriate design and management of open spaces, especially in urban areas deficient in natural habitats. The need to create new habitats in such areas was emphasised.

It will be no surprise to learn that the importance of nature to local people figured highly in these policies. It was argued that selection of important sites should not only be based on their ecological features, but also on their value as a source of inspiration and enjoyment for the local community. The range of policies was not restricted to nature conservation but also included ecological policies relevant to mineral extraction, waste disposal, flood alleviation and the use of vacant and derelict land. These policies were first published in a popular handbook on ecology and nature conservation (GLC, 1984). Although revisions to the London Plan never came into effect, because of the demise of the GLC in 1986, nevertheless London boroughs subsequently adopted many of these policies in their local plans. After the GLC was abolished implementation of the overall strategy for nature conservation in London became the responsibility of the London Ecology Unit, which continued the ecological work of the GLC. The ecological database was maintained and updated regularly and the Unit provided advice to the boroughs on hundreds of planning cases every year. (For further details on how this developed see Chapter 14.)

By the mid-1980s virtually all the metropolitan counties had produced a nature conservation strategy. Some just managed it before these counties were abolished, along with the Greater London Council in 1986. But despite the counties being short-lived these documents had great significance. They provided a much needed framework and philosophy, not only for their successor authorities, but also for other planning authorities elsewhere who were fast getting in on the act. Many smaller towns and cities developed official programmes for nature conservation and by 1989 these included Leicester, Nottingham, Norwich, Newport, Bristol and Edinburgh. Even the small town of St Helens in Merseyside identified 97 sites of wildlife interest in its 'Policy for Nature'. The urban wildlife unit of Landlife, together with the St Helens and Knowsley Groundwork Trust, helped to produce a plan that was way ahead of its time, especially the policy for 'encouraging local communities and voluntary groups to participate in the management of sites of existing and potential wildlife interest' (St Helens Borough Council, 1986).

All these strategies recognised the need for protection of habitats of value, enhancement of existing areas of open land for wildlife, the creation of new habitats in areas of particular need, and provision of an ecological database for planning. They all emphasised the value of nature to the residents of urban areas. Indeed this was often the main justification for their nature conservation policies. In 1987 these new initiatives were recognised by central government for the first time. Revised advice on nature conservation for planning authorities in England and Wales listed some of these recent initiatives by local authorities. They included habitat surveys and databases, provision of specialist ecological advisors, preparation of local nature conservation strategies, creation of new wildlife habitats and promoting greater public awareness of nature conservation. Protection of locally important sites was not specifically mentioned, but two years later the DoE suggested that London Boroughs refer to the Ecology Handbooks published by the London Ecology Unit in preparing their Unitary Development Plans. For London this gave the go-ahead for statutory planning documents to include measures for the protection of locally important wildlife sites.

CREATING NEW HABITATS

By 1980 the William Curtis Ecological Park at Tower Bridge had been going
for four years and much was being learnt. Max Nicholson had insisted from
the start that detailed monitoring should be carried out to record changes in
flora and fauna, and the park's annual reports make fascinating reading. During
construction of the park about 150 different plant species were introduced to
create a range of habitats including a small spinney of birches, mixed woodland
with elder, poplar, aspen, willow, and hazel, as well as osier beds and a shallow
pool. But the rate of natural colonisation was surprising. During the next two
years the number of species increased significantly and by 1980 almost 350 species
had been recorded. Some were early colonisers of the bare ground like chickweed,
shepherd's purse and pineapple weed, which gradually disappeared, whilst
others came at a later stage. One of the most notable features was the vigorous
establishment of clover and vetches. After only four years 27 species of these
leguminous plants had colonised the open habitats. Records also show that of the
900 trees that had been planted, nearly 600 died during these first few years due
to drought. This was caused by drying
out of shallow soil over the buried
basements of buildings, exacerbated by
high summer temperatures due to heat
reflecting off surrounding buildings.
Much had to be learnt about urban
ecology.

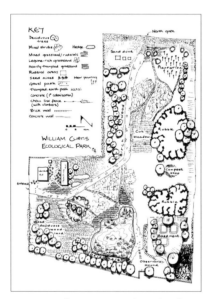

FIG 200. William Curtis Ecological Park: a
map of the habitats (Ecological Parks Trust
Annual Report 1984).

Of all the changes that occurred,
the gradual colonisation of the park by
butterflies was most impressive. During
the first year after the new habitats were
created in 1976 only six species were
recorded, all of which were common
and predictable in central London. The
following year a further six occurred
including common blue, wall, Essex
skipper and speckled wood. Next year
saw four more additions, small copper,
comma, green-veined white and painted
lady. So the number of species gradually
increased, until by 1983 a total of

21 species had been recorded, 16 of which occurred regularly in subsequent years. This was partly a response to increasing maturity of the new habitats, but more particularly to the abundance of nectar-yielding legumes such as clovers, black medic, common vetch and alfalfa. Colonisation by other invertebrates was also impressive with over 200 species recorded by 1980. The pond was particularly successful and pond dipping quickly became one of the most popular pursuits for school parties.

This was at a time when inner city schoolchildren had virtually no contact with the natural world and the park made huge advances in environmental education. It was a great success with local schools and during the eight years of its existence catered for over 120,000 visits by school children. The two teachers Pam Morris and Anne Heaton developed a range of projects for both primary and secondary level, providing guidance for others developing similar schemes elsewhere in the country. For many of the children the park was a great delight, something they will never forget. But the project had its setbacks too. Not all the local children appreciated nature in ways that we might hope. One weekend Pam Morris was devastated to find some of the older children playing tennis with the frogs! But the park provided an inspiration and joy for many, and when it was due to close down they organised a massive rescue operation for the wildlife, taking buckets of frogspawn and minibeasts to other local ponds.

It soon became clear that Nicholson had a bigger agenda than the park at Tower Bridge. Early in 1981 the Ecological Parks Trust published its first report, in which he made clear his aim for the Trust to become a national advisory body on urban ecology, with an ambitious programme for city nature parks. The Trust had already acquired two other sites, in Southwark at Lavender Pond and Dulwich Upper Wood. Now he had plans for a new ecological park as part of the Trafford Park Trading Estate in Manchester. By the time that the William Curtis Ecological Park closed in July 1985 plans were also well advanced for construction of a much larger park in the Surrey Docks at Rotherhithe. Later that year the name was changed to the Trust for Urban Ecology (TRUE), which soon found itself responsible for running seven ecological parks in London. But by then the idea of ecology parks had become widely accepted, and new examples were springing up all over the country.

On the day I started work at the Greater London Council in July 1982 I was told that the planning committee had decided that a derelict coal yard on the banks of the Regents Canal at the back of King's Cross station was to become an ecology park, rather than a parking space for long-distance coaches. So it was over to me to turn this patch of inner-city wasteland into an ecological park for use by schools and the local community. That was my first introduction to

Camley Street Natural Park, which became one of the best-known examples
in the country (see also Chapter 15). Other cities too had their nature parks,
including Benwell in Newcastle, Brandon Hill in Bristol, Norman Street Park in
Birmingham, Spinney Hill Park and Rally Nature Garden in Leicester.

So by the time the London-based Trust for Urban Ecology was set up, there
were many local initiatives, and a number of other organisations willing to take
the lead in providing a national advisory service. One of these was Landlife in
Liverpool which had grown from small beginnings as the Rural Preservation
Association to become a major force with a huge range of ground-breaking
activities. Like TRUE it was also devoted to understanding the science of urban
ecology, but had made greater use of government funding available from the
Job Creation Programme and employed well over 100 people in a wide variety of
projects putting this knowledge into practice.

Much of its success was due to the enthusiasm and single mindedness of
Grant Luscombe who led the organisation in the early days and remained its
Director until 2012. In remembering all that went on during the early pioneering
years he talks about 'those heady days of feverish activity when everything was
new and so much could be achieved'. In 1995, on Landlife's twentieth anniversary,
he wrote:

FIG 201. Landlife's National Wildflower Centre in Liverpool, 2010.

FIG 202. Displays of cornfield annuals at the Wildflower Centre: poppies, corn marigold and cornflower (left); Bird's-foot trefoil (below left) attracting red-tailed bumble bees.

There can surely be few experiences more depressing than life in the inner city or in the urban fringe, where so often the grey bleakness of concrete and decay dominates the landscape. That is why people have stared in disbelief at the stunning fields of wildflowers which local children and their families have helped us create on former derelict sites in Merseyside.

Over the years his team had landscaped sixty of these derelict sites and created a further ten nature study areas. In doing so Landlife built up a considerable body of experience in creative conservation and has had enormous influence in the development of new techniques, such as the novel practice of using soil inversion to create low nutrient conditions (Luscombe et al., 2008).

One milestone in their early years was winning the Gold Medal and Prize of Honour for their Wildlife Garden at the Liverpool International Garden Festival in 1984. The team had already produced an urban nature conservation strategy for Liverpool (the first in the UK) and went on to carry out detailed studies of derelict industrial sites with a view to them becoming urban nature reserves,

FIG 203. Professor Tony Bradshaw (left) receiving the Institute of Ecology's Medal in 2007 from Sir John Harman for his lifetime of work in Applied Ecology. (Jason Reeves)

including colliery spoil tips around St Helens. In 1982 Landlife spread its wings by developing a six-acre wildflower nursery, and started trading in wildflower plants and seeds, which proved to be enormously successful. It later broadened its scope to become the National Wildflower Centre based at Court Hey Park in Liverpool. Good ecological horticulture based on sound science has always been at the centre of their work and Landlife is still producing innovative solutions for dealing with urban landscapes (Luscombe & Scott, 2011).

Why Liverpool? Permeating much of the work on Merseyside was the thinking of one man, Tony Bradshaw. As Professor of Botany at the University of Liverpool he had become a national expert on the ecological restoration of derelict land. But during the 1980s he became increasingly involved in problems of the urban environment, and brought his understanding of applied ecology to bear on the management of urban green spaces. He had a great knack for finding simple solutions that worked. For instance, it was he who first pointed out that lack of nitrogen was the main problem when trying to get vegetation going on thin urban soils composed of brick rubble, cement and mortar. He found the most effective technique was to establish clovers and vetches, particularly *Trifolium repens,* which can rapidly accumulate nitrogen in the soil. His work not only provided the basis for many reclamation schemes, but also explained the characteristic vegetation communities, rich in legumes, developed on urban wastelands. Tony Bradshaw's research into urban soils and vegetation provided the foundation for a whole new approach to urban landscaping using low nutrient soils for maintenance of floristic diversity. But he was just as happy creating attractive new plant communities in urban nature reserves and ecological gardens, like St James's Garden by the Anglican Cathedral to which he latterly devoted much of his time.

But as mentioned earlier, Merseyside had other protagonists at this time. The landscape architects responsible for developing Warrington New Town had decided that the new landscape should be designed and managed on ecological principles, as had been so successful in some Dutch cities. Woodland belts were established three years before any houses were built, and these naturalistic habitats provided a strikingly different kind of environment from traditional new housing estates (Scott *et al.*, 1986). The trees used were predominantly native species including oak, ash, birch, rowan and alder, which were used to create belts and fingers of woodland enclosing small groups of houses, car parks and play areas. The overall effect was to provide a strong sense of living within a natural landscape. At the time this was one of the largest examples of ecological landscaping in the country, and the pioneering work at Warrington soon caught the attention of landscape designers elsewhere. The use of native trees not only proved very successful, but was also found to be extremely cost effective. An intense debate was stimulated within the landscape profession when it was argued that the ecological approach should be applied widely in urban renewal schemes. In 1981 a workshop held at Risley Moss summarised current experience in creating such landscapes and the resulting publication, produced by Allan Ruff of Manchester University, remains one of the key documents of the time (Ruff & Tregay, 1982).

By the end of the 1980s natural open spaces had proliferated enormously in towns and cities. As well as nature reserves, natural parks and ecological parks there were many small patches such as community nature gardens, informal green spaces and linear parks that were now being used by local people, instead of being left as urban wasteland. A study of the way people used these places (Millward & Mostyn, 1989) showed a great deal of variety. As well as providing great opportunities for contact with nature, they provided adventure playgrounds for children and a focus for community activities and socialising in ways that did not occur in more formal parks. Reasons given why people liked such places were the peace and quiet; natural countryside feel; presence of nature and wildlife; openness and trees. All of which contrasted sharply with their everyday urban surroundings.

SPREADING THE MESSAGE.

Conferences and publications played a vital role in promoting urban conservation. One of the first major conferences was a joint meeting of the Landscape Institute and British Ecological Society held in 1983 to explore ways in which ecological knowledge might be incorporated more successfully in landscape design. This attracted both academics and practitioners and was enormously successful in highlighting what for many members of the landscape profession were completely new approaches. The resulting book, *Ecology and Design in Landscape*, produced by the BES, turned out to be one of its most successful publications (Bradshaw *et al.*, 1986).

Urban ecology was the theme of the second European Ecological symposium, held in Berlin in 1980 (Bornkamm *et al.*, 1982). This was the first time that urban ecological studies were given such prominence by professional ecologists. The meeting attracted 400 participants and contributions reflected a wide range of newly developing interests within the field of urban ecology. Examples from the UK included studies of urban fox populations, invertebrate diversity of urban habitats, and the colonisation by orchids of industrial waste tips in south Lancashire. So for the first time academic ecologists were getting involved. Perhaps more significant was the international conference on *Greening the City* held in Liverpool at the same time as the Garden Festival in 1984. Here practitioners and academics met to explore new ways of dealing with urban landscapes, and particularly the role of nature in raising the quality of life in towns and cities. Following closely on the heels of inner city riots in Toxteth and Brixton, it was used by Michael Heseltine, then Minister for the Environment, to announce the setting up of a national Groundwork Foundation which would provide task forces to revitalise urban landscapes. This was based on the model of the St Helens and Knowsley Groundwork Trust led by John Handley, which had pioneered this approach.

International conferences in the USA, Canada and London in 1986–7 demonstrated that urban nature conservation was rapidly becoming established in many developed countries. In the USA the National Institute for Urban Wildlife led the way. Its Director Lowell Adams was responsible for bringing together a mixture of practitioners and academics who were able to chart the remarkable progress that had been made in the States over the previous twenty years. An international gathering in Toronto in 1987 was another very significant event that stimulated action in many countries (Gordon, 1990). At the same time *Urban Wildlife News*, produced by George Barker, who was by then the NCC's Urban Wildlife Co-ordinator, was circulated to 38 countries, and a new journal *Urban Wildlife* was also launched that year. This spate of activity was assisted by major international bodies, such as the Council of Europe, which commissioned the Institute of Ecology in Berlin to produce two critical reviews of urban ecological knowledge that became standard works for practitioners (Sukopp & Werner, 1982, 1987). UNESCO also had an important role at this time. The Man and Biosphere Programme, referred to as 'MAB 11', led by John Celecia, was an attempt to analyse how cities function in order to develop sustainable solutions. The approach was heavily dependent on knowledge of urban ecology and led to the gathering of much vital data on urban ecosystems. George Barker was quick to see the value of such an approach and set up a UK Urban Forum under the UNESCO banner, which still has considerable influence today (see UK Man and Biosphere

FIG 204. Oliver Gilbert: one of the most successful pioneers in the academic study of urban ecology.

Committee Urban Forum website at www.ukmaburbanforum.co.uk).

Books followed thick and fast. One was an extraordinarily detailed compendium of information on *Promoting Nature in Cities and Towns*, produced by the Trust for Urban Ecology, which provided chapter and verse on practically everything you needed to know about setting up and running urban wildlife sites (Emery, 1986). Then there was David Nicholson-Lord's more philosophical account of the growth of this new movement in *The Greening of the Cities* (1987). More popular were *The Wild Side of Town* by Chris Baines and my own book on London's natural history, *Wild in London*, both published in 1986. I also reviewed progress in urban nature conservation (Goode, 1989). To cap them all Oliver Gilbert produced *The Ecology of Urban Habitats* in 1989, which has remained the definitive text on urban ecology. For anyone working in this field in the 1980s there was no lack of material.

So where did this take us? There is no doubt that the intense activity of the 1980s resulted in radical changes in the way that nature conservation was perceived, not only by the official agencies but also by a whole raft of organisations that had not previously been involved. The very fact that such bodies now included town councils and local residents groups speaks for itself. Urban nature conservation was certainly put firmly on the map, and had a solid base from which to grow. Town councils had ecology committees. Nature reserves and environmental centres proliferated. The ecological basis of design began to permeate the landscape profession, resulting in exciting new naturalistic landscapes, rather than the standard close-mown grasslands which had for so long been the norm. The creation of new wildlife habitats was becoming commonplace. At the heart of all this was the concept that nature should be accessible to people living in towns and cities. That means nature on the doorstep rather than in the countryside.

CHAPTER 14

Planning for Nature

I F PLACES FOR NATURE ARE to survive within towns and cities it is essential that safeguards be provided within the planning process. Urban local authorities, at every level from county to local borough, were quick to adopt strategic policies for nature conservation in the 1980s, described in Chapter 13. These policies have provided the bedrock for effective conservation of locally important sites and have been central to the success of urban nature conservation programmes throughout Britain. The essence of this approach was to identify a series of Sites of Importance for Nature Conservation, (SINCS) which complements the national series of SSSIs at the local level. They include representatives of the important habitats within a local authority area and are listed in local development plans. While such designations do not have the same degree of statutory protection as SSSIs, they nevertheless provide an important framework for conservation. Much of the bread and butter work of local authorities on wildlife conservation is concerned with designating such sites and responding to planning applications affecting them. Their importance has been recognised increasingly at a national level. Wildlife trusts and urban wildlife groups are also heavily involved in casework affecting these sites. Many local authorities have also designated some of their most notable sites as statutory Local Nature Reserves.

There have also been attempts to improve people's access to nature. The idea that everyone living in an urban area should have access to a wildlife site within walking distance from home has gradually gained acceptance. It became a statutory part of planning in London in 2004 and was promoted nationally by Natural England in *Nature Nearby* (2010). Yet another strand affecting urban wildlife habitats is the recognition that such habitats can have a crucial role in maintaining the ecological integrity of urban areas. Planners who may have had little regard for the wildlife value of urban river valleys and woodlands, are now producing detailed master plans of the same 'green infrastructure' as a means of coping with the effects of climate change. Meanwhile nature conservation has developed its own kind of planning with the advent of Local Biodiversity Action Plans to address priority issues at the local level. This chapter describes these different strands, with examples from selected towns and cities.

LONDON'S NATURE CONSERVATION STRATEGY

One of the most successful strategies for protection of important urban wildlife sites was the programme developed in London, which is used as an example to illustrate the processes involved. Although the Greater London Council started the work, the London Ecology Unit carried out the main programme from 1986 to 2000 on behalf of the London boroughs. One of the key objectives was to ensure that nature conservation became part of strategic planning in London. When the work commenced in 1982 there was no reference to nature or wildlife in London's strategic development plan. Although provision was made for protection of open space for public enjoyment, the emphasis was largely on landscape and visual amenity rather than the natural environment or ecology. A priority task for the GLC, therefore, was to produce a set of policies on ecology and nature conservation for use by London boroughs in their local plans (GLC, 1984).

The policy to identify and protect sites of nature conservation value was crucial. But at that time knowledge of London's ecology was patchy and incomplete. So the GLC embarked on a comprehensive survey and evaluation of wildlife habitats throughout the capital. London Wildlife Trust was commissioned to do the job, which was carried out in 1984/85 by a team of six ecologists who got to know London's habitats in extraordinary detail and came up with some remarkable finds. From an initial desk study using air photographs 1,850 'sites' were selected for survey, totalling about 300 km², or 20 per cent of the land area of Greater London. It was a daunting prospect! The survey concentrated on areas of open land of potential significance for nature conservation, including woodlands, heaths, meadows, marshes and reservoirs, but also including a wide range of post industrial habitats such as disused docks and wharves, sewage farms and even the odd arsenal. Formal parks, private gardens, playing fields and arable farmland with little wildlife interest, were all excluded. For every site surveyors recorded the types of habitat present, dominant plant species, richness of species, presence of rare or unusual species, current land-use and accessibility.

FIG 205. Richmond Park: perhaps the most outstanding Site of Metropolitan Importance for Nature Conservation in London.

The wildlife habitat survey provided the first complete picture of London's natural habitats (GLC, 1986). Unimproved grassland was found to be the most extensive habitat, with a total area of nearly 13,000 hectares, most of it neutral grassland. Acid grassland totalled about 1,000 hectares and chalk grassland only 250 hectares. Woodland covered some 7,000 hectares, and parkland had a similar figure of 6,000 hectares. Other habitats were much less extensive, but there were notable examples of ruderal and tall herb communities on post-industrial sites totalling about 1,300 hectares. Wetland habitats, such as reedbeds, were limited to only 200 hectares.

For the first time it was possible to distinguish variants within each of the main habitat types. Native woodlands demonstrate such differences particularly well. Hornbeam woods predominate across a swathe of north London from Ruislip Woods in the west to Epping and Hainault forests in the east. Further south on the London clay, oak becomes dominant forming traditional woodland of coppice with standards. Around the southern edge of London on the chalk hills there are beech hangers. Extensive alder woodlands occur in two very different settings, in river valleys such as the Colne and Ingrebourne north of the Thames, and along the spring line of the chalk escarpment in the south. Small pockets of willow occur locally where they are spring-fed. Ancient wood pasture is well represented by Richmond Park. Examples of all these various types were identified and described (see also Chapter 2).

Although many sites were already well known, the survey team discovered a large number of important sites that were not well documented, and others that were completely new to London's naturalists. Highlights were the extensive hay meadows of Totteridge Fields in Barnet, herb-rich fields by the Yeading Brook in Hillingdon and a number of wasteland sites, including derelict wharves along the Thames, and a disused railway marshalling yard in Hounslow that proved to be exceptionally rich floristically.

But the main value of the survey was the fact that it was comprehensive. The results formed the basis for the first strategic nature conservation plan for Greater London and provided the starting point for selection of Sites of Importance for Nature Conservation. A methodology for deciding which areas were important was published (GLC, 1985) and this remained the basis of the system used by the London Ecology Unit from 1986–2000. A standardised set of criteria was used for comparing and evaluating sites. Although many of these criteria are similar to those developed by UK government agencies for selecting nationally important sites (such as species richness, size and presence of rare species), there are some essential differences. Public access and value for environmental education are examples. Details of these criteria and the way in which they were applied are given in Goode (1999, 2005).

Although some changes have occurred in the detailed approach, the methodology remains much the same and it has been widely accepted as the basis for nature conservation planning in London (LEU, 1994). Though non-statutory, it was endorsed in 1995 by the London Planning Advisory Committee for use by London Boroughs in their Unitary Development Plans. The same policy, criteria and procedures for identifying nature conservation sites were adopted by the Mayor of London in his Biodiversity Strategy for the capital (GLA, 2002), and now form part of the statutory London Plan (GLA, 2004).

During the 1990s the strategy was successfully tested at numerous public inquiries. The results set important precedents for London in favour of nature conservation. Examples included disused railway land and industrial sites, as well as long established habitats such as woods, meadows and marshland. In many cases it was the value of these places to local people that won the day, rather than scientific arguments about rare habitats or species. Such cases were important in illustrating newly emerging values and helped to establish the validity of nature conservation in heavily built-up urban areas (Goode, 2005, 2007). New approaches with a strong social dimension that had been pioneered by the GLC, and which

FIG 206. The meadows and woods of Horsenden Hill in Ealing are designated as a Site of Metropolitan Importance for Nature Conservation.

were seen at first as a radical departure from traditional nature conservation, became standard practice and were adopted by many London boroughs as an integral part of their local plans.

The data have been updated periodically through more detailed surveys of each individual London borough. Over the past 25 years the database provided a vital tool in strategic planning and for advising on the ecological implications of proposed new developments. The London Ecology Unit provided advice on many hundreds of planning applications every year. But its work is probably best known for the series of Ecology Handbooks, an ecological equivalent of Pevsner, which describe in great detail all the important wildlife sites in each London Borough. Thirty-one handbooks were published between 1985 and 2000. The full database is probably the most detailed for any part of the British Isles, and continues to provide essential information for implementation of the Mayor's biodiversity strategy for the capital.

The strategy is based on a hierarchy of sites at three levels: London-wide; Borough; and Local. Those of London-wide strategic significance are called 'Sites of Metropolitan Importance for Nature Conservation'. There are about 140 of these sites totalling 15,000 hectares, which represents 9 per cent of London's land area. They include nationally protected sites, such as National Nature Reserves and Sites of Special Scientific Interest, as well as many other important sites, which together provide the best examples of all the main habitats occurring in Greater London. Many of these are well known and well protected. They include Epping Forest, Hampstead Heath, the Royal Parks and Wimbledon Common. Other examples, such as Feltham Marshalling Yards, Yeading Brook Fields, Crayford Marshes and Kempton Waterworks may be less well known. But they are all significant in a London-wide context.

These top-level sites occur throughout London and vary in size from only a few hectares to over 1,000 hectares. Most are less than 100 hectares. A few were lost to development shortly after the London Ecology Committee first agreed the list (LEU, 1988). Most of these were wasteland sites that were already scheduled for development. Additional sites have been added over the years as individual boroughs have been surveyed in greater detail. The Mayor of London (2002) endorsed the list of Metropolitan Sites and they are all given statutory protection by policies in the London Plan (GLA, 2004).

FIG 207. The corridor of the River Crane, one of the lesser-known sites of London-wide importance. Crane Park Island is a nature reserve run by the London Wildlife Trust: the Shot Tower provides an environmental study centre.

The second category, 'Sites of Borough Importance', includes by far the largest number of sites in London. These are chosen from the mix of sites in each individual borough and represent the best examples of the major habitats in the borough. A third category, 'Sites of Local Importance', is for places valued by local residents, schools or community groups at the neighbourhood level. They tend to be small sites that provide opportunities for direct contact with nature within walking distance of home or school.

Detailed surveys were completed for 31 of the 33 London boroughs. This resulted in 1,160 sites being selected at borough or local level, which comprise 8 per cent of the land area of London. Together with the Metropolitan sites the overall London-wide strategy identifies

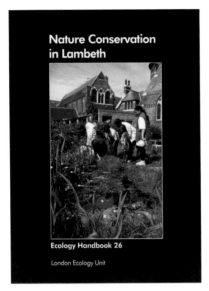

Nature Conservation in Lambeth

Ecology Handbook 26

London Ecology Unit

FIG 208. Nature Conservation Strategies were published during the 1990s for nearly all the 33 London Boroughs, providing an unrivalled description of London's ecology.

1,300 sites, totalling 27,000 hectares, or 17 per cent of London's land area. All of these are recognised as being of importance for nature conservation in borough plans. The use of the three different categories, i.e. Metropolitan, Borough and Local, is an attempt not only to protect the best sites in London, but also to provide each area of London with accessible wildlife sites so that people are able to have access to nature within their local neighbourhood

Success in developing this strategy was dependent on ensuring that the system was accepted as part of the planning process, even though it had little statutory basis. Given the lack of statutory powers, it is extraordinary how much was achieved. Compared with the position in the early 1980s when ecology and nature conservation did not figure at all in strategic planning in London, there was a sea change in the attitude of London Boroughs. By the 1990s nature conservation had become embedded in all their local plans and became a statutory part of the London Plan in 2004.

Fundamental to all of this was the need for both political and public support for the programme. The series of ecology handbooks published by the London Ecology Unit were crucial to gaining such support. The first ecology handbook set the scene and was instrumental in gaining political support within the Greater London Council (GLC, 1984). The series of handbooks for individual London boroughs, published over a period of fifteen years, maintained the public and political support necessary to ensure long-term success of the programme. They did two vital jobs. One was to supply the definitive input on nature conservation for each Borough Plan. Secondly they provided a popular account of London's natural history, which assisted enormously in raising public awareness of biodiversity issues. Later examples included a series of walks for people wishing to visit natural areas in different parts of London. The final handbook, describing the London Borough of Brent (Yarham & Game, 2000), includes a full list of all the handbooks.

Success also depended on the fact that the London Ecology Unit was a part

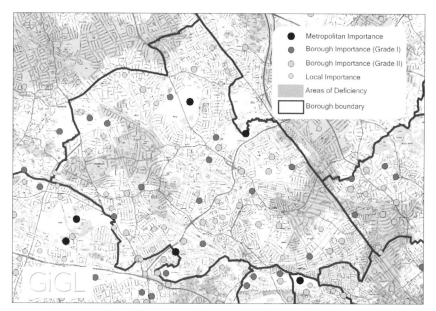

FIG 209. Locations of Sites of Importance for Nature Conservation (SINCs) in Brent, February 2014. SINCs have been identified since 1986 and the categorisation of sites is related to their protected status in the land-use planning system. The boundaries and site grades reflect the most recent consideration of each site. This information is managed by Greenspace Information for Greater London (GiGL) on behalf of local authorities and the GLA and may change as new information becomes available. *Note*: On this map, dots approximately illustrate locations of SINCs, and some SINCs are linear. Areas of Deficiency (AoD) are defined as built-up areas more than one kilometre walking distance from an accessible Metropolitan or Borough SINC. GiGL is responsible for periodically updating the AoD in line with SINC data using automated methods, redefined in collaboration with the GLA and London Boroughs Biodiversity Forum in 2013. (Contains Ordnance Survey data © Crown Copyright and database right 2014)

of local government. The Unit answered to a Joint Committee of the London Boroughs, which gave it a formal status within the planning process. Ecological advice came from professional ecologists, who could if necessary give expert advice at public inquiries, and the work of the Unit was held in high regard by planners and others in local government. The fact that the system is now a statutory part of planning in London came about as a result of the new arrangements for London government introduced in 2000. A duty was placed on the newly elected mayor to produce an action plan for conservation of London's biodiversity as part of his overall strategic plan for the capital. Since the London Ecology Unit was absorbed into the new Greater London Authority it was a small step for the mayor to adopt the system developed by the LEU. As a result London became the only part of the UK where sites of regional and local importance for nature conservation are given statutory protection through planning.

STRATEGIES FOR CITIES

Most towns and cities have similar schemes, often run in conjunction with their local Wildlife Trust and biological record centre. Local authorities take the lead in designating important wildlife sites. Some large conurbations have dedicated teams of ecologists. Manchester is fortunate to have had its own Ecology Unit since 1986, which advises the ten 'unitary authorities' that jointly comprise Greater Manchester. A total of 538 Sites of Biological Importance have been designated and the ecologists deal with over 800 planning applications each year. The sites include a great variety of habitats, such as fragments of raised bog; patches of derelict land now colonised by swathes of orchids; wooded ravines complete with dippers; disused railway sidings; and numerous ponds lakes and reservoirs. There are also extensive tracts of moorland where Manchester laps up onto the Pennines. District authorities in Merseyside have their own Environment Advisory Service, which does a similar job.

On the other side of the Pennines, Sheffield has been operating an extremely detailed strategy for nature conservation since 1991. Over 250 local wildlife sites are identified, including five major river valleys. The city is particularly fortunate that many areas of ancient woodland survive along these valleys, bringing a special character to a city that is perhaps better known for its industrial history. But the post-industrial legacy brings with it a range of unusual habitats, and it was here that Oliver Gilbert coined the term 'urban commons'. City ecologists deal with over 200 planning consultations every year. The Sheffield Wildlife Trust, which started life as the city's Wildlife Group in 1985, has been enormously successful in setting up 'Friends' groups in local neighbourhoods, who take responsibility for running local wildlife sites. Much of this success stems from an effective partnership with the City Council. There is a similar relationship in Bristol, where 87 wildlife sites are designated, and again the city's ecologists deal with over 200 planning cases annually. The range of sites includes cliff vegetation with many endemic species on the Avon Gorge; wet meadows and marshlands of Ashton Vale on the edge of the urban sprawl; the famous Arnos Vale cemetery; and post-industrial habitats at Troopers Hill. One of the sites is birch woodland colonising a disused railway viaduct at Royate Hill, which must be one of the oddest urban wildlife sites in the country.

Another good example is Brighton and Hove, which has 61 designated wildlife sites, of which eleven lie within the urban area. Wild Park, Stanmer Park, Whitehawk Hill and the Sheepcote valley are important natural areas, much appreciated by local people. Stanmer Park has ancient woodland and historic parkland with a long established arboretum. Sheepcote Valley was Brighton's rubbish tip, re-landscaped in the 1990s to create an attractive naturalistic area with a mixture of habitats including scrubland that is well known to local birders as a good place to see spring and autumn migrants, such as wrynecks and flycatchers. Whitehawk Hill is a piece of the South Downs chalk escarpment, complete with an ancient hill fort, which is now totally surrounded by modern housing estates, including one of the most deprived communities in the UK. The chalk grassland still supports notable butterfly species, including Adonis blue, small blue, dark green fritillary and both dingy and grizzled skippers and the local authority has plans to introduce grazing to maintain the grassland. In contrast Brighton marina is becoming well known as a place to see deep-water marine species including sea horses. On a smaller scale the city of Norwich has twenty-nine wildlife sites including eight LNRs, mostly wet meadowland and fen along the river valleys that ramify through the city. Here the city ecologist is faced with trying to maintain traditional grazing by cattle on sites that are becoming surrounded by urban development.

All these places have rigorous arrangements for identifying important sites and the designations have now become well embedded in the local planning system. The need for this 'second tier' of wildlife sites at the local level is particularly acute in urban areas, for a number of reasons. Although the value of nature for people living in urban areas has become widely appreciated and is now an accepted element of nature conservation policy at national level, this does not sit easily with national policies that give priority to habitats and species of international and national importance. Hardly any of the many important wildlife sites in towns and cities qualify as Sites of Special Scientific Interest in the national context. Sites in the urban environment barely register on the national scale of values and this is reflected by the fact that only 2 per cent of SSSIs in England are in urban areas.

There are several reasons why this is so. Many of the semi-natural habitats that survive in urban areas are heavily modified and are relatively poor examples in terms of their intrinsic scientific interest. Secondly, the habitats that are important, especially those associated with post-industrial landscapes, tend to be undervalued or ignored in the national scheme of things because traditionally they have not been recognised as having nature conservation value. Many of these are poorly described in the National Vegetation Classification (Rodwell 2000), so selection of SSSIs gives inadequate recognition to these specialised urban habitats. A few outstanding examples have achieved SSSI designation, as in the case of invertebrate populations at Canvey Wick in Essex, but these are exceptional cases. Finally, there are the social and cultural values, which need to be taken into account in urban areas, but which do not apply to SSSIs. In many ways this is the most significant distinction, for it is the value of urban wildlife sites to local people that makes them so important. The network of SSSIs does very little to cater for the needs of the vast majority of people in Britain who live in urban areas.

The importance of 'Local Sites' was at last recognised by central government in England and Wales, when guidance on the selection and protection of local sites was issued for local authorities (Defra, 2006). This went a long way to formalising what had already become accepted practice in many towns and cities. It recognised the value of such sites in urban areas by stating,

> In populous areas that are poorer in high quality natural environment, sites of lesser intrinsic ecological interest may still be of substantive nature conservation value for the opportunities they provide for the appreciation of nature.

It also specifically recognised the value of such sites for environmental education. One of its key recommendations was that greater weight should be given to social criteria. So in addition to the long established criteria based on intrinsic scientific features, it proposed four new criteria for selecting local sites, which were: recorded history and cultural associations; connectivity within the landscape; value for appreciating nature; and value for learning.

The four new criteria are particularly important in the context of urban areas. *Recorded history and cultural associations* allows for recognition of local historical features which may include industrial archaeology, or other aspects of local history which has a bearing on the present day ecology. *Connectivity* is important in providing linkages through the urban environment. This is particularly important for protection of the green infrastructure, especially in terms of urban streams and rivers, but also for provision of recreational cycle and walking routes linking Local Sites. *Value for appreciation of nature, and value for learning* are of paramount importance in the urban context, allowing for protection of a range of sites of truly local importance but which together provide a national resource of immense value. The inclusion of these four criteria in national policies helped considerably in the development and implementation of programmes for urban nature conservation.

But things do not always flow in one direction. The decision by the Coalition Government to streamline planning regulations in England and

Wales with a new National Planning Policy Framework in 2012 could seriously undermine local authorities' ability to protect important urban wildlife sites as the Framework pays little attention to sites of local importance. More recent proposals to introduce Biodiversity Offsets, which would allow development on important biodiversity sites by compensating elsewhere, would inevitably reduce the number of wildlife sites in urban areas, as there are so few options available. The main threat to urban wildlife sites will be the lack of specialist ecologists in district councils who can properly interpret plans and policies. The only way that urban wildlife sites can survive is for them to be fully protected. Interestingly some local communities have recognised the danger and have listed important wildlife sites as 'community assets'.

Garden cities offer other possibilities. The vision of Ebenezer Howard in his *Garden Cities of To-morrow* (1902) has influenced the development of many new towns and remains with us today. Although his emphasis was more concerned with social issues and the value of a garden city as a living environment there have been implications for nature. Hampstead Garden Suburb in London is just one of many examples where there have been distinct advantages for wildlife. On a much larger scale Milton Keynes in Buckinghamshire demonstrates how a new city can accommodate a rich array of wildlife. It is exceptional in the amount of green space that has been protected and created within the new townscape, and in the diversity and quality of wildlife habitats involved. The Parks Trust, which has responsibility for managing over 2,000 hectares of green space, is proud of the fact that 'no one in Milton Keynes is more than half a mile from a park'. From the outset the 'New City' was planned to ensure that important habitats such as ancient woodlands, meadows and washlands were managed to retain and enhance their value for wildlife. One of the ancient woodlands is designated as an SSSI, but the whole group of woodlands is significant as it supports populations of notable species, including the black hairstreak butterfly. Green spaces support 34 breeding species of butterflies. Some of the most significant habitats lie along the two river valleys of the Great Ouse and the Ouzel, both of which now form linear parks. Part of the Great Ouse valley is being re-landscaped in partnership with Hanson Aggregates, to create an extensive flood-plain forest with a naturalistic landscape of pools, backwaters, marshland, reedbeds and ponds alongside the river. Otters have already been seen in the Ouzel valley only one kilometre from the city centre. The Parks Trust also manages 130 km of landscaped roadside corridors which have considerable ecological and amenity value.

The Parks Trust itself provides an innovative model. It was created in 1992 and receives its funding from a substantial endowment which the Trust manages and invests, that enables it to spend about £5 million per year on managing the green landscape. Unlike most other towns and cities, where annual expenditure on parks

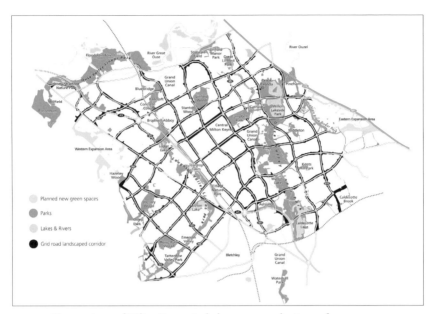

FIG 210. The new town of Milton Keynes includes over 2,000 hectares of green areas including ancient woodlands, meadows and washlands, as well as 130 km of landscaped roadsides. (The Parks Trust)

and green spaces has to compete with other council priorities, in Milton Keynes the Parks Trust endowment fund ensures that the parks, woodlands and other green spaces are protected and managed in perpetuity, independent of local taxation.

ACCESS TO NATURE

One of the main aims of urban nature conservation is that it should improve people's access to nature in the local area where they live or work. One way of doing this is to create more statutory Local Nature Reserves (LNRs). These reserves, which are designated by local authorities, are particularly important for several reasons. Not only do they give a greater degree of long term protection and a sense of permanence to these reserves; but they also emphasise that the primary land use is for nature conservation and that these nature reserves are there for the local community. Trooper's Hill in Bristol, Poet's Walk in Clevedon, Risley Moss in Warrington, Benwell Nature Park in Newcastle and Queen's Wood in London all have signboards describing the wildlife to be seen, and encouraging people to become involved in local projects. All have the official status of Local Nature Reserve and with this comes a degree of pride on the part of the local authority. But the greatest value of these reserves lies in their key function to promote public access to nature. As well as providing information about the wildlife most LNRs have paths and trails. Some have elaborate visitor facilities, including hides for viewing birds. Many have loyal groups of volunteers running everything from dawn chorus walks, and evening bat watches, to beetle safaris and even a 'city critter circus play day'.

It is interesting to look back at the original recommendations for LNRs made in 1947 in the report of the Government's Wildlife Conservation Special Committee which said,

> We attach great importance to stimulating local efforts to establish nature reserves for the enjoyment and education of the public and to give opportunities for local scientific and natural history investigations.

The report went on to recommend that local authorities be given powers for the establishment of such reserves (Ministry of Town and Country Planning, 1947). These powers were included in the 1949 Act that established the Nature Conservancy. Although local authorities gained the powers they were slow to take action and by 1970 there were only 24 LNRs in the UK. By 1990 the number had grown to 236, reaching 629 in 1997. But after that there was a surge of activity, particularly in England. This was mainly due to the Wildspace grant scheme funded by the Big Lottery, which channelled over £7 million to promote more LNRs, and took the total to about 1,500 reserves by 2007. A key feature was the funding of 'community liaison officers', whose job was to stimulate local groups of 'Friends' to take responsibility for embedding new reserves into the heart of local communities. Most of these newer LNRs are close to centres of population or well within urban areas. The prize for the tiniest LNR in the UK goes to the artificial nesting platform for kittiwakes on Tyneside!

In London the number of LNRs started to increase rather earlier than elsewhere prompted by the work of the GLC in the 1980s. In 1982 Perivale Wood and Ruislip were the only LNRs, but over the next 10 years the number grew to 28, with another 12 in the pipeline. During the 1990s there was a steady increase but since 2000 the number has grown dramatically. There are now over 140 reserves designated by London Boroughs and there is no doubt that many local communities have benefited. Many are small sites, but even very small reserves are valuable, not only in terms of their ecological and educational benefits, but also through their contribution to people's health and well-being (Box *et al.* 2007). Two of the smallest in London are Railway Fields in Haringey and Camley Street

Natural Park in Camden, both of which have provided inspirational leadership on environmental matters for local communities (see also Chapter 15).

English Nature (1996) set a target for a minimum provision of one hectare of statutory local nature reserve for every 1,000 residents as a green space standard for towns and cities. Although at the time this looked impossibly ambitious, many local authorities have since met this target. Some have even exceeded it, and prior to changes in planning regulations introduced in 2012 it was beginning to look achievable right across the country. Members of the Wildlife Conservation Special Committee would have been delighted to see such progress, even though it had taken more than fifty years to achieve.

Related to this is the more theoretical idea that everyone should have access to a natural area within a few minutes walk of home. Some of the Metropolitan Counties advocated such an approach in the 1980s and in London a scheme has been in use since 1985 using one kilometre as the minimum distance from home to an accessible wildlife site (GLC, 1985). A paper with the catchy title *Natural Spaces in Urban Places* (Box & Harrison, 1993) reduced the target distance to 500 m, which was revised again to only 300 m (Harrison *et al.*, 1995) and adopted by English Nature in 1996. In 2010 its successor body Natural England recommended a national standard for accessible natural greenspace as follows. Everyone, wherever they live, should have an accessible natural greenspace:

- of at least 2 hectares in size, no more than 300 m (5 minutes walk) from home;
- at least one accessible 20 hectare site within 2 km of home;
- one accessible 100 hectare site within 5 km of home;
- and one accessible 500 hectare site within 10 km of home; plus
- a minimum of one hectare of statutory Local Nature Reserves per thousand population.

Meanwhile the system developed in London has been adopted as part of the official London Plan (GLA, 2008). Areas lacking access, within one kilometre, to a high quality wildlife site (of at least borough level importance) are referred to as 'Areas of Deficiency in Access to Nature'. Whilst unfamiliar in the context of nature conservation, the concept of deficiency is stock in trade for planners dealing with strategic targets for parks, playing fields and other amenities. Maps showing the Areas of Deficiency in Access to Nature assist planners in London boroughs to identify where action can be taken to alleviate the situation. This can be done in a number of ways:

- improving the ecological quality of an accessible site;

- creating new habitats to provide a significant experience of nature;
- providing new entrance points to an existing site, so increasing the catchment;
- opening up access to a restricted site;
- improving access through areas surrounding a site, so extending the catchment.

An example was the construction of a footbridge over the railway at Gillespie Park Nature Reserve in Islington, which made it possible for large numbers of people from the other side of the railway to have easy access to the park. In another case new wetland habitats were created to replace the concrete channel of the River Ravensbourne at Brookmill Park in Lewisham. The result is a new high quality wildlife site, accessible to large numbers of people. In both cases large areas of deficiency have been substantially reduced, which is one of the stated objectives of the London Plan.

GREEN INFRASTRUCTURE AND ECOSYSTEM SERVICES

Planners have also started to look at green spaces in towns and cities as a means of coping with the effects of climate change and at the same time providing networks for informal recreation. The planning process deals with green areas according to their primary functions such as parks, playing fields, allotments, cemeteries, golf courses, river and canal corridors, as well as more extensive tracts designated as metropolitan open land or green belt. There is also derelict or contaminated land, much of which falls into the category of brownfield sites.

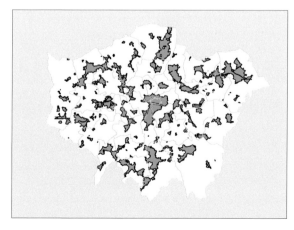

FIG 211. Areas of Deficiency in Access to Nature in London. (Greater London Authority)

Each has its own set of criteria for planning purposes and the more fundamental ecological benefits of soft landscapes have not generally been recognised. However times are changing. The advent of more sustainable approaches to urban design, together with challenges of climate change, are causing planners to look at things in a more unified way, especially in terms of the functions of urban ecosystems such as woodlands, river valleys and green corridors. The whole range of soft landscapes described in Chapter 1 has become known as the 'green infrastructure' (Goode, 2006).

The benefits of green networks were recognised by George Barker (1997) in a research report that stimulated new approaches to greenspace planning. He suggested that a range of functions could be accommodated in green networks including river and wildlife corridors, together with local cycle and walking routes and extensive areas of amenity greenspace. Such networks might connect locally important wildlife sites and provide greater opportunities for people to have access to natural areas. The potential health benefits of urban green space were also seen as part of an integrated package. Since then these ideas have been broadened to include the ecological functions of green networks.

In ecological terms an urban area can be viewed according to its underlying physical characteristics, the ecological elements of green space and the interacting variables of climate and hydrology. As pointed out in Chapter 1, local climatic and hydrological conditions are strongly influenced by the character of urban areas. The hard surfaces of buildings, roads, car parks and other solid structures can strongly modify these conditions. The larger the urban area the more pronounced will be its effects on local climate, in particular by promoting an urban heat-island effect. Similarly there are pronounced effects on hydrological conditions through reduced infiltration and more rapid run-off, leading to increased intensity of spate conditions on urban watercourses. The large-scale patterns of land-use, particularly the amount of greenspace and green networks, strongly affect local ecological conditions. They provide crucial components that can form the ecological basis for improved urban planning, design and management.

Some cities have been adopting an ecological approach for many years. Since 1994 Berlin has had a broad Biotope Strategy for city-wide planning, with the primary objective of using the green infrastructure to deliver ecological services (TCPA, 2004). The different climatic zones within the city were mapped, illustrating variations in average air temperature, humidity and soil moisture. Five broad zones were identified reflecting the moderating influences of greenspace. These provide the basis for long term planning to counter the effects of climate change.

There is now general agreement that soft landscapes can provide a range of benefits that help to maintain more sustainable conditions in the urban environment. These include provision of sustainable drainage systems and enhanced flood alleviation, local climatic amelioration, improved air quality, providing conditions for urban biodiversity, and provision of green space for a variety of uses, including the growing of food. There is also considerable evidence that green networks have an important role in maintaining people's health and wellbeing, by lowering stress levels and providing opportunities for exercise.

Natural England has promoted the concept of Green Infrastructure as a way of delivering a wide range of benefits for people and the natural environment together. It argues that green infrastructure should be provided as an integral part of all new development, alongside utilities and transport networks, and should also form a key part of proposals to regenerate existing urban areas. In Scotland too the body responsible for urban greenspace is addressing many of the same issues. Greenspace Scotland (which is jointly sponsored by the Scottish Centre for Regeneration, the Scottish NHS [Health Scotland] and Scottish Natural Heritage) has developed a strategy that goes well beyond traditional approaches to greenspace management. It uses green infrastructure as a means of promoting urban renewal, together with environmental and social benefits. This broad agenda may seem far removed from the specifics of urban nature conservation, yet it has made striking progress in this field by encouraging local people to become directly involved in the management of important wildlife sites, and by successfully promoting far greater use of green networks for recreation.

LOCAL BIODIVERSITY ACTION PLANS

One of the results of the 'Earth Summit' held in Rio de Janeiro in 1992 was the Convention on Biological Diversity, which required countries to implement national programmes for biodiversity conservation. After Rio the UK government was keen to develop a national strategy. The process was strongly influenced by the RSPB and Wildlife Trusts, who argued strongly for targets and action plans to be agreed for nationally endangered habitats and species. But the steering committee also included members from local authorities, who had a rather different agenda. They wanted to ensure that the UK programme promoted action on the ground at the local level, as well as encouraging greater public awareness of biodiversity issues. Local Biodiversity Action Plans (LBAPs) were suggested as a way of doing this. It was hoped that they would not only help to deliver the national plan at the local level, but also engage a wider range of people in biodiversity conservation, and cater for local rather than national needs.

In the event these local plans provided a great stimulus for urban nature conservation. They were extremely effective in bringing biodiversity into the work of urban local authorities. Within five years of guidance being issued most local authorities had embarked on production of a local biodiversity action plan. With government reorganisation of local planning in 2002 local authorities were required to include biodiversity planning within their community strategies. As a result many urban authorities found themselves having to address biodiversity issues for the first time. In England and Wales this was reinforced in 2006 by a new duty placed on all public bodies, including local authorities, to have regard to biodiversity in their decision making and in carrying out their functions. A similar duty was introduced in Scotland, under the Nature Conservation (Scotland) Act 2004, which requires public authorities to further the conservation of biodiversity.

Most towns and cities have Local Biodiversity Action Plans, reflecting their local priorities. Plans for habitats and species are designed to address urgent problems with a clear timetable for achieving positive results. Habitat action plans include parks, cemeteries, private gardens, wastelands, railwaysides, docklands and even green roofs. Action plans for species include bats, swift, house martin, black redstart, song thrush, house sparrow and peregrine falcon, as well as a number of locally significant plants and invertebrates.

A novel feature of these plans is that they rely on a much wider partnership than the mainstream conservation bodies such as the RSPB and Wildlife Trusts. They include an unusual mix of organisations, such as water companies, housing corporations, transport operators, port authorities, waterway managers and regional health authorities, along with local business and industry. For them biodiversity conservation may be a small part of their overall work. But all of them need to be involved because between them they have a huge influence on the extent to which nature can exist and thrive in towns and cities.

These local partnerships are in most cases led by the relevant local authority. Success of local action plans has depended on engagement with all these players to ensure that they are directly involved in biodiversity conservation in ways that did not occur before. Individual partners are encouraged to take responsibility for particular action plans. Some towns and cities have gone further by seeking to ensure that partners sign up to a 'Biodiversity Charter'. This reliance on local partnerships is particularly appropriate in view of the community-based philosophy of urban nature conservation.

FIG 212. London's Local Biodiversity Action Plan.

In London a Biodiversity Action Plan was launched in 1996, which developed programmes for the conservation of priority habitats and species that are of particular significance in the capital. The plan was implemented by the London Biodiversity Partnership, which illustrates very well the breadth of organisations involved. The Partnership was led by the London Ecology Unit and included the London Wildlife Trust, London Natural History Society, RSPB and the Royal Parks, but also on board were some less likely bodies such as Peabody Trust, London Underground and University College London.

The overall programme provides a set of targets for nature conservation in London aimed at conserving and enhancing the status of critical habitats and species, and encouraging greater public participation in wildlife conservation. Some habitats are chosen to reflect national priorities, notably heathlands and chalk grasslands, whilst others provide opportunities for Londoners to enjoy contact with nature such as private gardens, parks and city squares, and churchyards and cemeteries. Species are selected for a variety of reasons. Some are priority species in the national biodiversity plan that have significant populations in London, such as tower mustard, black poplar, bats, water vole and stag beetle. The black redstart is included because it is particularly characteristic of London. Others, like the house sparrow, are included because they have suffered a substantial recent decline. Sparrows and peregrines both offer an opportunity to raise public awareness of biodiversity issues, though for very different reasons. Some of the action plans may seem rather specific, but actually address broad issues of urban development. The black redstart is a case in point. As mentioned in Chapter 9 these nationally protected birds tend to be associated with derelict buildings and urban wasteland and their habitat is under threat through redevelopment. One of the options to cater for this species is to create artificial wasteland habitats on roofs of buildings and these 'black redstart roofs' have helped to encourage the wider development of green roofs.

TABLE 4. The London Biodiversity Action Plan

Habitat Action Plans	Species Action Plans
Woodland	Bats
Chalk Grassland	Water Vole
Heathland	Grey Heron
Wasteland	Peregrine Falcon
Acid Grassland	Sand Martin
Tidal Thames	Black Redstart
Canals	House Sparrow
Churchyards and Cemeteries	Stag Beetle
Private Gardens	Tower Mustard
Parks, Squares and Amenity Grassland	Mistletoe/Reptiles/Black Poplar

As well as the overall London Biodiversity Action Plan, individual Boroughs have developed their own local action plans to cater for their specific needs. Examples are those for Tower Hamlets and Westminster, both of which are heavily built-up parts of the capital. In Tower Hamlets (2003) there are few examples of semi-natural habitats and the main emphasis is on habitats which are clearly urban in character, including parks, city squares, cemeteries, gardens, school grounds, the built environment (including green and brown roofs), commercial areas and brownfield land. Species action plans include bats, black redstart, bird's foot trefoil, brimstone butterfly and a southern European species of jumping spider (*Macaroeris nidicolens*) for which Mile End Park is the only known locality in the UK. In Westminster the list of Habitat Action Plans is much the same, but here there is an additional category of veteran trees and decaying wood reflecting the importance of old trees in some of the long established parks and squares. Emphasis is also placed on improving aquatic habitats of parkland lakes and the Thames foreshore. Species Action Plans include tawny owl, hedgehog, house sparrow and a nationally rare moth, the buttoned snout moth (*Hypena rostralis*) that occurs along railway and canal corridors and in one of the borough's cemeteries.

FIG 213. Heron: a key species in the London Biodiversity Action Plan.

Other cities may have more wide ranging action plans. Edinburgh is very different, partly because of the great variety of habitats from seashore to mountaintop, but also because several nationally rare species occur in the city. The unusual range of habitats within the boundary of the city includes a variety of coastal habitats, notably rocky shores and islands; wetlands, including mesotrophic and oligotrophic lakes and even examples of raised bog; semi-natural grasslands and rock faces on the hills of volcanic rock such as Arthur's Seat and Castle Rock; and extensive woodlands in river valleys and on some of the hills. Many of these habitats are of considerable conservation value and there are numerous notable species associated with them.

The biodiversity plan for Edinburgh also contains detailed action plans for strictly urban habitats. The list is similar to many other cities, including parks, gardens, cemeteries, allotments, school grounds, golf courses, business premises, cyclepaths and footpaths, railway lines and minor water courses.

Some species with very particular requirements have their own Species Action Plans. An example, (described in more detail in Chapter 3), is the sticky catchfly (*Lychnis viscaria*) which has a very restricted distribution in the UK. A small number of these plants still grow on the volcanic rocks of Arthur's Seat and the object of the action plan is to manage existing sites to encourage this species, and to reintroduce the plant to other suitable habitats in Edinburgh. Action plans for species have also been produced for juniper, rock whitebeam, maiden pink and adder's tongue fern. The swift has received special attention owing to a recent reduction in its numbers in Scotland. Special efforts are now being made, working with the city council and developers, to provide nest boxes on existing buildings and to incorporate swift bricks in new developments. Other species singled out for special treatment include otter and badger. After an absence until the early 1990s, otters are gradually recolonising Edinburgh's rivers and the action plan aims to identify and establish a series of refuge areas with artificial holts. Small populations of badgers are present even in heavily built-up areas of the city, especially around Corstorphine Hill and some of the wooded valleys. The action plan includes guidance for planners, developers and land managers on their legal responsibilities for badgers in relation to development.

Local biodiversity action plans have been one of the great success stories for urban nature conservation. They have engaged sectors that have never been involved before, and it is extraordinary how many organisations have taken it upon themselves to do their own local plan. The idea has caught on, from parish councils to port authorities, and from carmakers to power stations, they have all produced plans, and made substantial changes that will benefit wildlife. Even the London Olympics in 2012 had a Biodiversity Action Plan to guide development of the Olympic Park (see Chapter 16).

I pointed out earlier that urban habitats were not adequately catered for in national policies for nature conservation. When the original list of National Priority Habitats was published in 1998 as part of the UK plan for biodiversity it did not include any urban habitats. But in 2007 a new category was added to cater specifically for urban biodiversity: it was given the somewhat cumbersome title 'Open Mosaic Habitats on Previously Developed Land'. Defra commissioned research to define the kinds of area that would fall into this category and a preliminary report was published which was intended to assist in identifying places that might be particularly valuable (Riding *et al.*, 2009).

In the meantime the Invertebrate Conservation Trust, Buglife, has become increasingly concerned at the loss of brownfield sites and in 2009 it issued a best-practice guide for planners and developers alerting them to the importance of invertebrates (Buglife, 2009). It also embarked on a series of studies of brownfield

FIG 214. A characteristic brownfield species, the brown-banded carder bee. (Steven Falk/ Buglife)

sites, concentrating initially on places around the Thames Estuary, an area that was already identified as nationally important for invertebrates (see Chapter 5). It became clear that about 40 per cent of the sites in the Thames Gateway were of significance for invertebrate populations. But the pace of development has been destroying sites almost as quickly as their importance has become appreciated. In September 2013, Buglife issued a report highlighting the loss of important brownfield sites in the Thames Gateway. Over the past six years more than half of these sites have been lost, damaged or are under immediate threat. Buglife argues that 'the very best wildlife sites should be protected from development and that sympathetic and sustainable development should be delivered on other brownfield sites'. With increasing pressure on brownfield land for housing the protection of nationally important sites becomes ever more urgent. But it isn't only development for housing and industry that threatens such sites. Many areas of industrial dereliction have been landscaped to create new parks and open spaces with the resulting loss of valuable habitats that could easily have been incorporated. Although the benefits of ecological landscaping have become widely accepted there is still a need for much greater integration between designers and ecologists.

CHAPTER 15

Connecting with Nature

T HE WORK OF AN URBAN ecologist is remarkably varied. In London it means that as well as dealing with everything from ancient woodlands to pigeons and parakeets there are meetings to be had with all manner of organisations, from the Corporation of the City of London to local community groups in some of the most deprived parts of the capital. So it was that I found myself one day in 1982 travelling with some trepidation from a formal session in the Guildhall to a meeting with residents of Somers Town, at that time a district of ill-repute lying between Euston and St Pancras Stations. My brief was to explain the Greater London Council's plans to convert the derelict coal yards of Camley Street into an Ecology Park. But I was well aware that in this neighbourhood it could easily result in ridicule or worse. As some protection I removed my jacket and tie and walked in with shirt-sleeves rolled up. I showed slides to illustrate the kind of place that might be created. At that time there were few other examples to draw on but I included shots of the William Curtis Ecology Park at Tower Bridge with children pond-dipping. My vision was to produce a mini wetland alongside the Regents Canal, so I used a variety of photos of wetland habitats around the country, including the fen at Malham Tarn in Yorkshire. Nothing could be further from the urban setting of Camley Street, but they were the best I had. When the lights came on there was silence. Then there came a deep chuckle from the depths of an armchair and a lady said: 'Do you know, this is the first beautiful thing that has happened to us here.'

That was the moment when I knew we had local residents on side. They were even happier to find themselves represented on the management committee. Some were involved for many years. Creating Camley Street Natural Park taught

FIG 215. Entrance gates to Camley Street Natural Park. (Mike Waite)

me many things, but the most important was the need not just to engage with the local community but to have local residents involved in every aspect of the project. When we excavated to make the ponds we found a Victorian rubbish dump full of bottles and broken pottery. People fell upon them with glee and nearby houses are still full of these artefacts. Children from local schools made a mural from the fragments. As each stage in creating the park was completed we celebrated with a barbecue or other festivity. Having a full time Warden working with local people whilst the park was being built was crucial to our success.

At that time the concept of an ecology park was still very new. Fergus Carnegie, one of the GLC's team of landscape designers, was assigned to the job but he freely admitted that he knew very little about ecology. My knowledge of landscape design was equally lacking. But between us we came up with a workable plan. Indeed the result was a great credit to Carnegie who managed to create a remarkably intimate yet natural feel within the confines of a very small site. The fact that it is still there today is largely due to the effectiveness of the original design and the considerable care that went into its construction. Ensuring that we got the ecology right was another matter. It was my job to select suitable plants. That's easy in theory but we soon ran up against problems of obtaining native species from horticultural suppliers. Deliveries of Purple-loosestrive, ragged robin and marsh marigold all turned out to be cultivars, and there seemed to be no way of obtaining common pond sedge or reedmace. That was early 1984. Thirty years later the situation is totally different with many suppliers providing native stock for a wide variety of habitats. With these early frustrations overcome the landscaping was completed very quickly and like many other newly created wetland habitats the area had a remarkably natural feel within only 18 months. I remember an excited phone call from the resident teacher telling me that a heron had arrived. It was standing precisely as portrayed by the artist in our publicity brochure. It seemed we had its stamp of approval.

The park was opened by Ken Livingstone, with great celebration by the local community, in May 1985 and it became an immediate success. After abolition of the GLC in 1986 it was leased to the London Wildlife Trust and quickly became one of their flagship nature centres. The main purpose of the park was to provide an opportunity for children in central London to have direct contact with nature. It was soon booked solid by local schools, attracting 10,000 schoolchildren every year by 1990. It also attracted visitors from far and wide as a demonstration project. As interest in urban nature grew worldwide Camley Street achieved a certain fame among practitioners and brought an endless stream of visitors from Europe, Japan, South Africa, North America and more recently from China. But it was also popular with local people of Camden and Islington as a place of peace and quiet at weekends. The local community has always been closely involved. Volunteers have ensured that the park is kept open at weekends and there has been a succession of environmental festivals and other events for local people. Some of the young children who were involved at the beginning continued to take an interest as teenagers, and I remember one incident where a youngster confronted others saying: 'Don't you touch those trees. I planted those!'

FIG 216. Ken Livingstone opening Camley Street Natural Park 7 May 1985.

FIG 217. Pond dipping at Camley Street Natural Park, 1986.

Camley Street Natural Park is still there today despite a succession of planning proposals threatening its existence, including the extension of St Pancras Station for the Channel Tunnel rail link. Local people who recognise that they have something very special have persisted in fighting them all off. So what is it that makes it so special? In essence it is having nature on the doorstep. For people living in one of the most deprived neighbourhoods of inner London it provides a remarkable link with the natural world. I met a family there one Sunday evening. They were busy. The children, who had already visited the park with their school, had taken their parents and grandparents pond dipping. By the end of the evening their grandad was extremely proud to tell me that he had identified four species of dragonfly and he had never set eyes on one before. He was entering a new world.

Camley Street Natural Park was just one of several pioneer projects aimed at connecting people with nature. Others established in the 1980s are mentioned earlier (see Chapter 13). Since then it has become commonplace for new habitats to be created even in the most densely built-up parts of town. Examples include the Wildlife Garden at the British Museum of Natural History in London; ecological parks on the Greenwich Peninsula, at Bow Creek on the River Lea, and Gillespie Park near the Arsenal football stadium; new wetland habitats at the Cardiff Bay Barrage; Pickerings Pasture, an area of spring and summer meadow created on an industrial and household waste tip beside the River Mersey at Widnes; and converted railway yards which now form the Jupiter Urban Wildlife Centre in the midst of industrial Grangemouth in Scotland. Many other habitat creation schemes have been developed in towns and cities elsewhere.

Bringing new wildlife habitats into the urban landscape can happen at every level. It doesn't have to be an ecology park. Growing wild flowers on roadside verges or roundabouts, on drab expanses of grass surrounding tower blocks, or even in inner-city courtyards can produce dramatic results. Their conversion to

FIG 218. Bow Creek Ecology Park

colourful hay meadows has revitalised local communities and provides a powerful image of ecological renewal. The attractive report *Flowers in the Grass* (Ash *et al.*, 1992) had considerable influence in promoting this new approach. As I mentioned earlier Landlife was one of the pioneers in such work, and many other cities are now adopting similar approaches (Luscombe & Scott, 2004, 2011). One of the best examples in Liverpool is in Knowsley where wildflowers have transformed huge areas of heavily mown or neglected grassland into visually stunning displays much appreciated by local people. Questionnaire surveys in 2009, after six years of these displays, resulted in a 98 per cent response in favour of the project and a widespread feeling that it had improved local community spirit. The *Kirkby Times*, a local community newspaper, included numerous letters from people who felt the benefit. A more formal letter came from a local medical centre:

> *The doctors and staff in the practice would like to let you know how impressed we were by the display of wildflowers near Quarry Green Heights earlier this summer. The display was uplifting and enormously improved the feel of the environment. Such activities are vitally important in making a community worth living in and encouraging people to value their environment. Those of us who have worked in Kirby for many years know how badly such initiatives are needed.* (Burls et al., 2010)

In east London the landscape of a council housing estate in Hackney was redesigned to encourage annual and perennial wildflowers to replace the regular and unsightly herbicide treatment of fence-lines and borders along paths. A

FIG 219. Landlife wildflower displays at Quarry Green Heights, Kirkby, in Liverpool. (Landlife)

FIG 220. Mathew Frith: One of the leading figures in urban nature conservation, working at every level from nature reserve warden to national specialist with English Nature, the Peabody Trust and currently with London Wildlife Trust.

reproduction of one of these street corner plots was awarded a Silver Gilt medal at the 2007 Chelsea Flower Show. The annual Chelsea show has provided a measure of changing attitudes to wildlife gardening since the 1980s when I remember the first 'Wildlife Garden' causing indignation amongst visitors. 'But it's just weeds!' was the cry. Now a well-designed wildlife garden is just as likely to gain a gold medal as the most sophisticated formal garden. This reflects the enormous advances that have been made over the past thirty years in ecological horticulture and habitat creation techniques, a subject that I return to in the next chapter. But the creation of more natural landscapes in inner-city housing estates requires social skills as well as ecological expertise, as demonstrated ably by Mathew Frith whilst working with the Peabody Trust.

Successes in improving town parks for wildlife were mentioned earlier, particularly those involving river restoration. The Environment Agency has been responsible for a number of schemes to restore sections of rivers within public parks by converting concrete lined channels to more natural conditions and in one case 'daylighting' a river that had been culverted. Case studies (Environment Agency, 2002) have demonstrated considerable environmental and social benefits. New wetland habitats have been created and flood risk has been substantially reduced by increased storage capacity. The visual appearance has been greatly improved and a range of wetland habitats created which are easily accessible and much enjoyed by local people. These projects bring nature right into the heart of the urban community. Local schools also use the new habitats for environmental education. Following restoration of one of these parks, Sutcliffe Park in Greenwich, the Environment Agency found that there was substantial support for the programme. Before restoration it was a rather dull expanse of grass with the River Quaggy running in an underground culvert. Following the improvements the number of visits increased substantially and it is clear that day-to-day contact with nature was important for many families.

But there are other ways in which parks can be improved to provide contact with nature. Mile End Park in Tower Hamlets is a good example. The park was remodelled during the late 1990s when extensive areas of herb-rich grassland were created with a wide variety of shrubs and trees, mostly native, that have produced an extremely attractive new naturalistic landscape. The park even has its own environmental centre, together with reedbeds and pond. It demonstrates very clearly that there are alternatives to the more formal park landscapes to which we have become accustomed and such areas are proving to be extremely popular with local people. The park is used by thousands of people every day. It also provides a focus for more specialised environmental activities such as bug hunts and spider safaris for children and there are public bird walks.

A current study of one area of grassland by spider expert Edward Milner demonstrates how invertebrate populations benefit from absence of mowing. Over a period of only eight years spider populations have changed from early colonisers to more mature communities including wolf spiders and others associated with newly established anthills. Milner estimates that the total biomass of spiders has doubled and points out that abundance of larger wolf spiders makes these habitats attractive to foraging birds such as robin, dunnock, wren and possibly house sparrow. Mile End Park has now become so well established that it was designated in 2013 as one of London's top-tier sites for nature conservation. Those

FIG 221. Mile End Park, a new kind of town park: with contributors to the Tower Hamlets Biodiversity Action Plan.

responsible for the designation recognised that 'the park provides excellent access to nature, with a great diversity of habitats and the possibility for large numbers of people to experience them. In particular the park clearly demonstrates how to design a large, modern, multi-functional park for biodiversity.'

Practical projects aimed at increasing people's access to nature have been backed up by social scientists who have investigated public perceptions of the natural world. The popularity of numerous Local Nature Reserves and natural parks demonstrates a huge change that has happened in attitudes to nature conservation over the past twenty years. Carolyn Harrison put her finger on the problem in the early 1990s when she recognised that public arguments pursued by conservation institutions were framed by the rhetoric and language of science and not by the language of natural history. She argued that despite the strength of the natural history tradition, its deep-seated roots were ignored in favour of scientific arguments and nature conservation was in danger of losing touch with the concerns of a wider public. She suggested that:

nature conservation matters because people benefit spiritually, emotionally, intellectually, physically and socially when nature is accessible. Getting this argument right and rehearsing it in ways that different audiences will understand is just as important as assembling the scientific evidence.

Harrison went on to suggest that the philosophy and practice of nature conservation would gain in significance for lay and specialist audiences if nature conservation realigned itself with the enthusiasms and concerns of the natural history tradition. She concluded that 'urban nature conservation has its roots in the right place' (Harrison, 1993). There is no doubt that such a realignment has taken place, and that lessons learnt from initiatives in towns and cities have had a profound effect on broader issues of nature conservation in the UK.

Building links between local communities and nature in the multicultural societies of our towns and cities has had its difficulties. There was for many years reluctance on the part of some ethnic minorities to engage with biodiversity projects in urban greenspaces. There are great differences in the cultural traditions of the many ethnic groups involved. Understanding these differences and promoting projects that involve ethnic minorities in ways that draw on their own cultural background has encouraged people to become more involved. The Black Environment Network (BEN) has done much to enable ethnic groups to participate in creating green spaces and to be fully involved in their care and improvement. The sense of belonging that comes from being involved in looking after a nature park or wildlife garden can contribute substantially to local community cohesion. In many places minority ethnic groups are now thoroughly involved, bringing a diverse range of activities stemming from their own cultural and spiritual sources. The Hidden Garden in Glasgow uses beautiful artwork to portray spiritual connections between people and nature in a multi-faith context, demonstrating how different traditions have found meaning in the indigenous plants of their homelands (BEN, 2005). Other projects put the emphasis on food production as, for example, Ashram Acres in Birmingham which was well known as one of the first places in the UK to grow Asian vegetables. In a few places ethnic communities are involved in running Friends Groups for urban green spaces. Women and children run the Friends of St Georges Park at Lozells in Birmingham and the Friends Group at St Agnes Park in Bristol is mainly African Caribbean people.

There is increasing evidence that urban green spaces and natural landscapes in the city bring health benefits to those who use them (Douglas *et al.*, 2011). This may result simply from a view out of a window, or from regular visits to a local park or natural area. Having contact with nature brings psychological benefits, lowering stress levels and increasing general wellbeing. The benefits of regular use of urban greenspace include a reduction in strokes and heart disease. Therapeutic use of such areas in treating problems of mental health is becoming accepted. There is now an extensive literature on the psychological and health benefits of urban nature and greenspace (e.g. Ulrich, 1984; Kaplan, 1985, 2011; Bird, 2004).

One small example will suffice to illustrate what is possible. Meanwhile Gardens, near Paddington Station in London, is a small park created by local residents in 1976 as a temporary community garden. But it is still thriving today. The local branch of MIND, the National Association for Mental Health, manages part of the park as a wildlife garden. Individuals with severe or enduring mental health problems who can benefit from the therapeutic aspects of gardening are offered an opportunity to gain horticultural and other skills working with a horticultural tutor and training co-ordinator. Working as a team they look after all aspects of the garden, from path maintenance and planting of summer flowering meadows, to pruning and beekeeping. The Wildlife Garden has received several awards, including in 2008 the national Urban Wildlife Award for Excellence. What started as a small community project has become a showcase of good practice in terms of mental health, ecological education and social transformation.

Creating new wildlife habitats in densely built-up areas that have little wildlife is one way of making nature more accessible. But, as I have described in earlier chapters, there are many long established natural areas in towns and cities that are managed by Wildlife Trusts, or by local authorities as Local Nature Reserves. In London alone there are over 140 LNRs and the London Wildlife Trust has 45 nature reserves. They have a vital role in encouraging people to become involved. Local 'Friends' groups carry out a huge range of activities, such as running visitor centres, organising wildlife investigations for children, providing specialist guidance on topics such as bird song or butterfly identification; and there is always the need for hard physical work in managing the habitats. For some office workers getting into a pair of waders to clear out an overgrown pond is their idea of a perfect weekend.

Some of the best nature reserves are also the smallest. Railway Fields in Haringey is one of these. Wedged between a railway line and the New River just north of Finsbury Park in north London it is a tiny plot, but one that means a great deal to the local community. Once a coal yard, it has served as the borough's environmental education centre since 1986, catering for visits from around 1,200 primary school children every year. It is a fine blend of small-scale habitat creation together with remnants of the post-industrial environment. There is a large pond fully equipped for pond dipping, a small marsh, flower-rich meadows and patches of secondary woodland. David Bevan, who ran the centre for many years, found that these habitats support a good range of flora and fauna. Species lists now include more than 200 flowering plants, 67 birds and 23 butterflies. The butterflies are monitored each year along specific transects. New species recorded since 2005 include marbled white and ringlet, both of which appear to be spreading in London. As a result of detailed investigations over many years Bevan found a number of notable plants, especially alien species, including one which was 'new to science' known as Haringey knotweed (*Fallopia × conollyana*), a hybrid between Japanese knotweed and Russian vine, first discovered here in 1987.

But Railway Fields is much more than a collection of unusual plants and animals, remarkable though some of these are. Step through its impressive wrought iron entrance gates on Green Lanes (which depict some of the plants and animals to be found within), and you enter a world far removed from the noisy traffic-filled high road that you have just left. For local people, the reserve has become an important oasis of peace and tranquillity in a heavily built-up part of the borough. It gained a Green Flag Award in 2004 for the sensitive management of the reserve and has retained this prestigious award ever since. There is an active Friends group that helps to organise a varied programme of events throughout the year. An annual fungus foray, now in its 23rd year, is always held on the last Sunday in October, visiting some of the wilder patches of Haringey and returning to Railway Fields at the end of the day to have a 'fry-up' and sample some of the fungi. A winter 'tree-dressing' day includes a candle-lit procession through the reserve, which is very popular with local people. Ecologically themed events continue through the summer, including a butterfly day, bat walk, dawn chorus morning and a range of wild flower walks. In summer 2002 the poet Katherine Gallagher was appointed Writer in Residence and organised a series of poetry events on green themes. This resulted in a number of poems dedicated to Railway Fields and there have been annual Poetry Days ever since. Conservation Volunteers (formerly the BTCV) have been based at the reserve since 2012. They now continue the practice of providing high quality environmental education for the borough's primary schools.

A similar story could be told in many nature areas in towns and cities elsewhere. Railway Fields provides a perfect example of what is possible, even on a very limited budget and with basic facilities. Its success was largely due to there being an enthusiastic and dedicated individual who made it all happen. In a review of *Nature Areas for City People*, Jacklyn Johnston (1990) identified ten things that are crucial for the successful management of urban nature areas. The first of these is the Key Person or Group to provide the driving force to fight for all that is required: funding, security of tenure, staffing and buildings. Such leadership is also needed to build partnerships within the local community and with national

FIG 222. Spider Hunt with the London Natural History Society.

agencies to generate funding and support. In times when local authority funding is severely limited the work of some urban nature areas will be threatened. Ensuring that a wildlife site is 'owned' by the local community could be crucially important for its survival. Johnston emphasises that 'such areas should be promoted as everyday places, not as nature reserves for specialists. They need to be open to the public every day to encourage people to drop by at any time.' Wildlife Trusts working in towns and cities now offer a huge array of activities to encourage contact with nature. Special days with bug hunts and barbecues are always popular. They also help to forge links and promote active participation from local people. But nature is always there on the doorstep for those who wish to find it, and increasingly there are local initiatives, such as the innovative project in Bath called 'Nature Moments', that encourage people from all walks of life to explore their immediate surroundings. In his acclaimed book *The Thunder Tree* American ecologist Robert Pyle (1993) refers to the loss of personal contact with nature among urban dwellers as 'the extinction of experience'. It is heartening to see new community initiatives such as Nature Festivals and Neighbourhood Wildlife Watch offering opportunities for people to rediscover their personal links with nature.

Field meetings of natural history societies provide opportunities of a more specialised kind. Those that I am familiar with in London and Bath include everything from early morning expeditions to hear the dawn chorus, to special interest groups devoted to spiders, dragonflies, grasshoppers, the flora of walls and pavements and even the plants that have become established in London Zoo. One particularly enjoyable excursion was a spider hunt around Brent Reservoir in 2009 guided by Edward Milner, London's spider recorder, during which we found forty-three species in two hours. For me highlights of the visit included the tiny green spider *Nigma walckenaeri,* that makes its web on ivy leaves. It is thought to have been introduced a hundred years ago via Kew Gardens and is gradually spreading northwards into the Midlands. A larger green spider was the cucumber spider (*Araniella cucurbitina*). The sharp eyes of our youngest participant, six-year-old Alice, spotted a fine specimen of the yellow and black striped wasp spider (*Argiope bruennichi*), which has spread dramatically since its arrival in the UK.

I quizzed Milner about the absence of spiders with large webs between trees and bushes. It seems that there are some spiders, such as *Araneus marmoreus,* that are completely missing from London's open spaces as the webs get disturbed or broken. Its relative *Araneus quadratus* occurs locally in places that are less disturbed. The meadow by the Ladies Pool on Hampstead Heath had a few individuals in a rough patch in 1991 and Milner recommended that it be left uncut. This secluded corner has provided just the right habitat for this species and there are now 185 specimens. You can learn a lot on a field trip. Milner is not just a recorder, but has a huge understanding about the ecology of these lesser-known creatures. He regularly publishes his observations in the *London Naturalist* (e.g. Milner, 2000) and is an excellent mentor for budding naturalists.

Heading homeward and imbued with Milner's enthusiasm I made a detour to see the large tube-web spiders (*Segestria florentina*) that have colonised the ornate lamp standards along the Thames Embankment in Westminster. A group of schoolchildren sitting nearby became curious to know what I was doing and I demonstrated how the spiders would emerge with great alacrity if you tickled the spokes of their web with a piece of grass. There was much excitement, not without shrieks and screams, at which point the teacher in charge started to take an interest. But some of the children were fascinated and I suspect those spiders will have been one of the highlights of their trip.

The next month a botanical field meeting was held just across the river along the streets between Waterloo Station and the Imperial War Museum. Nick Bertrand, who knows the vagaries of Lambeth's flora better than anyone, led a large group that included specialists on alien plants as well as newcomers to inner-city botany. Rough corners produced the usual array of common mallow, hoary mustard and perennial wall rocket, but there were a number of surprises, including Chinese silver grass (*Miscanthus sinensis*) growing in a pavement crack; passion flower rooted high up in the fork of a London plane tree; and the high point of the day, some plants of navelwort, a western species that is virtually unknown in the Home Counties, which provided a new record for London. The increasing number of ferns was also noted, especially on railway architecture, including harts-tongue, maidenhair spleenwort, wall rue, male fern and a house holly fern.

FIG 223. Trooper's Hill Bug Hunt in Bristol.

In an average year the London Natural History Society organises over eighty field meetings in London (and others further afield). Other societies may not be so ambitious, but most have a programme of field visits and records are published in newsletters, journals and websites. Some of the meetings aim to provide data for local or national atlases on specific groups such as birds, butterflies, dragonflies and plants. Many local natural history societies work closely with regional biological record centres, feeding local records into national recording schemes. This form of citizen science is now well established in the UK with a multitude of people involved as recorders. They are the dedicated naturalists whose specialist knowledge is essential for accuracy to be maintained.

For many people one of the most direct ways of making contact with nature is through their gardens. This can include a wide range of activities from wildlife gardening, contributing to national projects such as the BTO's Garden BirdWatch, indulging in the pleasures of watching birds at close quarters on feeders, setting up cameras in nest-boxes or recording night-time visitors such as foxes or badgers. The possibilities are growing almost by the day.

Wildlife gardening has become extremely fashionable over the past thirty years. There is now a considerable body of literature on the subject and garden centres provide a vast array of material in the form of wildflower seeds, bird-boxes, insect houses, birdfeeders and all the paraphernalia needed to construct the perfect wildlife pond. There are also specialist centres devoted to the practice of wildlife gardening and the use of wildflowers for habitat creation. The London Wildlife Trust has run a Centre for Wildlife Gardening since 1989, promoting a range of local projects involving all sectors of the community, including family events, children's activities and adult classes. A range of mini-habitats demonstrates what is possible in town gardens and tiny patios. The National Wildflower Centre run by Landlife at Court Hey Park in Liverpool provides

FIG 224. London Wildlife Trust Centre for Wildlife Gardening.

a national focus for creative conservation, much of which is aimed at wildlife gardening. The Royal Horticultural Society (RHS) has fine examples of wildflower meadows and other wildlife habitats in its gardens at Wisley and Harlow Carr. There are similar examples at Kew Gardens and Wakehurst Place.

The concept of a wild garden is not new. The first edition of William Robinson's *The Wild Garden* was published in 1870 and ran to seven editions during his lifetime (1838–1935). It was hugely influential in its day, coming 'as a breath of fresh air into the gardening world of the time, extolling the beauties of English wild flowers to a society obsessed with ranks of geraniums and pelargoniums, palms and bamboo groves' (Brown, 1982). His emphasis on the importance of local influences in guiding garden design and his close links with the British Arts and Crafts Movement provided a strong ethos. He also had considerable influence through his weekly journal *The Garden* which he launched in 1871 and edited for nearly thirty years. Gertrude Jekyll became a lifelong friend from the start of her gardening career and her own garden at Munstead Wood embraced many of his wild garden concepts. Robinson's own garden at Gravetye Manor 'was an amazing example of how one could gracefully combine both formal and informal elements in a designed landscape' and was much admired by Jekyll (Tankard, 2011). It is also suggested that Frederick Law Olmsted was influenced by Robinson's ideas when he and Calvert Vaux designed The Ramble in the middle of New York's Central Park. Robinson's book has left an enduring legacy. It was recently updated and expanded to provide 'a sound basis for sustainable garden design and management in the 21st century'.

The recent surge of interest in wildlife gardening came largely from wildlife enthusiasts rather than conventional gardeners. In particular there were strong links with the urban nature conservation movement. Some of the early books on creating wildlife gardens by Baines (1985), Chambers (1987) and Gibbons (1988) still stand the test of time. More recently there has been detailed guidance on how to attract birds to your garden (Moss & Cottridge, 1998) and a complete guide on gardening for wildlife from the RSPB (Thomas, 2010). So much has been written that it seems superfluous to add anything more. A good summary of current practice is the section on creating habitats in the garden in *Science in the Garden* (Ingram *et al.*, 2008). Specific guidelines and suggested species-lists of native plants are given for creation of a range of habitats, namely woodland margins, hedgerows, wild flower meadows, cornfield annuals and ponds and marshes, in part based on information given by Baines. Examples are also given of plants (both native and exotic) that are attractive to birds and bumble bees. A list of nectar plants most commonly used as a food source by butterflies in gardens throughout the British Isles was published by Vickery (1995) and reproduced by Buczacki (2007). Such lists, based on direct observations organised by Butterfly Conservation, are particularly valuable.

There has been something of a debate about the value to wildlife of native plant species as compared with exotic garden flowers as a result of the Sheffield BUGS Project referred to in Chapter 7. Their findings showed that the number and variety of invertebrates recorded was hardly influenced by whether a garden had few or many native wild flowers (Thompson, 2007). This has a bearing on whether creation of natural habitats with native species attracts a richer diversity of wildlife than traditional gardens. But it is not quite as simple as that. It is quite clear from Owen's work that traditional gardens with their great variety of exotic plant species provide considerable resources for wildlife, either as a source of nectar or providing other food for invertebrates. There is no doubt that traditional gardens support a vast array of wildlife. But we can also expect that host specific species will benefit from presence of native plant species. Some insect groups may benefit more than others. Butterflies are remarkably well tuned to particular plant species which they can recognise by their feet. What we don't know is how significant native plant species are in terms of the number of native species of invertebrates that are critically dependent on them. There is more work to do. The

RHS is running a Plants for Bugs experiment using native, near native and exotic plants to investigate which species are good for wildlife. As Ingram points out the debate could also be informed by the research of private gardeners.

Whatever the outcome of that debate there are other reasons for wildlife gardening. A great deal of it is done to create a naturalistic environment that has a different ambience from the usual, and generally more formal, garden setting. It brings nature closer to home. A well-designed wildlife pond can provide hours of enjoyment, even in the tiniest garden. Similarly conversion of part of the garden to a woodland glade allows people to connect with nature in ways that are deep seated in the human psyche.

For many people wildlife in the garden means birds. In January 2013 the annual Big Garden Birdwatch organised by the RSPB attracted nearly 590,000 participants. Every year people are asked to spend one hour recording the birds in their garden, or in a local park, and to note the highest number of each species seen at any one time. The results are fascinating, providing a snapshot of the birds seen in gardens throughout the UK in the last weekend of January. Lists are produced for many towns and cities with the species in order of frequency. I have amalgamated the lists for eighteen urban areas to provide the average position of the top twenty species, in cities ranging from Aberdeen to Bristol and including some major conurbations such as London, Manchester and Merseyside (Table 5). The individual lists are remarkably consistent throughout Britain for these top twenty species, but below that level there is more variation, such as the greater frequency of fieldfare, waxwing and siskin in Scottish cities, which is to be

TABLE 5. Results of the RSPB Big Garden Birdwatch 2013: the twenty birds most frequently seen in urban areas of the UK. (RSPB data)

1	House sparrow	11	Feral pigeon
2	Blackbird	12	Long-tailed tit
3	Blue tit	13	Coal tit
4	Starling	14	Collared dove
5	Woodpigeon	15	Dunnock
6	Magpie	16	Crow
7	Chaffinch	17	Greenfinch
8	Great tit	18	Wren
9	Goldfinch	19	Song thrush
10	Robin	20	Siskin

expected. The RSPB reported that this single annual count could detect changes in the numbers of individual species. Compared with 2012 the numbers of several species had declined. In particular the number of starlings fell by 16 per cent, house sparrows by 17 per cent, bullfinches by 20 per cent and dunnocks by 13 per cent. One interesting feature of the lists is that ring-necked parakeets were remarkably widespread. In 2013 they occurred in all the towns and cities listed and even made it into the top twenty species in several places, including Newport, Cardiff and Dundee. The results demonstrate the valuable role played by amateur bird watchers in gathering ecological data.

The British Trust for Ornithology has run its more sophisticated Garden BirdWatch since 1994 with thousands of dedicated recorders who provide detailed weekly information on birds and other wildlife seen in their gardens. They are asked to make their observations at about the same time (or times) each week. The maximum number of individuals seen at any one time is recorded for each week. Results are published quarterly for different geographical areas of the UK. An example for the London area is given in Table 6. The position of any species can be compared with the average for all the previous years since 2002. It has now become rather more than a bird-watch. 'Other wildlife' includes mammals, reptiles, amphibians, butterflies, bumblebees, hornet, stag beetle, cockchafer, dragonflies and hummingbird hawk-moth. The BTO also organises special one-off surveys, as in the case of house sparrows.

The results have provided the basis for detailed research on bird populations that could not have been done in any other way. As well as demonstrating population trends for individual species, the results help to throw light on seasonal patterns in the use of garden habitats. Garden BirdWatch has also provided a means of monitoring changes in the populations of species considered to be of conservation importance, such as blackbird, starling, house sparrow and song thrush. Other special projects include an initiative on Wildlife Health, jointly with the Zoological Society of London, RSPB and Froglife. It is hoped that this will help to identify new and emerging threats such as finch trichomonosis, which has recently affected populations of greenfinch.

One of the aims of the BTO in promoting Garden BirdWatch is 'to introduce people to wildlife recording and monitoring, allowing them to record observations that can be used to determine conservation policy'. This is Citizen Science of a sophisticated kind. Through involvement in detailed monitoring programmes it is hoped that people will become more aware of ecological issues and support positive action for conservation.

Which brings me to the final part of this chapter. It is now possible for individuals with little taxonomic experience to identify many species of plants

TABLE 6. Results of the BTO Garden BirdWatch in London for the breeding season 2013. (Data reproduced with permission, from BTO Garden BirdWatch www.bto.org/gbw)

Ranking	Species	Reporting rate	Avg. rep. rate	Avg. rank
1	Woodpigeon	90.6%	85%	2.7
2	Blue Tit	89.3%	90%	2.1
3	Robin	89.1%	80%	4.5
4	Blackbird	89.0%	90%	1.8
5	Great Tit	82.7%	75%	5.4
6	Magpie	68.8%	67%	7.0
7	Dunnock	60.2%	53%	9.4
8	Starling	57.5%	70%	6.0
9	Goldfinch	56.3%	26%	16.4
10	Feral Pigeon	51.2%	46%	11.7
11	House Sparrow	49.3%	65%	7.4
12	Collared Dove	44.1%	52%	10.0
13	Greenfinch	41.6%	47%	11.1
14	Carrion Crow	39.8%	38%	13.4
15	Chaffinch	38.2%	32%	14.6
16	Great Spotted Woodpecker	27.9%	22%	17.2
17	Coal Tit	21.4%	20%	17.9
18	Jay	20.9%	25%	16.3
19	Wren	18.5%	24%	16.8
20	Long-tailed Tit	17.6%	11%	19.8
21	Jackdaw	11.0%	4%	24.4
22	Blackcap	10.4%	4%	24.1
23	Nuthatch	5.9%	4%	22.9
24	Song Thrush	5.4%	13%	19.7
25	Siskin	4.6%	1%	30.7
26	Goldcrest	3.7%	3%	25.7
27	Sparrowhawk	3.0%	3%	24.8
28	Black-headed Gull	1.5%	1%	33.5
29	Pied Wagtail	1.3%	1%	33.1
30	Mistle Thrush	1.3%	2%	27.1

and animals by posting a photograph on iSpot. This is a powerful tool that could well revolutionise the study of natural history. Social networking of the kind promoted by iSpot offers the opportunity for anyone with a mobile phone to become a naturalist. It is a new kind of society, linked by a common interest where beginners feel comfortable. It might even provide the means by which existing natural history societies survive. Most of them have an ageing population with few young recruits. They also have taxonomic experts whose knowledge is crucial to the study of local natural history. These are the people who can act as mentors for a new generation of naturalists using new technology. It has been suggested that the smart phone is the new butterfly net. It certainly offers enormous opportunities for citizen science.

Why is this relevant to towns and cities? The fact is that most people live in urban areas and that is where young people will find their most immediate contact with nature. They don't have to go off into the wilds to photograph unusual creatures. Indeed many photos are done with the support of teachers at schools in their local neighbourhood. One of the commonest photos on iSpot is a species of ladybird now commonly found in houses and gardens, though it only recently arrived in the UK.

The prospects for community-based science programmes are enormous. Mobile phones provide satellite location down to a few metres and the internet can provide expertise and keys for identification of species. Already there are numerous apps for identifying birds, plants and many other groups of species. It has become possible to develop recording schemes using citizen science on a scale never contemplated before. They could be designed to investigate and record biological responses to climate change, using a large number of observers all contributing to the same data bank. Similarly the public could be encouraged to record the spread of introduced pests and diseases (as is already happening in the case of Ash Dieback), or to catalogue newly colonising species; or simply to map the distribution of popular species in towns and cities. Every city could have an ID app for major groups such as plants, birds, butterflies, dragonflies and other common insects.

The approach is very different from anything that natural history societies have traditionally done before, but it gives hope that the pursuit of natural history can be revitalised. It is possible too that the role of specialists or mentors will take on a new significance. Many naturalists will tell you that it was a particular teacher or enthusiast who set them on the road to natural history. The expertise of specialists in natural history societies could be one of our greatest assets in generating enthusiasm among the younger generation. Opportunities presented by the internet have enormous implications for learning about the natural history and ecology of places where people live. They may even ensure a future for the pursuit of natural history itself.

CHAPTER 16

New Ecological Landscapes

IN TRACING THE PROGRESS OF urban nature conservation we have seen that newly created wildlife habitats have become an increasingly significant part of urban design during the past thirty years. We have now reached the point where new habitats are being constructed in the very heart of the urban environment. Some of these provide traditional nature reserves, others provide new kinds of park landscape that will hopefully make them more sustainable in the face of climate change. Yet others provide new habitats on roofs and walls in the middle of the built environment. This final chapter describes some of these new initiatives and offers possibilities for the future development of towns and cities.

THE LONDON WETLAND CENTRE

The London Wetland Centre, created during the late 1990s to replace the redundant Barn Elms reservoirs at Barnes in west London, is one of the most impressive habitat creation projects anywhere in Britain. The original concrete lined reservoirs covering 42 hectares were totally replaced by newly created habitats, designed to provide a range of conditions for a variety of wetland birds and other species. Alongside these natural features high quality facilities are provided for public access and viewing. The whole project has been remarkably successful, and is now one of the premier bird-watching locations in London. It is all the more remarkable when one realises that it lies only four miles from Buckingham Palace.

FIG 225. London Wetland Centre: a statue of Sir Peter Scott stands at the entrance.

Early last century Barn Elms Reservoirs were known to attract a range of unusual birds and over the years the site became well known to London's bird watchers. The reservoirs were constructed in 1897, at a time when black headed gulls were first congregating along the Thames, and they soon became a favourite roosting site. Max Nicholson describes how in the 1920s he tracked down this roost by following winter flight lines of gulls from different parts of London (Nicholson, 1995). By the 1930s the numbers of ducks using the reservoirs during the winter had grown significantly, with 2,000 tufted duck and pochard, rising to over 3,000 after the war. But the reservoirs were particularly famous as a wintering place for smew, with numbers varying from 50 to 100 birds in the early 1950s. For about 30 years, until the mid-1970s, Barn Elms was one of the principal wildfowl wintering sites in London. Populations of tufted duck, pochard and smew were sufficiently high for it to be notified as an SSSI in 1975. It was also designated as Metropolitan Open Land in 1976. Because of being on a flight-line following the Thames valley, the reservoirs attracted a great variety of migrant birds, not only aquatic species such as black tern, red-necked grebe and even Bewick's swans, but also many other rarities such as desert wheatear and red throated pipits. A total of 217 species were recorded since the reservoirs were constructed.

With construction of a new ring main for London's water supply the reservoir became redundant by the mid-1980s and plans were made for it to be decommissioned. Happily this coincided with a visit by Sir Peter Scott and his wife Philippa who were invited to join a boat trip on the Thames with environmental organisations. During our trip down the river he asked where in London it might be possible to develop a Wetland Trust centre like Slimbridge. I knew that the reservoirs at both Stoke Newington and Barn Elms were due to become redundant, and told him that there may well be an opportunity to

FIG 226. Aerial view of the London Wetland Centre looking west. (Wildfowl and Wetlands Trust/Berkeley Homes)

develop a new centre at one of these. Because of its ornithological history Barn Elms was the obvious choice. He was tremendously excited at the prospect of developing a wetland centre in London and soon after this the Wildfowl and Wetlands Trust (WWT) entered into negotiations with Thames Water to create a new wetland at Barnes.

Draft proposals for a Wetland Centre were exhibited to the public in June 1990 and, with some amendments, were submitted jointly by Thames Water and WWT for consideration by the London Borough of Richmond upon Thames in 1991. Planners had already insisted that the whole of the area notified as an SSSI should be retained for conservation, and this became a key element of the plan. The other critical element was that the scheme was to be funded from income generated by building houses on adjacent Thames Water land. A partnership was forged with Berkeley Homes in 1993 and the proposals gained planning approval in 1995. Under these plans Berkeley Homes built about 340 luxury houses and flats on nine hectares of land, thereby providing funding of £11 million for construction of the Wetland Centre on the 42 hectares previously occupied by the reservoirs.

In the meantime staff of WWT had been hard at work drawing up plans for creation of new habitats that would replace the concrete reservoirs. Much of the subsequent success is due to the painstaking detail of these plans and the accuracy with which they were implemented. The object was to construct a range of different wetland habitats from open-water lakes, reedbed and carr woodland, to seasonally inundated grazing marsh, open mudflats and a variety of small ponds of varying depths, which would provide suitable conditions for a wide range of wetland species. If this was not ambitious enough in itself, it was compounded by a planning condition precluding any export or import of soil or other materials from the site, including all the concrete waste. The project involved detailed engineering to provide the right hydrological conditions, with construction of 27 sluices for controlling water levels. Earthmoving commenced in November 1995 and the substrates were all in place ready for planting within a year. Before flooding each of the water bodies the edges were sculpted, often by hand, to increase the level of diversity along the water's edge. It was this attention to detail that paid off as the site matured over the years.

All the plant communities were designed to replicate natural conditions and were based on the national vegetation classification. The range of communities included seven submerged or floating leafed communities with pondweeds, water crowfoot and water lilies, and four emergent aquatic or swamp communities including greater tussock-sedge, common reed, greater pond- sedge and lesser pond-sedge, together with associated species such as branched bur-reed, meadowsweet, angelica, purple loosestrife, valerian, marsh marigold and reed canary

FIG 227. The Wetland Centre is one of the most successful habitat creation projects of recent years.

FIG 228. Winter scene with herons and black-headed gulls.

grass. The range of species involved and the number of individual plants supplied provide some indication of the enormous changes that have affected ecological projects since the early 1980s, as described in Chapter 15. Construction involved planting some 250,000 individual plants (including trees and shrubs) of which 50,000 were plugs of common reed. Planting started in May 1997 and continued for two seasons. Wetland construction was completed by the end of 1998. Work on the buildings commenced in 1996, first the two main hides, sluices and walkways, followed by the visitor centre. Even during construction in 1997 a number of birds moved in to breed, including several pairs of little ringed plovers, lapwings and great crested grebes. Sir David Attenborough opened the centre in May 2000.

In its first year 135 species of birds were recorded, a total which rose to over 200 by 2008. Visitor numbers rose from 80,000 in the first year, to about 150,000 for the next few years, rising to over 220,000 in 2007–8. For serious bird-watchers the range of hides, including a triple-decker tower with lift for wheelchair access, are extremely effective. They are strategically placed to ensure that most of the wild areas of the wetland are visible from at least one of the hides, and they are populated daily by a regular team of observers known as the Barn Elms Natural History Group. Their detailed daily records make this one of the best-recorded sites in London, providing invaluable information not only on bird populations, but also on a range of other groups including amphibians, butterflies, moths, dragonflies and flowering plants.

FIG 229. Bittern, a bird that everyone hopes to see. (Mark Turnbull)

FIG 230. Artificial sand martin bank. (Anne and Chris Algar/WWT)

Records of dragonflies demonstrate the changes currently occurring as a result of climate change. Two species, the ruddy darter and red-eyed damselfly, which were rare or uncommon in London, have now become established as breeding species. Other invertebrate species showing a similar expansion of their range include the long winged conehead (*Conocephalus discolor*), Roesels bush cricket (*Metrioptera roeselii*), and wasp spider (*Argiope bruennichi*), all of which are regularly recorded on the site.

Since the first plantings the vegetation has gradually matured, with growth of extensive reed beds, willow carr and thickets of birch. The result is most impressive. As well as large numbers and a great variety of ducks, a vast array of other wetland species now occur regularly, including bittern, heron, water rail, lapwing, snipe and little ringed plover. Even avocets have nested successfully. The numbers of gadwall and shoveler using the new wetland was particularly high in the early years, with maxima of nearly 250 for each in 2001, and this prompted

FIG 231. Some birds, like this moorhen, become remarkably tame at the Wetland Centre.

English Nature to reinstate the SSSI designation in 2002. Other species that have benefited from the new wetland are wigeon, with 100–200 birds recorded every year since 2002; teal with over 300 every year and over 900 in 2005; heron with 10–20 birds recorded regularly and a maximum of 38 in 2002. The Wetland Centre is one of the most reliable places in London to see water rails, which were first recorded breeding in 2001, and now has a substantial population with up to 26 birds recorded. On one of my visits a water rail was feeding inside a duck feeder in the American pen. It remained undetected for most of the afternoon only yards away from crowds of visitors. The centre has also become a regular haunt of wintering bitterns that provide great entertainment when they come into the open, but can also be frustratingly elusive.

An artificial bank for sand martins was constructed in 2003, which proved extremely successful for a species that has suffered significant fluctuations in numbers in the UK over the past 30 years. From small beginnings, with only 10 pairs in 2004, the population grew to 44 pairs in 2006, reaching 81 pairs in 2008. Most of the 95 holes were in use in 2007–8, including second broods. Sadly success can also have its drawbacks. Young birds provide easy prey for the small number of hobbys which frequent the centre during late August and September in most years and it seems they are devastating the population. On a more positive note the Wetland Centre has provided a focus for re-introducing water voles as part of the detailed Action Plan for this species in London.

The London Wetland Centre provides a model for similar projects in other towns and cities. It demonstrates very clearly that it is possible to create high quality habitats on a grand scale and attract a wealth of wildlife within a totally urban environment. Its success is not restricted to its ecology. It has become a major visitor attraction in the capital and a fine example of making connections with nature for people of every age.

QUEEN ELIZABETH OLYMPIC PARK

You may think that Olympic Games are all about sport and have little to do with nature. But you would be wrong. London's bid for the 2012 Olympics put enormous emphasis on sustainability. It was conceived as the 'One Planet Olympics' which meant that catering for biodiversity became a significant issue. The whole approach was designed to ensure that there was no net loss of biodiversity and every opportunity was taken to improve opportunities for wildlife in the future. So construction of the Olympic Park in east London, with its various sports arenas and 'athletes village', included a range of newly created naturalistic habitats as part of an integrated plan for the lower Lea Valley where the venue was situated. It is said to be one of the largest urban parks created in Europe for over 150 years.

The Queen Elizabeth Olympic Park is designed to enhance the wildlife and amenity of the whole area by providing a major public park alongside a mixture of residential, sporting and commercial developments. This ecological landscape incorporates flood storage, sustainable drainage schemes, green roofs and forty-five hectares of wildlife habitat, as part of a much larger area of newly accessible public open space. So as well as supporting wildlife it also provides effective 'ecological services'. The functional aspects of this 'green infrastructure' which have been built into the urban landscape of the Olympic Park are particularly important. Whereas the London Wetland Centre, described previously, was created specifically to provide a habitat for people to see wetland wildlife, here in the Lea Valley the aim was to create a sustainable urban landscape within which nature could thrive.

One of the legacies of the Olympics has been to revitalise a part of London that had suffered from severe post-industrial blight. The section of the Lea Valley chosen for the main Olympic venue presented huge challenges. For the past 150 years it has had a history of industrial development, followed by decline and neglect, and in the immediate post-war years became a dumping ground for demolition rubble from London's bomb-sites, along with a great mixture of waste materials. Part of the site was known locally as 'Fridge Mountain'. With declining industrial use the area became derelict wasteland, with countless disused factory sites and railway yards, much of which was contaminated by petrol, oil and tar, together with severely toxic materials such as arsenic and lead. Ground water and surface deposits were heavily polluted. The area was also crossed by a complex infrastructure of services including a network of pylon lines carrying electricity supply cables, as well as gas and water mains and the main sewer carrying sewage from the whole of north London. This part of the Lea Valley is also bisected by a number of branches of the River Lea all of which were heavily polluted. River edges were colonised by swathes of invasive plants including giant hogweed, Himalayan balsam and Japanese knotweed. Chinese mitten crabs occurred in the waterways.

But in the midst of this post-industrial landscape there were patches that had value for nature conservation. The London Ecology Unit identified a number of such sites in the Nature Conservation Strategy for Newham (Archer & Yarham, 1991) and the borough designated these as sites of value for nature conservation in its Local Plan. They amounted to a total of forty-five hectares within the area to be developed for the Olympics. The sites contained a number of key species listed in the London Biodiversity Action Plan and in the local action plan for Newham borough. So when planning permission was sought for the Olympic venue the proposal contained a specific Biodiversity Action Plan (BAP) for the whole 230 hectares of the Olympic Park, with a requirement to create 45 ha of new habitats as replacement for important sites that would be lost, and detailed action plans for twenty six species that required special conditions for their survival. To have a Biodiversity Action Plan as part of the master plan for a major urban development was a new innovation and developers and contractors were faced with a steep learning curve. On one occasion a contractor was in touch with the

FIG 232. New wetland habitats in the Queen Elizabeth Olympic Park 2012.

ecologists asking: 'What's a tumbling flower beetle and what's it to do with me?' The BAP was supplemented by detailed guidance for every individual structure, translating the targets in the BAP into the final design.

The policy of no net loss of biodiversity meant that substantial areas of new high-quality habitats were created. These are mainly wetland communities and various kinds of flower-rich grasslands capable of surviving in a future parkland environment. Attempts were also made to replicate conditions of urban wasteland by creating stony banks and areas of rubble capable of supporting a range of critical plants and invertebrate species typical of 'brownfield' land, such as the brown-banded carder bee and toadflax brocade moth.

Nearly 700 bird and bat boxes were incorporated into the built structures such as gabions of bridges, to accommodate species such as swift, house sparrow, starling and one of the local rarities, the black redstart. Elsewhere there are artificial banks for kingfishers and sand martins, and holts for otters. By the time the Games took place in 2012 reed warblers and reed buntings had already colonised the newly created reedbeds.

This is all far removed from one's normal perception of Olympic Games! But it is not all about building new habitats for nature. The whole park has been designed using principles of sustainability and the result is a model of what is possible in new urban developments.

NATURE ON ROOFTOPS

Although ecological approaches have become increasingly significant as part of urban design, one of the most obvious opportunities has until recently been one of the slowest to be exploited. This is the huge potential offered by rooftops. Look down on any major city in the UK and you will see vast areas of rooftops almost entirely devoid of any greenery. Yes there are occasional roof gardens bringing life to this arid environment, but they are few and far between. However, if we look at new urban development schemes some have significant areas of roofs swathed in vegetation. They are an indication of what is possible. Go to some European cities, especially in Germany and Switzerland, and the picture is very different. Here we find many buildings covered in vegetation. They are leading the way in a novel approach which could in time change the character of towns and cities, bringing nature back into the heart of the built environment. The creation of green roofs may seem incongruous, but the approach is gaining considerable momentum in the UK as a means of achieving greater sustainability within the built environment.

The idea is not new. Turf roofs have been used traditionally on houses in Scandinavia, Iceland, Kurdistan and parts of China for many centuries, and their insulation benefits have long been well known. But creating new habitats on the roofs of city buildings is rather different. So how has this new approach come about? As with so many new ideas it stemmed from cross fertilisation between several disciplines, in this case a blend of ecology, horticulture and innovative architecture, together with inspiration from some outstanding artists and landscape designers. The realisation that green roofs have many environmental benefits, especially for conservation of energy and water resources, as well as providing opportunities for nature to thrive in the city, has led to this new approach being used to achieve key aspects of sustainability. But other earlier influences have also played their part.

Derry and Toms' Roof Garden

The landscape designer's concept of *rus in urb* (literally, 'country in the city') was central to the design of many roof gardens, none more so than the famous gardens constructed in the 1930s on the roof of Derry and Toms department store in Kensington, London. This large roof has several contrasting gardens, a Spanish Garden with Moorish pergolas and fountains, linked by Tudor-style

FIG 233. The Woodland Garden; part of the famous 'Garden in the Sky' on Derry and Toms in Kensington, constructed in the 1930s.

colonnades to a formal English Garden. On the other side of the roof is the Woodland Garden with a stream and ponds complete with ducks and flamingos. When first constructed it was the largest roof garden in Europe and quickly achieved great fame as the 'garden in the sky' (Scrivens, 1980).

Built at a time when the more refined departmental stores were vying with one another to attract international customers it is said that the architect of Derry and Toms took his inspiration from the 'Gardens of the Nation' on the 11th floor of the Rockefeller Center in New York. The idea came from Raymond Hood, a principal architect at the Center, who was an ardent supporter of urban gardening. At the time he had ambitious plans for linking the roofs of Manhattan skyscrapers with bridges to create a park in the sky! The British landscape architect Ralph Hancock, who was responsible for much of the installation and planting of the Rockefeller gardens, also designed the gardens on Derry and Toms (Duterloo-Morgan, 1998).

As it happened the Derry and Toms building was designed for seven floors, but only six were built owing to fire safety limits, so the building had the structural potential for another floor. The garden was created on top of a conventional flat roof over a layer of waterproof asphalt. Soil depth varied from 600 mm to 1 m. Some 33 different tree species were planted as standards, including ash, birch, field maple, sycamore, willow and yew, as well as more ornamental specimens of cherry, apple, mulberry, ginkgo and fig. Many of these are now sizable specimens. The stream was originally stocked with fish, but had to be covered with netting to stop the depredations of herons. Despite being six floors up the gardens were quickly colonised by birds, including blackbird, song thrush, dunnock, robin, wren and house sparrow. Waterbirds such as moorhen, mallard and grey wagtail also became established and the gardens continue to provide an unusual natural sanctuary.

It is an extraordinary experience to visit this garden. Entering the lift at street level amongst the crowds of shoppers and traffic of Kensington High Street one emerges in the leafy enclave of the woodland garden where a stream winds amongst the trees and the songs of blackbird, robin and wren fill the air. Its success is all the more striking because of the incongruity of bringing nature into the very heart of the metropolis in such an unexpected way. The garden remains one of the wonders of London.

The influence of Friedensreich Hundertwasser

Emphasis on the unexpected is even more pronounced in the case of the Hundertwasser House in Vienna which has become such a landmark in the links between ecology and the built environment. It demonstrates what is possible through the vision of a man who as both artist and architect was committed to an ecological lifestyle. Hundertwasser's 1973 painting of a house inhabited by 'tree tenants' fed by rainwater filtered through humus from organic toilets was way ahead of its time (Schmied, 2005). Wherever he lived he made his ecological principles a reality, making the most of even the smallest patch to grow trees and meadows on the roof. So when he embarked on the creation of Hundertwasser House in 1979 he had clear ideas of what it would be. His concept of making a building truly ecological, with rainwater filtration to feed trees growing within the fabric of the building was revolutionary. With some of the most conservative architects of Austria pitted against him, Hundertwasser persevered with his vision and the result is a truly iconic building which now has a special place in the development of green architecture.

The building contains 52 flats, 5 shops and a doctor's surgery and is situated on one of Vienna's busy main streets. What distinguishes it from the surrounding traditional buildings is the overall design (Schmied, 2005). The flats are stacked on top of each other, but overlapping in a series of steps like houses on the slopes of a hill, creating about 20 roof terraces at different levels. Each of these was planted with trees, so that at first sight it appears as if the building is covered in woodland. Some 250 trees and bushes were planted in a layer of humus 0.5 to 1 m deep contained in a concrete shell with insulating and waterproof layers. Other trees, the so-called 'tree tenants', were planted in deep tubs contained in specially constructed balconies integrated into the building, so that they have the appearance of growing out of the windows. Climbers such as ivy and Virginia creeper were also planted and now cover parts of the façade.

Added to all of this was Hundertwasser's determination to get away from regular geometry and standardised layout. Instead he went for diversity, variety and irregularity, resulting in a higgledy-piggledy configuration of the apartments, each of which had its own colour on the outside. His aim was to replicate the variety in nature, rather than impose rigid lines. The result was a building that defied convention and inevitably it brought much criticism from the media and the architectural profession. Interestingly the public reaction was less severe and with time the building has taken its place as more than just a curiosity. It has in fact become one of Austria's greatest tourist attractions.

This was an artist's attempt to bring nature into the city. The influence which Hundertwasser had on the subsequent development of green roofs is difficult to judge, but there is no doubt that he did much to foster a greater awareness of the opportunities for 'greening the city' through the many buildings which he designed. The fact that he had a large following, particularly among young people, may well have helped to sow the seeds of change that enabled others to benefit.

The ecology of green roofs

In fact much was already happening in Germany. Ecologists in Berlin had become aware that flat roofs of apartment blocks built in the late nineteenth century that had become naturally colonised by plants were proving to be extremely resilient (Wells & Grant, 2005). By the 1970s other researchers in Germany found that greening of roofs had many environmental benefits, particularly in terms of energy conservation and the effective management of water resources. Several German firms were already well established, providing roofing services and carrying out research. In one case the main objective was to replace landscapes lost to built development by making the most of unused roof areas and planting them with vegetation. A Green Roof Study Group was set up as early as 1977 within the German Society for Landscape Construction Research. Another German company Erisco Bauder was the first to introduce lightweight 'extensive' green roofing technology into the UK in 1982.

At that time few people in Britain had heard of green roofs. There were some spectacular roof gardens, often built as expensive luxuries for prestigious buildings, but these were of the traditional kind with load bearing roofs capable of supporting a significant depth of soil and substantial trees. Most of these gardens

FIG 234. An extensive green roof: Sedum mat on a garden centre in Bath.

were designed to be accessible and in many cases they performed the same function as small parks or gardens on the ground. Few, if any, of these gardens were designed specifically to cater for wildlife. Because they require a high level of maintenance such gardens have become known as 'intensive' green roofs.

The new style 'extensive' green roofs introduced by Erisco Bauder were quite different, with an emphasis on thin lightweight substrates supporting a ground cover of low-growing grasses, mosses or herbaceous plants, especially drought-tolerant succulents such as stonecrop. They provided a simple and effective means of creating vegetation cover on rooftops, most often through laying thin rolls of Sedum matting complete with an appropriate freely draining substrate. Being lightweight they required little additional support and because the vegetation was adapted to the harsh rooftop environment little maintenance was needed. Such roofs were not generally intended for human access.

This approach was first popularised in Britain by Kathy Stansfield (1988) in an article aimed at local government, in which she pointed out the environmental benefits. These were later explained in greater detail in the London Ecology Unit's landmark publication *Building Green* (Johnston & Newton, 1993). This was the first attempt to summarise the German literature in English, and did much to promote acceptance of these ideas. Four main kinds of benefits were identified: amenity, ecological, technical and financial. The amenity category included provision of

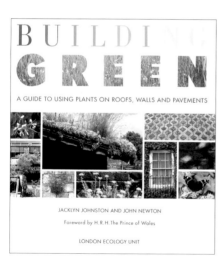

accessible rooftop gardens, improved visual amenity, and psychological benefits deriving from a green landscape. Ecological advantages included slowing and reduction of storm-water run-off, reduction of the urban heat island effect, provision of wildlife habitats and reduction in air pollution. Technical advantages included thermal and acoustic insulation and protection of roof surfaces from damaging effects of ultra-violet radiation. Additionally there were reduced long-term maintenance costs.

Many of these advantages have little bearing on biodiversity, but have profound significance for urban sustainability. However, when

FIG 235. *Building Green* (1993) was instrumental in promoting green roofs to a sceptical architectural profession.

Building Green was published in 1993 I was asked to give a lecture at the RIBA and well remember the hostile reaction of many architects who dismissed these ideas as flights of fancy. It took another 10 years before British architects were willing to accept such ideas as a normal part of their practice. Interestingly this was largely due to the value of such roofs for biodiversity, and in particular for black redstarts. This happened because the black redstart was chosen as one of the critical species in the London Biodiversity Action Plan. As described earlier (Chapter 9) this is a bird of derelict land and post-industrial habitats, with a large percentage of its UK breeding population in east London. An advice note (Frith *et al.*, 1999) alerted those involved in urban development to the special measures needed for its conservation. One of the authors was Dusty Gedge who had carried out detailed surveys of black redstarts in London and was rapidly becoming a national expert on the species. Production of the action plan very quickly focussed on creating new habitats on roofs, mimicking those of brownfield land, as a means of maintaining black redstart populations in the face of continuing loss of important ruderal habitats. So it was that the black redstart action plan became a key driving force in making green roofs an acceptable part of urban development. Such roofs even became known among architects as 'black redstart roofs'. Gedge went on to become the national champion of green roofs, setting up and running a national website: www.livingroofs.org (Gedge, 2003).

Why green roofs?

Since 2000 there has been a surge of activity promoting green roofs, commencing with a report by English Nature (Grant *et al.*, 2003) reviewing the current situation and explaining the environmental benefits. Potential benefits for biodiversity were described more fully than in *Building Green*, with recognition that green roofs in densely built-up urban areas could provide important habitats in districts otherwise lacking any wildlife habitat. They might also provide links, or stepping-stones, facilitating dispersal of species and might provide significant habitats for rare or endangered species, particularly those of urban wastelands. As well as protected species such as the black redstart (Frith & Gedge, 2000; Wells, 2001), this could include specialist invertebrate assemblages with many nationally scarce species such as those recently discovered on brownfield sites in the East Thames Corridor (Harvey, 2001, 2004). Living roofs thus offer unique opportunities for creation of typically urban habitats, as mitigation for loss of ruderal habitats on brownfield land through development. Creation of 'biodiverse roofs' (including living-roofs to replicate post-industrial urban habitats) is now becoming accepted within the urban development professions and what started with small scale examples on roofs around Deptford Creek in London has now been adopted in many other places.

Although it has been very significant, biodiversity is only one of the factors encouraging the creation of green roofs in the UK. Over the past ten years the number of green roofs being built has increased enormously, mainly because they are seen as achieving sustainable solutions in urban design, and the approach has now become firmly accepted within the development industry. Their value in regulating storm water discharge rates as part of sustainable drainage schemes has been one of the main reasons for their adoption. Green roofs are now being created at all scales from bus shelters and roofs of individual houses, to large-scale roofing of business parks and showpiece buildings in key locations. The Olympic Village in London has an area of about 1.2 ha of green roofs rich in biodiversity as an integral feature of the development.

A National Green Roof Centre was established in Sheffield in 2008 to provide guidance on best practice for architects and developers, drawing on the horticultural and ecological expertise in the University of Sheffield. It originated from small-scale university research projects in 1999, since when research activity increased dramatically and Sheffield City Council became very active in policy development and promotion of green roofs. Groundwork Sheffield joined the team as another powerful green roof advocate, and the city now contains a number of landmark green roof projects. Not to be outdone, Manchester City Council promoted an ambitious Green Roofs Programme in 2009 in conjunction with property developers. Since 2003 international conferences have been held annually, keeping architects and developers abreast of new approaches in what has become a rapidly expanding new industry.

Green roofs achieved national recognition when the Royal Commission on Environmental Pollution (sadly abolished in 2010) recommended to Government that it should promote their use (RCEP, 2007). At the same time detailed advice by the construction industry research association (CIRIA) demonstrated the wide range of benefits through case studies, including roofs at Canary Wharf and London Zoo (Newton *et al.*, 2007). In London a policy was included in the statutory London Plan requiring new developments to include provision for living roofs and the GLA published detailed advice for developers (Mayor of London, 2008). A recent audit estimated that the capital contained over 60,000 m² of intensive roof gardens and almost 33,000 m² of extensive green roofs, with a further 80,000 m² of green roofs planned as mitigation for loss of urban habitats.

Advantages for wildlife

So what are the advantages of green roofs for wildlife? Evidence from the UK is patchy owing to the recent nature of most green roofs and the paucity of systematic studies, but there is good evidence from some long established roofs in Europe, particularly in Switzerland. Though unintended, the roofs of the

Moos water filtration plant in Zurich, built in 1914, provide one of the most spectacular examples. The original intention was simply to cool the filtration beds by having a vegetated roof. The concrete ceiling and waterproof layer was covered with 5 cm of sand and gravel to provide drainage, covered by 15–20 cm of topsoil from surrounding farmland. Through natural colonisation over the years the roofs have developed into flower-rich meadows which now include many rare and endangered species. Some 175 grassland species occur, with nine species of orchids, including about 6,000 plants of the green winged orchid which is no longer found in the local district. The flora of these roofs reflects the biological diversity of the local landscape of the early twentieth century, which has gradually been lost through agricultural intensification and urban development (Brenneisen, 2003). These roofs, which cover an area of three hectares, have now been given special protection because of the large number of critical species which they support. More recent work in Switzerland has demonstrated that many green roofs more than 10 years old support important populations of orchids that have become established naturally. Eleven species of orchid were recorded from thirty-one roofs examined, all of which are on the Red List of endangered species in Switzerland.

Switzerland also provided one of the first investigations into the biodiversity value of newly created green roofs (Brenneisen, 2001, 2003). Twenty-four green roofs were examined in Basel and Lucerne, which included some well established turf roofs from the 1970s, together with modern Sedum-mat roofs, and some specially designed 'biodiverse' roofs using local soils and substrates such as rubble. Beetles and spiders were chosen as biological indicators and birds were also investigated. Over a three-year period, 78 spiders and 254 beetle species were recorded. Fourteen (18 per cent) of the spiders and twenty-seven (11 per cent) of the beetles were categorised as rare or endangered. When compared with nearby brownfield habitats, such as railway sidings or derelict land, there was little difference in the number of spiders and beetles recorded. The study concluded that diversity of invertebrates was largely dependent on variation in depth of the substrate. Thin substrates supported a narrow range of drought tolerant species, whilst deeper substrates retained more moisture. They produced structurally more diverse vegetation cover and supported a greater range of species. Not surprisingly older roofs tended to be more diverse than younger ones and the best were those with greatest variety in substrate conditions and vegetation structure.

Of the birds the most frequently recorded species were black redstart, white wagtail, carrion crow, house sparrow, feral pigeon and magpie. Other species also use green roofs in Germany and Switzerland, including crested lark, little ringed plover, lapwing, skylark, common tern, meadow pipit, wheatear and greenfinch.

Yet another example from Switzerland illustrates how protected reptiles can be accommodated on green roofs. When a railway station in Zurich was to be extended it was found that the track supported protected wall lizards and rare invertebrates. The solution was to create replacement habitats on the canopies above the platforms, with lizard ladders to allow them to move up and down from the track to the roofs. Ballast on the roof provided the basis for a pioneer community similar to that of many brownfield sites.

The Swiss work prompted similar studies of the spider fauna of green roofs in London (Kadas, 2002). An initial investigation of six Sedum-mat roofs found 59 species of spider (representing 9 per cent of the UK and 26 per cent of the Greater London spider fauna). The list included widespread species, together with some which are nationally rare, such as *Pardosa agrestis* and *Bianor aurocintus*. Although the smallest (100 m^2) of the six, the roof of the education centre at the Greenwich Peninsula Ecology Centre was the most diverse in species composition. It was originally laid with Sedum matting, with a relatively deep substrate of 9 cm and had been reseeded with herbs which provided more structural diversity than the other roofs.

Kadas went on to study spiders and other selected invertebrates from a range of other green roofs in London from 2003–6. These included three recently created 'biodiverse' roofs (designed specifically to cater for biodiversity), together with several Sedum-mat roofs of different ages. It was found that the diversity of spider species, and the number of spider families represented, was higher on biodiverse roofs than on Sedum roofs. The number of locally or nationally important species was also higher on the biodiverse roofs, reaching nearly 20 per cent of the spiders recorded, compared with only 10 per cent on Sedum roofs. Over the three-year period the spider fauna of Sedum roofs was initially high but declined as the Sedum mat dried out, whilst spiders on biodiverse roofs became more diverse as the plant communities became established with time. Kadas concluded that biodiverse roofs could play an important role not only in creating additional wildlife spaces in urban areas

FIG 236. Roofs can even have pools to diversify the habitat. (Fleur Timmer)

but also in the conservation of rare or endangered species. Her studies showed that green roofs support a large variety of invertebrates, at least 10 per cent of which are nationally rare or scarce (Kadas, 2006).

As a result of these studies some general principles for design of green roofs for biodiversity have been established. The most important factor is the nature and depth of the substrate. Low nutrient, well-drained substrates support species-rich plant communities akin to the flower rich habitats of urban wastelands. Commercially available substrates now include a range of pH, including some that are suitable for calcareous flower-rich meadow communities. Variations in the substrate depth and provision of a range of wet and dry conditions help to maximise biodiversity. In contrast the relatively uniform Sedum-mat roofs that have become widely used are of less value for biodiversity. However, by seeding these with appropriate species of grasses and herbs such roofs can make a significant contribution. Some recommend that biodiverse roofs need to be seeded with locally appropriate native seed mixes that are matched to the substrate and suited to the geographical region. The 'London living roofs mixture' advocated by the London Biodiversity Partnership is an example. Buglife has produced a 'best practice guide' on how to create green roofs for biodiversity which summarises the key issues (Gedge *et al.*, 2012).

FIG 237. Aerial view of the Olympic Village, an integrated scheme of ecological urban design. (Olympic Delivery Authority)

Others have questioned the need for locally sourced native species and argue for use of a wider variety of plants, including alien species, which bring more variety and colour to the roofs, whilst still providing an important source of nectar for foraging insects (Dunnet, 2006). That debate will continue on the rooftops just as it has in the gardens.

There is no doubt that green roofs, living walls and rain gardens are now well established as a new form of ecological architecture. Examples in recent years show that such features can contribute substantially to the sustainable management of water within urban areas and at the same time provide habitats for wildlife. The Athlete's Village at the London Olympics now called East Village is a good example. This was designed to incorporate green roofs on all buildings, including five different habitat types. At ground level the large areas of new green landscape are all rich in biodiversity, with herb-rich meadows, dry and wet woodland and marsh. They also have an important hydrological role in treating waste-water for re-use in landscape irrigation.

This is a rapidly developing field with new ideas proliferating in cities throughout the world. Many of the new initiatives are aimed at finding cost-effective sustainable solutions for future urban design. I don't expect they will revolutionise the landscapes of our towns and cities overnight, but they do provide an indication of what we might expect to see in the future as architects grapple with the impacts of climate change. There is every likelihood that as these new habitats become firmly established they will develop their own characteristic wildlife features. We can also be confident that some of the species will be incomers, new to the UK, making the most of these new surroundings. But if ecologists and architects work together in this new form of urbanism who knows what might be possible? Cities of the future could be remarkably rich in wildlife if we work with nature to create them.

References

Andrews, J. & Kinsman, D. (1993). *Gravel pit restoration for wildlife*. RSPB.

Archer, J., Britton, B., Burley, R., Hare, T. & Yarham, I. (1989). *Nature Conservation in Southwark*. Ecology Handbook 12. London Ecology Unit, London.

Archer, J. & Curson, D. (1993). *Nature Conservation in Richmond*. Ecology Handbook 21. London Ecology Unit, London.

Archer, J. & Yarham, I. (1991). *Nature Conservation in Newham*, Ecology Handbook 17. London Ecology Unit, London.

Archer, J. & Yarham, I. (2000). *Nature Conservation in Lewisham*. Ecology Handbook 30. London Ecology Unit, London.

Ash, H.J. (1983). *The Natural Colonisation of Derelict Industrial Land*. PhD thesis, University of Liverpool.

Ash, H., Gemmell, R.P. & Bradshaw, A.D. (1994). The introduction of native plant species on industrial waste heaps: a test of immigration and other factors affecting primary succession. *J. App. Ecol.* 31, 74–84.

Ash, H.J., Bennett, R. & Scott, R. (1992). *Flowers in the grass. Creating and managing grasslands with wildflowers*. Nature Conservancy Council, Peterborough.

Ash, H.J. (1991). Soils and vegetation in urban areas. In: *Soils in the Urban Environment*. Eds Bullock, P. & Gregory, P. 153–172. Blackwell, Oxford.

Baines, C. (1985). *How to make a Wildlife Garden*. Elmtree Books, London.

Baines, C. (1986). *The Wild Side of Town*. BBC &Elm Tree Books, London.

Baker, H. (1985). The status of the Canada Goose in the London area. *London Bird Report* 49: 111–26. LNHS, London.

Baker, H. (1992). Status of the Canada Goose, Greylag Goose and other introduced geese in Greater London and Middlesex, 1991. *London Bird Report* 56: 175–82. LNHS, London.

Baker, H. (2004). LNHS House Sparrow Monitoring: 1995–2003. *London Bird Report* 69, 158–65. LNHS, London.

Balmer, D.E. et al. (2013). *Bird Atlas 2007–11: the breeding and wintering birds of Britain and Ireland*. BTO Books, Thetford.

Barker, F. & Gay, J. (1984). *Highgate Cemetery, Victorian Valhalla*. John Murray, London.

Barker, G. (1997). *A framework for the future: green networks with multiple uses in and around towns and cities*. English Nature Research Report 256, Peterborough.

Barker, G. (2007). Preface to Shirley, P., *The Endless Village Revisited*. Wildlife Trust for Birmingham and the Black Country, Birmingham.

Batten, L.A. (1972). The past and present bird life of Brent Reservoir and its vicinity. *The London Naturalist* 50: 8–62. London Natural History Society, London.

Batten, L., Beddard, R., Colmans, J. & Self, A. (Eds) (2002). *Birds of Brent Reservoir*. Welsh Harp Conservation Group, London.

Bell, C. P., Baker, S. W., Parkes, N. G., Brook, M. DeL. & Chamberlain, D. E. (2010). The role of the Eurasian Sparrowhawk (*Accipiter nisus*) in the decline of the House sparrow (*Passer domesticus*) in Britain. *The Auk*, 127: 411–20.

BEN (2005). *Ethnic Communities and Green Spaces: Guidance for green space managers.* Black Environment Network, Llanberis.

Bender, D. A. & Edwards, P. J. (1981). *Wildlife in the Suburbs: Perivale Wood Local Nature Reserve.* The Selborne Society.

Bevan, D. (1993). Conserving Nature in London. *The London Naturalist,* 72: 9–14. LNHS, London.

Bevan, D. (2008). Out of the ashes – the greening of the City's bombed sites. In: *London's changing Natural History* ed. M. Burgess, 51–2. London Natural History Society, London.

Bevan, D. (2011). Coppicing Haringey's ancient woodlands. *The London Naturalist,* 90, 55–81. LNHS.

Bird, W. (2004). *Natural Fit.* RSPB, Sandy.

Bornkamm, R., Lee, J. A. & Seaward, M. R. D. (Eds) (1982). *Urban Ecology.* Blackwell, Oxford.

Box, J. & Harrison, C. (1993). Natural Spaces in Urban Places. *Town and Country Planning* 62: (9) 231–235.

Box, J., Berry, S., Angus, I., Cush, P., & Frost, P. (2007). Planning local nature reserves. *Town and Country Planning.* November. 392–5.

Bradshaw, A. D., Goode, D. A. & Thorp, E. H. P. (Eds) (1986). *Ecology and Design in Landscape.* Symposium of British Ecological Society, Blackwell, Oxford.

Brenneisen, S. (2001). *Vogel, Kafer und Spinnen auf Dachbegrunengen: Nutzungsmoglichkeiten und Einrichtungsoptimeierungen.* Geographisches Institut, Universitat Basel.

Brenneisen, S. (2003). The benefits of biodiversity from green roofs: key design consequences. In: *Proc. 1st Annual Conf. Greening Rooftops for Sustainable Communities.* Chicago.

Briggs, J. (2012). Canals under new management: A review of wildlife value, issues and opportunities. *British Wildlife* 23 315–323.

Brown, J. (1982). *Gardens of a Golden Afternoon.* Allen Lane.

Bullock, R. (2011). *Bird records from the London Wetland Centre.* Unpublished.

Burls, A., Luscombe, G. & Millward, A. (2010). *Discover Yourself Outside.* UK MAB Urban Forum, Manchester.

BTO (2005). *BTO News,* 257, p7. British Trust for Ornithology, Thetford.

Buczacki, S. (2007). *Garden Natural History.* Collins, London.

Buglife (2009). *Planning for brownfield biodiversity: a best practice guide.* Buglife, The Invertebrate Conservation Trust, Peterborough.

Butler, A. (1896). *British Birds with their Nests and Eggs.* Brumby and Clarke, London.

Butler, C. (2002). Breeding parrots in Britain. *British Birds* 95: 377–83.

Butler, C. J. (2003). *Population Biology of the Introduced Rose-ringed Parakeet (Psittacula krameri) in the UK.* Thesis submitted for DPhil, University of Oxford.

Cabot, D. (2009). *Wildfowl.* Collins, London.

Castell, C. P. (1947). Nature conservation in the London Area. *The London Naturalist* 26: 17–41. LNHS, London.

Chambers, J. (1987). *Wild Flower Garden.* Elm Tree Books, London.

Chandler, R. J. (1979). Pied wagtail roosts and numbers in the London area in winter. *London Bird Report* 44: 85–90. LNHS, London.

Chamberlain, D. E. et al. (2009). Avian productivity in urban landscapes: a review and meta-analysis. *Ibis* 151, 1–18.

Chater, A. O., Oswald, P. H. & Preston, C. D. (2000). Street floras in Cambridge and Aberystwyth. *Nature in Cambridgeshire* 42, 3–26.

Chinery, M (1977). *The Natural History of the Garden.* Collins, London.

Chinery, M. (2007). *Garden Wildlife of Britain and Europe.* Collins.

Chislett, R. (1952). *Yorkshire Birds.* Brown & Son, Hull.

Cocker, M. & Mabey, R. (2005). *Birds Britannica.* Chatto and Windus, London.

Cole, L. (1978). *Nature Conservation in Urban Areas.* Nature Conservancy Council, London.

Cole, L. (1980). Urban Nature Conservation: The role of the Nature Conservancy Council. *Landscape Research* 5 (2) 28–9.

Cramp, S. (1971). Gulls nesting on buildings in Britain and Ireland. *British Birds* 64: 476–87.

Cramp, S. (1975). The influence of cleaner air on breeding birds of Inner London. *London Bird Report* 38: 65–72. LNHS, London.

Cresswell, W. J. & Harris, S. (1988). Foraging behaviour and home range utilisation in a suburban Badger (*Meles meles*) population. *Mammal Review* 18: 37–49.

Crick, H., Banks, A. & Coombes, R. (2003). Findings of the National Peregrine Survey 2002. *BTO News* 248:8–9.

Crick, H. Q. P., Robinson, R. A., Appleton, G. F., Clark, N. A. & Rickard, A. D. (2002). *Investigation into the causes of the decline of starlings and house sparrows in Great Britain.* BTO Research Report 290.

Curl, J. S. (Ed.) (2001). *Kensal Green Cemetery. The Origins and Development of the General Cemetery of All Souls, Kensal green, London, 1824–2001.* Phillimore, Chichester.

Curtis, W. (1771). *Flora Londinensis.* London.

Dagley, J. R. (2007). Les trognes de la forêt d'Epping. *Les trognes en Europe*, pp. 46–52. Maison Botanique, Vendome, France.

Darlington, A. (1981). *Ecology of Walls.* Heinemann Educational Books, London.

Davies, H. (1983). *A Walk Round London's Parks.* Hamish Hamilton, London.

Davies, Z. G., et al. (2009). A national scale inventory of resource provision for biodiversity within domestic gardens. *Biological Conservation* 142: 761–771.

Davis, B. N. K. (1976). Wildlife, urbanisation and industry. *Biological Conservation* 10 249–291.

Davison, J., et al. (2008). Restricted ranging behaviour in a high-density population of urban badgers. *Journal of Zoology* 277: 46–63.

Dawson, D. and Gittings, T. (1990). *The effect of suburban residential density on birds.* Report commissioned by London Borough of Sutton. London Ecology Unit.

Defra (2006). *Local Sites: guidance on their identification, selection and management.* Defra, London

Dickson, J. H. (1991). *Wild Plants of Glasgow: Conservation in the City and Countryside.* Mercat Press, Edinburgh.

Dickson, J. H., Macpherson, P. & Watson, K. J. (2000). *The Changing Flora of Glasgow.* Edinburgh University Press.

Douglas, I., Goode, D., Houck, M. C. & Wang, R. (Eds) (2011). *The Routledge Handbook of Urban Ecology.* Routledge, London.

Drakeford, T. & Sutcliffe, U. (Eds) (2000). *Wimbledon Common and Putney Heath: A Natural History.* Wimbledon and Putney Commons Conservators, London.

Drewitt, E. J. A. & Dixon, N. (2008). Diet and prey selection of urban-dwelling Peregrine Falcons in south west England. *British Birds* 101: 58–67.

Drewitt, E. (2014). *Urban Peregrines.* Pelagic Publishing, Exeter.

Dunnett, N. (2006). Green Roofs for Biodiversity: Reconciling Aesthetics with Ecology. In: *Proc 4th Annual Conf. Greening roof tops for sustainable communities.* Boston.

Duterloo-Morgan, F. (1998). Kensington's Babylon: Derry and Toms Roof Garden. *London Gardener* 4: 39.

Emery, M. (1986). *Promoting nature in cities and towns: A practical guide.* Croom Helm, London.

English Nature (1995). *Badgers: Guidelines for Developers.* English Nature, Peterborough.

English Nature (1996). *A place for nature.* English Nature, Peterborough.

Environment Agency (2002). *River Restoration: A Stepping Stone to Urban Regeneration highlighting the opportunities in South London.* Environment Agency, London.

Fairbrother, N. (1970). *New Lives, New Landscapes.* Architectural Press, London.

Farmer, A. (1984). *Hampstead Heath.* Historical Publications, London.

FERA. (2009). Rose-ringed parakeets in England: A scoping study of potential damage to agricultural interests and management measures. *Management,* 100.

Fitter, R. S. R. (1945). *London's Natural History.* Collins, London.

Fitter, R. S. R. (1949). Check-List of the Mammals, Reptiles and Amphibia of the London Area, 1900–1949. *The London Naturalist* 28: 98–115. LNHS, London.

Fitter, R. S. R. (1965). The breeding status of the Black Redstart in Britain. *Brit Birds* 58: 481–92.

Freed, T. (1997). *Butterfly Ecology in an Urban Cemetery; four illustrated projects researched at Kensal Green Cemetery.* Ph D Thesis. Royal College of Art, London.

Freed, T. (2001). The Land Use History and Flora and Fauna of Kensal Green Cemetery. In: *Kensal Green Cemetery,* J. S.Curl (Ed.). Phillimore, Chichester.

Frith, M., Sinnadurai, P. & Gedge, D. (1999). Advice on the conservation of Black Redstarts in London. London Wildlife Trust.

Frith, M. & Gedge, D. (2000). The black redstart in urban Britain; a conservation conundrum? *British Wildlife* 11: 381–8.

Game, M. & Whitfield, J. (1996). *Nature Conservation in Tower Hamlets.* Ecology Handbook 27. London Ecology Unit, London.

Gedge, D. (2003). From rubble to redstarts. In: *Proc.1st Annual Conf. Greening roof tops for sustainable communities.* Chicago.

Gedge, D., Grant, G., Kadas, G. & Dinham, C. (2012). *Creating Green Roofs for Biodiversity: A best practice guide.* Buglife. Available as PDF from www.buglife.org.uk

Gemmell, R.P. (1982). The origin and botanical importance of industrial habitats. In: *Urban*

Ecology. Bornkamm, R., Lee, J. A. and Seaward, M. R. D (Eds), 33–39. Blackwell, Oxford.

Gibbons, B. & L. (1988). *Creating a Wildlife Garden.* Chancellor Press, London.

Gilbert, O. (1983). The wildlife of Britain's wasteland. *New Scientist*, 67, 824–9.

Gilbert, O. L. (1989). *The Ecology of Urban Habitats.* Chapman and Hall, London.

Gilbert, O. & Bevan, D. (1997). The effect of urbanisation on ancient woodlands. *British Wildlife* 8, 213–218.

Gillham, M. (2002). *A Natural History of Cardiff: Exploring along the River Taff.* Lazy Cat Publishing, Caerphilly.

GLA (2002). *Connecting with London's Nature: The Mayor's Biodiversity Strategy.* Greater London Authority, London. (Available from www.london. gov.uk).

GLA (2004). *The London Plan: Spatial Development Strategy for Greater London.* Greater London Authority, London. (Available from www.london. gov.uk).

GLA (2008). *Improving Londoners' Access to Nature.* London Plan Implementation Report. Greater London Authority, London. (Available from www.london.gov.uk).

GLC (1984). *Ecology and nature conservation in London.* Ecology Handbook 1. Greater London Council, London.

GLC (1985). *Nature Conservation Guidelines for London*, Ecology Handbook 3. Greater London Council, London.

GLC (1986). *A nature conservation strategy for London; woodland, wasteland, the tidal Thames and two London Boroughs.* Ecology Handbook 4. Greater London Council, London.

Goode, D. (1986). *Wild in London.* Michael Joseph, London.

Goode, D. A. (1989). Urban Nature Conservation in Britain. *Journal of Applied Ecology* 26: 859–873.

Goode, D. A. (1999). Habitat survey and evaluation for nature conservation in London. *Deinsea* 5: 27–40. Natural History Museum of Rotterdam.

Goode, D. (2005). Connecting with nature in a capital city: The London Biodiversity Strategy. In: *The Urban Imperative* (Ed. Trzyna, T.), 75–85. California Institute of Public Affairs & IUCN.

Goode, D. A. (2006). *Green Infrastructure.* Report Commissioned by the Royal Commission on Environmental Pollution. www.rcep.org.uk

Goode, D. (2007). Nature conservation in towns and cities. In: *Contemporary Rural Geographies* (ed. Clout, H.), 111–128. Routledge, London.

Gooders, J. (1968). The Swift in central London. *London Bird Report* 32: 93–8. LNHS, London.

Gordon, D. (1990). *Green Cities.* Black Rose Books, Montréal.

Gosling, A. P. (1986). A study of the movements and site fidelity of foreign ringed Black-headed gulls in St. James's Park, 1983–86. *London Bird Report* 50, 156–169.

Grant, G., Engleback, L. & Nicholson, B. (2003). *Green Roofs: their existing status and potential for conserving biodiversity in urban areas.* English Nature Research Reports No. 498. English Nature, Peterborough.

Greater Manchester Council (1986). *A nature conservation strategy for Greater Manchester: Policies for the protection, development and enjoyment of wildlife resources.* Greater Manchester Council, Manchester.

Greenwood, J. (2010). Black Guillemots at Bangor, Co. Down: a 25-year study. *British Wildlife.* 21, 153–158.

Greenwood, E. F. & Gemmell, R. P. (1978). Derelict industrial land as a habitat for rare plants in S Lancs (v.c. 59) and W. Lancs. (v.c. 60). *Watsonia*, 12, 33–40.

Hadden, R. M. (1978). Wild flowers of London W1. *London Naturalist* 57: 26–33. LNHS, London.

Hansell, J. (2003). *Images of the Dove.* Millstream Books, Bath.

Hare, T. (Ed.) (1988). *London's Meadows and Pastures (Neutral Grassland).* Ecology Handbook 8. London Ecology Unit, London.

Harris, S. (1984). Ecology of urban badgers *Meles meles*: distribution in Britain and habitat selection, persecution, food and damage in the City of Bristol. *Biological Conservation* 28: 349–75.

Harris, S. & Baker P. (2001). *Urban Foxes.* 2nd Edn., Whittet Books, Stowmarket.

Harris, S. & Cresswell, W. J. (1988). Bristol's Badgers. *Proceedings of the Bristol Naturalists' Society* 48: 17–30.

Harris, S. & Rayner, J. M. V. (1986). Urban fox (*Vulpes vulpes*) population estimates and habitat requirements in several British cities. *J. Applied Ecol.* 24, 75–86.

Harris, S. & Woollard, T. (1988). Bristol's Foxes. In: *Bristol's Urban Ecology. Proc. Bristol Naturalists' Society.* 48, 3–15.

Harrison, C. (1993). Nature Conservation, Science and Popular Values. In: *Conservation in Progress*, Goldsmith, F. B. & Warren, A. (Eds) 35–49. Wiley

Harrison, C., Burgess J., Millward, A., & Dawe, G. (1995). *Accessible natural greenspace in towns and cities: A review of appropriate size and distance criteria.* English Nature Research Reports Number 153. English Nature, Peterborough.

Harrison, G. & J. (2005). *The new Birds of the West Midlands.* West Midland Bird Club.

Harvey, P. (2001). The East Thames Corridor; a nationally important invertebrate fauna under threat. *British Wildlife* 12: 91–8.

Harvey, P. (2004). Brown roofs for invertebrates. *Essex Naturalist (New Series)* 21 79–88.

Haskins, L. (2000). Heathlands in an urban setting: effects of urban development on heathlands of south-east Dorset. *British Wildlife* 11 (4), 229–237.

Henke, H. & Sukopp, H. (1986). A natural approach in cities. In: *Ecology and Design in Landscape.* Bradshaw, A. D., Goode, D. A. & Thorp, E. H. P. (Eds), 307–324. Symposium of British Ecological Society, Blackwell, Oxford.

Hewlett, J., Archer, J. & Dawson, D. (1995). *City of Westminster Nature Conservation Survey 1995.* London Ecology Unit Report. London.

Hewlett, J. (Ed.) (2002). *The Breeding Birds of the London Area.* London Natural History Society, London.

Holmes, Mrs. B. I. (1896). *The London burial grounds.* Fisher Unwin, London.

Homes, R.C. (1964). *The Birds of the London Area.* (Revised Edition of London Natural History Society, 1957). Hart-Davis, London.

Hoskins, W.G. & Stamp, L.D. (1963). *The Common Lands of England and Wales.* Collins, London.

Howard, E. (1902). *Garden Cities of To-morrow.* New revised edition (1985). Attic Books, Eastbourne.

Hudson, W.H. (1898). *Birds in London.* Longmans, Green. London.

Ingram, D. S., Vince-Prue, D. & Gregory, P. J. (Eds) (2008). *Science in the Garden.* 2nd Edn. Royal Horticultural Society. Blackwell, Oxford.

Innes, R. (2012). Bird highlights at Staines Reservoirs. *London Bird Report for 2009,* 74. 226–8. LNHS, London.

Jefferies, R. (1889). *Nature near London.* Chatto and Windus, London.

Johnston, J. (1989). *Nature areas for city people.* Ecology Handbook 14. London Ecology Unit, London.

Johnston, J. & Newton, J. (1993). *Building Green.* London Ecology Unit, London.

Jones, A.W. (1958). The flora of the City of London bombed sites. *The London Naturalist* (for 1957) 37:189–210. LNHS, London.

Jones, M. (2009). *Sheffield's Woodland Heritage.* Fourth Edition (first published 1989, Sheffield City Libraries), Wildtrack, Sheffield.

Kadas, G. (2002). *Study of invertebrates on green roofs: How roof design can maximise biodiversity in an urban environment.* MSc Thesis, University College London.

Kadas, G. (2006). Rare invertebrates colonising green roofs in London. *Urban Habitats* 4. (electronic journal).

Kaplan, R. (1985). Nature at the doorstep: Residential satisfaction and the nearby environment. *Journal of Architectural and Planning Research.* 2, 115–127.

Kaplan, R. (2011). Intrinsic and aesthetic values of urban nature: A psychological perspective. In: *The Routledge Handbook of Urban Ecology.* Eds Douglas, I., Goode, D., Houck, M.C. & Wang, R., 385–393. Routledge, London.

Kieran, J. (1959). *A Natural History of New York City.* Houghton Mifflin, Boston.

Kruuk, H. & Parish, T. (1981). Feeding specialization in the European Badger *Meles meles* in Scotland. *Journal of Animal Ecology* 50: 773–788.

Lack, D. (1956). *Swifts in a Tower.* Methuen, London.

Lancaster, R. (2007). A natural remedy. *The Garden* December 2007, 806–9

Latham, J.B. (1984). A Survey of the Flora of Kensal Green and St. Mary's Cemeteries, 1981–1983. *The London Naturalist* 63: 53–67. LNHS, London.

Laurie, I. C. (Ed.) (1975). *Nature in Cities.* Proc. Symp. Landscape Research Group, Manchester University.

Laurie, I. C. (Ed.) (1979). *Nature in Cities.* Wiley, Chichester.

Lawton, J. H. et al. (2010). *Making Space for Nature: A review of England's Wildlife Sites and Ecological Network.* Report to Defra.

Lee, J. A. & Greenwood, E. (1976). The colonization by plants of calcareous wastes from the salt and alkali industry in Cheshire, England. *Biological Conservation* 10, 131–149.

Lever, C. (1977). *The Naturalised Animals of the British Isles.* Hutchinson.

LEU (1988). *Sites of Metropolitan Importance for Nature Conservation as identified by the London Ecology Unit.* Unpublished report, London Ecology Unit, London.

LEU (1994). *Policy, criteria and procedures for identifying nature conservation sites in London.* London Ecology Unit, London.

London Natural History Society (1957). *The Birds of the London Area since 1900.* New Naturalist Special Volume. Collins, London.

Loudon, J.C. (1843). *On the Laying Out, Planting, and Managing of Cemeteries.* Facsimile edition 1981, Ivelet Books, Redhill.

Lousley, E. (1971). Mitcham Common and its Conservation. *Proc. Croydon Nat. Hist. Sci. Soc.* 15 (3) 35–46.

Luscombe, G. & Scott, R. (2004). *Wildflowers Work: A guide to creating and managing new wildflower landscapes.* Landlife, Liverpool.

Luscombe, G., Scott, R. & Young, D. (2008). *Soil inversion works.* Landlife, Liverpool.

Luscombe, G. & Scott, R. (2011). Creative conservation. In: *The Routledge Handbook of Urban Ecology.* Eds Douglas, I., Goode, D., Houck, M.C. & Wang, R., 221–232. Routledge, London.

Mabey, R. (1973). *The Unofficial Countryside.* Collins, London.

MacDonald, D. (1987). *Running with the fox.* Unwin Hyman, London.

MacDonald, D. W. & Newdick, M. T. (1982). The distribution and ecology of foxes, *Vulpes vulpes* (L.), in urban areas. In: *Urban Ecology.* Bornkamm, R., Lee, J. A. and Seaward, M. R .D (Eds), 123–135. Blackwell, Oxford.

MacLeod, R., Barnett, P., Clark, J. & Cresswell, W. (2006). Mass-dependent predation risk as a mechanism for house sparrow declines? *Biol. Lett.* 2: 43–6.

Marren, P. (2002). *Nature Conservation.* Collins, London.

Mayer, E. (2004). The decline of the Common Swift. *British Birds* 97: 417 – 418.

Mayor of London (2002). *Sites of Metropolitan Importance for Nature Conservation in London.* Greater London Authority, London.

Mayor of London (2008). *Living roofs and walls.* Technical report supporting London Plan Policy. Greater London Authority.

McHarg, I. (1969). *Design with Nature.* Doubleday Natural History Press.

Meadows, B.S. (1970). Breeding distribution and feeding ecology of the Black Redstart in London. *London Bird Report* (for 1969) 34: 72–9. LNHS, London.

Millward, A. & Mostyn, B. (1989). People and Nature in Cities: the social aspects of planning and managing natural parks in urban areas. *Urban Wildlife Now* 2. Nature Conservancy Council, Peterborough.

Ministry of Town and Country Planning (1947). *Conservation of Nature in England and Wales. Report of the Wild Life Conservation Special Committee.* Command 7122. HMSO.

Milner, J. E. (2000). Spiders in London: observations on their occurrence, phenology, habitat preference and response to disturbance, from the results of 82 12-month pitfall samples. *The London Naturalist* 79. LNHS, London.

Milner, J. E. (2006). Spiders of Hampstead Heath: an ongoing story of ecological change. *The London Naturalist* 85. LNHS, London.

Mitchell, I. P., Newton, S. F., Ratcliffe, N & Dunn, T.E. (2004). *Seabird populations of Britain and Ireland.* Poyser, London.

Monaghan, P. & Coulson, J.C. (1977). The status of large gulls nesting on buildings. *Bird Study* 24: 89–104.

Montier, D. J. (Ed.) (1977). *Atlas of Breeding Birds of the London Area.* Batsford, London.

Morgan, D. H. W. (1993). Feral Rose-ringed Parakeets in Britain. *British Birds* 86: 561–64.

Morgan, R. A. & Glue, D.E. (1981). Breeding survey of Black Redstarts in Britain, 1977. *Bird Study* 28: 163–168.

Mostyn, B.J. (1979). *Personal benefits and satisfactions derived from participation in urban wildlife projects: a qualitative evaluation.* Research report, Nature Conservancy Council, London.

Moss, S. & Cottridge, D. (1998). *Attracting Birds to your Garden.* New Holland, London.

Murphy, K. J. & Eaton, J. W. (1983). Effects of pleasure-boat traffic on macrophyte growth in canals. *J. App. Ecol.,* 20: 713–729.

Murton, R. K., Thearle, R. J. P. & Thompson, J. (1972). Ecological studies of the Feral Pigeon *Colomba livia* var. *J. App. Ecol.* 9 835–874.

Myles, S. L. (Ed.) (2000). *The Flora of the Bristol Region.* Pisces Publications.

Natural England (2010). *Nature Nearby: Accessible Natural Greenspace Guidance.* Natural England. (www.naturalengland.org.uk/publications).

NCC (1979). *Nature conservation in urban areas: Challenge and opportunity.* Nature Conservancy Council, London.

NCC (1980). *Fifth Annual Report, 1978–9.* Nature Conservancy Council, HMSO, London.

NCC (1984). *Inventory of Ancient Woodland in Greater London.* Nature Conservancy Council.

NCC (1988). *Tyne and Wear Nature Conservation Strategy*. Nature Conservancy Council, Peterborough.

Nelson, T. H. (1907). *The Birds of Yorkshire*. A Brown & Sons, London.

Newton, J., Gedge, D., Early, P., & Wilson, S. (2007). *Building Greener: Guidance on the use of green roofs, green walls and complementary features on buildings*. CIRIA, London.

Nicholson, E. M. (1995). *Bird watching in London*. London Natural History Society, London.

Nicholson-Lord, D. (1987). *The Greening of the Cities*. Routledge, London.

Owen, J. (1991). *The ecology of a garden*. Cambridge University Press.

Owen. J. (2010). *Wildlife of a garden: A thirty-year study*. Royal Horticultural Society, London.

Pape, D. (1990). *Nature Conservation in Hounslow*. Ecology Handbook 15. London Ecology Unit, London.

Parr, D. (1972). *Birds in Surrey 1900–1970*. Batsford, London.

Parslow, J. L. F. (1967). Changes in the status among breeding birds in Britain and Ireland, part 3. *British Birds* 60: 177–202.

Pithon, J. A., & Dytham. C. (1999). Census of the British Ring-necked Parakeet *Psittacula krameri* population by simultaneous count of roosts. *Bird Study* 46: 112–115.

Plant, C. (Ed.) (1999). The Natural history of Buckingham Palace Garden, London. Part 1. *Supplement to The London Naturalist* 78. LNHS, London.

Plant, C. (Ed.) (2001). The Natural history of Buckingham Palace Garden, London. Part 2. *Supplement to The London Naturalist* 80. LNHS, London.

Project Parakeet (2011). *Newsletter* 3, August 2011. Imperial College London, Silwood Park.

Prowse, A. (2002). The urban decline of the House Sparrow. *Brit. Birds* 95: 143146.

Pyle, R. M. (1993). *The Thunder Tree: lessons from an urban wildland*. Houghton Mifflin Company, Boston.

Rackham, O. (2006). *Woodlands*. Collins, London.

Ratcliffe, D. A. (Ed.) (1977). *A Nature Conservation Review*. Cambridge University Press.

Ratcliffe, D. A. (1993). *The Peregrine Falcon*. 2nd edn. Poyser, London.

Raven, S. J. & Coulson, J. C. (1997). The distribution and abundance of *Larus* gulls nesting on buildings in Britain and Ireland. *Bird Study* 44: 13–44.

RCEP (2007). *The Urban Environment*. Royal Commission on Environmental Pollution, London.

Riding, A., Critchley, N., Wilson, L. & Parker, J. (2009). *Definition and mapping of open mosaic habitats on previously developed land: Phase one*. Final Report. ADAS UK, Wolverhampton.

Ritchie, J. (1961). Duddingston Loch Bird Sanctuary. In: The Birds of Duddingston Loch Edinburgh. Special Supplement to *Scottish Birds* 1 395–400.

Robinson, R. A., Siriwardena, G. M. & Crick, H. Q. P. (2005). Size and trends of the House Sparrow *Passer domesticus* population in Great Britain. *Ibis*, 147 552–562.

Robinson, W. (1870). *The Wild Garden*. Murray. Expanded edition. Darke R. (Ed.) (2009) Timber Press.

Rock, P. (2005). Urban gulls: problems and solutions. *British Birds* 98: 338–355.

Rodwell, J. S. (Ed.) (2000). *British Plant Communities*. Vol. 5. Cambridge University Press.

Roper, T. J. (2010). *Badger*. Collins, London.

RSPB (2003). Where Have All Our Sparrows Gone? Survey Report: London 2002. RSPB, Sandy.

Ruff, A. (1979). *Holland and the ecological landscapes*. Deanwater, London.

Ruff, A. & Tregay, R.J. (Eds) (1982). *An Ecological Approach to Urban Landscape Design*. Occasional Paper 8. Department of Town and Country Planning, Manchester University.

Salisbury, E.J. (1943). The flora of bombed areas. *Nature* 151: 462–66.

Sanderson, R. (1999). Birds in Buckingham Palace Garden. In: The Natural History of Buckingham Palace Garden. Supplement to *The London Naturalist* 78. LNHS, London.

Sanderson, R. (2001). Further declines in an urban population of House Sparrows. *British Birds*, 94, 507.

Sanderson, R. (2005). Autumn bird counts in Kensington Gardens 2005. *London Bird Report* 70 168–176.

Sanderson, R. (2013). Buckingham Palace Garden Birds, 1995–2011. *London Bird Report 2011* 76, 186–192. LNHS, London.

Sandwith, C.I. (1933). The Adventive Flora of the Port of Bristol. Buncle & Co.

Sargent, C. (1984). *Britain's Railway Vegetation*. Institute of Terrestrial Ecology, NERC, Cambridge.

Schmied, W. (2005). *Hundertwasser*. Taschen, Koln.

Scott, D., Greenwood, R.D., Moffatt, J.D. & Tregay, R.J. (1986). Warrington New Town: an ecological approach to landscape design and management. In: *Ecology and Design in Landscape*. Bradshaw, A. D., Goode, D. A. & Thorp, E. H. P. (Eds). Symposium of British Ecological Society, Blackwell, Oxford.

Scott, R. (2004). *Wild Belfast: on safari in the city*. Blackstaff Press, Belfast.

Scrivens, S. (1980). Roof gardens: Derry and Toms. *Architects Journal* 15 October.

Shaw, P. (1994). Orchid Woods and Floating Islands – The Ecology of Fly Ash. *British Wildlife* 5: 149–157.

Shirley, P. (1988). *Wildlife Walkabout: Birmingham and the Black Country*. Wayside Books, Clevedon.

Shirley, P. (2007). *The Endless Village revisited*. Wildlife Trust for Birmingham and the Black Country, Birmingham.

Silvertown, J. (1978). The History of Woodlands in Hornsey. *London Naturalist* 57: 11–25. LNHS, London.

Simms, E. (1979). *The Public Life of the Street Pigeon*. Hutchinson, London.

Smith, D. (1974). *Brocky the Bathwick badger*. Privately published, Bath.

Smyth, B. (1987). *City Wildspace*. Hilary Shipman, London.

St Helens Borough Council (1986). *A Policy for Nature*. St. Helens Borough Council.

Stace, C. (1997). *New Flora of the British Isles*. Second Edition. Cambridge University Press, Cambridge.

Stansfield, K. (1988). Going Green on Top. *Local Government News* June 1988.

Stubbs, D. (1996). *An Environmental Management Programme for Golf Courses*. European Golf Association Ecology Unit. Dorking.

Sukopp, H. & Werner, P. (1982). *Nature in Cities*. Nature and Environment Series 28. Council of Europe, Strasbourg.

Sukopp, H. & Werner, P. (1987). *Development of flora and fauna in urban areas*. Nature and Environment Series 36. Council of Europe, Strasbourg.

Summers-Smith, J. D. (1963). *The House Sparrow*. New Naturalist Monograph, Collins, London.

Summers-Smith, J. D. (1999). Current status of the House Sparrow in Britain. *Brit. Wildlife* 10: 381–86.

Summers-Smith, J. D. (2003). The decline of the House Sparrow: a review. *British Birds* 96, 439–46.

Tankard, J. B. (2011). *Gertrude Jekyll and the Country House Garden*. Aurum Press, London.

TCPA. (2004). *Biodiversity by Design. A guide for sustainable communities*. Town and Country Planning Association.

Teagle, W. G. (1967). The Fox in the London suburbs. *London Naturalist* 46: 44–68. LNHS, London.

Teagle, W. G. (1969). The Badger in the London area. *London Naturalist* 48: 48–75. LNHS, London.

Teagle, W. G. (1978). *The Endless Village*. Nature Conservancy Council, Shrewsbury.

Thomas, A. (2010). *RSPB Gardening for Wildlife*. A & C Black, London.

Thompson, K. (2007). *No nettles required: The truth about wildlife gardening*. Transworld, London.

Tinbergen, N. (1953). *The Herring Gull's World*. Collins, London.

Trueman, I., Poulton, M. & Reade, P. (2013). *Flora of Birmingham and the Black Country*. Pisces Publications, Newbury.

Ulrich, R. S. (1984). View through a window may influence recovery from surgery. *Science*. 224, 420–1.

Vickery, M. (1995). Gardens; the neglected habitat. In: *Ecology and conservation of butterflies*. Pullen A. S. (Ed.). Chapman & Hall, London.

Vincent, K. (2005). *Investigating the causes of the decline of the urban House Sparrow Passer domesticus population in Britain*. PhD Thesis, De Montfort University, Leicester.

Waite, M., Keech, D. & Game, M. (1993). *Nature Conservation in Camden*. Ecology Handbook 24. London Ecology Unit, London.

Wells, M. J. (2001). Rarity on the roof? Finding partial solutions to challenges of brownfield site redevelopment. *In Practice*. 33 pp 14–15. IEEM, Winchester.

Wells, M. & Grant, G. (2005). Biodiverse vegetated architecture worldwide: status, research and advances. *Proc. IEEM Conference* Bournmouth. IEEM, Winchester.

West Midlands County Council (1984). *The Nature Conservation Strategy for the County of West Midlands*. WMCC, Birmingham.

Wheater, C. P. (2011). Walls and paved surfaces. In: *The Routledge Handbook of Urban Ecology*, Douglas, I., Goode, D., Houck, M.C. & Wang, R. (eds), 239–51. Routledge, London.

Wheeler, A. (1979). *The Tidal Thames – The history of a River and its fishes*. Routledge and Kegan Paul.

White, G. (1789). *The Natural History and Antiquities of Selborne*. (Letter to the Hon Daines Barrington, 28 September 1774.)

White, J. & Hodson, J. (Eds) (2007). *Paradise Preserved: An introduction to the assessment, evaluation, conservation and management of historic cemeteries.* English Heritage and Natural England.

Wills, D. L. & Kettle, R. H. (1997). The birds of Wimbledon Common and Putney Heath, 1974 to 96. *London Bird Report* 61: 212–28. LNHS, London.

Wilmore, G. T. D. (2000). *Alien Plants of Yorkshire.* Yorkshire Naturalists' Union.

Wiltshire, E. & Reynolds, J.D. (2006). Bird predation on Turkish crayfish in central London. *The London Naturalist* 85, 121–4.

Woodward, I, & Arnold, R. (2012). The changing status of the breeding birds of the Inner London area. *British Birds* 105, 433–457.

Wrighton, F. E. (1948). City bombed sites survey: First Year. Plant ecology at Cripplegate, 1947. *London Naturalist* 27: 44–48. LNHS, London.

Yarham, I. & Game, M. (2000). *Nature Conservation in Brent.* Ecology Handbook 31. London Ecology Unit, London.

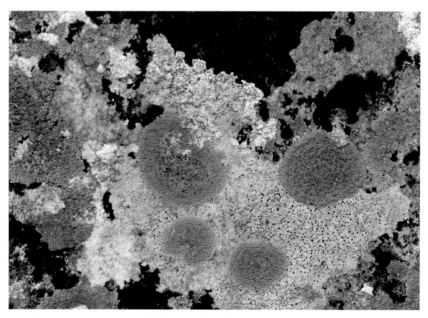

FIG 238. An attractive mosaic of lichens on a headstone at Smallcombe Cemetery in Bath including the orange *Caloplaca flavescens*, along with several species of *Verrucaria* and other species typically found on limestone.

Index

GENERAL INDEX

This index includes reference to species that feature significantly in the text.

Ecological Parks Trust 298,
301, 318–9
ecological recombination 130
Edinburgh 1, 66–9, 100, 137–8,
157, 198, 201, 220, 237, 241,
248, 269, 270, 317, 347, 348
Arthur's Seat 66–7
Habitat Action Plan for Rock
Faces 67
Local Biodiversity Action
Plan 347–8
Water of Leith 68–9
encapsulated countryside
16–18
Effects of urbanisation 18, 54
Endless Village, The 292–5,
310–14
English Heritage 99
English Nature 248, 340, 356,
377, 386
Environment Agency 357
Epping Forest 30, 32, 33, 37–9,
197, 230–1, 248, 250, 286, 331
estuaries 70
European Habitats Directive
65, 160
Evelyn, John 162, 191
exhaust emissions,
methyl tertiary butyl ether
(MTBE) 271
extinction of experience 362

F
Fairbrother Group 314
Fairbrother, Nan 288–9, 314
Fairburn Ings 140
Farmer, Alan 53
Feltham Marshalling Yard
108, 109, 331
feral pigeon 258–66
Fifer, Joy 310, 311
Fitter, Richard ix, 224, 260,
287, 289
Forest Hill railway cutting,
London 103
Forth and Clyde Canal (Port
Dundas) 83
founder effect 121
fox 248–57
attacks on babies and
children 257
colonisation of towns and
cities 248–50
diet 254–5
life expectancy 254

fox *cont.*
mange 253
territory size and density
251–3
Freed, Tim 94–6
Frith, Mathew 356, 357, 386

G
Game, Dr Meg 35
Garden BirdWatch (BTO) 364,
368, 369
Garden Cities of To-morrow 337
gardens 173–80, 364–9
BUGS project in Sheffield
178–9
Owen's 30-year study 176–8
value for wildlife 173–180
wildlife gardening 364–7
Gargoyle Wharf, London 123,
124, 130
Gas Street Basin, Birmingham
73
Gedge, Dusty 386
Gilbert, Oliver x, 41, 101, 105,
114, 120, 121, 325, 334
Gilbert White Memorial
Reserve, Perivale Wood 34
Gillespie Park, London 341,
354
Glasgow 1, 43, 68, 82–4, 88–9,
94–5, 98, 110, 122–3, 127, 139,
269, 298, 313, 359
colliery tips 127
disused railway land 110
inner-city wastelands 122–3
Necropolis 84, 88, 89
Port Dundas 83
Possil Marsh 139
River Kelvin 68–69
Gosling, Audley 164
golf courses 18–19
Grand Union Canal 34, 78,
199
gravel pits 144, 187, 191
Attenborough Lakes,
Nottingham 142–4
Sevenoaks, Kent 144
grazing marsh 46–7
great-crested grebe 187–189
Greater London Authority
(GLA) vii, 18, 329, 331, 333,
334, 340, 341, 387
Greater London Council
(GLC) x, , 132, 133, 227, 304,
307, 319, 351–3

Camley Street Natural Park
351–54
ecological policies 315–7
ecology programme 316,
339–40
GLC *cont.*
nature conservation strategy
327–334
wasteland survey 82, 123,
wildlife habitat survey 327–9
woodland survey 35–6
Greater London Development
Plan (GLDP) 316
Greater Manchester 72, 113,
229, 315, 334
Green Belt 32, 39, 46, 48, 288
green infrastructure 341–3
green roofs 378–91
Greenspace Information for
Greater London 333
Greenspace Scotland 343
Greenwich Peninsula Ecology
Park 389
Greenwood, Julian 222
greylag goose 195–6
Groundwork Foundation 324
gulls, roof-nesting 211–220
Gunnersbury Triangle 106,
300–8

H
Habitat Action Plans 67,
344–48,
habitat creation 24
Hainault Forest 35
Hampstead Garden Suburb
29, 337
Hampstead Heath 51–53,
60–2, 167, 198–9, 230–1, 239,
286, 331, 363
battles to save the heath 53,
60
ecology 60–2
Hampstead Heath Act of
1871 53
Handley, John 324
Harborne Line Walkway
106–7
Harris, Stephen 241–3, 251–5
Harrison, Carolyn 358
Harrogate 1, 54
Hawk and Owl Trust 207–8
hay meadows 11, 45, 47–50,
60–1, 170, 329, 355
health benefits 359–60

The New Naturalist Library

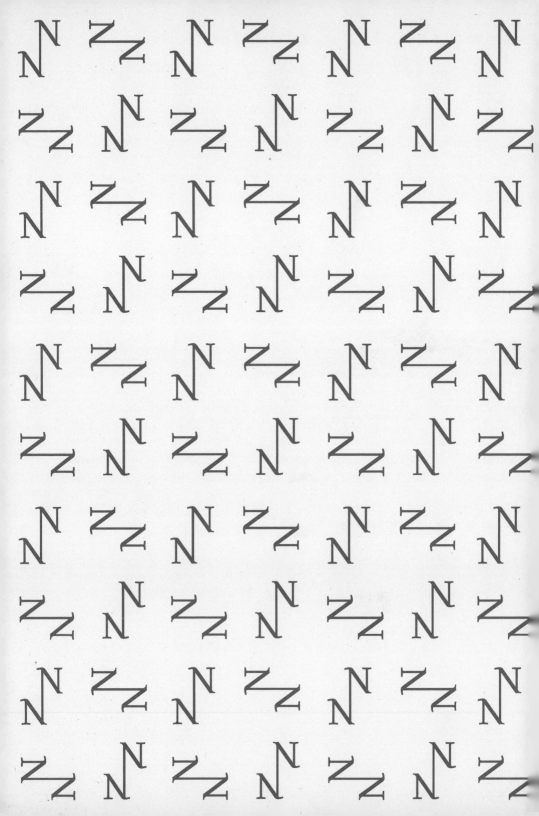